Clashing Views
on

Abnormal Psychology
A Taking Sides® Custom Reader

Susan Nolen-Hoeksema

Dushkin/McGraw-Hill
A Division of The McGraw-Hill Companies

Photo Acknowledgments

Cover photo © Daniel Nivens

Cover Art Acknowledgment

Charles Vitelli

Manufactured in the United States of America

First Edition

10 9 8 7 6 5 4 3 2 1

Library of Congress Cataloging-in-Publication Data

Main entry under title:
Clashing views on abnormal psychology: A Taking Sides® custom reader/
selected and with introduction by Susan Nolen-Hoeksema.—1st ed.
    Includes bibliographical references and index.
    1. Psychology, Pathological. I. Nolan-Hoeksema, Susan, *comp.*

616.89
97-068714

0-07-289545-4

 Printed on Recycled Paper

Editors

The material presented in this volume is a compilation of the works of leading psychologists, sociologists, educators, and health care professionals whose works have been reviewed for content, level, and appropriateness for this volume and edited for length and level when necessary. The following academics all played a part in selecting the readings and pairing them into a pro/con format to represent the controversies that exist in the current issues of the day.

Susan Nolen-Hoeksema is a professor of psychology and the director of the Gender and Mental Health Training Program at the University of Michigan in Ann Arbor, Michigan. She received her B.A. in 1982 from Yale University and her Ph.D. in 1986 from the University of Pennsylvania. She is well known across the world for her work on gender differences in mood disorders, coping with depression, bereavement, and childhood depression. She has published 4 books and over 35 articles and chapters.

Brent Slife is a clinical psychologist and a professor of psychology at Brigham Young University in Provo, Utah. A fellow of the American Psychological Association, he has authored over 60 articles and books, his most recent being *Time and Psychological Explanation* (State University of New York Press, 1993), which describes the overlooked influence of linear time on mainstream psychology. He has edited nine editions of *Taking Sides: Clashing Views on Controversial Psychological Issues.*

Raymond Goldberg has been a professor of health education at the State University of New York College at Cortland since 1977. He received his B.S. in health and physical education from Pembroke State University in 1969, his M.Ed. in health education from the University of South Carolina in 1971, and his Ph.D. in health education from the University of Toledo in 1981. He is the author of *Drugs Across the Spectrum* (West Educational Publishing, 1994), and he has edited three editions of *Taking Sides: Clashing Views on Controversial Issues in Drugs and Society.*

Robert T. Francoeur has taught human sexuality at colleges and high schools for over 20 years. He is currently a professor of biological and allied health sciences at Fairleigh Dickinson University in Madison, New Jersey, and he is the author of 7 books on human sexuality, including *A Descriptive Dictionary and Atlas of Sexology* (Greenwood, 1992) and *An International Handbook of Sexuality* (Greenwood, 1994). He has edited five editions of *Taking Sides: Clashing Views on Controversial Issues in Human Sexuality.*

Eileen L. Daniel, a registered dietitian, is an associate professor in and the chair of the Department of Health Science at the State University of New York College at Brockport. She has authored or coauthored over 30 articles on issues of health, nutrition, and health education in such professional journals as the *Journal of Nutrition Education*, the *Journal of School Health*, and the *Journal of Health Education*, and she has edited three editions of *Taking Sides: Clashing Views on Controversial Issues in Health and Society*.

Staff

David Dean	List Manager
David Brackley	Developmental Editor
Ava Suntoke	Developmental Editor
Tammy Ward	Administrative Assistant
Brenda S. Filley	Production Manager
Juliana Arbo	Typesetting Supervisor
Diane Barker	Proofreader
Lara Johnson	Graphics
Richard Tietjen	Publishing Systems Manager

PREFACE

The study of psychological disorders is fascinating and often troubling. Researchers must grapple with questions such as, How do we decide when someone has a mental disorder? Why are some people vulnerable to psychological problems when other people are not? What is the best way to help people who have psychological disorders? Most people would like to think that science has provided clear answers to these questions. Otherwise, people might be wrongly labeled (or not labeled) as having a mental disorder, experts might not understand the underpinnings of psychological disorders, or a clinician might prescribe the wrong treatment for a person with psychological disorders. In other words, people's lives are affected by the answers to these questions. Unfortunately, however, we do not yet have definitive answers to questions such as these.

The 12 issues debated in this book reflect some of the hottest scientific and philosophical debates in abnormal psychology. Students who wish to know the "right" answers to questions they have about psychological disorders may be frustrated by these debates. Yet a critical part of education is learning how to weigh conflicting arguments and evidence to come to your own opinions about the best answers to important questions. The debates presented in this book will challenge students to apply what they are learning in class and their own analytical skills to evaluate the arguments presented by each side of the debates. These skills will help students in class and in evaluating new information on psychological disorders that they hear about in the future.

Plan of the book   *Clashing Views on Abnormal Psychology: A Taking Sides® Custom Reader* is designed to be used for courses in abnormal psychology or clinical psychology that use the textbook *Abnormal Psychology* by Susan Nolen-Hoeksema. The issues chosen for this custom reader are intended to complement issues raised in the textbook. They are organized into four parts that parallel the four parts of *Abnormal Psychology*. Part 1 focuses on defining and treating abnormality. Part 2 focuses on anxiety and mood disorders, schizophrenia, dissociative and somatoform disorders, and personality disorders. Part 3 focuses on childhood disorders, eating disorders, sexual disorders, substance use disorders, and disorders involving physical health and cognitive impairment. And Part 4 focuses on researching abnormality and current legal controversies in abnormal psychology. Several issues are concerned explicitly with gender.

Each issue begins with an *introduction* that provides some background about the controversy, briefly describes the authors, and gives a brief summary of the positions reflected in the issue. Each issue concludes with a set of *challenge questions* that encourage students to think deeply about the arguments made on both sides of the issue. These issues can be studied consecutively or in any order, and each is designed to be independent of the others.

A word to the instructor   Multiple-choice and essay questions for this volume can be found in the Instructor's Course Planner that accompanies *Abnormal Psychology*, by Susan Nolen-Hoeksema, which is available through the publisher. A general guidebook, called *Using Taking Sides in the Classroom*, which discusses methods and techniques for integrating the pro/con approach into any classroom setting, is also available.

Psychology titles that are available through Dushkin/McGraw-Hill are listed on the back cover. If you are interested in seeing the table of contents for any of these titles, please visit the Dushkin/McGraw-Hill Web site at http://www.dushkin.com/.

Acknowledgments   I thank Meera Dash and David Dean for inspiring this custom reader and assisting in the selection of the issues. I look forward to receiving feedback on *Clashing Views on Abnormal Psychology: A Taking Sides® Custom Reader* from both faculty and students. I can be reached via email at nolen@umich.edu.

Susan Nolen-Hoeksema
University of Michigan

CONTENTS IN BRIEF

CONTENTS

Rosenhan argues that patients labeled as schizophrenic are seen as such by
mental health workers regardless of the true state of the patients' mental
health. Spitzer argues that diagnostic labels are necessary and valuable.

DeLeon and his colleagues argue that the public would benefit greatly from
psychologists' obtaining prescription privileges. DeNelsky maintains that
prescription privileges for psychologists would harm the discipline's ability
to serve the public.

Kramer advocates prescribing Prozac to improve people's moods. Mauro argues that Prozac does not get at the root of people's problems—that it is only a temporary fix.

Wartik asserts that the combined evidence of biological factors strongly supports the existence of premenstrual syndrome (PMS). Tavris argues that the bodily changes that women experience during their menstrual cycles are normal, not symptoms of an illness requiring treatment.

Johnstone contends that schizophrenia is a biological disease. Sarbin argues that schizophrenia is actually a social construct developed to make sense of a variety of behaviors.

Bernstein and Kelley claim that medical problems related to environmental and chemical exposure are currently affecting thousands of soldiers who fought in the Persian Gulf War. Fumento argues that medical experts have not found any evidence to support the existence of a syndrome related to the war.

Straus finds a relationship between physical punishment in childhood and
violent behavior in the teenage and adult years. McCord concludes that neglected children, not those who are physically punished, become the most
violent adults.

Berg contends that yo-yo dieting, or weight cycling, is associated with an
elevated risk of physical and mental health problems. The National Task
Force on the Prevention and Treatment of Obesity maintains that there is no
convincing evidence that weight cycling has any major effects on health.

Logli argues that pregnant women who use drugs should be prosecuted because they may harm the life of their unborn children. Norton-Hawk contends
that there is more opportunity to help pregnant addicts and their babies if they
can come for prenatal care and drug treatment without fearing prosecution.

Henkin asserts that there is no such thing as an addiction to sex. Carnes argues that a significant number of people have identified themselves as sexual addicts.

Laurence and Weinhouse claim that women have been excluded from most research on new drugs and medical treatments. Kadar argues that women actually receive more medical care and benefit more from medical research than do men.

Bass and Davis assert that even a faint or vague memory of sexual abuse is prime evidence that sexual abuse has occurred. Coleman argues that "memories" of sexual abuse that never occurred can be created in therapy with the encouragement of mental health professionals.

INTRODUCTION

Controversy in Abnormal Psychology

Susan Nolen-Hoeksema

When a person is suffering, he or she will often seek a label for that suffering, an explanation for the suffering, and a proven treatment to stop the suffering. In medicine, great strides have been made in identifying and labeling diseases, understanding their causes, and developing reliable treatments, although there is much work yet to be done.

Great strides are also being made in classifying, understanding, and treating psychological suffering. There are many unresolved issues in clinical or abnormal psychology, however. Psychological problems pose many challenges that make them more difficult to study and treat than many medical problems. First, the very definition of psychological problems is rooted in cultural and gendered norms for acceptable and healthy behavior. Several of the essays in this book address the biases and subjective judgments involved in labeling certain behaviors as abnormal. For example, Issue 1, "Do Diagnostic Labels Hinder Treatment?" presents a classic debate over a study apparently showing that once a person is labeled as having a psychological disorder, all of his or her subsequent behaviors are interpreted in line with that label. Issue 10, "Is Sex Addiction a Myth?" addresses the impact of societal norms on determining when a person is *too* interested in sex.

Second, whereas many medical problems are identifiable through objective tests, the assessment of psychological problems often requires information that is subjective and available only to the person who is suffering—information about feelings, thoughts, memories, and self-evaluations. This absence of "hard" pathology that can be quantified or viewed under a microscope makes it much more difficult to say definitively that a person does or does not have a disorder. It also contributes to the ambivalence that we as a society still have toward people with psychological problems. Sometimes we view them with compassion just as we would regard someone with an identifiable medical disease. At other times we view them with contempt or fear, as if they are faking their suffering or bringing it upon themselves. Issue 6, "Is the Gulf War Syndrome Real?" highlights these tensions in a discussion of a modern phenomenon that some people say is real and represents a biological disease and that other people say is not real, in the biological sense, but represents some people's way of manifesting psychological distress.

Third, most psychological problems probably have multiple biological, psychological, and social causes, and specifying the relative contribution of any one cause can be nearly impossible. Still, our belief about whether or not a given factor contributes to psychological problems influences our social policies. Issue 7, "Do Physically Punished Children Become Violent Adults?" focuses on a social factor that some researchers argue contributes to later psychological problems in children. If we believe that physical punishment does contribute to later violence in children, then we may be willing to make social policies to reduce physical punishment—for example, arresting and prosecuting parents who physically punish their children—even though these policies may contradict other beliefs in our society, such as the belief that parents should be able to raise their children as they wish. If we do not believe that physical punishment contributes to later violence in children, then we will be much less willing to make social policies that intrude on parents' freedom to raise their children as they wish.

Some of the unresolved issues in abnormal psychology eventually may be resolved through scientific observation and experimentation. As our technologies for investigating the human brain improve, and our databases on the social and psychological characteristics of people who develop psychological disorders expand, we may be better able to identify, understand, and treat psychological disorders.

Many of the unresolved issues in abnormal psychology cannot be resolved through science, however, because these issues involve fundamental philosophical questions. Many of these questions have to do with how we interpret the role of biology in psychological disorders. There is increasing evidence that biology plays a role in most psychological disorders. In most cases, biological factors seem to increase certain people's risk for psychological disorders, but they are not absolutely determinate. When we find that biology influences people's vulnerability to a psychological disorder, does that mean that the psychological disorder is basically a biological disorder? If the answer is yes, then how do we explain why psychological treatments can be as effective as biological treatments for many psychological disorders? If we accept that biology can affect psychology, then should people be allowed to change their psychology through biological interventions even if they do not have a disorder? For example, should people be able to take pills to make them more self-confident, less shy, or more outgoing (see Issue 3)?

Another philosophical question at the heart of several unresolved issues in abnormal psychology concerns society's attitudes toward women's bodies and psychology. The ongoing debate reflected in Issue 4, "Is Premenstrual Syndrome a Medical Disorder?" is flanked on one side by people who argue that society has long dismissed women's reports of premenstrual distress as some form of female hysterics and on the other side by people who argue that society always finds ways to pathologize women's natural reproductive functioning. Issue 9, "Should Drug Use by Pregnant Women Be Considered Child Abuse?" raises questions about women's rights to rule their own bodies and society's obligations to fetuses.

A DIALECTICAL APPROACH

Much of education today involves memorization of information presented as facts. There are some facts in abnormal psychology, scientifically derived pieces of information, that students need to learn. Many of these facts are presented in the textbook *Abnormal Psychology*. But, as I have just discussed, there are many unresolved issues and philosophical questions in abnormal psychology as well. Several of these issues and questions are raised in *Abnormal Psychology*, in descriptions of the research on specific disorders and in the critical thinking questions throughout the textbook.

Clashing Views on Abnormal Psychology: A Taking Sides® Custom Reader presents the unresolved issues in abnormal psychology through a different approach—a dialectical approach. The unresolved issues are presented with two distinct, opposing sides. Students are asked to familiarize themselves with both sides of an issue, look at the supporting evidence on both sides, and engage in constructive conversation about possible resolutions. This approach to education requires students to take an active role in making sense of the issues. In so doing, students benefit in several ways.

First, students come to a richer understanding of the subject matter of abnormal psychology. By realizing that there can be two (or more) firmly held, well-argued viewpoints on important issues in abnormal psychology, students can appreciate the complexity and subjectivity inherent in most of the phenomena studied in abnormal psychology.

Second, students develop a healthy respect for both sides of a debate. There is a natural tendency to underestimate reasonable arguments on one side or the other of a debate. Of course, the side one favors often appears to be the "most reasonable." The issues in this book have reasonable people and reasonable arguments on both sides. That is, these issues are issues in psychology precisely because they have reasonable arguments and evidence on either side. This is not to say that both sides are correct. It is to say, rather, that a proper appreciation of both sides is necessary to understand what is at issue and thus to begin to find a resolution.

A third benefit of the dialectical approach is that students better understand the nature of psychological knowledge in general. Although contemporary psychologists have taken up the scientific challenge of exploring behavior and mind, many questions are still far from being answered. Psychology's parent, like that of all sciences, is philosophy. Hence, philosophical (or theoretical) issues always lurk behind the activities of psychologists. Issues such as mind versus body, free will versus determinism, nature versus nurture, and the philosophy of science are both philosophical and psychological questions. Students will necessarily have to entertain and explicate these types of issues as they learn about and advance within the discipline.

Fourth, students become more aware of alternative views on controversial psychological issues. People often do not even realize that there is another point of view to an issue or evidence to the contrary. This realization, however, can help students to be more cautious in their knowledge. As the dialectician Socrates once noted, this caution is sometimes the first step toward true wisdom—knowing what it is that you do not know.

Finally, the dialectical approach promotes critical thinking skills. Finely honed critical skills give students a better position from which to examine the psychological literature critically and to select or develop their own positions on important psychological issues.

On the Internet . . .

Clinical Psychology Resources
This page contains Internet resources for clinical and abnormal psychology, behavioral medicine, and mental health. *http://www.psychologie.uni-bonn.de/kap/links_20.htm*

Psych Web!
This Web site contains lots of psychology-related information for students and teachers of psychology. *http://www.gasou.edu/psychweb/psychweb.htm*

The Effectiveness of Psychotherapy:
A *Consumer Reports* Study
Martin E. P. Seligman, a professor in the Department of Psychology at the University of Pennsylvania, responds to a *Consumer Reports* study on psychotherapy. He examines the methodological virtues and drawbacks of the large-scale survey and contrasts it with the more traditional efficacy study. He concludes that the survey complements the efficacy method and that the best features of these two methods can be combined into a more ideal method that will best provide empirical validation of psychotherapy. *http://www.apa.org/journals/seligman.html*

Psychological Screening Criteria from
MED-TOX Health Services
MED-TOX Health Services specializes in several areas of job and ergonomic analysis, occupational and environmental health and safety, and medical/physical standards development. This page presents criteria for the evaluation of psychological testing services, prepared by Vernon R. Padgett, Ph.D. *http://home.earthlink.net/%7Emedtox/psych.html*

PART 1

Understanding Abnormality and Its Treatment

Who is allowed to label behaviors or people as abnormal? And who is allowed to provide treatment for these behaviors or people? There is tremendous power vested in the hands of the people given authority to label others as abnormal and to treat people with psychological disorders.

Labeling individuals as abnormal can result in their losing opportunities and perhaps even personal freedom. On the other hand, refusing to acknowledge individuals' psychological suffering and disabilities may result in their not receiving needed help.

People who provide treatment for psychological disorders clearly should have the appropriate training. But how much training is the appropriate amount? And does it matter that the people providing treatment have a professional degree, or just that they know how to provide the treatment?

■ Classic Dialogue: Do Diagnostic Labels Hinder Treatment?

■ Should Psychologists Be Allowed to Prescribe Drugs?

ISSUE 1

Classic Dialogue: Do Diagnostic Labels Hinder Treatment?

YES: D. L. Rosenhan, from "On Being Sane in Insane Places," *Science* (January 13, 1973)

NO: Robert L. Spitzer, from "On Pseudoscience in Science, Logic in Remission and Psychiatric Diagnosis: A Critique of 'On Being Sane in Insane Places,'" *Journal of Abnormal Psychology* (vol. 84, 1975)

ISSUE SUMMARY

YES: Psychologist D. L. Rosenhan describes an experiment that, he contends, demonstrates that once a patient is labeled as schizophrenic, his behavior is seen as such by mental health workers regardless of the true state of the patient's mental health.

NO: Psychiatrist Robert L. Spitzer argues that diagnostic labels are necessary and valuable and that Rosenhan's experiment has many flaws.

Traditionally, the first step in treating a disorder is to diagnose it. When a disorder is diagnosed, presumably the most effective treatment can then be applied. But diagnosis often involves classifying the person and attaching a label. Could such a label do more harm than good?

How would you think and behave if you were introduced to someone described as a high school dropout? A heroin addict? A schizophrenic? What would you think and how would you behave if, having recently taken a series of personality tests, you were told by an expert that you were schizophrenic?

Some people believe that diagnostic labels may actually serve as self-fulfilling prophecies. Labels seem to have a way of putting blinders on the way a problem is seen. Those who are labeled may behave differently toward others or develop self-concepts consistent with the diagnosis—and thereby exaggerate, or even create anew, behavior considered to be "abnormal."

In the following selections, D. L. Rosenhan asks the question, "If sanity and insanity exist, how shall we know them?" He then describes an experiment that he conducted to help answer this question. Rosenhan interprets the results of his investigation as demonstrating that "the normal are not detectably sane" by a mental hospital staff because "having once been labeled schizophrenic, there is nothing the [patient] can do to overcome this tag." He believes that mental institutions impose a specific environment in which the meaning of even normal behaviors can be construed as abnormal. If this is so, Rosenhan wonders, "How many people are sane ... but not recognized as such in our psychiatric institutions?"

Robert L. Spitzer criticizes Rosenhan's experiment on many grounds and, in fact, contends that "a correct interpretation of his own [Rosenhan's] data contradicts his conclusions." Rosenhan's data, Spitzer contends, show that in "a psychiatric hospital, psychiatrists are remarkably able to distinguish the 'sane' from the 'insane.'" Although Spitzer recognizes some of the dangers of diagnostic classification, he believes that Rosenhan has not presented fairly the purpose and necessity of diagnoses. The misuse of diagnoses, he maintains, "is not a sufficient reason to abandon their use because they have been shown to be of value when properly used." They "enable mental health professionals to communicate with each other ... , comprehend the pathological processes involved ... , and control psychiatric disorders," says Spitzer.

POINT	COUNTERPOINT
• Psychiatric diagnoses are in the minds of the observers and do not reflect the behavior of the patients.	• A diagnosis based on real or false symptoms *is* based on a patient's behavior.
• A diagnosis can become a self-fulfilling prophecy for the doctor or the patient.	• Competent diagnoses derive from a necessary classification of the symptoms of disorder.
• In the setting of a mental institution, almost any behavior could be considered abnormal.	• Mental patients *do* eventually get discharged when they continue to show no symptoms of behavior pathology.
• Diagnostic labels serve no useful purpose, especially in view of the harm they do.	• Diagnoses enable psychiatrists to communicate, comprehend, and control disorders.

YES

D. L. Rosenhan

ON BEING SANE IN INSANE PLACES

If sanity and insanity exist, how shall we know them?

The question is neither capricious nor itself insane. However much we may be personally convinced that we can tell the normal from the abnormal, the evidence is simply not compelling. It is commonplace, for example, to read about murder trials wherein eminent psychiatrists for the defense are contradicted by equally eminent psychiatrists for the prosecution on the matter of the defendant's sanity. More generally, there are a great deal of conflicting data on the reliability, utility, and meaning of such terms as "sanity," "insanity," "mental illness," and "schizophrenia." Finally, as early as 1934, Benedict suggested that normality and abnormality are not universal. What is viewed as normal in one culture may be seen as quite aberrant in another. Thus, notions of normality and abnormality may not be quite as accurate as people believe they are.

To raise questions regarding normality and abnormality is in no way to question the fact that some behaviors are deviant or odd. Murder is deviant. So, too, are hallucinations. Nor does raising such questions deny the existence of the personal anguish that is often associated with "mental illness." Anxiety and depression exist. Psychological suffering exists. But normality and abnormality, sanity and insanity, and the diagnoses that flow from them may be less substantive than many believe them to be.

At its heart, the question of whether the sane can be distinguished from the insane (and whether degrees of insanity can be distinguished from each other) is a simple matter: do the salient characteristics that lead to diagnoses reside in the patients themselves or in the environments and contexts in which observers find them? From Bleuler, through Kretchmer, through the formulators of the recently revised *Diagnostic and Statistical Manual* of the American Psychiatric Association, the belief has been strong that patients present symptoms, that those symptoms can be categorized, and, implicitly, that the sane are distinguishable from the insane. More recently, however, this belief has been questioned. Based in part on theoretical and anthropological considerations, but also on philosophical, legal, and therapeutic ones, the view has grown that psychological categorization of mental illness is useless at best and downright harmful, misleading, and pejorative at worst. Psychiatric diagnoses, in this view, are in the minds of the observers and are not valid summaries of characteristics displayed by the observed.

Gains can be made in deciding which of these is more nearly accurate by getting normal people (that is, people who do not have, and have never suffered, symptoms of serious psychiatric disorders) admitted to psychiatric hospitals and then determining whether they were discovered to be sane and, if so, how. If the sanity of such pseudopatients were always detected, there would be prima facie evidence that a sane individual can be distinguished from the insane context in which he is found. Normality (and presumably abnormality) is distinct enough that it can be recognized wherever it occurs, for it is carried within the person. If, on the other hand, the sanity of the pseudopatients were never discovered, serious difficulties would arise for those who support traditional modes of psychiatric diagnosis. Given that the hospital staff was not incompetent, that the pseudopatient had been behaving as sanely as he had been outside of the hospital, and that it had never been previously suggested that he belonged in a psychiatric hospital, such an unlikely outcome would support the view that psychiatric diagnosis betrays little about the patient but much about the environment in which an observer finds him.

This article describes such an experiment. Eight sane people gained secret admission to 12 different hospitals. Their diagnostic experiences constitute the data of the first part of this article; the remainder is devoted to a description of their experiences in psychiatric institutions. Too few psychiatrists and psychologists, even those who have worked in such hospitals, know what the experience is like. They rarely talk about it with former patients, perhaps because they distrust information coming from the previously insane. Those who have worked in psychiatric hospitals are likely to have adapted so thoroughly to the settings that they are insensitive to the impact of the experience. And while there have been occasional reports of researchers who submitted themselves to psychiatric hospitalization, these researchers have commonly remained in the hospitals for short periods of time, often with the knowledge of the hospital staff. It is difficult to know the extent to which they were treated like patients or like research colleagues. Nevertheless, their reports about the inside of the psychiatric hospital have been valuable. This article extends those efforts.

PSEUDOPATIENTS AND THEIR SETTINGS

The eight pseudopatients were a varied group. One was a psychology graduate student in his 20s. The remaining seven were older and "established." Among them were three psychologists, a pediatrician, a psychiatrist, a painter, and a housewife. Three pseudopatients were women, five were men. All of them employed pseudonyms, lest their alleged diagnoses embarrass them later. Those who were in mental health professions alleged another occupation in order to avoid the special attentions that might be accorded by staff, as a matter of courtesy or caution, to ailing colleagues. With the exception of myself (I was the first pseudopatient and my presence was known to the hospital administrator and chief psychologist and, so far as I can tell, to them alone), the presence of pseudopatients and the nature of the research program was not known to the hospital staffs.

The settings were similarly varied. In order to generalize the findings, admission into a variety of hospitals was sought. The 12 hospitals in the sample are located in five different states on the East and West coasts. Some were old and shabby, some were quite new. Some were research-oriented, others not. Some had good staff-patient ratios, others were quite understaffed. Only one was a strictly private hospital. All the others were supported by state or federal funds or, in one instance, by university funds.

After calling the hospital for an appointment, the pseudopatient arrived at the admissions office complaining that he had been hearing voices. Asked what the voices said, he replied that they were often unclear, but as far as he could tell they said "empty," "hollow," and "thud." The voices were unfamiliar and were of the same sex as the pseudopatient. The choice of these symptoms was occasioned by their apparent similarity to existential symptoms. Such symptoms were alleged to arise from painful concerns about the perceived meaninglessness of one's life. It is as if the hallucinating person were saying, "My life is empty and hollow." The choice of these symptoms was also determined by the *absence* of a single report of existential psychoses in the literature.

Beyond alleging the symptoms and falsifying name, vocation, and employment, no further alterations of person, history, or circumstances were made. The significant events of the pseudopatient's life history were presented as they had actually occurred. Relationships with parents and siblings, with spouse and children, with people at work and in school, consistent with the aforementioned exceptions, were described as they were or had

been. Frustrations and upsets were described along with joys and satisfactions. These facts are important to remember. If anything, they strongly biased the subsequent results in favor of detecting sanity, since none of their histories or current behaviors were seriously pathological in any way.

Immediately upon admission to the psychiatric ward, the pseudopatient ceased simulating *any* symptoms of abnormality. In some cases, there was a brief period of mild nervousness and anxiety, since none of the pseudopatients really believed that they would be admitted so easily. Indeed their shared fear was that they would be immediately exposed as frauds and greatly embarrassed. Moreover, many of them had never visited a psychiatric ward; even those who had, nevertheless had some genuine fears about what might happen to them. Their nervousness, then, was quite appropriate to the novelty of the hospital setting, and it abated rapidly.

Apart from that short-lived nervousness, the pseudopatient behaved on the ward as he "normally" behaved. The pseudopatient spoke to patients and staff as he might ordinarily. Because there is uncommonly little to do on a psychiatric ward, he attempted to engage others in conversation. When asked by staff how he was feeling, he indicated that he was fine, that he no longer experienced symptoms. He responded to instructions from attendants, to calls for medication (which was not swallowed), and to dining-hall instructions. Beyond such activities as were available to him on the admissions ward, he spent his time writing down his observations about the ward, its patients, and the staff. Initially these notes were written "secretly," but as it soon became clear that no one much cared, they were subsequently written on standard tablets of paper in such public places as the day-room. No secret was made of these activities.

The pseudopatient, very much as a true psychiatric patient, entered a hospital with no foreknowledge of when he would be discharged. Each was told that he would have to get out by his own devices, essentially by convincing the staff that he was sane. The psychological stresses associated with hospitalization were considerable, and all but one of the pseudopatients desired to be discharged almost immediately after being admitted. They were, therefore, motivated not only to behave sanely, but to be paragons of cooperation. That their behavior was in no way disruptive is confirmed by nursing reports, which have been obtained on most of the patients. These reports uniformly indicate that the patients were "friendly," "cooperative," and "exhibited no abnormal indications."

THE NORMAL ARE NOT DETECTABLY SANE

Despite their public "show" of sanity, the pseudopatients were never detected. Admitted, except in one case, with a diagnosis of schizophrenia each was discharged with a diagnosis of schizophrenia "in remission." The label "in remission" should in no way be dismissed as a formality, for at no time during any hospitalization had any question been raised about any pseudopatient's simulation. Nor are there any indications in the hospital records that the pseudopatient's status was suspect. Rather, the evidence is strong that, once labeled schizophrenic, the pseudopatient was stuck with that label. If the pseudopatient was to be discharged, he must naturally be "in remission"; but he was not sane, nor, in the institution's view, had he ever been sane.

The uniform failure to recognize sanity cannot be attributed to the quality of the hospitals, for, although there were considerable variations among them, several are considered excellent. Nor can it be alleged that there was simply not enough time to observe the pseudo-patients. Length of hospitalization ranged from 7 to 52 days, with an average of 19 days. The pseudopatients were not, in fact, carefully observed, but this failure clearly speaks more to traditions within psychiatric hospitals than to lack of opportunity.

Finally, it cannot be said that the failure to recognize the pseudopatients' sanity was due to the fact that they were not behaving sanely. While there was clearly some tension present in all of them, their daily visitors could detect no serious behavioral consequences—nor, indeed, could other patients. It was quite common for the patients to "detect" the pseudopatients' sanity. During the first three hospitalizations, when accurate counts were kept, 35 of a total of 118 patients on the admissions ward voiced their suspicions, some vigorously. "You're not crazy. You're a journalist, or a professor [referring to the continual note-taking]. You're checking up on the hospital." While most of the patients were reassured by the pseudopatient's insistence that he had been sick before he came in but was fine now, some continued to believe that the pseudopatient was sane throughout his hospitalization. The fact that the patients often recognized normality when staff did not raises important questions.

Failure to detect sanity during the course of hospitalization may be due to the fact that physicians operate with a strong bias toward what statisticians call the type 2 error. This is to say that physicians are more inclined to call a healthy person sick (a false positive, type 2) than a sick person healthy (a false negative, type 1). The reasons for this are not hard to find: it is clearly more dangerous to mis-diagnose illness than health. Better to err on the side of caution, to suspect illness even among the healthy.

But what holds for medicine does not hold equally well for psychiatry. Medical illnesses, while unfortunate, are not commonly pejorative. Psychiatric diagnoses, on the contrary, carry with them personal, legal, and social stigmas. It was therefore important to see whether the tendency toward diagnosing the sane insane could be reversed. The following experiment was arranged at a research and teaching hospital whose staff had heard these findings but doubted that such an error could occur in their hospital. The staff was informed that at some time during the following 3 months, one or more pseudopatients would attempt to be admitted into the psychiatric hospital. Each staff member was asked to rate each patient who presented himself at admissions or on the ward according to the likelihood that the patient was a pseudopatient. A 10-point scale was used, with a 1 and 2 reflecting high confidence that the patient was a pseudopatient.

Judgments were obtained on 193 patients who were admitted for psychiatric treatment. All staff who had had sustained contact with or primary responsibility for the patient—attendants, nurses, psychiatrists, physicians, and psychologists—were asked to make judgments. Forty-one patients were alleged, with high confidence, to be pseudopatients by at least one member of the staff. Twenty-three were considered suspect by

at least one psychiatrist. Nineteen were suspected by one psychiatrist *and* one other staff member. Actually, no genuine pseudopatient (at least from my group) presented himself during this period.

The experiment is instructive. It indicates that the tendency to designate sane people as insane can be reversed when the stakes (in this case, prestige and diagnostic acumen) are high. But what can be said of the 19 people who were suspected of being "sane" by one psychiatrist and another staff member? Were these people truly "sane," or was it rather the case that in the course of avoiding the type 2 error the staff tended to make more errors of the first sort—calling the crazy "sane"? There is no way of knowing. But one thing is certain: any diagnostic process that lends itself so readily to massive errors of this sort cannot be a very reliable one.

THE STICKINESS OF PSYCHODIAGNOSTIC LABELS

Beyond the tendency to call the healthy sick—a tendency that accounts better for diagnostic behavior on admission than it does for such behavior after a lengthy period of exposure—the data speak to the massive role of labeling in psychiatric assessment. Having once been labeled schizophrenic, there is nothing the pseudopatient can do to overcome this tag. The tag profoundly colors others' perceptions of him and his behavior.

From one viewpoint, these data are hardly surprising, for it has long been known that elements are given meaning by the context in which they occur. Gestalt psychology made this point vigorously, and Asch demonstrated that there are "central" personality traits (such as "warm" versus "cold") which are so powerful that they markedly color the meaning of other information in forming an impression of a given personality.

"Insane," "schizophrenic," "manic-depressive," and "crazy" are probably among the most powerful of such central traits. Once a person is designated abnormal, all of his other behaviors and characteristics are colored by that label. Indeed, that label is so powerful that may of the pseudopatients' normal behaviors were overlooked entirely or profoundly misinterpreted. Some examples may clarify this issue.

Earlier I indicated that there were no changes in the pseudopatient's personal history and current status beyond those of name, employment, and, where necessary, vocation. Otherwise, a veridical description of personal history and circumstances was offered. Those circumstances were not psychotic. How were they made consonant with the diagnosis of psychosis? Or were those diagnoses modified in such a way as to bring them into accord with the circumstances of the pseudopatient's life, as described by him?

As far as I can determine, diagnoses were in no way affected by the relative health of the circumstances of a pseudo-patient's life. Rather, the reverse occurred: the perception of his circumstances was shaped entirely by the diagnosis. A clear example of such translation is found in the case of a pseudopatient who had had a close relationship with his mother but was rather remote from his father during his early childhood. During adolescence and beyond, however, his father became a close friend, while his relationship with his mother cooled. His present relationship with his wife was characteristically close and warm.

Apart from occasional angry exchanges, friction was minimal. The children had rarely been spanked. Surely there is nothing especially pathological about such a history. Indeed, many readers may see a similar pattern in their own experiences, with no markedly deleterious consequences. Observe, however, how such a history was translated in the psychopathological context, this from the case summary prepared after the patient was discharged:

> This white 39-year-old male... manifests a long history of considerable ambivalence in close relationships, which begins in early childhood. A warm relationship with his mother cools during his adolescence. A distant relationship to his father is described as becoming very intense. Affective stability is absent. His attempts to control emotionality with his wife and children are punctuated by angry outbursts and, in the case of the children, spankings. And while he says that he has several friends, one senses considerable ambivalence embedded in these relationships also....

The facts of the case were unintentionally distorted by the staff to achieve consistency with a popular theory of the dynamics of a schizophrenic reaction. Nothing of an ambivalent nature had been described in relations with parents, spouse, or friends. To the extent that ambivalence could be inferred, it was probably not greater than is found in all human relationships. It is true the pseudopatient's relationships with his parents changed over time, but in the ordinary context that would hardly be remarkable —indeed, it might very well be expected. Clearly, the meaning ascribed to his verbalizations (that is, ambivalence, affective instability) was determined by the diagnosis: schizophrenia. An entirely different meaning would have been ascribed if it were known that the man was normal.

All pseudopatients took extensive notes publicly. Under ordinary circumstances, such behavior would have raised questions in the minds of observers, as, in fact, it did among patients. Indeed, it seemed so certain that the notes would elicit suspicion that elaborate precautions were taken to remove them from the ward each day. But the precautions proved needless. The closest any staff member came to questioning these notes occurred when one pseudopatient asked his physician what kind of medication he was receiving and began to write down the response. "You needn't write it," he was told gently. "If you have trouble remembering, just ask me again."

If no questions were asked of the pseudopatients, how was their writing interpreted? Nursing records for three patients indicate that the writing was seen as an aspect of their pathological behavior. "Patient engages in writing behavior" was the daily nursing comment on one of the pseudopatients who was never questioned about his writing. Given that the patient is in the hospital, he must be psychologically disturbed. And given that he is disturbed, continuous writing must be a behavioral manifestation of that disturbance, perhaps a subset of the compulsive behaviors that are sometimes correlated with schizophrenia.

One tacit characteristic of psychiatric diagnosis is that it locates the sources of aberration within the individual and only rarely within the complex of stimuli that surrounds him. Consequently, behaviors that are stimulated by the environment are commonly misattributed to the patient's disorder. For example, one kindly nurse found a pseudopatient pacing the long hospital corridors. "Nervous, Mr. X?" she asked. "No, bored," he said.

The notes kept by pseudopatients are full of patient behaviors that were misinterpreted by well-intentioned staff. Often enough, a patient would go "berserk" because he had, wittingly or unwittingly, been mistreated by, say, an attendant. A nurse coming upon the scene would rarely inquire even cursorily into the environmental stimuli of the patient's behavior. Rather, she assumed that his upset derived from his pathology, not from his present interactions with other staff members. Occasionally, the staff might assume that the patient's family (especially when they had recently visited) or other patients had stimulated the outburst. But never were the staff found to assume that one of themselves or the structure of the hospital had anything to do with a patient's behavior. One psychiatrist pointed to a group of patients who were sitting outside the cafeteria entrance half an hour before lunchtime. To a group of young residents he indicated that such behavior was characteristic of the oral-acquisitive nature of the syndrome. It seemed not to occur to him that there were very few things to anticipate in a psychiatric hospital besides eating.

A psychiatric label has a life and an influence of its own. Once the impression has been formed that the patient is schizophrenic, the expectation is that he will continue to be schizophrenic. When a sufficient amount of time has passed, during which the patient has done nothing bizarre, he is considered to be in remission and available for discharge. But the label endures beyond discharge, with the unconfirmed expectation that he will behave as a schizophrenic again. Such labels, conferred by mental health professionals, are as influential on the patient as they are on his relatives and friends, and it should not surprise anyone that the diagnosis acts on all of them as a self-fulfilling prophecy. Eventually, the patient himself accepts the diagnosis, with all of its surplus meanings and expectations, and behaves accordingly.

The inferences to be made from these matters are quite simple. Much as Zigler and Phillips have demonstrated that there is enormous overlap in the symptoms presented by patients who have been variously diagnosed, so there is enormous overlap in the behaviors of the sane and the insane. The sane are not "sane" all of the time. We lose our tempers "for no good reason." We are occasionally depressed or anxious, again for no good reason. And we may find it difficult to get along with one or another person—again for no reason that we can specify. Similarly, the insane are not always insane. Indeed, it was the impression of the pseudopatients while living with them that they were sane for long periods of time—that the bizarre behaviors upon which their diagnoses were allegedly predicated constituted only a small fraction of their total behavior. If it makes no sense to label ourselves permanently depressed on the basis of an occasional depression, then it takes better evidence than is presently available to label all patients insane or schizophrenic on the basis of bizarre behaviors or cognitions. It seems more useful, as Mischel has pointed out, to limit our discussions to *behaviors*, the stimuli that provoke them, and their correlates.

It is not known why powerful impressions of personality traits, such as "crazy" or "insane," arise. Conceivably, when the origins of and stimuli that give rise to a behavior are remote or unknown, or when the behavior strikes us as immutable, trait labels regarding the *behaver* arise. When, on the other hand, the origins and stimuli are known and available, discourse is limited to the behavior itself. Thus, I may hallucinate because I am sleeping, or I may hallucinate because I have ingested a peculiar drug. These are termed sleep-induced hallucinations, or dreams, and drug-induced hallucinations, respectively. But when the stimuli to my hallucinations are unknown, that is called craziness, or schizophrenia—as if that inference were somehow as illuminating as the others.

THE EXPERIENCE OF PSYCHIATRIC HOSPITALIZATION

The term "mental illness" is of recent origin. It was coined by people who were humane in their inclinations and who wanted very much to raise the station of (and the public's sympathies toward) the psychologically disturbed from that of witches and "crazies" to one that was akin to the physically ill. And they were at least partially successful, for the treatment of the mental ill *has* improved considerably over the years. But while treatment has improved, it is doubtful that people really regard the mentally ill in the same way that they view the physically ill. A broken leg is something one recovers from, but mental illness allegedly endures forever. A broken leg does not threaten the observer, but a crazy schizophrenic? There is by now a host of evidence that attitudes toward the mentally ill are characterized by fear, hostility, aloofness, suspicion, and dread. The mentally ill are society's lepers.

That such attitudes infect the general population is perhaps not surprising, only upsetting. But that they affect the professionals—attendants, nurses, physicians, psychologists, and social workers—who treat and deal with the mentally ill is more disconcerting, both because such attitudes are self-evidently pernicious and because they are unwitting. Most mental health professionals would insist that they are sympathetic toward the mentally ill, that they are neither avoidant nor hostile. But it is more likely that an exquisite ambivalence characterizes their relations with psychiatric patients, such that their avowed impulses are only part of their entire attitude. Negative attitudes are there too and can easily be detected. Such attitudes should not surprise us. They are the natural offspring of the labels patients wear and the places in which they are found.

Consider the structure of the typical psychiatric hospital. Staff and patients are strictly segregated. Staff have their own living space, including their dining facilities, bathrooms and assembly places. The glassed quarters that contain the professional staff, which the pseudopatients came to call "the cage," sit out on every dayroom. The staff emerge primarily for caretaking purposes—to give medication, to conduct a therapy or group meeting, to instruct or reprimand a patient. Otherwise, staff keep to themselves, almost as if the disorder that afflicts their charges is somehow catching.

So much is patient-staff segregation the rule that, for four public hospitals in which an attempt was made to measure the degree to which staff and patients mingle, it was necessary to use "time out of the staff cage" as the operational measure. While it was not the case that all time spent out of the cage was spent mingling with patients (attendants, for example, would occasionally emerge to watch television in the dayroom), it was the only way in which one could gather reliable data on time for measuring.

The average amount of time spent by attendants outside of the cage was 11.3 percent (range, 3 to 52 percent). This figure does not represent only time spent mingling with patients, but also includes time spent on such chores as folding laundry, supervising patients while they shave, directing ward clean-up, and sending patients to off-ward activities. It was the relatively rare attendant who spent time talking with patients or playing games with them. It proved impossible to obtain a "percent mingling time" for nurses, since the amount of time they spent out of the cage was too brief. Rather, we counted instances of emergence from the cage. On the average, daytime nurses emerged from the cage 11.5 times per shift, including instances when they left the ward entirely (range, 4 to 39 times). Late afternoon and night nurses were even less available, emerging on the average 9.4 times per shift (range, 4 to 41 times). Data on early morning nurses, who arrived usually after midnight and departed at 8 a.m., are not available because patients were asleep during most of this period.

Physicians, especially psychiatrists, were even less available. They were rarely seen on the wards. Quite commonly, they would be seen only when they arrived and departed, with the remaining time being spent in their offices or in the cage. On the average, physicians emerged on the ward 6.7 times per day (range 1 to 17 times). It proved difficult to make an accurate estimate in this regard, since physicians often maintained hours that allowed them to come and go at different times.

The hierarchical organization of the psychiatric hospital has been commented on before, but the latent meaning of that kind of organization is worth noting again. Those with the most power have least to do with patients, and those with the least power are most involved with them. Recall, however, that the acquisition of role-appropriate behaviors occurs mainly through the observation of others, with the most powerful having the most influence. Consequently, it is understandable that attendants not only spend more time with patients than do any other members of the staff—that is required by their station in the hierarchy —but also, insofar as they learn from their superiors' behavior, spend as little time with patients as they can. Attendants are seen mainly in the cage, which is where the models, the action, and the power are.

I turn now to a different set of studies, these dealing with staff response to patient-initiated contact. It has long been known that the amount of time a person spends with you can be an index of your significance to him. If he initiates and maintains eye contact, there is reason to believe that he is considering your requests and needs. If he pauses to chat or actually stops and talks, there is added reason to infer that he is individuating you. In four hospitals, the pseudopatient approached the staff member with a request which took the following form: "Pardon me, Mr. [or Dr. or Mrs.] X, could you tell me when I will be eligible for grounds privileges?" (or " ... when I will be presented at the staff meeting?" or " ... when I am likely to be discharged?"). While the content of the question varied according to the appropriateness of the target and the pseudopatient's (apparent) current needs, the form was always a courteous and relevant request for information. Care was taken never to approach a particular member of the staff more than once a day, lest the staff member become suspicious or irritated. In examining these data, remember that the behavior of the pseudopatients was neither bizarre nor disruptive. One could indeed engage in good conversation with them.

The data for these experiments are shown in Table 1, separately for physicians (column 1) and for nurses and attendants (column 2). Minor differences between these four institutions were overwhelmed by the degree to which staff avoided continuing contacts that patients had initiated. By far, their most common response consisted of either a brief response to the question offered while they were "on the move" and with head averted, or no response at all.

The encounter frequently took the following bizarre form: (pseudopatient) "Pardon me, Dr. X. Could you tell me when I am eligible for grounds privileges?" (physician) "Good morning Dave. How are you today?" (moves off without waiting for a response).

It is instructive to compare these data with data recently obtained at Stanford University. It has been alleged that large and eminent universities are characterized by faculty who are so busy that they have no time for students. For this comparison, a young lady approached individual faculty members who seemed to be walking purposefully to some meeting or teaching engagement and asked them the following questions.

1. "Pardon me, could you direct me to Encina Hall?" (at the medical school: " ... to the Clinical Research Center?").

Table 1

Self-Initiated Contact by Pseudopatients With Psychiatrists and Nurses and Attendants, Compared With Other Groups

Contact	Psychiatric hospitals		University campus (nonmedical)	University medical center Physicians		
	(1) Psychiatrists	(2) Nurses and attendants	(3) Faculty	(4) "Looking for a psychiatrist"	(5) "Looking for an internist"	(6) No additional comment
Responses						
Moves on, head averted (%)	71	88	0	0	0	0
Makes eye contact (%)	23	10	0	11	0	0
Pauses and chats (%)	2	2	0	11	0	0
Stops and talks (%)	4	0.5	100	78	100	90
Mean number of questions answered (out of 6)	*	*	6	3.8	4.8	4.5
Respondents (No.)	13	47	14	18	15	10
Attempts (No.)	185	1283	14	18	15	10

*Not applicable

2. "Do you know where Fish Annex is?" (there is no Fish Annex at Stanford).
3. "Do you teach here?"
4. "How does one apply for admission to the college?" (at the medical school: "... to the medical school?").
5. "Is it difficult to get in?"
6. "Is there financial aid?"

Without exception, as can be seen in Table 1 (column 3), all of the questions were answered. No matter how rushed they were, all respondents not only maintained eye contact, but stopped to talk. Indeed, many of the respondents went out of their way to direct or take the questioner to the office she was seeking, to try to locate "Fish Annex," or to discuss with her the possibilities of being admitted to the university.

Similar data, also shown in Table 1 (columns 4, 5, and 6), were obtained in the hospital. Here too, the young lady came prepared with six questions. After the first question, however, she remarked to 18 of her respondents (column 4), "I'm looking for a psychiatrist," and to 15 others (column 5), "I'm looking for an internist." Ten other respondents received no inserted comment (column 6). The general degree of cooperative responses is considerably higher for these university groups than it was for pseudopatients in psychiatric hospitals. Even so, differences are apparent with the medical school setting. Once having indicated that she was looking for a psychiatrist, the degree of cooperation elicited was less than when she sought an internist.

POWERLESSNESS AND DEPERSONALIZATION

Eye contact and verbal contact reflect concern and individuation: their absence, avoidance and depersonalization. The data I have presented do not do justice to the rich daily encounters that grew up around matters of depersonalization and avoidance. I have records of patients who were beaten by staff for the sin of initiating verbal contact. During my own experience, for example, one patient was beaten in the presence of other patients for having approached an attendant and told him, "I like you." Occasionally, punishment meted out to patients for misdemeanors seemed so excessive that it could not be justified by the most radical interpretations of psychiatric canon. Nevertheless, they appeared to go unquestioned. Tempers were often short. A patient who had not heard a call for medication would be roundly excoriated, and the morning attendants would often wake patients with, "Come on, you m—— f——s, out of bed!"

Neither anecdotal nor "hard" data can convey the overwhelming sense of powerlessness which invades the individual as he is continually exposed to the depersonalization of the psychiatric hospital. It hardly matters *which* psychiatric hospital —the excellent public ones and the very plush private hospital were better than the rural and shabby ones in this regard, but again, the features that psychiatric hospitals had in common overwhelmed by far their apparent differences.

Powerlessness was evident everywhere. The patient is deprived of many of his legal rights by dint of his psychiatric commitment. He is shorn of credibility by virtue of his psychiatric label. His freedom of movement is restricted. He cannot initiate contact with the staff, but may only respond to such overtures as they make. Personal privacy is minimal. Patient quarters and possessions can be entered and examined by any staff member, for whatever reason. His personal history and anguish are available to any staff member (often including the "grey lady" and "candy striper" volunteer) who chooses to read his folder, regardless of their therapeutic relationship to him. His personal hygiene and waste evacuation are often monitored. The water closets may have no doors.

At times, the depersonalization reached such proportions that pseudopatients had the sense that they were invisible, or at least unworthy of account. Upon being admitted, I and other pseudopatients took the initial physical examination in a semipublic room, where staff members went about their own business as if we were not there.

On the ward, attendants delivered verbal and occasionally serious physical abuse to patients in the presence of other observing patients, some of whom (the pseudopatients) were writing it all down. Abusive behavior, on the other hand, terminated quite abruptly when other staff members were known to be coming. Staff are credible witnesses. Patients are not.

A nurse unbuttoned her uniform to adjust her brassiere in the presence of an entire ward of viewing men. One did not have the sense that she was being seductive. Rather, she didn't notice us. A group of staff persons might point to a patient in the dayroom and discuss him animatedly, as if he were not there.

One illuminating instance of depersonalization and invisibility occurred with regard to medications. All told, the pseudopatients were administered nearly 2100 pills, including Elavil, Stelazine, Compazine, and Thorazine, to name but a few. (That such a variety of medications should have been administered to patients presenting identical symptoms is itself worthy of note.) Only two were swallowed. The rest were either pocketed or deposited in the toilet. The pseudopatients were not alone in this. Although I have no precise records on how many patients rejected their medications, the pseudopatients frequently found the medications of other patients in the toilet before they deposited their own. As long as they were cooperative, their behavior and the pseudopatients' own in this matter, as in other important matters, went unnoticed throughout.

Reactions to such depersonalization among pseudopatients were intense. Although they had come to the hospital as participant observers and were fully aware that they did not "belong," they nevertheless found themselves caught up in and fighting the process of depersonalization. Some examples: a graduate student in psychology asked his wife to bring his textbooks to the hospital so he could "catch up on his homework"—this despite the elaborate precautions taken to conceal his professional association. The same student, who had trained for quite some time to get into the hospital, and who had looked forward to the experience, "remembered" some drag races that he had wanted to see on the weekend and insisted that he be discharged by that time. Another pseudopatient attempted a romance with a nurse. Subsequently, he informed the staff that he was applying for admission to graduate school in psychology and was very likely to be admitted, since a graduate professor was one of his regular hospital visitors. The same person began to engage in psychotherapy with other patients—all of this as a way of becoming a person in an impersonal environment.

THE SOURCES OF DEPERSONALIZATION

What are the origins of depersonalization? I have already mentioned two. First, are attitudes held by all of us toward the mentally ill—including those who treat them—attitudes characterized by fear, distrust, and horrible expectations on the other. Our ambivalence leads us, in this instance as in others, to avoidance.

Second, and not entirely separate, the hierarchical structure of the psychiatric hospital facilitates depersonalization. Those who are at the top have least to do with patients, and their behavior inspires the rest of the staff. Average daily contact with psychiatrists, psychologists, residents, and physicians combined ranged from 3.9 to 25.1 minutes, with an overall mean of 6.8 (six pseudopatients over a total of 129 days of hospitalization). Included in this average are time spent in the admissions interview, ward meetings in the presence of a senior staff member, group and individual psychotherapy contacts, case presentation conferences, and discharge meetings. Clearly, patients do not spend much time in interpersonal contact with doctoral staff. And doctoral staff serve as models for nurses and attendants.

There are probably other sources. Psychiatric installations are presently in serious financial straits. Staff shortages are pervasive, staff time at a premium. Something has to give, and that something is patient contact. Yet, while financial stresses are realities, too much can be made of them. I have the impression that the psychological forces that result in depersonalization are much stronger than the fiscal ones and that the addition of more staff would not correspondingly improve patient care in this regard. The incidence of staff meetings and the enormous amount of record-keeping on patients, for example, have not been as substantially reduced as has patient contact. Priorities exist, even during hard times. Patient contact is not a significant priority in the traditional psychiatric hospital, and fiscal pressures do not account for this. Avoidance and depersonalization may.

Heavy reliance upon psychotropic medication tacitly contributes to depersonalization by convincing staff that treatment is indeed being conducted and that further patient contact may not be necessary. Even here, however, caution needs to be exercised in understanding the role of psychotropic drugs. If patients were powerful rather than powerless, if they were viewed as interesting individuals rather than diagnostic entities, if they were socially significant rather than social lepers, if their anguish truly and wholly compelled our sympathies and concerns, would we not *seek* contact with them, despite the availability of medications? Perhaps for the pleasure of it all?

THE CONSEQUENCES OF LABELING AND DEPERSONALIZATION

Whenever the ratio of what is known to what needs to be known approaches zero, we tend to invent "knowledge" and assume that we understand more than we actually do. We seem unable to acknowledge that we simply don't know. The needs for diagnosis and remediation of behavioral and emotional problems are enormous. But rather than acknowledge that we are just embarking on understanding, we continue to label patients "schizophrenic," "manic-depressive," and "insane," as if in those words we had captured the essence of understanding. The facts of the matter are that we have known for a long time that diagnoses are often not useful or reliable, but we have nevertheless continued to use them. We now know that we cannot distinguish insanity from sanity. It is depressing to consider how that information will be used.

Not merely depressing, but frightening. How many people, one wonders, are sane but not recognized as such in our psychiatric institutions? How many have been needlessly stripped of their privileges of citizenship, from the right to vote and drive to that of handling their own accounts? How many have feigned insanity in order to avoid the criminal consequences of their behavior, and, conversely, how many would rather stand trial than live interminably in a psychiatric hospital—but are wrongly thought to be mentally ill? How many have been stigmatized by well-intentioned, but nevertheless erroneous, diagnoses? On the last point, recall again that a "type 2 error" in psychiatric diagnosis does not have the same consequences it does in medical diagnosis. A diagnosis of cancer that has been found to be in error is cause for celebration. But psychiatric diagnoses are rarely found to be in error. The label sticks, a mark of inadequacy forever.

Finally, how many patients might be "sane" outside the psychiatric hospital but seem insane in it—not because craziness resides in them, as it were, but because they are responding to a bizarre setting, one that may be unique to institutions which harbor nether people? Goffman calls the process of socialization to such institutions "mortification"—an apt metaphor that includes the processes of depersonalization that have been described here. And while it is impossible to know whether the pseudopatients' responses to these processes are characteristic of all inmates—they were after all, not real patients—it is difficult to believe that these processes of socialization to a psychiatric hospital provide useful attitudes or habits of response for living in the "real world."

SUMMARY AND CONCLUSIONS

It is clear that we cannot distinguish the sane from the insane in psychiatric hospitals. The hospital itself imposes a special environment in which the meanings of behavior can easily be misunderstood. The consequences to patients hospitalized in such an environment—the powerlessness, depersonalization, segregation, mortification, and self-labeling—seem undoubtedly countertherapeutic.

I do not, even now, understand this problem well enough to perceive solutions. But two matters seem to have some promise. The first concerns the proliferation of community mental health facilities, of crisis intervention centers, of the human potential movement, and of behavior therapies that, for all of their own problems, tend to avoid psychiatric labels, to focus on specific problems and behaviors, and to retain the individual in a relatively nonpejorative environment.

Clearly, to the extent that we refrain from sending the distressed to insane places, our impressions of them are less likely to be distorted. (The risk of distorted perceptions, it seems to me, is always present, since we are much more sensitive to an individual's behaviors and verbalizations than we are to the subtle contextual stimuli that often promote them. At issue here is a matter of magnitude. And, as I have shown, the magnitude of distortion is exceedingly high in the extreme context that is a psychiatric hospital).

The second matter that might prove promising speaks to the need to increase the sensitivity of mental health workers and researchers to the *Catch-22* position of psychiatric patients. Simply reading materials in this area will be of help to some such workers and researchers. For others, directly experiencing the impact of psychiatric hospitalization will be of enormous use. Clearly, further research into the social psychology of such total institutions will both facilitate treatment and deepen understanding.

I and the other pseudopatients in the psychiatric setting had distinctly negative reactions. We do not pretend to describe the subjective experiences of true patients. Theirs may be different from ours, particularly with the passage of time and the necessary process of adaptation to one's environment. But we can and do speak to the relatively more objective indices of treatment within the hospital. It could be a mistake, and a very unfortunate one, to consider that what happened to us derived from malice or stupidity on the part of the staff. Quite the contrary, our overwhelming impression of them was of people who really cared, who were committed and who were uncommonly intelligent. Where they failed, as they sometimes did painfully, it would be more accurate to attribute those failures to the environment in which they too, found themselves than to personal callousness. Their perceptions and behavior were controlled by the situation, rather than being motivated by a malicious disposition. In a more benign environment, one that was less attached to global diagnosis, their behaviors and judgments might have been more benign and effective.

NO

Robert L. Spitzer

ON PSEUDOSCIENCE IN SCIENCE, LOGIC IN REMISSION AND PSYCHIATRIC DIAGNOSIS

Some foods taste delicious but leave a bad aftertaste. So it is with Rosenhan's study, "On Being Sane in Insane Places" (Rosenhan, 1973a), which, by virtue of the prestige and wide distribution of *Science*, the journal in which it appeared, provoked a furor in the scientific community. That the *Journal of Abnormal Psychology*, at this late date, chooses to explore the study's strengths and weaknesses is a testament not only to the importance of the issues that the study purports to deal with but to the impact that the study has had in the mental health community.

Rosenhan apparently believes that psychiatric diagnosis is of no value. There is nothing wrong with his designing a study the results of which might dramatically support this view. However, "On Being Sane in Insane Places" is pseudoscience presented as science. Just as his pseudopatients were diagnosed at discharge as "schizophrenia, in remission," so a careful examination of this study's methods, results, and conclusions leads me to a diagnosis of "logic, in remission."

Let us summarize the study's central question, the methods used, the results reported, and Rosenhan's conclusions. Rosenhan (1973a) states the basic issue simply: "Do the salient characteristics that lead to diagnoses reside in the patients themselves or in the environments and contexts in which observers find them?" Rosenhan proposed that by getting normal people who had never had symptoms of serious psychiatric disorders admitted to psychiatric hospitals "and then determining whether they were discovered to be sane" was an adequate method of studying this question. Therefore, eight "sane" people, pseudopatients, gained secret admission to 12 different hospitals with a single complaint of hearing voices. Upon admission to the psychiatric ward, the pseudopatients ceased simulating any symptoms of abnormality.

The diagnostic results were that 11 of the 12 diagnoses on admission were schizophrenia and 1 was manic-depressive psychosis. At discharge, all of the patients were given the same diagnosis, but were qualified as "in remission."[1]

From Robert L. Spitzer, "On Pseudoscience in Science, Logic in Remission and Psychiatric Diagnosis: A Critique of 'On Being Sane in Insane Places,'" *Journal of Abnormal Psychology*, vol. 84 (1975), pp. 442–452. Copyright © 1975 by The American Psychological Association. Reprinted by permission.

Despite their "show of sanity" the pseudopatients were never detected by any of the professional staff, nor were any questions raised about their authenticity during the entire hospitalization.

Rosenhan (1973a) concluded: "It is clear that we cannot distinguish the sane from the insane in psychiatric hospitals" (p. 257). According to him, what is needed is the avoidance of "global diagnosis," as exemplified by such diagnoses as schizophrenia or manic-depressive psychosis, and attention should be directed instead to "behaviors, the stimuli that provoke them, and their correlates."

THE CENTRAL QUESTION

One hardly knows where to begin. Let us first acknowledge the potential importance of the study's central research question. Surely, if psychiatric diagnoses are, to quote Rosenhan, "only in the minds of the observers," and do not reflect any characteristics inherent in the patient, then they obviously can be of no use in helping patients. However, the study immediately becomes confused when Rosenhan suggests that this research question can be answered by studying whether or not the "sanity" of pseudopatients in a mental hospital can be discovered. Rosenhan, a professor of law and psychology, knows that the terms "sane" and "insane" are legal, not psychiatric, concepts. He knows that no psychiatrist makes a diagnosis of "sanity" or "insanity" and that the true meaning of these terms, which varies from state to state, involves the inability to appreciate right from wrong—an issue that is totally irrelevant to this study.

DETECTING THE SANITY OF A PSEUDOPATIENT

However, if we are forced to use the terms "insane" (to mean roughly showing signs of serious mental disturbance) and "sane" (the absence of such signs), then clearly there are three possible meanings to the concept of "detecting the sanity" of a pseudopatient who feigns mental illness on entry to a hospital, but then acts "normal" throughout his hospital stay. The first is the recognition, when he is first seen, that the pseudopatient is feigning insanity as he attempts to gain admission to the hospital. This would be detecting sanity in a sane person simulating insanity. The second would be the recognition, after having observed him acting normally during his hospitalization, that the pseudopatient was initially feigning insanity. This would be detecting that the currently sane never was insane. Finally, the third possible meaning would be the recognition, during hospitalization, that the pseudopatient, though initially appearing to be "insane," was no longer showing signs of psychiatric disturbance.

These elementary distinctions of "detecting sanity in the insane" are crucial to properly interpreting the results of the study. The reader is misled by Rosenhan's implication that the first two meanings of detecting the sanity of the pseudopatient to be a fraud, are at all relevant to the central research question. Furthermore, he obscures the true results of his study—because they fail to support his conclusion—when the third meaning of detecting sanity is considered, that is, a recognition that after their admission as "insane," the pseudopatients were not psychiatrically disturbed while in the hospital.

Let us examine these three possible meanings of detecting the sanity of the pseudopatient, their logical relation to the central question of the study, and the actual results obtained and the validity of Rosenhan's conclusions.

THE PATIENT IS NO LONGER "INSANE"

We begin with the third meaning of detecting sanity. It is obvious that if the psychiatrists judged the pseudopatients as seriously disturbed while they acted "normal" in the hospital, this would be strong evidence that their assessments were being influenced by the context in which they were making their examination rather than the actual behavior of the patient, which is the central research question. (I suspect that many readers will agree with Hunter who, in a letter to *Science* (Hunter, 1973), pointed out that, "The pseudopatients did *not* behave normally in the hospital. Had their behavior been normal, they would have walked to the nurses' station and said, 'Look, I am a normal person who tried to see if I could get into the hospital by behaving in a crazy way or saying crazy things. It worked and I was admitted to the hospital, but now I would like to be discharged from the hospital'" [p. 361].)

What were the results? According to Rosenhan, all the patients were diagnosed at discharge as "in remission."[2] The meaning of "in remission" is clear: It means without signs of illness. Thus, all of the psychiatrists apparently recognized that all of the pseudopatients were, to use Rosenhan's term, "sane." However, lest the reader appreciate the significance of these findings, Rosenhan (1973a) quickly gives a completely incorrect interpretation: "If the pseudopatient was

to be discharged, he must naturally be 'in remission'; but he was not sane, nor, in the institution's view, had he ever been sane" (p. 252). Rosenhan's implication is clear: The patient was diagnosed "in remission" not because the psychiatrist correctly assessed the patient's hospital behavior but only because the patient had to be discharged. Is this interpretation warranted?

I am sure that most readers who are not familiar with the details of psychiatric diagnostic practice assume, from Rosenhan's account, that it is common for schizophrenic patients to be diagnosed "in remission" when discharged from a hospital. As a matter of fact, it is extremely unusual. The reason is that a schizophrenic is rarely completely asymptomatic at discharge. Rosenhan does not report any data concerning the discharge diagnoses of the real schizophrenic patients in the 12 hospitals used in his study. However, I can report on the frequency of a discharge diagnosis of schizophrenia "in remission" at my hospital, the New York State Psychiatric Institute, a research, teaching, and community hospital where diagnoses are made in a routine fashion, undoubtedly no different from the 12 hospitals of Rosenhan's study. I examined the official book that the record room uses to record the discharge diagnoses and their statistical codes for all patients. Of the over 300 patients discharged in the last year with a diagnosis of schizophrenia, not one was diagnosed "in remission." It is only possible to code a diagnosis of "in remission" by adding a fifth digit (5) to the 4-digit code number for the subtype of schizophrenia (e.g., paranoid schizophrenia is coded as 295.3, but paranoid schizophrenia "in remission" is coded as 295.35). I therefore realized that a psychiatrist might intend to make a discharge diagnosis of "in remission" but fail to use the fifth digit, so that the official recording of the diagnosis would not reflect his full assessment. I therefore had research assistants read the discharge summaries of the last 100 patients whose discharge diagnosis was schizophrenia to see how often the term "in remission," "recovered," "no longer ill," or "asymptomatic" was used, even if not recorded by use of the fifth digit in the code number. The result was that only one patient, who was diagnosed paranoid schizophrenia, was described in the summary as being "in remission" at discharge. The fifth digit code was not used.

To substantiate my view that the practice at my hospital of rarely giving a discharge diagnosis of schizophrenia "in remission" is not unique, I had a research assistant call the record room librarians of 12 psychiatric hospitals, chosen catch as catch can.[3] They were told that we were interested in knowing their estimate of how often, at their hospital, schizophrenics were discharged "in remission" (or "no longer ill" or "asymptomatic"). The calls revealed that 11 of the 12 hospitals indicated that the term was either never used or, at most, used for only a handful of patients in a year. The remaining hospital, a private hospital, estimated that the terms were used in roughly 7 percent of the discharge diagnoses.

This leaves us with the conclusion that, because 11 of the 12 pseudopatients were discharged as "schizophrenia in remission," a discharge diagnosis that is rarely given to real schizophrenics, the diagnoses given to the pseudopatients were a function of the patients' behaviors and not of the setting (psychiatric hospital) in which the diagnoses were made. In

fact, we must marvel that 11 psychiatrists all acted so rationally as to use at discharge the category of "in remission" or its equivalent, a category that is rarely used with real schizophrenic patients.

It is not only in his discharge diagnosis that the psychiatrist had an opportunity to assess the patient's true condition incorrectly. In the admission mental status examination, during a progress note or in his discharge note the psychiatrist could have described any of the pseudopatients as "still psychotic," "probably still hallucinating but denies it now," "loose associations," or "inappropriate affect." Because Rosenhan had access to all of this material, his failure to report such judgments of continuing serious psychopathology strongly suggests that they were never made.

All pseudopatients took extensive notes publicly to obtain data on staff and patient behavior. Rosenhan claims that the nursing records indicate that "the writing was seen as an aspect of their pathological behavior." The only datum presented to support this claim is that the daily nursing comment on one of the pseudopatients was, "Patient engaged in writing behavior." Because nursing notes frequently and intentionally comment on nonpathological activities that patients engage in so that other staff members have some knowledge of how the patient spends his time, this particular nursing note in no way supports Rosenhan's thesis. Once again, the failure of Rosenhan to provide data regarding instances where normal hospital behavior was categorized as pathological is remarkable. The closest that Rosenhan comes to providing such data is his report of an instance where a kindly nurse asked if a pseudopatient, who was pacing the long hospital corridors because of boredom, was "nervous." It was, after all, a question and not a final judgment.

Let us now examine the relation between the other two meanings of detecting sanity in the pseudopatients: the recognition that the pseudopatient was a fraud, either when he sought admission to the hospital or during this hospital stay, and the central research question.

DETECTING "SANITY" BEFORE ADMISSION

Whether or not psychiatrists are able to detect individuals who feign psychiatric symptoms is an interesting question but clearly of no relevance to the issue of whether or not the salient characteristics that lead to diagnoses reside in the patient's behavior or in the minds of the observers. After all, a psychiatrist who believes in a pseudopatient who feigns a symptom *is* responding to the pseudopatient's behavior. And Rosenhan does not blame the psychiatrist for believing the pseudopatient's fake symptom of hallucinations. He blames him for the diagnosis of schizophrenia. Rosenhan (1973b) states:

> The issue is not that the psychiatrist believed him. Neither is it whether the pseudopatient should have been admitted to the psychiatric hospital in the first place.... The issue is the diagnostic leap that was made between the single presenting symptom, hallucinations, and the diagnosis schizophrenia (or in one case, manic-depressive psychosis). Had the pseudopatients been diagnosed "hallucinating," there would have been no further need to examine the diagnosis issue. The diagnosis of hallucinations implies only that: no more. The presence of hallucinations does not itself define

the presence of "schizophrenia." And schizophrenia may or may not include hallucinations. (p. 366)

Unfortunately, as judged by many of the letters to *Science* commenting on the study (Letters to the editor, 1973), many readers, including psychiatrists, accepted Rosenhan's thesis that it was irrational for the psychiatrists to have made an initial diagnosis of schizophrenia as *the most likely condition* on the basis of a single symptom. In my judgment, these readers were wrong. Their acceptance of Rosenhan's thesis was aided by the content of the pseudopatients' auditory hallucinations, which were voices that said "empty," "hollow," and "thud." According to Rosenhan (1973a), these symptoms were chosen because of "their apparent similarity to existential symptoms [and] the *absence* of a single report of existential psychoses in the literature" (p. 251). The implication is that if the content of specific symptoms has never been reported in the literature, then a psychiatrist should somehow know that the symptom is fake. Why then, according to Rosenhan, should the psychiatrist have made a diagnosis of hallucinating? This is absurd. Recently I saw a patient who kept hearing a voice that said, "It's O.K. It's O.K." I know of no such report in the literature. So what? I agree with Rosenhan that there has never been a report of an "existential psychosis." However, the diagnoses made were schizophrenia and manic-depressive psychosis, not existential psychosis.

DIFFERENTIAL DIAGNOSIS OF AUDITORY HALLUCINATIONS

Rosenhan is entitled to believe that psychiatric diagnoses are of no use and therefore should not have been given to the pseudopatients. However, it makes no sense for him to claim that within a diagnostic framework it was irrational to consider schizophrenia seriously as the most likely condition without his presenting a consideration of the differential diagnosis. Let me briefly give what I think is a reasonable differential diagnosis, based on the presenting picture of the pseudopatient when he applied for admission to the hospital.

Rosenhan says that "beyond alleging the symptoms and falsifying name, vocation, and employment, no further alterations of person, history, or circumstances were made" (p. 251). However, clearly the clinical picture includes not only the symptom (auditory hallucinations) but also the desire to enter a psychiatric hospital, from which it is reasonable to conclude that the symptom is a source of significant distress. (How often did the admitting psychiatrist suggest what would seem to be reasonable care: outpatient treatment? Did the pseudopatient have to add other complaints to justify inpatient treatment?) This, plus the knowledge that the auditory hallucinations are of 3 weeks duration,[4] establishes the hallucinations as significant symptoms of psychopathology as distinguished from so-called "pseudohallucinations" (hallucinations while falling asleep or awakening from sleep, or intense imagination with the voice heard from inside of the head).

Auditory hallucinations can occur in several kinds of mental disorders. The absence of a history of alcohol, drug abuse, or some other toxin, the absence of any signs of physical illness (such as high fever), and the absence of evidence of distractibility, impairment in concentration, memory or orientation, and a negative neurological examination all make an organic psychosis extremely unlikely. The absence of a recent precipitating stress rules out a transient situational disturbance of psychotic intensity or (to use a nonofficial category) hysterical psychosis. The absence of a profound disturbance in mood rules out an effective psychosis (we are not given the mental status findings for the patient who was diagnosed manic-depressive psychosis).

What about simulating mental illness? Psychiatrists know that occasionally an individual who has something to gain from being admitted to a psychiatric hospital will exaggerate or even feign psychiatric symptoms. This is a genuine diagnostic problem that psychiatrists and other physicians occasionally confront and is called "malingering." However, with the pseudopatients there was no reason to believe that any of them had anything to gain from being admitted into a psychiatric hospital except relief from their alleged complaint, and therefore no reason to suspect that the illness was feigned. Dear Reader: There is only one remaining diagnosis for the presenting symptom of hallucinations under these conditions in the classification of mental disorders used in this country, and that is schizophrenia.

Admittedly, there is a hitch to a definitive diagnosis of schizophrenia: Almost invariably there are other signs of the disorder present, such as poor premorbid adjustment, affective blunting, delusions, or signs of thought disorder. I would hope that if I had been one of the 12 psychiatrists presented with such a patient, I would have been struck by the lack of other signs of the disorder, but I am rather sure that having no reason to doubt the authenticity of the patients' claim of auditory hallucinations, I also would have been fooled into noting schizophrenia as the most likely diagnosis.

What does Rosenhan really mean when he objects to the diagnosis of schizophrenia because it was based on a "single symptom"? Does he believe that there are real patients with the single symptom of auditory hallucinations who are misdiagnosed as schizophrenic when they actually have some other condition? If so, what is the nature of that condition? Is Rosenhan's point that the psychiatrist should have used "diagnosis deferred," a category that is available but rarely used? I would have no argument with this conclusion. Furthermore, if he had presented data from real patients indicating how often patients are erroneously diagnosed on the basis of inadequate information and what the consequences were, it would have been a real contribution.

Until now, I have assumed that the pseudopatients presented only one symptom of psychiatric disorder. Actually, we know very little about how the pseudopatients presented themselves. What did the pseudopatients say in the study reported in *Science*, when asked as they must have been, what effect the hallucinations were having on their lives and why they were seeking admission into a hospital? The reader would be much more confident that a single presenting symptom was involved if Rosenhan had made available for each pseudopatient the actual admission work-up from the hospital record.

DETECTING SANITY AFTER ADMISSION

Let us now examine the last meaning of detecting sanity in the pseudopatients, namely, the psychiatrist's recognition, *after* observing him act normally during his hospitalization, that the pseudopatient was initially feigning insanity and its relation to the central research question. If a diagnostic condition, by definition, is always chronic and never remits, it would be irrational not to question the original diagnosis if a patient were later found to be asymptomatic. As applied to this study, if the concept of schizophrenia did not admit the possibility of recovery, then failure to question the original diagnosis when the pseudopatients were no longer overtly ill would be relevant to the central research question. It would be an example of the psychiatrist allowing the context of the hospital environment to influence his diagnostic behavior. But neither any psychiatric textbook nor the American Psychiatric Association's *Diagnostic and Statistical Manual of Mental Disorders* (American Psychiatric Association, 1968) suggests that mental illnesses endure forever. Oddly enough, it is Rosenhan (1973a) who, without any reference to the psychiatric literature, says: "A broken leg is something one recovers from, but mental illness allegedly endures forever" (p. 254). Who, other than Rosenhan, alleges it?

As Rosenhan should know, although some American psychiatrists restrict the label of schizophrenia to mean chronic or process schizophrenia, most American psychiatrists include an acute subtype. Thus, the *Diagnostic and Statistical Manual*, in describing the subtype, acute schizophrenic episode, states that "in many cases the patient recovers within weeks."

A similar straw man is created when Rosenhan (1973a) says,

The insane are not always insane... the bizarre behaviors upon which their (the pseudopatients) behaviors were allegedly predicated constituted only a small fraction of their total behavior. If it makes no sense to label ourselves permanently depressed on the basis of an occasional depression, then it takes better evidence than is presently available to label all patients insane or schizophrenic on the basis of behaviors or cognitions. (p. 254)

Who ever said that the behaviors that indicate schizophrenia or any other diagnostic category comprise the total of a patient's behavior? A diagnosis of schizophrenia does not mean that all of the patient's behavior is schizophrenic anymore than a diagnosis of carcinoma of the liver means that all of the patient's body is diseased.

Does Rosenhan at least score a point by demonstrating that, although the professional staff never considered the possibility that the pseudopatient was a fraud, this possibility was often considered by other patients? Perhaps, but I am not so sure. Let us not forget that all of the pseudopatients "took extensive notes publicly." Obviously this was highly unusual patient behavior and Rosenhan's quote from a suspicious patient suggests the importance it had in focusing the other patients' attention on the pseudopatients: "You're not crazy. You're a journalist or a professor (referring to the continual note-taking). You're checking up on the hospital." (Rosenhan, 1973a, p. 252)

Rosenhan presents ample evidence, which I find no reason to dispute, that the professional staff spent little time actually with the pseudopatients. The note-taking may easily have been overlooked, and therefore they developed no suspicion that the pseudopatients had simulated illness to gain entry into the hospital. Because there were no pseudopatients who did not engage in such unusual

behaviors, the reader cannot assess the significance of the patients' suspicions of fraud when the professional staff did not. I would predict, however, that a pseudopatient in a ward of patients with mixed diagnostic conditions would have no difficulty in masquerading convincingly as a true patient to both staff and patients if he did nothing unusual to draw attention to himself.

Rosenhan presents one way in which the diagnosis affected the psychiatrist's perception of the patient's circumstances: Historical facts of the case were often distorted by the staff to achieve consistency with psychodynamic theories. Here, for the first time, I believe Rosenhan has hit the mark. What he described happens all the time and often makes attendance at clinical case conferences extremely painful, especially for those with a logical mind and a research orientation. Although his observation is correct, it would seem to be more a consequence of individuals attempting to rearrange facts to comply with an unproven etiological theory than a consequence of diagnostic labeling. One could as easily imagine a similar process occurring when a weak-minded, behaviorally-oriented clinician attempts to rewrite the patient's history to account for "hallucinations reinforced by attention paid to patient by family members when patient complains of hearing voices." Such is the human condition.

One final finding requires comment. In order to determine whether "the tendency toward diagnosing the sane insane could be reversed," the staff of a research and teaching hospital was informed that at some time during the following three months, one or more pseudopatients would attempt to be admitted. No such attempt was actually made. Yet approximately 10 percent of the 193 real patients were suspected by two or more staff members (we are not told how many made judgments) to be pseudopatients. Rosenhan (1973a) concluded: "Any diagnostic process that lends itself so readily to massive errors of this sort cannot be a very reliable one" (p. 179). My conclusion is that this experimental design practically assures only one outcome.

ELEMENTARY PRINCIPLES OF RELIABILITY OF CLASSIFICATION

Some very important principles that are relevant to the design of Rosenhan's study are taught in elementary psychology courses and should not be forgotten. One of them is that a measurement or classification procedure is not reliable or unreliable in itself but only in its application to a specific population. There are serious problems in the reliability of psychiatric diagnosis as it is applied to the population to which psychiatric diagnoses are ordinarily given. However, I fail to see, and Rosenhan does not even attempt to show, how the reliability of psychiatric diagnoses applied to a population of pseudopatients (or one including the threat of pseudopatients). The two populations are just not the same. Kety (1974) has expressed it dramatically:

> If I were to drink a quart of blood and, concealing what I had done, come to the emergency room of any hospital vomiting blood, the behavior of the staff would be quite predictable. If they labeled and treated me as having a bleeding peptic ulcer, I doubt that I could argue convincingly that medical science does not know how to diagnose that condition. (p. 959)

(I have no doubt that if the condition known as pseudopatient ever assumed epidemic proportions among admittants to psychiatric hospitals, psychiatrists would in time become adept at identifying them, though at what risk to real patients, I do not know.)

ATTITUDES TOWARD THE INSANE

I shall not dwell on the latter part of Rosenhan's study, which deals with the experience of psychiatric hospitalization. Because some of the hospitals participated in residency training programs and were research oriented, I find it hard to believe that conditions were quite as bad as depicted, but they may well be. I have always believed that psychiatrists should spend more time on psychiatric wards to appreciate how mind dulling the experience must be for patients. However, Rosenhan does not stop at documenting the horrors of life on a psychiatric ward. He asserts, without a shred of evidence from his study, that "negative attitudes [toward psychiatric patients] are the natural offspring of the labels patients wear and the places in which they are found." This is nonsense. In recent years large numbers of chronic psychiatric patients, many of them chronic schizophrenics and geriatric patients with organic brain syndromes, have been discharged from state hospitals and placed in communities that have no facilities to deal with them. The affected communities are up in arms not primarily because they are mental patients labeled with psychiatric diagnoses (because the majority are not recognized as ex-patients) but because the behavior of some of them is sometimes incomprehensible, deviant, strange, and annoying.

There are at least two psychiatric diagnoses that are defined by the presence of single behaviors, much as Rosenhan would prefer a diagnosis of hallucinations to a diagnosis of schizophrenia. They are alcoholism and drug abuse. Does society have negative attitudes toward these individuals because of the diagnostic label attached to them by psychiatrists or because of their behavior?

THE USES OF DIAGNOSIS

Rosenhan believes that the pseudopatients should have been diagnosed as having hallucinations of unknown origin. It is not clear what he thinks the diagnosis should have been if the pseudopatients had been sufficiently trained to talk, at times, incoherently, and had complained of difficulty in thinking clearly, lack of emotion, and that their thoughts were being broadcast so that strangers knew what they were thinking. Is Rosenhan perhaps suggesting multiple diagnoses of (a) hallucinations, (b) difficulty thinking clearly, (c) lack of emotion, and (d) incoherent speech... all of unknown origin?

It is no secret that we lack a full understanding of such conditions as schizophrenia and manic-depressive illness, but are we quite as ignorant as Rosenhan would have us believe? Do we not know, for example, that hallucinations of voices accusing the patient of sin are associated with depressed affect, diurnal mood variation, loss of appetite, and insomnia? What about hallucinations of God's voice issuing commandments, associated with euphoric affect, psychomotor excitement, and accelerated and disconnected speech? Is this not also an entirely different condition?

There is a purpose to psychiatric diagnosis (Spitzer & Wilson, 1975). It is to enable mental health professionals to (a) communicate with each other about the subject matter of their concern, (b) comprehend the pathological processes involved in psychiatric illness, and (c) control psychiatric disorders. Control consists of the ability to predict outcome, prevent the disorder from developing, and treat it once it has developed. Any serious discussion of the validity of psychiatric diagnosis, or suggestions for alternative systems of classifying psychological disturbance, must address itself to these purposes of psychiatric diagnosis.

In terms of its ability to accomplish these purposes, I would say that psychiatric diagnosis is moderately effective as a shorthand way of communicating the presence of constellations of signs and symptoms that tend to cluster together, is woefully inadequate in helping us understand the pathological processes of psychiatric disorders, but does offer considerable help in the control of many mental disorders. Control is possible because psychiatric diagnosis often yields information of value in predicting the likely course of illness (e.g., an early recovery, chronicity, or recurrent episodes) and because for many mental disorders it is useful in suggesting the best available treatment.

Let us return to the three different clinical conditions that I described, each of which had auditory hallucinations as one of its manifestations. The reader will have no difficulty in identifying the three hypothetical conditions as schizophrenia, psychotic depression, and mania. Anyone familiar with the literature on psychiatric treatment will know that there are numerous well-controlled studies (Klein

& Davis, 1969) indicating the superiority of the major tranquilizers for the treatment of schizophrenia, of electroconvulsive therapy for the treatment of psychotic depression and, more recently, of lithium carbonate for the treatment of mania. Furthermore, there is convincing evidence that these three conditions, each of which is often accompanied by hallucinations, are influenced by separate genetic factors. As Kety (1974) said, "If schizophrenia is a myth, it is a myth with a strong genetic component."

Should psychiatric diagnosis be abandoned for a purely descriptive system that focuses on simple phenotypic behaviors before it has been demonstrated that such an approach is more useful as a guide to successful treatment or for understanding the role of genetic factors? I think not. (I have a vision. Traditional psychiatric diagnosis has long been forgotten. At a conference on behavioral classification, a keen research investigator proposes that the category "hallucinations of unknown etiology" be subdivided into three different groups based on associated symptomatology. The first group is characterized by depressed affect, diurnal mood variation, and so on, the second group by euphoric mood, psychomotor excitement....)

If psychiatric diagnosis is not quite as bad as Rosenhan would have us believe, that does not mean that it is all that good. What is the reliability of psychiatric diagnosis prior to 1972 (Spitzer & Fleiss, 1974) revealed that "reliability is only satisfactory for three categories: mental deficiencies, organic brain syndrome, and alcoholism. The level of reliability is no better than fair for psychosis and schizophrenia, and is poor for the remaining categories." So be it. But where did Rosenhan get the idea that

psychiatry is the only medical specialty that is plagued by inaccurate diagnosis? Studies have shown serious unreliability in the diagnosis of pulmonary disorders (Fletcher, 1952), in the interpretation of electrocardiograms (Davis, 1958), in the interpretation of X-rays (Cochrane & Garland, 1952; Yerushalmy, 1947), and in the certification of causes of death (Markush, Schaaf, & Siegel, 1967). A review of diagnostic unreliability in other branches of physical medicine is given by Garland (1960) and the problem of the vagueness of medical criteria for diagnosis is thoroughly discussed by Feinstein (1967). The poor reliability of medical diagnosis, even when assisted by objective laboratory tests, does not mean that medical diagnosis is of no value. So it is with psychiatric diagnosis.

Recognition of the serious problems of the reliability of psychiatric diagnosis has resulted in a new approach to psychiatric diagnosis—the use of specific inclusion and exclusion criteria, as contrasted with the usually vague and ill-defined general descriptions found in the psychiatric literature and in the standard psychiatric glossary of the American Psychiatric Association. This approach was started by the St. Louis group associated with the Department of Psychiatry of Washington University (Feighner, Robins, Guze, Woodruff, Winokur, & Munoz, 1972) and has been further developed by Spitzer, Endicott, and Robins (1974) as a set of criteria for a selected group of functional psychiatric disorders, called the Research Diagnostic Criteria (RDC). The Display shows the specific criteria for a diagnosis of schizophrenia from the latest version of the RDC.[5]

DIAGNOSTIC CRITERIA FOR SCHIZOPHRENIA FROM THE RESEARCH DIAGNOSTIC CRITERIA

1. At least two of the following are required for definite diagnosis and one for probable diagnosis:

   a. Thought broadcasting, insertion, or withdrawal (as defined in the RDC).
   b. Delusions of control, other bizarre delusions, or multiple delusions (as defined in the RDC), of any duration as long as definitely present.
   c. Delusions other than persecutory or jealousy, lasting at least 1 week.
   d. Delusions of any type if accompanied by hallucinations of any type for at least 1 week.
   e. Auditory hallucinations in which either a voice keeps up a running commentary on the patient's behaviors or thoughts as they occur, or two or more voices converse with each other (of any duration as long as definitely present).
   f. Nonaffective verbal hallucinations spoken to the subject (as defined in this manual).
   g. Hallucinations of any type throughout the day for several days or intermittently for at least 1 month.
   h. Definite instances of formal thought disorder (as defined in the RDC).
   i. Obvious catatonic motor behavior (as defined in the RDC).

2. A period of illness lasting at least 2 weeks.
3. At no time during the active period of illness being considered did the patient meet the criteria for either probable or definite manic or depressive syndrome (Criteria 1 and 2 under Major Depressive or Manic Disorders) to such a degree that it was a prominent part of the illness.

Reliability studies using the RDC with case record material (from which all cues as to diagnosis and treatment were removed), as well as with live patients, indicate high reliability for all of the major categories and reliability coefficients generally higher than have ever been reported (Spitzer, Endicott, Robins, Kuriansky, & Garland, in press). It is therefore clear that the reliability of psychiatric diagnosis can be greatly increased by the use of specific criteria. (The interjudge reliability [chance corrected agreement, K] for the diagnosis of schizophrenia using an earlier version of RDC criteria with 68 newly admitted psychiatric inpatients at the New York State Psychiatric Institute was .88, which is a thoroughly respectable level of reliability). It is very likely that the next edition of the American Psychiatric Association's *Diagnostic and Statistical Manual* will contain similar specific criteria.

There are other problems with current psychiatric diagnosis. The recent controversy over whether or not homosexuality per se should be considered a mental disorder highlighted the lack of agreement within the psychiatric profession as to the definition of a mental disorder. A definition has been proposed by Spitzer (Spitzer & Wilson, 1975), but it is not at all clear whether a consensus will develop supporting it.

There are serious problems of validity. Many of the traditional diagnostic categories, such as some of the subtypes of schizophrenia and of major affective illness, and several of the personality disorders, have not been demonstrated to be distinct entities or to be useful for prognosis or treatment assignment. In addition, despite considerable evidence supporting the distinctness of such conditions as schizophrenia and manic-depressive illness, the boundaries separating these conditions from other conditions are certainly not clear. Finally, the categories of the traditional psychiatric nomenclature are of least value when applied to the large numbers of outpatients who are not seriously ill. It is for these patients that a more behaviorally or problem-oriented approach might be particularly useful.

I have not dealt at all with the myriad ways in which psychiatric diagnostic labels can be, and are, misused to hurt patients rather than to help them. This is a problem requiring serious research which, unfortunately, Rosenhan's study does not help illuminate. However, whatever the solutions to that problem the misuse of psychiatric diagnostic labels is not a sufficient reason to abandon their use because they have been shown to be of value when properly used.

In conclusion, there are serious problems with psychiatric diagnosis, as there are with other medical diagnoses. Recent developments indicate that the reliability of psychiatric diagnosis can be considerably improved. However, *even with the poor reliability of current psychiatric diagnosis, it is not so poor that it cannot be an aid in the treatment of the seriously disturbed psychiatric patient.* Rosenhan's study, "On Being Sane in Insane Places," proves that pseudopatients are not detected by psychiatrists as having simulated signs of mental illness. This rather remarkable finding is not relevant to the real problems of the reliability and validity of psychiatric diagnosis and only serves to obscure them. A correct interpretation of his own data contradicts his conclusions. In the setting of a psychiatric hospital, psychiatrists are remarkably able to distinguish the "sane" from the "insane."

NOTES

1. The original article only mentions that the 11 schizophrenics were diagnosed "in remission." Personal communication from D. L. Rosenhan indicates that this also applied to the single pseudopatient diagnosed as manic-depressive psychosis.

2. In personal communication D. L. Rosenhan said that "in remission" referred to a use of that term or one of its equivalents, such as recovered or no longer ill.

3. Rosenhan has not identified the hospitals used in this study because of his concern with issues of confidentiality and the potential for ad hominem attack. However, this does make it impossible for anyone at those hospitals to corroborate or challenge his account of how the pseudopatients acted and how they were perceived. The 12 hospitals used in my mini-study were: Long Island Jewish-Hillside Medical Center, New York; Massachusetts General Hospital, Massachusetts; St. Elizabeth's Hospital, Washington, D.C.; McLean Hospital, Massachusetts; UCLA, Neuropsychiatric Institute, California; Meyer-Manhattan Hospital (Manhattan State), New York; Vermont State Hospital, Vermont; Medical College of Virginia, Virginia; Emory University Hospital, Georgia; High Point Hospital, New York; Hudson River State Hospital, New York, and New York Hospital-Cornell Medical Center, Westchester Division, New York.

4. This was not in the article but was mentioned to me in personal communication by D. L. Rosenhan.

5. For what it is worth, the pseudopatient would have been diagnosed as "probable" schizophrenia using these criteria because of 1(f). In personal communication, Rosenhan said that when the pseudopatients were asked how frequently the hallucinations occurred, they said "I don't know." Therefore, Criterion 1(g) is not met.

REFERENCES

American Psychiatric Association. *Diagnostic and statistical manual of mental disorders* (2nd ed.). Washington, D.C.: American Psychiatric Association, 1968.

Cochrane, A. L., & Garland, L. H. Observer error in interpretation of chest films: International Investigation. *Lancet*, 1952, 2, 505–509.

Davies, L. G. Observer variation in reports on electrocardiograms. *British Heart Journal*, 1958, 20, 153–161.

Feighner, J. P., and Robins, E., Guze, S. B., Woodruff, R. A., Winokur, G., & Munoz, R. Diagnostic criteria for use in psychiatric research. *Archives of General Psychiatry*, 1972, 26, 57–63.

Feinstein, A. *Clinical judgment*. Baltimore, Md.: Williams & Wilkins, 1967.

Fletcher, C. M. Clinical diagnosis of pulmonary emphysema—an experimental study. *Proceedings of the Royal Society of Medicine*, 1952, 45, 577–584.

Garland, L. H. The problem of observer error. *Bulletin of the New York Academy of Medicine*, 1960, 36, 570–584.

Hunter, F. M. Letters to the editor. *Science*, 1973, 180, 361.

Kety, S. S. From rationalization to reason. *American Journal of Psychiatry*, 1974, 131, 957–963.

Klein, D., & Davis, J. *Diagnosis and drug treatment of psychiatric disorders*. Baltimore, Md.: Williams & Wilkins, 1969.

Letters to the editor. *Science*, 1973, 180, 356–365.

Markush, R. E., Schaaf, W. E., & Siegel, D. G. The influence of the death certifier on the results of epidemiologic studies. *Journal of the National Medical Association*, 1967, 59, 105–113.

Rosenhan, D. L. On being sane in insane places. *Science*, 1973, 179, 250–258. (a)

Rosenhan, D. L. Reply to letters to the editor. *Science*, 1973, 180, 365–369. (b)

Spitzer, R. L., Endicott, J., & Robins, E. *Research diagnostic criteria*. New York: Biometrics Research, New York State Department of Mental Hygiene, 1974.

Spitzer, R. L., Endicott, J., Robins, E., Kuriansky, J., & Garland, B. Preliminary report of the reliability of research diagnostic criteria applied to psychiatric case records. In A. Sudilofsky, B. Beer, & S. Gershon (Eds.), *Prediction in psychopharmacology*, New York: Raven Press, in press.

Spitzer, R. L. & Fleiss, J. L. A reanalysis of the reliability of psychiatric diagnosis. *British Journal of Psychiatry*, 1974. 125, 341–347.

Spitzer, R. L., & Wilson, P. T. Nosology and the official psychiatric nomenclature. In A. Freedman & H. Kaplan (Eds.), *Comprehensive textbook of psychiatry*. New York: Williams & Wilkins, 1975.

Yerushalmy, J. Statistical problems in assessing methods of medical diagnosis with special reference to X-ray techniques. *Public Health Reports*, 1947, 62, 1432–1449.

CHALLENGE QUESTIONS

Classic Dialogue: Do Diagnostic Labels Hinder Treatment?

1. Would society be better off if there were no names (such as "normal" or "abnormal") for broad categories of behavior? Why, or why not?

2. Who would you consider best qualified to judge a person's mental health: a parent, a judge, or a doctor? Why?

3. If a person at any time displays symptoms of a mental disorder, even fraudulently, is it helpful to consider that the same symptoms of disorder may appear again? Why, or why not?

4. Is there any danger in teaching the diagnostic categories of mental behavior to beginning students of psychology? Explain.

ISSUE 2

Should Psychologists Be Allowed to Prescribe Drugs?

YES: Patrick H. DeLeon et al., from "The Case for Prescription Privileges: A Logical Evolution of Professional Practice," *Journal of Clinical Child Psychology* (vol. 20, no. 3, 1991)

NO: Garland Y. DeNelsky, from "The Case Against Prescription Privileges for Psychologists," *Psychotherapy in Private Practice* (vol. 11, no. 1, 1992)

ISSUE SUMMARY

YES: Psychologist and lawyer Patrick H. DeLeon and his colleagues argue that psychologists and the public would benefit greatly from psychologists' obtaining prescription privileges.

NO: Clinical psychologist Garland Y. DeNelsky opposes prescription privileges for psychologists on the grounds that they are likely to harm the discipline of psychology and its ability to serve the public.

A recent and highly controversial proposal to expand the role of the psychologist entails the prescribing of drugs. Drugs have been increasingly recognized as contributing to the effective treatment of mental disorders. Because such treatment has traditionally been the province of psychology, many psychologists have advocated that they should be allowed to use all the effective treatments available, including prescription medications.

The most controversial aspect of this proposal, however, is that within the mental health field, only psychiatrists (and a few other allied professions) are currently permitted to prescribe drugs. With this proposal, the psychologist would be moving into the professional and economic "turf" of the psychiatrist. Psychiatrists are medical doctors who have their primary training in the anatomy and physiology of the human body. Psychologists, on the other hand, are trained in human relations. Although some psychologists receive considerable education in pharmacology (the study of medications) and related topics, few have the training necessary to enable them to competently prescribe drugs. However, the question arises: What if an appropriate level of training were obtained? Couldn't psychologists, then, prescribe drugs to their patients?

Patrick H. DeLeon and his colleagues, in the following selection, answer this question affirmatively. The authors cite research as well as their own personal experiences to demonstrate that psychologists can successfully and competently prescribe medications. The federal government has allowed some psychologists under certain circumstances to assume the role of drug prescriber; DeLeon et al. argue that these experiences should be reviewed to determine whether or not psychologists should in general assume this role. Almost without exception, the authors argue, these experiences have been positive. The unique perspective of the psychologist, the authors contend, provides an important complement to the perspective of other drug prescribers.

Garland Y. DeNelsky contends that giving psychologists prescription privileges would mean the downfall of the field of psychology. Currently, many consumers find psychology attractive because it successfully treats people without the use of potentially dangerous drugs. This attractiveness would be undermined by prescription privileges. Thus, instead of psychology increasing its role in the treatment of mental disorders, DeNelsky asserts, psychology could find itself without a role at all.

POINT	COUNTERPOINT
• The vast majority of child psychologists feel that prescription privileges should be granted with specialized training.	• Recent surveys indicate that a majority of practicing psychologists do not favor obtaining prescription privileges.
• Psychologists will do a better job of prescribing than the general practitioners who now prescribe psychoactive drugs.	• Psychologists will likely be held to higher standards, leading to more liability problems.
• Prescription privileges will more effectively address the public's mental health needs.	• Prescription privileges will make psychology less attractive to the public it serves.
• The profession of psychology has now matured sufficiently to responsibly administer psychotropic medications.	• Drugs can detract from psychotherapeutic efforts by implying that benefits come from external agents.
• The unique perspective of the psychologist will complement that of other drug prescribers.	• The "war" with psychiatry will detract from the development of other distinctively psychological treatments.

YES

Patrick H. DeLeon et al.

THE CASE FOR PRESCRIPTION PRIVILEGES: A LOGICAL EVOLUTION OF PROFESSIONAL PRACTICE

As psychology has become more intimately involved in addressing society's pressing needs and has begun to conceptualize itself as a health care profession, it has become necessary collectively to rethink earlier self-imposed limits on its fundamental "scope of practice." Under our constitutional framework, psychologists employed within federal and state systems are not bound by the parameters of the various state practice acts, and certain psychologists have been able to demonstrate that, like their colleagues in a wide range of other professions, they can accept the clinical responsibility of utilizing psychoactive medications responsibly. To date, the profession's traditional training institutions have not accepted their responsibility of systematically providing relevant training experiences. Further, there is considerable disagreement within the practice community as to whether the profession should enter the prescription arena. However, recent legislative developments at the federal and state level would seem to ensure that this evolution will proceed....

THE FEDERAL GOVERNMENT AS A PROVIDER OF CARE

One of the fundamental roles the federal government currently fulfills in our society is to provide health services to various legislatively specified beneficiary populations (DeLeon & VandenBos, 1980)....

In the prescription arena, it has historically been the federal government's responsibility to determine which medications require prescriptions, and the responsibility of the various states to determine which health care practitioners would be authorized to prescribe and under what conditions (Burns, DeLeon, Chemtob, Welch, & Samuels, 1988). However, under our constitutional system of distinct federal–state responsibilities (powers), within

From Patrick H. DeLeon, Raymond A. Folen, Floyd L. Jennings, Diane J. Willis, and Rogers H. Wright, "The Case for Prescription Privileges: A Logical Evolution of Professional Practice," *Journal of Clinical Child Psychology*, vol. 20, no. 3 (1991), pp. 254–258, 262–265. Copyright © 1991 by Lawrence Erlbaum Associates, Inc. Reprinted by permission. References omitted.

federal health care institutions the various disciplines are not limited by the constraints of their particular state "scope of practice" acts, unless either the administration or the Congress has specifically so designated. Similarly, with the rare exception of overtly grievous or heinous incidents of malfeasance, it has historically been extraordinarily difficult to sue any governmental entity successfully for alleged "malpractice." Thus, from a health policy frame of reference, the federal system presents an excellent laboratory in which to test out new models of care (DeLeon, 1986, 1988b). And, we would further point out that the same flexibility is inherent within our various state governmental systems.

INNOVATIVE HEALTH MANPOWER DEMONSTRATIONS

In addition to providing direct care, another of the responsibilities of government has been to explore the development of innovative health human resources and service delivery initiatives. For example, the need of the VA for ready access to quality mental health care following World War II led to a major influx of training funds to our nation's clinical and counseling psychology programs (Cranston, 1986; Larson, 1986). Similarly, the health manpower interests of the then-Department of Health, Education, and Welfare (HEW) lead to the establishment of the nurse practitioner (NP) initiatives of the mid-1960s. In this context, we feel that as the various facets of psychology debate whether or not our profession should seek to obtain prescription privileges, it is important that the field as a whole step back and collectively look at the broader picture. In essence, we are proposing that

organized psychology learn from the experiences of the other nonphysician, or alternative, health care providers in this arena (DeLeon, 1988a; DeLeon, Kjervik, Kraut, & VandenBos, 1985; DeLeon, Wakefield, Schultz, Williams, & VandenBos, 1989).

In the mid-1970s, the state of California utilized its health human resources demonstration power to test out whether nonphysicians might be properly authorized to utilize prescriptive authority. On July 1, 1973 the state of California's Health Manpower Pilot Project Program became operational. Its *Final Report to the Legislature, State of California and to the Healing Arts Licensing Boards: Prescribing and Dispensing Pilot Projects* (State of California, 1982) was submitted in November, 1982. The authors reported that:

> None of the projects, to date, have received the intense scrutiny that these 10 prescribing and dispensing projects have received. Over one million patients have been seen by these prescribing and dispensing trainees over the past three years. At least 50% of these patients have had drugs prescribed for them or dispensed to them by these professionals. (p. i)

The report noted that the health professionals participating in the pilot projects received additional educational experiences provided by project staff. The principal teaching methods were lectures and seminars, varying from 16 hr to 95 hr in length. It was further noted that only 56% of the trainees had graduated from academic programs with a bachelors degree or higher; that is, they possessed considerably less educational training than doctoral-level psychologists.

Most of the patients seen were female (96%). They were clearly comfortable with the trainees' performance (99.5%), and 84% indicated that they received more information from the trainees than from physicians. The supervising physicians were similarly consistent in their judgment that permitting these physician associates to prescribe and dispense drugs had increased the availability of care and was cost effective. In fact, the state of California's (1982) final report concluded that: "Even when the cost of having physician supervision and pharmacist consultation... is computed, the annual savings to the health care delivery system is at least $2 million per year" (p. ii). Not surprisingly, the California Office of Statewide Health Planning and Development specifically recommended that clear statutory authority be enacted for the prescribing and dispensing of drugs by appropriately prepared registered nurses, physician assistants, and pharmacists.

Psychology should understand that this particular demonstration project was not conducted in a health policy vacuum. The state of California's report also cited literature on nurse practitioner prescription practices, which had found that there was total agreement between the recommendations of pediatric nurse practitioners and consulting pediatricians in 86% of the cases reviewed, and further, that in only two instances, or 0.7% of the cases, was the difference between the nurse and the physician assessment considered significant (Duncan, Smith, & Silver, 1971). Another study cited reported that nurse practitioners in primary care settings could handle two-thirds of the patient care episodes without consulting a physician and that there was no significant difference found in patient physi-

cal capacity, social function, or emotional function (Spitzer et al., 1974).

Independent reviews conducted by the Office of Technology Assessment (OTA; U.S. Congress, OTA, 1981, 1986c), which is the scientific policy arm of the Congress, have reached similar positive conclusions:

> the quality of care provided by NPs functioning within their areas of training and expertise tends to be as good as or better than care provided by physicians.... researchers found that NPs prescribe and use medications less frequently than do physicians, and that NPs tend to prescribe only well-known and relatively simple drugs. (U.S. Congress, OTA, 1986c, p. 19)

And, as one concrete example, we would point out that currently our nation's Certified Registered Nurse Anesthetists (CRNAs) provide care to more than 65% of all patients undergoing surgical or other medical intervention that necessitates the services of an anesthetist. CRNAs are the sole anesthesia provider in approximately 33% of the hospitals in the U.S., and they provide between 80% and 90% of the anesthesia received by Medicare beneficiaries (Jordan, 1990). Although most psychologists are not aware of the legislative struggles that CRNAs experience with their anesthesiologist (MD) colleagues, we would suggest that these are probably only second in intensity to those that our optometrist colleagues experienced with opthamologists (MDs) during their over 50-year successful struggle to obtain prescription privileges.

As we indicated earlier, we feel that it is important that psychology's practice and educational leadership take a careful look at what already exists in the health care (health manpower) literature, rather than allow themselves to enter into hypothetical and/or emotional debates as to whether our practitioners can (or should) be appropriately trained to accept this important clinical responsibility. And, we would further suggest that because our current training programs do not effectively control their own clinical facilities (e.g., we do not possess "teaching nursing homes" or administer "model in-patient wards"), most of our educational leadership does not currently possess sufficient clinical expertise to reach appropriate policy conclusions without consultation with other health care disciplines (Raymond, DeLeon, VandenBos, & Michael, in press).

PSYCHOLOGISTS WITHIN THE INDIAN HEALTH SERVICE

One of the authors (Floyd L. Jennings) served in the Indian Health Service (IHS) from May 1988 through May 1989; while in that capacity he was granted the legal authority to prescribe. In 1986 the IHS Santa Fe Indian Hospital and Service Unit had modified its hospital bylaws to specifically provide authority for qualified psychologists to prescribe under standing orders from a specified limited formulary (i.e., from a predetermined listing of approved medications). This approach (model) is common within the professional nursing community. Its application to psychology was at the behest of physicians in that particular hospital, had the active and enthusiastic support of the IHS area psychiatrist, and received cautious agreement from those in the psychology field! ...

During the period from August 1, 1988 thru May 3, 1989, when Jennings kept detailed records of his prescription protocols, 46% of his patient contacts were on an inpatient basis, and 25% of the patient contacts involved psychotropic medication (total number of patient contacts was 378). The vast majority of the prescriptions he ordered were for antidepressants, either tricyclics or second generation antidepressants such as trazodone, as 28% of all patient contacts involved a diagnosis of depression. There were significant sex differences in medications prescribed. For the 37 medication contacts with males, 51% involved neuroleptics. The medications he utilized included: amitriptyline, desipramine, doxepin, imipramine, trazodone, chlorpromazine, haldol, haldol decanoate, prolixin decanoate, stelazine, and thioridazine. Throughout this period the bottom line was that no major adverse experiences were encountered! Further, significant time was spent alleviating problems created by "less than appropriate treatment" provided by his physician colleagues.

Interestingly, when our colleague requested a ruling from the New Mexico Psychological Association as to whether he was functioning in an ethical manner when prescribing, the committee responded, in part, that:

It appears from your statements that you are practicing within relevant APA [American Psychological Association] ethical principles in your employment by the Indian Health Service. The Ethics Committee, however, believes that it is unable to make a definitive statement about the ethics of psychologists, or any particular psychologist, prescribing medication because psychology has not adopted any standards of education or practice as reference criteria. We recognize that general standards exist within the medical profession but we cannot assume that these standards represent criteria for psychologists as another profession. (J. P. Cardillo, personal communication, fall 1988)

From a health policy frame of reference, one might suggest that when Jennings prescribed, he was writing orders trading on the license and supervision (collaboration) of the hospital medical staff in general, and the clinical director, in particular.…

From a purely interprofessional/political frame of reference, it is interesting to note that when the fact of Jennings' prescribing practice came to the attention of psychiatry's political leadership, they worked closely with their colleagues throughout organized medicine and in the administration to stop this practice, notwithstanding the fact that there had not been a single incident of adverse care reported. On December 9, 1988 a memorandum was sent out to the field from the associate director, Office of IHS Health Programs, noting that:

> In a limited number of service units, clinical psychologists have been allowed by medical staff by-laws to prescribe psychotropic medications independent of physician supervision.… Therefore … I am hereby advising you that effective with the date of this letter, it is IHS policy that no psychologist may be permitted to prescribe medications independent of physician supervision. Operationally, this policy means at a minimum that any order for medication written for inpatients or outpatients by psychologists must be countersigned by a physician, preferably a psychiatrist.

For psychology, the IHS has already provided an operational answer to the question "Can we responsibly prescribe?"— We already have! And, it clearly remains IHS Policy that our practitioners can legally prescribe. The policy debate has moved to the issue of "under what conditions."…

THE CURRENT DEBATE WITHIN PSYCHOLOGY

A number of articles presenting opinions (Adams, 1986; Brandsma & Frey, 1986a, 1986b; Fox, 1986; Gay, 1978; Handler, 1988; Jones, 1984; Kotler-Cope, 1989) and opinion surveys (Bascue & Zlotowski, 1981; Folen, 1989; Massoth, McGrath, Bianchi, & Singer, 1990; Piotrowski, 1989; Piotrowski & Lubin, 1989) have recently been published within the psychological literature, and they generally report that significant numbers of psychologists have strong views on both sides of the policy issue of whether or not our profession should seek prescription privileges. Articles are also beginning to surface that raise the more fundamental question as to whether any profession (including psychology) should utilize psychotropic medications (Greenberg & Fisher, 1990; Klosko, Barlow, Tassinari, & Cerny, 1990). Some of the generic issues raised have been whether malpractice premiums would escalate needlessly versus whether the absence of prescription authority might result in greater liability (Dorken, 1990); whether as a practical matter it is possible to provide adequate training in medications without radically altering professional psychology's current training programs; and whether as a profession we would be in danger of losing our uniqueness (behavioral science and/or humanism) if we obtained this particular clinical responsibility (Platman, Dorgan, & Gerhard, 1976; Wiggins, 1980). And, of course, the issue of whether the political price required for eventual success would be worth it (DeLeon, 1986, 1988b).

The Section on Clinical Child Psychology of Division 12 (Section 1) experienced the same diversity of opinion among its executive committee and recently decided to form a task force to study the issue comprehensively. The committee agreed to explore the advantages and disadvantages of prescription privileges, to discuss the issues involved in the debate, and to survey clinical child psychologists about their opinions concerning the issue. Under the leadership of then-Section 1 President Russell Barkley, the task force reviewed the relevant literature, surveyed the Section membership, and concluded its work by issuing a report on the role of clinical child psychologists in the prescribing of psychoactive medication for children (Barkley et al., 1990). Barkley et al. sent out surveys to 950 Section members, of whom 56.2% responded. Results of the survey suggested that a majority of clinical child psychologists are consulted by, or consult with, a physician on medication issues, and a majority assist in evaluating, or monitoring, the effects of medications. Slightly more than 65% of the respondents felt that prescription privileges should be granted with specialized training in psychopharmacology at a postdoctoral level. Over 80% of those surveyed felt that services to underserved children, or children in rural areas, would improve if psychologists had such prescription privileges.

Clinical child psychologists, by the nature of their training in child development, behavioral assessment/intervention, and research are indeed involved in medication issues in a variety of ways as the Section 1 survey demonstrated (Conners, 1988). Research by Barkley et al. demonstrates the roles psychologists already play in monitoring behavioral effects of medication. In one of these studies the response of aggressive and nonaggressive attention deficit hyperactivity disorder (ADHD) children to two doses of methylphenidate was explored (Barkley, McMurray, Edelbrock, & Robbins, 1989). In another study, Barkley, Fischer, Newby, and Breen (1988) developed a multimethod clinical protocol for assessing stimulant drug responding in attention deficit disorder (ADD) children. The use of psychostimulant medication in treating ADHD children has been studied extensively, and the results demonstrate both the efficacy of treatment by medication (Barkley, 1977; Gadow, 1986; Gadow & Pomeroy, 1990) and the important role played by psychologists in monitoring medication effects.

Paralleling the debate on prescription privileges is the debate on whether children should be medicated. There are a variety of justifiable reasons for medicating children as indicated in the Barkley et al. (1990) report. Medication certainly may eliminate or decrease seizure activity in a child, thus modifying a dysfunctional neurological problem that may contribute to atypical behavior. Drugs used to treat anxiety or depression in children and adolescents may prevent them from harming themselves or others. Drugs for children also may suppress disrupting and embarrassing behavior such as seen in selected cases of Tourette's syndrome. Children who are diagnosed as having ADHD often are socially and behaviorally disruptive, and medication permits them to be placed in regular classrooms or at least in less restrictive environments (Barkley, 1990).

If medication is to be used with children, care must be taken in deciding what conditions indicate the appropriate use of medication. The Barkley et al. (1990) report provides a brief overview of changes in psychopathology and the special considerations in assessing the child prior to the decision to medicate. For example, one special consideration is to determine who the client might be. Parents who report that they cannot manage the child's behavior may be reflecting their own stress levels and not the activity level of the child. Thus, one cannot over-rely on one set of observations. Secondarily, one must be assured of the correct clinical diagnosis (e.g., one would not use medication with oppositional defiant disorder with anxious features and one might with ADHD children; Carlson, 1990). Clinical child psychologists generally have the training and knowledge to make these differential diagnoses. Training in psychopharmacology is a logical extension of working with children and would round out our care of a particular child.

Research is needed to further our knowledge about the appropriate use of medication with children. Clinical child and pediatric psychologists are in a unique position, not only in the assessment area but in the research area. Clinical child psychologists could initiate and collaborate in the pediatric psychopharmacology field. Areas woefully understudied include medication effects with adolescents and the mentally retarded (Campbell & Spencer, 1988). Because many studies dealing with these populations, especially with the mentally retarded, are already conducted by psychologists, a new field of research could be, and should be, initiated. But to be involved in this type of research clinical child psychologists must know something about medications, such as special considerations in pharmacokinetics, the efficacy of child psychoactive drugs, and issues to consider in deciding to medicate children. Barkley et al. (1990) clearly suggested that clinical child psychologists will seek retraining in psychopharmacology when this becomes a viable option, with over 45% responding affirmatively. With this new clinical authority, undoubtedly additional treatment will be provided to underserved populations, and important new research studies on the efficacy of child psychoactive drugs will be undertaken.

Depending on the particular clinical needs of the beneficiary population that one plans to serve, the context of the debate, and the necessary training model required, appear to differ substantially. For example, those working with the chronically mentally ill would have different needs than those working within comprehensive medical centers with the physically handicapped. Similarly, those working in rural America, where there is the necessity for truly comprehensive services (DeLeon et al., 1989) would have different requirements than those specializing in the unique needs of children, where behavior is such a predominant concern (Campbell & Spencer, 1988; U.S. Congress OTA, 1986a; Werry, 1982). Those interested in our nation's elderly are faced with statistics suggesting that (a) mental health problems are significant (U.S. Senate Special Committee on Aging, 1986, 1988) and are overlooked by general physicians in about 50% of elderly patients; (b) the American Medical Association (AMA) has publicly criticized general physicians' ability to prescribe psychotropic medications appropriately; and (c) the Inspector General of the U.S. has referred to the overmedication of the elderly as "our country's other drug problem." Each year drug over-doses cause 32,000 fractured hips from falls, 60,000 cases of Parkinson symptoms, and 15,000 cases of memory loss and dementia, not to mention 250,000 hospital admissions annually for adverse drug reactions (Office of the Inspector General, 1989; Welch, 1989b).

Notwithstanding the range of views that may exist within psychology on the underlying issue, it is clear that the elected political leadership of psychology is becoming increasingly supportive (Fox, 1988a; Graham, 1990a). A number of the practice division presidents have spoken out in favor of the movement (DeLeon, 1987d, 1987b, 1987c, 1987a, 1987e; Samuels, 1985; Wright, 1988), and arrangements have been made to increase significantly the presence of drug companies at relevant state association and divisional meetings. In November 1989 the APA Board of Professional Affairs (BPA) focused its fall retreat meeting on the issue of prescription privileges. After extensive consultation with relevant experts and deliberation, BPA (1989, p. 15) concluded that:

> ... BPA strongly endorses the immediate research and study intervention feasibility and curricula development in psychopharmacology for psychologists in order to provide broader service to the public and to address more effectively the public's psychological and mental health needs. And BPA strongly recommends moving to the highest APA priority a focused attention to the responsibility of preparing the profession of psychology to address the current and future needs of the public for psychologically managed psychopharmacological interventions.

During its August 1990 meeting, the APA Council of Representatives (the association's highest policy body) voted 118–2 to establish a prescription privilege task force.

In the most comprehensive survey conducted to date, the Practice Directorate arranged for an independent telephone interview of 1,505 APA members to be conducted by Frederick/Schneiders, Inc. (1990) between December 7 and December 22, 1990. Their key findings were:

1. There is very strong support for prescription privileges for psychologists (68%).
2. The proposition that psychologists could do a better job of prescribing than the general practitioners who now prescribe most psycho-active drugs is the most effective argument in support of prescription privileges (71%). A potential rise in malpractice rates is the strongest argument against the proposal (58%).
3. There is overwhelming support for a demonstration project on prescription privileges (78%). Even among opponents of the general proposal, a majority support the demonstration project (54%).

The authors concluded that: "There is nothing in these data to suggest that APA is getting too far out in front of the troops on this issue" (p. 28). They further concluded that: "This is overwhelming support for the only proposition that is currently on the table (the demonstration project). Supporting only the demonstration project at this time would be a very cautious and, certainly, very safe position for APA" (p. 23).

In our judgment, the next crucial development in this evolution will be the active participation of our educational training institutions. There can be little doubt that psychologists within the federal sector have (and will continue to) demonstrate that it is possible (and practical) to obtain this clinical privilege. Further, as the prescription privilege debate continues, those seriously interested in serving various underserved segments of our society (e.g., the chronically mentally ill, those in rural America, the elderly, and our nation's children) will come to appreciate the importance of this clinical modality to their collective goals. For some beneficiary populations, it is especially significant that: "the power to prescribe is also the power not to utilize medications" (B. F. Riess, personal communication).

To date, the missing component in the dialogue has been the practical one of how those who desire to obtain this clinical responsibility can obtain the necessary and appropriate training. Currently, at least 28 states authorize nurse practitioners/nurse clinical specialists to prescribe—including psychiatric nurses (American Nurses' Association [ANA], personal communication). Perhaps in one of these states we will soon find the state psychological association serving as a broker with a local nursing school in order to arrange the appropriate summer institute or continuing education courses, so that those of their membership who complete the training will have equivalent expertise to their nursing colleagues who can legally prescribe. Or perhaps the various state associations will pursue the route that Hawaii has chosen; that is, they will first seek legislative authority to prescribe and then develop appropriate training modules. In any case, however, it is clear that the APA Practice Directorate has already begun the process of making prescription privileges a state association legislative priority (Welch, 1989a).

SUMMARY

As Fox (1988b) pointed out, it may have been prudent and politically expedient 45 years ago, when efforts were directed to passing the first psychology licensing law, to adopt a dualism that placed all "hands-on" (i.e., physical) interventions beyond the scope of the practice of psychology. However, times (and knowledge) have changed dramatically since then, and in our judgment, the profession of psychology has now matured sufficiently to responsibly utilize psychotropic medications (BPA, 1981, 1986). Psychologists within the federal sector have demonstrated that our profession can prescribe and efforts are currently under way to develop appropriate training modules. Historically, the decision as to which health care professions should prescribe, and under which circumstances, has been a state responsibility. Psychologists in the state of Hawaii have been the first in the nation to attempt to modify their "scope of practice" act to allow prescription authority. Not surprisingly, Hawaii was not entirely successful during its first legislative attempt; however, notwithstanding strongly held divergent views within the broader psychological community, there are growing signs that Hawaii will soon be joined by other states in this quest (Brentar & McNamara, 1991; Wickramasekera, 1984).

NO

Garland Y. DeNelsky

THE CASE AGAINST PRESCRIPTION PRIVILEGES FOR PSYCHOLOGISTS

Several leading psychologists have spoken out strongly in favor of psychologists seeking prescription privileges. This paper presents the arguments against this position, including the potentially negative effects prescription privileges could have on the future course of the profession, the training of psychologists, the marketing of psychological services, and other issues of importance to psychology. It is concluded that attempting to obtain the right to prescribe psychoactive medications would involve an extremely expensive struggle that could change professional psychology in many ways, some of which might actually make it less attractive to the public is serves.

Several respected and visible psychologists have argued forcefully in favor of prescription privileges for psychologists (DeLeon, 1988; Fox, 1988a; Burns, DeLeon, Chemtob, Welch, & Samuels, 1988). APA's [American Psychological Association] Board of Professional Affairs recently endorsed the concept. APA's legislative body, the Council of Representatives, recently approved creation of a special Task Force on Psychopharmacology. There is movement toward psychologists getting prescription training through the Department of Defense (Buie, 1989b). Only a few writers have opposed this movement, despite the fact that recent surveys indicate that a majority of practicing psychologists are *not* in favor of psychologists obtaining prescription privileges (Piotrowski & Lubin, 1989; Boswell, Litwin & Kraft, 1988). The purpose of this paper is to provide a reasonably comprehensive exposition of the arguments against psychologists obtaining prescription privileges.

THE INFLUENCE OF PRESCRIPTION PRIVILEGES UPON THE FUTURE DIRECTIONS OF PSYCHOLOGY

If psychologists gained the right to prescribe psychoactive medications a shift is likely to occur in the direction in which professional psychology is evolving. Psychology could move from a predominantly behavioral field toward one increasingly similar to a medical specialty—psychiatry.

From Garland Y. DeNelsky, "The Case Against Prescription Privileges for Psychologists," *Psychotherapy in Private Practice*, vol. 11, no. 1 (1992), pp. 15–23. Copyright © 1992 by The Haworth Press, Inc., Binghamton, NY. Reprinted by permission. References omitted.

No consensus has yet emerged as to a single definition of professional psychology. One definition which has been widely circulated comes from Fox, Barclay, and Rodgers (1982). They proposed that "professional psychology is that profession which is concerned with enhancing the effectiveness of human functioning" (Fox, Barclay, & Rodgers, 1982, p. 307). Congruent with this definition, psychology has been producing a large number of well-trained practitioners who spend a substantial portion of their professional lives practicing psychotherapy and other types of psychological and behavioral interventions. Psychiatry, too, emphasized the practice of psychotherapy before the widespread use of psychoactive drugs. As psychiatry increased its reliance upon the use of medications it turned more and more away from psychotherapy. Psychoactive medications often produce "quick fixes"—reductions in symptoms, with little or no lasting changes in behavior or perception. In the short run, medications may be quicker, easier, and more profitable than the demanding work of psychotherapy. When a patient reports a symptom such as anxiety, depression, an obsessive-compulsive disorder, or a sleep problem, it is both easier and quicker to turn to a prescription pad than to those behavioral and psychotherapeutic interventions which have been demonstrated to be equally (or more) effective. The therapist feels he/she is doing something immediately, and the patient gains some quick symptomatic relief.

This rapid reinforcement of both therapist and patient can begin a pattern with far-ranging implications. For the therapist the message may become that medications provide a quick way to produce some symptomatic relief. It is possible that some therapists may gradually become influenced by another pattern of reinforcement: that regularly utilizing medications yields greater profits since shorter appointments are possible and hence more appointment times per day become available. The result could become a "short circuiting" of psychotherapeutic efforts, an effect that appears to have already influenced many within the field of psychiatry.

Medications also have some significant meanings for the patient, some of which may actually run counter to the processes of personal change and growth. Medications can subtly detract from psychotherapeutic efforts by implying that benefit comes from external agents, not from one's own efforts. As noted by Handler (1988, p. 47), "medication is a temporary solution which has powerful and sometimes peculiar control over consciousness; it teaches the patient little or nothing enduring about self control." The use of medications by psychologists could indeed change the direction in which psychology is evolving.

THE INFLUENCE OF PRESCRIPTION PRIVILEGES ON TRAINING

If training to prescribe becomes a routine part of the training of psychologists, it is highly likely that the educational process would have to be substantially longer than it is now. Training to prescribe medications will require a good deal more than providing a basic understanding of dosage and side effects, information that many practicing psychologists currently need to know. Education will have to focus a great deal more upon basic physiology, pharmacology, and physical diseases. This would result in increasing the length of graduate study, perhaps by a full year or more. Although one advocate of prescription privileges asserts that "addition of a special tract (to teach medications) would neither seriously distort our basic education in psychology nor necessarily require an extension in the length of time to earn the doctorate" (Fox, 1988b, p. 27), it is difficult to imagine how this goal could be realized unless there is a great deal of unessential material in current doctoral programs.

It should be noted that psychologists who prescribe medications will be held responsible for any and all complications that might arise from their use. Medication education will need to impart expertise regarding the potential interactions between medications and various medical conditions (e.g., hypertension, cardiac conditions, hormone therapy, diabetes, etc.). Although the majority of patients may present few if any such complications, psychologists will still have to learn how to deal with the difficult, medically complex patient. Because psychology will be "the new kid on the block," and a non-medical one at that, psychologists will likely be held to higher standards than is customary for physicians. Those standards can be expected to carry over to the courts. They will also be reflected in substantially higher malpractice rates for psychologists who prescribe and those who train others to prescribe; psychiatric malpractice rates currently range from three to 24 times higher than psychological malpractice coverage, depending on the state (Dorken, 1990).

The basic emphasis in our graduate education would likely change. The current emphasis is (or should be) upon psychologists becoming the preeminent specialists in human behavior change and psychotherapy. If psychology incorporates medication training into its graduate education, its training would shift from a primary emphasis upon behavioral change and personal growth through psychological interventions to, at best, a dual emphasis upon psychological and medical interventions. This dual emphasis could be expected to carry over into our postgraduate continuing education programs, too. Since there seems to be a new batch of medications each year or so, it is likely that the preponderance of continuing education programs would be devoted to medication, rather than behavioral change, psychotherapy, assessment, or other psychologically oriented topics. Practicing psychologists would be devoting less time to keeping up with new developments in psychology and more to acquiring new information about medications.

POLITICAL CONSIDERATIONS: A MAJOR WAR AHEAD?

Even the strongest proponents of prescription privileges for psychologist acknowledge that the struggle to secure such privileges would be a formidable one (Fox, 1988b). While it may be correctly argued that an independent profession does not allow other professions to determine its boundaries, the political implications and the potential costs involved in expanding those boundaries must be considered.

Seeking medication privileges would plunge psychology into a full-scale war with both psychiatry and medicine. In all likelihood, all of the previous conflicts psychology is engaged in now or in the past would be eclipsed—battles over licensure, third-party reimbursement, freedom of choice statutes, inclusion in Medicare, even hospital privileges. Medicine seems more than ever grimly committed to resisting all efforts to "encroach" on what it defines as its territory. It is true that other professionals such as dentists, optometrists, pharmacists, podiatrists, nurse practitioners, and physician assistants have been able to secure prescription privileges (Burns, DeLeon, Chemtob, Welch, & Samuels, 1988). However, these professions obtained prescription privileges at a time when organized medicine was not as rigidly committed to resisting further incursions into what it defined as its "turf." Perhaps even more significantly, psychologists with prescription privileges would *not* be viewed as "limited practitioners" such as those other providers with prescription privileges. If psychologists become able to prescribe medications, they will be capable of duplicating virtually everything that psychiatrists do-or at least that is how psychiatry and organized medicine would probably perceive them. None of the other nonmedical professions that have obtained prescription privileges pose such a complete threat to their corresponding medical specialties. In short, if organized psychology decides to push ahead for the right to prescribe, it will undoubtedly find itself locked in an immense struggle.

The financial cost of such a struggle would be overwhelming. It has been estimated that in one state alone—Massachusetts—upwards of four million dollars would be needed to finance the battle for prescription privileges (Tanney, 1987). Expand that figure to estimate the cost if all 50 states seek prescription privileges and it is not an overstatement to estimate that these battles could exhaust all of psychology's current assets and probably sink us deeply into debt.

In addition to the issue of financial cost is the matter of energy expenditure. If organized psychology decides to seriously pursue prescription privileges other issues will almost certainly receive diminished emphasis (Kovacs, 1988). Issues such as inclusion of psychological services in HMO's, hospital privileges, minimum mental health benefits, closing the ERISA loopholes, and marketing of psychological services will all have to assume reduced priority. When a profession is fighting a major war that requires all of its resources and more there is an obvious limit to how many other battles can be undertaken concurrently.

The war for prescription privileges might even cost psychology many of its hard earned gains of the past quarter century. All current psychology licensing laws are written in such a way as to preclude prescription of medications; they would have to be revised or amended (Fox, 1988b). These licensing laws would need to be "opened up" in the state legislatures at a time when psychology's opponents were mobilized against it. It is easy to imagine attempts to cripple existing psychology licensing laws in such a manner as to remove many of the significant gains of the past. Psychology could find itself with much less than it possessed before it sought prescription privileges.

Much greater divisiveness within psychology could also be an outcome if psychology actually obtained prescription privileges. If psychology gains prescription privileges, there would be some psychologists legally permitted to prescribe and some who could not. In view of the strong feelings likely to emerge on both sides of this issue, considerable discord is likely. For example, after having fought so hard and at such cost to earn the right to prescribe, it is easy to imagine that at least some psychologists will prescribe a great deal. That behavior is likely to draw considerable denunciation from others within the field. It is also possible that those psychologists who gain the right to prescribe may consider themselves "full practitioners" in comparison with their peers who are unable to prescribe, resulting in tensions within psychology not unlike those which frequently emerge between psychologist and psychiatrists. If gaining the right to prescribe really does lead those who have it to broader third-party reimbursement and easier access to hospital privileges (as has been argued by some proponents of prescription privileges) will those psychologists unable to prescribe feel relegated to a second-class status within their own profession?

MARKETING OF PSYCHOLOGY: EASIER OR MORE DIFFICULT?

The argument has been made by some that not securing the right to prescribe keeps psychology at a competitive disadvantage with psychiatry (Fox, 1988a). While this may be true in some cases, the overall record of psychology in the marketplace does not support this assertion. Recent figures from CHAMPUS indicate that in 1987 psychologists provided service for 34 percent of outpatient behavioral health visits compared with less than 22 percent for psychiatrists (Buie, 1989a). Five years earlier the figures had been reversed with psychiatrists providing service for 36 percent of the visits and psychologists for 28 percent. Without prescription privileges, psychology seems to be becoming the leading provider of outpatient mental health services. Psychiatry, with prescription privileges, has been steadily losing its market share over the past five years.

It has been asserted that the main reason clinical psychology has prospered is that it has built a reputation as being *different* from psychiatry (Handler, 1988). Handler further points out that there has been a steady increase averaging over ten percent each year in the number of clinical psychologists from 1966 to 1983. He attributes these increases to psychology being "independent and innovative in our training, our research, and in our service delivery ... to ape psychiatry in providing biological answers when our psychologically based answers are far more adequate for psychotherapeutic intervention is ill-advised" (Handler, 1988, p. 45).

Psychology is a vigorous, growing field that is perceived by many as a most viable alternative to the increasingly biological orientation of organized psychiatry. Instead of attempting to blur the differences between psychology and psychiatry in the public's mind, which gaining prescription privileges is likely to do, the argument can be made that psychology needs to sharpen the essential distinctions between the two fields. Practicing psychologists strive to help people learn about themselves and acquire more effective means of coping with stressors in their lives, since symptoms such as depression and anxiety frequently are indications of a mismatch between the demands of the environment and the individual's ability to cope with these demands (DeNelsky & Boat, 1986). Even where there may be biologic predisposing factors, such as with major mental disorders such as schizophrenia, appropriate psychological interventions can be quite effective (Paul & Lentz, 1977; Karon and VandenBos, 1981). It would certainly seem to be curious logic to engage in a monumental struggle to acquire a technique—prescription privileges—which seems to be leading those who have it to a diminishing share of the market which they once dominated!

THE FUTURE OF PRESCRIPTION PRIVILEGES

Without prescription privileges, and despite increasing competition from other disciplines such as social work and counseling, professional psychology has prospered. Psychologists today represent the largest pool of doctoral-level trained mental health practitioners in the United States. They have been steadily gaining in market share to where they now deliver more outpatient mental health care within CHAMPUS than any other group of providers (Dorken, 1989). Whatever some psychologists may perceive as a therapeutic deficiency because they lack prescription privileges is apparently not recognized as such by the general public. Although there is no clear evidence one way or the other on this issue, a case can be made that we have flourished *because* we offer a clear and distinct choice from psychiatry. To quote Handler (1988, p. 48): "I am not worried that we will be replaced by psychiatry if we cannot write prescriptions. I worry instead that we might sell our birthright by failing to value our professional individuality and our professional distinctiveness."

Gaining prescription privileges would likely change the trajectory of the profession of psychology from a field which relies primarily upon strategies of learning, adapting, and growing to a domain similar to the medical specialty of psychiatry. Approximately 20 years ago, psychiatry made a conscious decision to "medicalize." Since then there has been a noteworthy growth in non-medical mental health professions, while psychiatry itself has shown negligible growth. Might psychology fall prey to a similar fate if it turned away from its heritage and toward the prescription pad?

Gaining prescription privileges might help solve some problems for some psychologists, but seeking them is likely to create major ones for the field as a whole. The quest for such privileges would undoubtedly plunge psychology into a major war. At this time, when there is not even a clear majority of practicing psychologists in favor of psychology pursuing the right to prescribe, the quest for prescription privileges could become a costly, no-win situation—a "Viet Nam War" for professional psychology. And if psychology did manage to win the many battles and secure prescription privileges, would it gradually evolve into a field indistinguishable from psychiatry? If so, would such a metamorphose be in the interest of either the public or psychology? In the long run, winning the battles for prescription privileges might turn out to be infinitely less desirable than not going to war at all.

CHALLENGE QUESTIONS

Should Psychologists Be Allowed to Prescribe Drugs?

1. If psychologists were to obtain the privilege of prescribing medications, how would they be different from the profession of psychiatry? How might your answer affect psychology's future?

2. Underlying this issue is what some theorists call reductionism. Reductionism is the notion that all psychological entities (e.g., mind, feelings, unconscious) can be ultimately reduced to biological entities. How might this theoretical notion affect the current controversy, and how might one's stance on reductionism affect one's stance on this issue?

3. How does a profession like psychology balance the sometimes competing interests of its marketability and the good of the public?

4. DeNelsky claims that many people prefer a nonmedication treatment when they experience emotional disturbances. Would you prefer to be treated without medication if you were to experience emotional problems? Why, or why not?

5. How much should the issue of psychiatry's "turf" enter into this debate? That is, should the traditional boundaries between psychology and psychiatry be respected for any reason, or is this irrelevant?

On the Internet . . .

http://www.dushkin.com

Mental Health Infosource: Disorders
This no-nonsense page lists links to sites containing information on a number of psychological disorders, including anxiety, panic, phobic disorders, schizophrenia, and violent/self-destructive behaviors. *http://www.mhsource.com/disorders/*

The Personality Project
The Personality Project of William Revelle, director of the Graduate Program in Personality at Northwestern University, is meant to guide those interested in personality theory and research to the current personality research literature. *http://fas.psych.nwu.edu/personality.html*

The International Society for Traumatic Stress Studies (ISTSS)
Founded in 1985, the ISTSS provides a forum for the sharing of research, clinical strategies, public policy concerns, and theoretical formulations on trauma in the United States and around the world. The ISTSS is dedicated to the discovery and dissemination of knowledge and to the stimulation of policy, program, and service initiatives that seek to reduce traumatic stressors and their immediate and long-term consequences. *http://www.istss.com/*

Mind Tools
This site provides useful information on stress management. *http://www.gasou.edu/ psychweb/mtsite/smpage.html*

PART 2

Disorders of Anxiety, Mood, Psychosis, and Personality

Mood and anxiety disorders and schizophrenia are among the most debilitating conditions that people can suffer. They are also among the most researched conditions in abnormal psychology—psychologists know much more about these conditions than many others that people experience. Yet there are still many unanswered questions about these conditions.

Biological theories of abnormality are extremely popular these days, among laypeople as well as psychologists and psychiatrists. Indeed, biological explanations of everyday moods and thoughts are increasingly prominent. But is a bad mood fundamentally a psychological phenomenon or a biological phenomenon? Are strange or unusual ways of thinking the result of dysfunctioning neurons or an individual's social isolation and sense of purposelessness? Even if we accept that biological processes influence moods and thinking, do we necessarily want to change everyone's biology so that they no longer experience bad moods or uncommon ways of thinking?

■ Do the Advantages of Prozac Outweigh Its Disadvantages?

■ Is Premenstrual Syndrome a Medical Disorder?

■ Is Schizophrenia a Disease?

■ Is the Gulf War Syndrome Real?

ISSUE 3

Do the Advantages of Prozac Outweigh Its Disadvantages?

YES: Peter D. Kramer, from *Listening to Prozac: A Psychiatrist Explores Antidepressant Drugs and the Remaking of the Self* (Viking Penguin, 1993)

NO: James Mauro, from "And Prozac for All ...," *Psychology Today* (July/August 1994)

ISSUE SUMMARY

YES: Psychiatrist Peter D. Kramer considers Prozac to be very effective for relieving depression, and he advocates prescribing the drug to improve people's moods. Unlike mind-altering drugs that create self-absorption, Kramer says, Prozac opens depressed people up to pleasures normally experienced by people who do not suffer from depression.

NO: James Mauro, a former senior editor for *Psychology Today*, contends that Prozac is being prescribed too freely to people who have symptoms that do not fit the criteria of a disorder, such as feelings of discontent and irritability. Mauro further argues that Prozac does not get at the root of people's problems —that it is only a temporary fix.

One of the most common emotional problems in America is depression. It is estimated that approximately 10 percent of Americans experience some type of depression during their lives. The antidepressant drug most typically prescribed for treating depression is Prozac, whose generic name is fluoxetine. Developed in 1987, global sales of Prozac exceeded $1.2 billion by 1993. Nearly 1 million prescriptions for Prozac are written every month, and it is now the fifth most commonly prescribed drug in the world.

Although Prozac was originally developed for treating depression—for which it is believed to be about 60 percent effective—the drug has been prescribed for an array of other conditions. These conditions include eating disorders such as bulimia and obesity, obsessive-compulsive disorders, and anxiety. An important question about Prozac is currently under debate: Is Prozac being prescribed too casually? Some experts feel that physicians are giving Prozac to patients who do not need chemical treatment to overcome their afflictions. Sherwin Nuland, a professor at Yale University, believes that Prozac is relatively safe for its approved applications but that it is inappropriate for less severe problems.

As with most other drugs, Prozac can produce a number of adverse side effects, though they are reportedly fewer and less severe than other antidepressants. These effects include hypotension (low blood pressure), weight gain, and irregular heart rhythms. Short-term effects from Prozac may include headaches, sweating, fatigue, anxiety, reduced appetite, jitteriness, dizziness, stomach discomfort, nausea, sexual dysfunction, and insomnia. Because it is a relatively new drug, long-term side effects have yet to be determined.

Several lawsuits have been filed against Eli Lilly and Company, Prozac's manufacturer, as a result of one of the drug's alleged side effects: the drug has been linked to violent and suicidal behavior. Some individuals charged with violent crimes have even used the defense that Prozac made them act violently and that they should not be held accountable for their actions while on the drug. Prozac has also been implicated in a number of suicides, though it is unclear whether Prozac caused these individuals to commit suicide or whether they would have committed suicide anyway. In 1990 the Prozac Survivors Support Group was formed to help people who have experienced adverse symptoms while on the drug.

Psychiatrist Peter R. Breggin, who feels that Prozac is being prescribed too frequently, has argued that Prozac and other antidepressant drugs are being used to replace traditional psychotherapy. Breggin claims that psychiatry has given in to the pharmaceutical companies. Compared to psychiatry, Prozac is far less expensive and more convenient. However, does Prozac get at the root of the problems that many people have? The U.S. Public Health Service recommends drug therapy for severe cases of depression but psychotherapy for mild or moderate cases of depression.

Psychiatrist Peter D. Kramer claims that Prozac brings about a positive transformation in the personalities of many individuals: people who are habitually timid seem more confident after taking the drug; sensitive people become more brash; and introverts improve their social skills. Kramer states that people become more real. Critics of this viewpoint ask, If one's personality changes as a result of a drug, what is that individual's real personality? Is the personality of a person on Prozac "real"? Also, does Prozac change one's personality or simply the way one perceives the world?

In the following selections, Kramer argues that Prozac is an invaluable drug that allows people to alter negative aspects of their personalities and to brighten their moods. He feels that it is solely a matter of time before the benefits of Prozac are recognized by most mental health professionals. James Mauro argues that Prozac is overprescribed and that it is being used simply to make perfectly well people feel better. He also contends that Prozac is employed as a quick fix solution and that people who take the drug are not confronting the source of their problems.

YES

Peter D. Kramer

THE MESSAGE IN THE CAPSULE

I think traditional medical ethics fails to pinpoint what it is about Prozac that makes us uneasy. Part of the problem lies in the phrase "mood brightener," which captures one aspect of Prozac's potential but at the same time mistakes the character of the drug. When we imagine a hypothetical mood brightener, we model the image on an actual drug, one that already exists. The tradition of medical ethics in the area of mood is to worry about heroin and cocaine; the antidepressants are different. The issue of mood enhancement really concerns hedonism—should we use drugs for pleasure? But the word "hedonism" contains the same ambiguity as the phrase "mood brightener." Stimulants, opiates, and antidepressants are all hedonic but in different ways.

Philosophers have long debated the nature of pleasure. Is it inherent in pleasurable acts, or is it a separable result of certain acts? The discovery ten years ago of endorphin receptors in the brain seemed to support the latter alternative, what the philosopher Dan Brock has called "the property-of-conscious-experience theory," of pleasure. According to this theory (which I will call "separability"), we engage in actions for the pleasure they bring. Pleasure is a state of the brain neurons—satiety or excitation, for example —that is separable from the actions people undertake to make themselves happy. Opiates and amphetamines shortcut the hedonic process: they allow us to have the pleasure without the pleasurable acts, and thereby cut us off from the realities of the world. "Mood brightener" implies a substance that makes people happy when they haven't done anything to earn happiness.

Separability is the basis of the usual argument not only against psychotropic drugs but against hedonism altogether. The concern is that people will pursue pleasure directly—orgies are the usual sin of hedonists—rather than achieve pleasure through "distinctly human"—intellectual, altruistic, planful—efforts for which pleasure is the reward. This case against pleasure as the direct goal in life is sometimes called the "swine objection," from John Stuart Mill's contention that hedonism is a doctrine "fit only for swine."

* * *

Just as the endorphin receptor revived interest in the idea that pleasure is separable from pleasurable acts, I expect Prozac to refocus attention on an alternative theory: that pleasure is to be found throughout (and not separable from) certain activities such as reading a book. There is no receptor that corresponds to the pleasure of reading a book, and no single state of the neurons. By this understanding, pleasure is a matter of preference among experiences. Though generally not used in connection with illicit drugs, what Brock calls the preference theory of pleasure could well apply. For instance, marijuana not only gives pleasure directly (separability); it also may enhance, or allow an anhedonic uptight person to enjoy, the inherent pleasure of a walk through the countryside.

The swine objection to hedonic drugs seems irrelevant in the face of drugs that draw people *toward* ordinary and even noble human activities. My sense is that the preference theory of pleasure has received little attention because the usual experience-enhancing mood altering drugs, like marijuana or LSD, encourage self-absorption. The experience they enhance is most often autistic. Prozac is different. It induces pleasure in part by freeing people to enjoy activities that are social and productive. And, unlike marijuana or LSD or even alcohol, it does so without being experienced as pleasurable in itself and without inducing distortions of perception. Prozac simply gives anhedonic people access to pleasures identical to those enjoyed by other normal people in their ordinary social pursuits.

* * *

My impression is that Prozac, because it gives pleasure indirectly, by enhancing hedonic capacity and lowering barriers to ordinary social intercourse, generally increases personal autonomy. Aranow and his colleagues have argued to the contrary, using a fascinating example to make their point.

They describe a woman, Ms. B., prescribed Prozac for trichotillomania, a syndrome in which a person cannot resist the impulse to pull out her own hair. Hair-pulling in moderation is a sign of anxiety; but the need to pull hair relentlessly, to the point of disfigurement, is recognized as an illness, related to obsessive-compulsive disorder. Besides hair-pulling, Ms. B. has a second concern: she is unmarried at age thirty-six, despite her "appropriate, if somewhat strenuous efforts to meet eligible men." On Prozac, Ms. B.'s hair-pulling diminishes, but so does her feeling of urgency about meeting men. Ms. B. does not isolate herself: on the contrary, she now enjoys time spent with people, such as her parents, with whom she argued in the past. She is more content with life, more reconciled to the possibility of never marrying, and, though still interested in men, is no longer driven.

Regarding Ms. B.'s social behavior on Prozac, Aranow and his colleagues ask whether she has been opiated into a cocoon. Aranow puts forth drivenness as a desirable human quality that produces, if not happiness, certain admirable accomplishments on which the species thrives.

The notion that Prozac diminishes autonomy because it diminishes drive is an important one: it echoes Walker Percy's concern about "not worrying the same old bone." But Ms. B.'s case is unusual, and not only because she has a rare illness. Heretofore, we have seen nothing but examples in which Prozac moves people toward courtship activity. In this story, it moves someone away.

I think we can dismiss the concern that Prozac diminishes social intercourse: the usual complaint against Prozac is that it leaves people too social, too little in touch with their solitary core. Even Ms. B. seems to arrive at a more comfortable relationship with her social strengths and possibilities. The story as told implies that her drive produced strenuous social efforts that were ineffectual; her measured approach on medication might well work better.

Inner drive can lead to great accomplishments. But often "being driven" indicates compromised autonomy (as indicated by our use of the passive participle, "driven," as if by an alien force). To be opiated into a cocoon is one thing, but to be granted peace where once you were neurotically compelled is quite another: there are instances in which contentment contains more autonomy than drive.

* * *

It happens that the psychiatrist who treated Ms. B. has also given an account of her recovery. He is Ronald Winchel, who introduced the theory that an "aloneness affect" spurs primates to affiliate. Winchel describes himself as having been surprised when he learned that his hair-pulling patient, who had for so long engaged in "mildly agitated spouse-pursuit," socialized less on medication:

> ... For the first time in her memory she felt perfectly relaxed and happy sitting at home reading books or listening to music and felt less of the free-floating anxiety that was previously quelled by going out. She then mentioned, parenthetically, that for the first time in her adult life, she considered that maybe marriage wasn't in her future—but, she felt, that was not necessarily bad. She would make her life happy, she considered, in other ways.

Off Prozac, Ms. B. bar-hopped in search of men. Prozac moderated her sense of aloneness and allowed her to enjoy a variety of social settings. In Winchel's account, Ms. B. is not opiated, merely spared the pain of social desperation.

* * *

If Ms. B.'s story is disturbing, it is because she took medication to treat one problem, hair-pulling, and found a change in a quite separate area, courtship. For her, mood brightening is something like a side effect, one about which an ethically punctilious clinician might warn: We can diminish your hair pulling, but I must warn you, you may feel more contented.

If Ms. B. had taken Prozac as a mood brightener—more precisely, if she had taken it because she felt she was overanxious about men—we would see the drug as a useful tool toward a desired end. The vignette illustrates an important quality of Prozac—namely that it often surprises us. Sometimes it will change only one trait in the person under treatment; but often it goes far beyond a single intended effect. You take it to treat a symptom, and it transforms your sense of self.

The medical ethicists approach Prozac as if it were a case of dull or bright, down or up. Unlike amphetamine, Prozac is not a case of down or up but of same or other. Prozac has the power to transform the whole person—illness and temperament, drive to pull hair and drive to affiliate, anxiety and hedonic capacity. When you take it, you risk widespread change.

The story of Ms. B. made me realize that the concept of mood brightener just will not do—it arises from the limited idea of an "antidepressant," when what we are dealing with is a thymoleptic, a drug that acts on personality. Instead of looking at mood and being surprised to discover that Prozac affects other areas, why not begin with the understanding that Prozac can induce the sort of widespread change ordinarily brought about by psychotherapy? There really is no way to assess Prozac without confronting transformation.

* * *

The idea of transformation leads us to address a new set of ethical issues. Who is Ms. B.? The change Prozac brings about in her is so profound that there are almost two different persons in the story, one discontented and driven, the other contented and complacent. Whose autonomy are we out to preserve?

Instinctively, we might want to say that the unmedicated woman has priority; this is the stance the ethicists take when they worry whether the patient has been opiated into a cocoon. But consider circumstances that might make us change our mind. If medication were not an issue, if Ms. B. had spontaneous mood swings, would we attend to her more closely in her driven or in her contented state? How would we see the matter if we considered her drivenness to be the result of a deficiency state—if we believed she "needed" more serotonin in the brain the way some people need vitamins or insulin or thyroid hormone? In that case, we would associate personhood with the medicated self. How would we understand Ms. B. if she were... to "discover" on Prozac that her man-chasing had been compulsive? Or if she were... to say she felt "like myself at last" on Prozac? Perhaps the most interesting case would arise if she reported she felt fully herself both on and off medication, so that the personality she chose would be purely a matter of preference.

There are many perspectives from which we might say that denial of medication would injure Ms. B.'s autonomy, precisely because we accept that Ms. B. as she is when medicated has the standing of personhood. If we believe that she is in fact transformed—one person when driven and one when contented—then we must determine how to choose between the autonomy of two distinct "persons," each fully human and deserving of autonomy. If Prozac has brought about a break between an individual and her humanity, the break may be so substantial that we are left asking, whose humanity is it?

My guess is that medical ethicists writing about Prozac have ignored the issue of personhood because they are hesitant to see in a medication this power to transform—and who can blame them? The idea is unlikely and uncomfortable.

* * *

Part of what may bother us is the nature of the changes that Prozac can accomplish. Michael McGuire hypothesized that low mood in dysthymic women results from a mismatch between the personality with which they enter adulthood and the one their culture rewards. It follows that a mood elevator for dysthymics, at least one that works through altering temperament, will necessarily be a drug that induces "conformity." I put "conformity" in quotation marks because here it means conformity to traits that society rewards, which might well be rebelliousness, egocentricity, radical self-confidence, or other qualities that lead to behaviors we ordinarily call nonconformist. (The evolutionary model entails certain paradoxes. It holds that in a given society an "antidepressant" is any chemical that leads to a rewarded personality—different cultures may have quite different antidepressants. In a culture that rewards caution, a compulsiveness-inducing drug might produce the temperament that leads to social rewards and thus brightened mood.) What are the implications of a drug that makes a person better loved, richer, and less constrained —because her personality conforms better to a societal ideal? These moral concerns seem at least as complex as those attending a drug that just inherently makes a person happy. In terms of its interaction with cultural norms, a transforming drug might be even more ethically troubling than a mood brightener.

* * *

Consider the Greek widow who over the course of five years is given a chance to allow her feelings to attenuate. She lives in an affect-tolerant culture, though she may be far from affect-tolerant: the widow may be rejection-sensitive and for that reason in need of an especially long time to recover after the death of a husband. Perhaps rural Greek society is organized precisely to allow widows with low affect tolerance to recover at their own pace. In an affect-tolerant traditional culture, rejection-sensitivity might be an adaptive trait. A more assertive widow, or one quicker to heal, would find the society stifling and infuriating: she might be happier in a less affect-tolerant culture, and indeed might find that rural Greek society makes impossible demands that she is temperamentally ill-equipped to meet.

To say that our society is less affect-tolerant is to say that it favors different temperaments. The Greek society is not preferable, just more comfortable for certain people. But it may be in our society that what doctors do when they treat mourning with medication goes far beyond elevating mood: they are asking a fragile widow to adopt a new temperament—to be someone she is not.

* * *

Prozac highlights our culture's preference for certain personality types. Vivacious women's attractiveness to men, the contemporary scorn of fastidiousness, men's discomfort with anhedonia in women, the business advantage conferred by mental quickness—all these examples point to a consistent social prejudice. The ways in which our culture favors one style over another go far beyond impatience with grief.

A certain sort of woman, socially favored in other eras, does poorly today. Victorian culture valued women who were emotionally sensitive, socially retiring, loyally devoted to one man, languorous and melancholic, fastidious in dress and sensibility, and histrionic in response to perceived neglect. We are less likely to reward such women today, nor are they proud of their traits.

We admire and reward a quite different sort of femininity, which, though it has its representations in heroines of novelists from Jane Austen to Fay Weldon, contains attributes traditionally considered masculine: resilience, energy, assertiveness, an enjoyment of give-and-take. Prozac does not just brighten mood; it allows a woman with the traits we now consider "overly feminine," in the sense of passivity and a tendency to histrionics, to opt, if she is a good responder, for a spunkier persona.

The Mexican poet and essayist Octavio Paz has put the issue of American expectations of women in the context of our form of economic organization: "Capitalism exalts the activities and behavior patterns traditionally called virile: aggressiveness, the spirit of competition and emulation, combativeness. American society made these values its own." Paz acknowledges that the position of women under American capitalism is legally and politically superior to that of women under Mexican traditionalism. But American social equality, Paz contends, comes in the context of a masculine society, in terms of values and expectations; Mexican society, though deplorable in the way it treats women, is more open to values Paz calls feminine.

Does Prozac's ability to transform temperament foster a certain sort of social conformity, one dominated in this case by "masculine" capitalist values? Thymoleptics are feminist drugs, in that they free women from the inhibiting consequences of trauma. But the argument can be made that, in "curing" women of traditional, passive feminine traits and instilling in good responders the attributes of a more robust feminine ideal, Prozac reinforces the cultural expectations of a particularly exigent form of economic organization.

NO

James Mauro

AND PROZAC FOR ALL...

The year 1993 proved a big one for Eli Lilly & Co., makers of Prozac. *Listening to Prozac*, a testimonial to the drug's healing powers, make the best-seller list, while Peter Kramer, its author, touted his tiny benefactor on various talk shows. Again and again the pill popped up in endless *New Yorker* cartoons, computer-network discussions, even David Letterman jokes. In February, the pill itself graced a cover of *Newsweek*.

Slowly, stealthily, Prozac is slithering into more and more of our lives and finding a warm place to settle.

Even the most casually aware citizen can feel the shift in thinking brought about by the drug's ability to "transform" its users: We speak of personality change, we argue over the drug's benefits over psychotherapy (all those expensive hours of parent-bashing as compared to a monthly dash to the pharmacy); and we let ourselves imagine a world in which our pain is nullified, erased as easily and fully as dirty words on a school blackboard.

Most of all, we envision a race of people both frighteningly bland and joyously healed as the ultimate double-edged sword. While Prozac may indeed be our gift horse of the decade, at least we're staring it straight in the jagged molars.

Of all the fears and concerns, the one barely spoken of but no less valid apparently has more to do with the good news than the bad: It seems the drug is *more* effective, and works to relieve *more* symptoms, than previously imagined.

Without a doubt, Prozac is exiting the realm of clinical depression and entering the murkier world of subclinical, subsyndromal, sub-"sick" disorders. Clinicians in particular are worried that the definition of "subsyndromal" disorders (psychological complaints that fail to meet the criteria for a specific illness) is expanding to include more of what were once thought of as ordinary life stresses. (The unofficial term for this is "bracket creep.")

And as this illness invitation list grows, so, of course, do the numbers of patients who now fall into this category—people somewhere short of being honest-to-God sick but who are nevertheless in some sort of pain.

Robert Trestman, M.D., director of the outpatient program at Bronx VA Medical Center, sums up the dilemma: "There are many situations where people do not meet the minimum criteria for a disorder. Where a specific diagnosis may require five criteria, for instance, some people will have only two, perhaps even one. And yet they're suffering."

And receiving psychiatric medication when once they were shipped off to a therapist's couch. Trestman neatly breaks down the dividing lines between the sick and the uncomfortable:

- Traditional patients, who say, "Doc, can you fix me? I'm hurting."
- Nontraditional patients, who say, "I'm not broken, but make me better. I want to be more assertive, I want to feel better, I want to accomplish more."

In the past, both groups would be recommended for therapy. Now, more and more are being tried on Prozac. Because of its fewer side effects and lower toxicity, the risk-to-benefit ratio is a lot lower.

"It's lower," agrees Trestman, "but it's not zero. There are side effects, risks that raise concern in the medical community."

GOOD NEWS OR BAD?

Historically, the use of drugs as fixers of the world's private ills has run into serious, if unanticipated, snags. At the turn of the century, the medical community thought that cocaine was a completely appropriate, nonaddictive drug, and widely prescribed it. In the 1950s and '60s, first barbiturates and then amphetamines were doled out for various psychological maladies. We now know that each of these drugs came with significant risks. So what yet-to-be imparted knowledge may cause science, once again, to admit sheepishly that the exuberance over Prozac was somewhat premature, if not wholly overblown?

While much remains to be learned about Prozac, so far the bad news may be that there's no bad news. If, after all, it does turn out to have no serious drawbacks, what are the implications of a drug that is a shortcut to healing?

It is a concern that potentially affects all psychologists, who may find themselves short of angst-laden clients in the coming years; that places dubious power in the hands of primary care physicians, who may prescribe the drug without a fully articulated understanding of their patients' distress; and that strikes a chord of defensive fervor in the hearts and minds of everyone raised with the Judeo-Christian ethics—that nothing in life can be worthwhile, or effective, unless you *work* for it.

There's more to the story. Questions abound regarding the drug and its chemical cousins, Zoloft and Paxil: What other types of disorders, aside from clinical depression, are they being prescribed for? Do the medications work? What other options exist? What are the potential risks to individuals and to society?

I'M DYSTHYMIC, YOU'RE DYSTHYMIC

Of all the distresses, ailments, and infirmities patients complain of nowadays, perhaps none is so broad or so muddy in definition as "dysthymia"—a chronic discontent involving either depression (but not *clinical* depression) or irritability. Its symptoms—not eating or eating too much, not sleeping or oversleeping, poor concentration or difficulty making decisions—reveals the unexclusivity of its rank and file. In terms of requirements for diagnosis, dysthymia may be the only club that would have Groucho Marx for a member.

According to a recent survey, approximately 48 percent of Americans—almost half the population—has experienced some form of dysthymic disorder. And all of them may qualify for Prozac. Robert Millman, M.D., professor of psychiatry and public health at Cornell, sees the irony of it: "There's *nobody* nonsyndromal. You can give Prozac to anyone you want."

Which is anathema to what medical science is supposed to be about. "We try to convince people there's some specificity to what we do," says Millman. "But this is embarrassing."

And the list doesn't stop there. Simon Sobo, M.D., director of psychiatry at New Milford Hospital, reports that "Prozac has been successfully used for obsessive hair-pulling, panic disorder, eating disorders, and social and other phobias. It has proven useful to people to free themselves from addictive relationships; to dispel doubts about performance; to overcome obstacles that once seemed impossible. I have even added it to my watering can and found geraniums grow better on it."

He's joking, of course, but only about the geraniums. Add obesity, gambling addiction, and PMS to the spectrum of complaints now being helped by Prozac.

BETTER RECEPTION?

If little is known yet of just how effective these drugs are for psychological distress, even less clear is the actual impact they have on those who benefit from them. Are they simply mood brighteners or are they re-regulating systems that are out of balance? Do they actually *change* personality, making you feel better than normal, or merely fine-tune it? Do people say, "Gee, I feel more myself on this drug" or "Gee, I'm a different person now"?

Some clinicians, such as Larry Siever, M.D., director of the Outpatient Psychiatry Division at Mt. Sinai School of Medicine in New York, offer an opinion between the two: "If you have a staticky, bland picture on your TV set, you can fix the reception by adjusting the tuning and contrast. Or simply change the channel. My understanding of the medications personally is more the former than the latter."

Of course the big fear surrounding the "channel-changing" aspect of the drugs is that society will evolve into a battalion of "happy soldiers." Exhumed by Kramer himself, the specter of Aldous Huxley's soma—*Brave New World's* fictional drug that anesthetized citizens into a content unawareness—continues to haunt us and cloud the argument surrounding Prozac. Yet to many, the analogy seems false.

"The drugs, if properly used," says Siever, "shouldn't dampen normal signals of anxiety, not even normal depression. It should not snow under in the way that a hypnotic does a person's normal level of arousal or awareness, but should allow all of these signals to emerge more clearly."

And, he continues, extending the argument, "If depression or other symptoms emerge, whether from psychological or social stresses, aren't people entitled to treatment for these conditions, just as they would get if they had an ulcer in relation to the stresses in their lives?"

Siever's example inadvertently reveals yet another controversy surrounding the use of drugs—any drugs—in fighting these disorders: the contention that pharmacology focuses on the individual rather than examining the larger societal problems that lie behind depression and other ills. Epidemiological studies have shown that more people are suffering from major depression that ever before—at ever-younger ages. Prozac, some argue, puts a Band-Aid on individual symptoms rather than addressing why people are seeking help in ever-increasing numbers.

The response of clinicians is to answer the question with a question: Why must one solution preclude any other?

The fundamental error, they argue, is to assume that the use of Prozac as a therapeutic tool equals an interest only in the biological causes of depression (or sub-depression, or just plain old feeling lousy). Those who can prescribe medication are, by profession, at least partly invested in biological *solutions*. And since Prozac is usually recommended along with some form of psychotherapy, the conclusion that interpersonal relationships are somehow ignored—or that individual brain chemistry is the one and only root being addressed—seems erroneous.

"We're not saying this is the *only* way to help," insists Trestman. "We're saying, 'This is one way, but of course there are others.' Many more people can be helped by changing the structure of society than through medicine. But we also have the ability apparently to help many more people with medication than before. Now we have to figure out should we? And for whom? And where does it stop?"

OUT OF THE WOODWORK

Other concerns stem from the staggering numbers of people for whom Prozac would prove beneficial. In 1991, this advertisement appeared in New York's *Times* and *Village Voice*.

"ARE YOU DEPRESSED? DO YOU SUFFER FROM FATIGUE? INABILITY TO CONCENTRATE? HAVE TROUBLE SLEEPING OR EATING? IF SO, CONTACT..."

The ad was placed to gather subjects for a study of the effectiveness of Prozac in treating dysthymia. The response, according to researcher Jesse Rosenthal, M.D., Director of psychopharmacology at Beth Israel Medical Center in New York, was "literally thousands of phone calls. It was amazing—all these bright, educated, hardworking people just came out of the woodwork. We found a mother lode of nice people who were able to function, but who were quite literally the walking wounded of New York."

After selecting a core group who met the criteria for dysthymia, Rosenthal and his team divided them up and gave one-half Prozac, the other half a placebo. Results? An astonishing 62 percent of the Prozac group showed significant improvement after only eight weeks (as opposed to 18 percent given placebos). Other studies conducted by Rosenthal have shown a more than 70 percent success rate.

The number of people who responded to the advertisement is evidence of widespread, if low-level, depression—and in greater numbers than were previously imagined. But what struck Rosenthal was that, while their average age was 36, almost 80 percent of them were single, and another 9 percent were divorced. Nearly 90 percent of them had been in therapy on and off over the years.

"They had a lot of insight," reports Rosenthal. "But they still had symptoms."

Which begs the question: Were these people dysthymic (read "unhappy") because they couldn't get themselves involved romantically, or were their persistent blues preventing them from successfully interacting with others?

The distinction is an important one, and crucial in the argument of a "drugs vs. societal change" approach to combating low-level depression. Romantic courtship may be more difficult now than ever before—which may lead many to remain single and unhappy. If so, working toward easier social interaction would benefit. If, however, the reverse were true, and the subjects' dysthymia was what prevented them from dating, then focusing on the individual—*in order to correct the social*—seems justified. "And that focus is not to be dismissed," stresses Trestman.

DOES PROZAC = LEARNING?

Whatever the root, one can see them, sipping Cranzac (Prozac and cranberry juice—a popular cocktail for those unable to tolerate full doses of the drug), nuzzling up to potential mates at the local singles' bar, smiling, their psychological wounds successfully sutured. Given time, wouldn't a more positive outlook lead to better interactions, and the potential relationships that developed continue to promote good cheer once Prozac is tapered off?

"Of course," agrees Trestman. "If people start responding differently to you, and you start feeling different about yourself, you set up new habit patterns that reinforce your changed state of affairs. It may be that Prozac resets the adjustment in the brain after a number of months, and that afterward people would be at this new point and could taper off without relapse."

In other words, first the drugs make you better, happier, more in control—then you do the rest of the work on your own. Cornell's Robert Millman concurs: "The drugs change a person's emotional reward system. Your sense of acceptance increases. Your feeling state is changed. Then hopefully you take this new ammunition and go out and use it on your own."

Wait a minute. What are we saying here? That "real learning" occurs on Prozac? That the drug does not simply solve your problems medically, but requires you to do half the legwork yourself? Yes, believes Millman, "So that even when you take away the medication, the same situation in life may create different responses in an individual. Where once the thought of initiating romance seemed too stressful, it now seems possible. Where once life seemed sad, lonely, and defeating, it now appears worthwhile and conquerable."

SYNDROME VS. CHARACTER

Still, there are fears. Is Prozac bringing to light the frightening number of people who suffer from some sort of distress? Or is it that what were once called "character traits" are now being reclassified as "syndromes"—because they can be smoothed out by medication? And, if such a trend continues, will there be anyone left who *isn't* "disordered"? Who *doesn't* need drugs?

Some doctors bristle at the distinction between syndrome and character. "It's a false and meaningless boundary," insists Steven Roose, M.D., of Columbia University. "People implicitly cross the border from, well, it's a syndrome, that means there's something wrong with the brain, to, well, that's just their character, their personality, so that's psychology."

Such dualism is destructive, believes Roose: "If somebody has a bad temper and works to control it, we don't say they're altering who they are. But there's a paranoia that somehow with medication, we're trying to control the essence of individuality, that we're manipulating someone."

No doubt the moral arguments about character altering are being applied more severely when treatment involves medication as opposed to psychotherapy. Consider one recent *New Yorker* cartoon: "If they had Prozac in the 19th century." One panel features Karl Marx saying, "Sure, capitalism could work out its kinks!" In another, Edgar Allen Poe is on friendly terms with the raven. A third shows Nietzsche outside a church with his mother, saying, "Gee, Mom, I like what the priest said about the little people."

The implicit message is that, without suffering, without the character quirks that made Poe poetic, for example, we would be deprived of his brooding masterworks. True, perhaps, but if suffering is so enlightening, if it is part of what makes us "us" and we should try our best to preserve it rather than medicate it away— isn't that also an argument against *any* kind of treatment? Shouldn't we then avoid seeking *any* kind of relief, for fear that we may be damaging, even destroying, the human spirit, the creative urge, that which defines all of us, the brilliant and the dullard?

"The notion that suffering is good is paternalistic and, at worst, sadistic," says Roose. But even if we take that moralistic, almost religious view, why point our swords only at the dragons marked "take as directed"? Why not apply the

same questions and concerns to psychotherapy? "The use of psychotherapy in this country has been grandfathered in," points out Bob Trestman. "It's been accepted already for many years, first in terms of counseling from religious leaders, and more recently in the practice of formal therapy. So that we no longer question either its intrusiveness on who we are or its relative safety."

Does psychotherapy have side effects? Is it intrusive? Does it change the essence of who we are? The answer is yes to all. "If psychotherapy couldn't manipulate or effect change, then it wouldn't work," states Roose. "The idea that therapy isn't intrusive, that we don't alter behavior or control people's thoughts is fundamentally untrue."

What about side effects? "By definition, if a treatment is powerful enough to work, it's powerful enough to have adverse effects. Every journal on psychotherapy will talk about people who regress in treatment, people who have psychotic reactions, people for whom therapy has caused deterioration rather than progress.

"Still," Roose continues, "because these so-called nonsyndromal disorders are considered to be in the realm of psychology, we don't think there's anything wrong in treating them with psychotherapy. We believe that *isn't* manipulation while medication is—regardless of outcome."

MANIPULATION VS. CHANGE

Yet what if the brain reacted, readjusted itself in the same way, whether in response to a pill or a therapeutic directive?

Last year, in the *Archives of General Psychiatry*, a research team headed by

UCLA's Lewis Baxter, M.D., reported a study of two groups suffering from obsessive-compulsive disorder (recurrent, unwanted thoughts accompanied by ritualized acts, such as excessive handwashing). In treatment, one group was given Prozac with no formal therapy, the other behavior therapy, in the form of exercises designed to prevent their compulsiveness, with no drugs. After 10 weeks, scans of their brains were compared with those taken at the beginning of treatment.

Approximately two-thirds of each group improved. More important, for those who did improve, rates of glucose metabolism (an indicator of brain activity) decreased in *exactly* the same areas of the brain, in statistically similar amounts, regardless of treatment. The behavioral techniques actually altered brain function —and did so no differently, no less intrusively, than Prozac.

"Some may wonder," writes Baxter et al, "how behavior therapy could produce brain-function changes similar to drugs. [But] the possibility of both having the same neural effects is not as farfetched as it might seem."

The brain is the organ of the mind, and its function affects personality. So how far do we go in treating its disorders and distresses, its syndromes and its character flaws? By all accounts, the resounding answer seems to be: as far as it is safe to go. The unanimous opinion among professionals is that more information is needed.

Yet what about the concern that we are entering an age when even the slightest wrinkle in character can be defined as a "disorder." Will we become a Prozac nation? Hardly, thinks Robert Millman, who does not believe the whole of society is going to became dependent upon these drugs. The reason? Evolution, which, over the course of time, has created in us the brain functions that dictate the way we deal with thoughts and emotions. That intricate interplay, he offers, is way beyond the primitive effects of any of these drugs.

"The system is so refined," believes Millman, "and drugs are so primitive, that one can never really replace the other. With drugs, you're always giving away more than you're getting—if you're not really debilitated. You're giving away sensitivity, receptivity, some capacity for pleasure. But it's a reasonable trade-off if you're in pain."

The only question, then, is for what degree of pain do we seek medical treatment. And, as Bob Trestman puts it, where will it end?

CHALLENGE QUESTIONS

Do the Advantages of Prozac Outweigh Its Disadvantages?

1. What is the ethical significance of identifying Prozac as a mood brightener rather than as a transforming drug?

2. Do you accept the idea that although "there are many situations where people do not meet the minimum criteria for a disorder" they should still receive mood enhancers? Why, or why not?

3. How would you answer Mauro's question, "What are the implications of a drug that is a shortcut to healing?"

4. What are the main objections to prescribing Prozac too broadly? Which line of argument do you feel is the strongest? Why?

ISSUE 4

Is Premenstrual Syndrome a Medical Disorder?

YES: Nancy Wartik, from "The Truth About PMS," *American Health* (April 1995)

NO: Carol Tavris, from "The Myth of PMS," *Redbook* (November 1991)

ISSUE SUMMARY

YES: Nancy Wartik, a contributing editor for *American Health*, asserts that although there is no clear, simple answer to what causes premenstrual syndrome (PMS), the combined evidence of biological factors strongly supports the existence of PMS.

NO: Social psychologist Carol Tavris argues that the bodily changes that women experience during their menstrual cycles are normal, not symptoms of an illness requiring treatment. She maintains that the myth of PMS is perpetuated by psychologists, nutritionists, and others who promote "cures" for PMS for profit.

In the 1950s Katherine Dalton, a British physician, became fascinated by the dangers of the extreme hormone fluctuations she observed and treated successfully in a few patients who displayed psychotic or near-psychotic antisocial behavior during their premenstrual period. She and a colleague coined the term *premenstrual syndrome,* or *PMS.*

Since its identification, PMS has become a topic of heated controversy. There is little agreement as to what causes PMS or even what the exact definition of PMS is. The debate that follows focuses on the issue of whether PMS is actually a syndrome (an illness) or simply natural bodily changes that are experienced to different degrees in different women.

Physicians and others who believe that PMS is an illness recently received support for their position from the fourth edition of the American Psychological Association's *Diagnostic and Statistical Manual of Mental Disorders* (APA *DSM-IV*), published in 1994. The manual includes a description of a condition identified as "premenstrual dysphoric disorder," or "PMDD." According to the *DSM-IV*, women with PMDD experience bouts of marked premenstrual depression, anxiety, sadness, or anger along with one or more physical symptoms, such as breast tenderness or bloating. Furthermore, these symptoms are so severe that they impair a woman's ability to "function socially or occupationally in the week prior to menses." The implication is that PMDD is really a severe form of what is popularly known as PMS and that the physical debilitation indicates an illness.

The PMDD diagnosis has itself become a topic of dispute. Critics have protested that the APA is identifying normal women's behavior as an illness. They further argue that although women may exhibit symptoms of PMS, there is no reason to classify them as being mentally ill, which is what many feel the PMDD label does. Another fear is that the PMDD diagnosis will reinforce the commonly held notion that women become "incompetent" once a month.

On the other side, some have argued that classifying severe PMS as a disorder will make it more likely that women suffering premenstrual discomfort will be taken seriously. Physicians and psychologists will be more likely to search for ways to treat the syndrome instead of dismissing the claims of PMS sufferers. Furthermore, officially recognizing PMS as an illness will lead to the development of research standards.

Medical and cross-cultural research has been done to determine whether or not women worldwide experience symptoms of PMS. In 1992, for example, researchers at the State University of New York at Buffalo reported their findings in the first large-scale comparison of women's premenstrual experiences. Women in the United States, Italy, and Bahrain reported experiencing menstrual cramps, water retention, emotional disruptions, and decreased activity before and during their menstrual periods. Although the Italian women had not heard of PMS, more than half reported symptoms similar to those experienced by the American women. However, there were intriguing differences. The Bahrainian women reported a lower incidence than the American women of all symptoms except backache, which was experienced by twice as many Bahrainians as Americans. Twice as many Italian women as Americans reported that PMS interfered with their work performance. And more American women than Italians reported premenstrual irritability, mood swings, and crying.

In the following selections, Nancy Wartik asserts that PMS is a medical disorder, and she suggests a number of approaches for treatment. Carol Tavris maintains that there is no reliable evidence that PMS exists and that PMS is often only a convenient excuse for negative emotions and behavior.

YES

Nancy Wartik

THE TRUTH ABOUT PMS

It's part of the universal language of women. Snap at a coworker, burst into tears or go on a chocolate-eating spree, and any fellow sufferer will sympathize once you utter three letters of the alphabet: PMS.

Premenstrual syndrome is an array of physical and psychological symptoms triggered by ovulation (the midcycle release of an egg from the ovary) and ending with menstruation. First identified in the 1930s, PMS has gained wide recognition—even notoriety—only in the past two decades, due in part to two British murder cases in the early 1980s in which the defendants invoked PMS as an extenuating circumstance.

Despite hundreds of PMS studies, the condition remains perplexing and controversial. It's estimated that 5% to 10% of all menstruating women are seriously affected, while at least that many more have symptoms that could benefit from treatment. Though it's undoubtedly linked to monthly hormonal fluctuations, there's little agreement on exactly what causes PMS or at what point ordinary premenstrual discomfort turns into a medical disorder. Some doctors question its very existence, while others feel that the severe depression, anxiety or violence it can trigger in its extreme form makes PMS a psychological illness.

Then there are those in the middle, who acknowledge the symptoms but question their classification as a medical disorder. "We're making a disease out of normal changes in mood and body," asserts Dr. Jerilynn Prior, an endocrinologist at the University of British Columbia in Vancouver. "The symptoms are real, but we shouldn't be labeling them as an illness. It's one of the many ways by which we've medicalized women's experience."

The debate continues, but in the meantime, women who seek help may find themselves facing questionable remedies, unethical practitioners, or treatments that aren't always appropriate, such as hysterectomy. Their best defense is to get the facts.

Dozens of symptoms have been attributed to PMS, including moodiness, fatigue, insomnia, broken concentration, food cravings, backaches and breast pain. (Menstrual cramps, however, are not considered part of PMS.) Women

who have asthma, migraine headaches or other chronic illnesses often find that these conditions worsen as their period approaches.

But for many women it's the emotional turmoil that's hardest to take. "Women may have sore breasts, bloating or food cravings, but that's not what they come in and complain about," says Dr. Ellen Freeman, codirector of the University of Pennsylvania Medical Center PMS program. "They talk about feeling like a different person in the premenstrual phase. They're afraid they'll hurt their children, they're angry and they're upset. Some get extremely depressed; they withdraw, want to sleep, don't want to leave the house."

"I've had people tell me PMS is just an excuse for being crabby," says Mary Brooks, 35, a St. Louis administrative assistant. "But if you're not in my shoes, it's hard to understand what it feels like. Each month like clockwork, 10 days before my period, I have a total personality change. I want to cry at the drop of a hat; I pick fights. It affects my work, because I'm tired as soon as I wake up. I don't have any energy. I have headaches, bloating. I walk into a room and can't remember what I wanted there."

* * *

No matter how many doctors insist that women only imagine such distress, new studies suggest that specific physiological changes, including variations in sleep patterns and body temperature, take place prior to menstruation in women who have PMS. What's more, the syndrome isn't limited to American women. When researchers at the State University of New York at Buffalo and other institutions compared women from the U.S.,

Italy and Bahrain (a Middle Eastern nation), they found that although many of the foreign women had never heard of PMS, they nevertheless reported many of its typical symptoms. "This supports the idea that PMS isn't simply a media-created phenomenon, as some have suggested," says Dr. Lisa Monagle, a certified nurse midwife, who headed the study.

Women who have had a major episode of depression or whose mothers or sisters have PMS may be more prone to develop the condition. Age also seems to play a role, though researchers don't know why. A 1992 study from the University of Calgary in Alberta, for instance, found that women in their late 20s to mid 30s are likeliest to experience mood problems.

* * *

There's little doubt that PMS is linked to hormonal changes during the menstrual cycle. Estrogen levels rise gradually during the first two weeks of the cycle. After ovulation, estrogen production decreases, while the other female hormone progesterone dominates the last two weeks. A decade ago, it was thought that PMS resulted from a progesterone deficiency. But scientists have so far failed to find evidence that women with PMS have different levels of progesterone—or of any other reproductive hormone—than unaffected women. It's now believed that some women may simply be extra sensitive to the effect of normal hormonal fluctuations and that the syndrome has multiple causes. These include:

Serotonin imbalance. Changing hormone levels may affect neurotransmitters (chemical messengers) in the brain. Serotonin imbalances, for example, have been linked to depression, violent

behavior, and appetite and sleep disturbances. PMS sufferers seem to have abnormally low levels of this chemical in the 10 days before menstruation.

Endorphins. The monthly hormonal tides may also affect endorphins, opiate-like compounds that act as natural pain relievers. It's possible that symptoms are triggered by an endorphin decline around the time of ovulation, mimicking what addicts experience during withdrawal from a drug: depression, anxiety, increased appetite and insomnia.

Body chemistry. Other possible PMS triggers include deficiencies or imbalances of nutrients, such as zinc or magnesium, or abnormal levels of prostaglandins, hormonelike substances with wide-ranging effects on body function.

Stress. Many experts believe psychological factors and life stresses contribute strongly to premenstrual woes. "If two individuals have the same degree of biochemical imbalance," says Dr. James Chuong, director of the PMS program at Baylor University College of Medicine in Houston, "but one woman has marriage or job problems, her symptoms will be more severe. It's not that PMS is only a psychological problem, but the way a woman experiences it has to do with a combination of biological and situational factors."

Dr. Joseph Mortola, a reproductive endocrinologist and psychiatrist at Harvard Medical School, disagrees. "Stress doesn't cause PMS," he says. "PMS causes stress. In the high-progesterone state preceding menstruation, a woman may be more reactive to the same event and experience it with more intensity. We've studied women over three consecutive cycles, and when we add up all the stress someone has in a given month, it's no prediction of how bad PMS will be that month. Your most stressful month is just as likely to be your mildest PMS month."

* * *

What should you do if you think you have PMS? First, since there are no specific tests for it, your best chance to identify it is by carefully charting your daily physical and emotional symptoms for two months. If you don't have at least a week's reprieve following the cessation of menstruation, PMS isn't your problem. In fact, more than 50% of women who see a doctor for suspected PMS discover they have a different ailment. "A lot of women think they have it, because they've seen so much about PMS in the media," says UCLA gynecologist Andrea Rapkin, author of *A Woman Doctor's Guide to PMS.* "About half turn out to have clinical depression or anxiety." Other conditions that may produce PMS-like symptoms include diabetes, thyroid disorders and anemia.

If you do have PMS, you may have to do some experimenting to find a treatment that's right for you. In some cases, simply identifying what's going on may help. That was true for a 30-year-old woman whose premenstrual moodiness was straining her marriage until her husband pointed out that their worst fights always happened before her period.

"Now when I get upset," she says, "I think, Does this have to do with the time of the month? I try to stay away from stressful situations, because I know if I start an argument when I have PMS, I can't control myself."

If you can't deal with the problem alone, talk with your gynecologist or

look for a PMS program at a local medical school. A team approach—including doctors, psychologists and registered dietitians—may be helpful. But be wary of those freestanding PMS clinics that are more interested in your wallet than in helping you. "If they give you an immediate diagnosis or try to sell you a treatment program or special PMS products right away, go elsewhere," warns Dr. John Renner, a board member at the National Council Against Health Fraud. Unless the problem is severe, experts advise taking a conservative approach to treatment, say, changing diet or exercise habits or trying stress reduction techniques.

Diet. Try cutting back on sugar, caffeine and alcohol during the premenstrual period, though it's unclear whether these substances exacerbate PMS or whether women use them as self-medication. Caffeine, however, is thought to aggravate breast tenderness. If bloating is a problem, decrease premenstrual salt intake. Snacking on several small meals during the day may help allay food cravings and have a beneficial effect on energy and mood....

Exercise. Vigorous activity may be one of the best PMS antidotes. A 1993 Duke University study compared a group of women who did aerobic exercise for one hour three times a week with a group who did strength training. PMS symptoms improved to some degree for all the women, but the aerobic group reaped especially significant benefits, particularly for depression.

Stress reduction. While the experts debate the role of stress in PMS, there's evidence that stress reduction techniques —say, meditation or deep breathing— can alleviate symptoms. A 1990 Harvard Medical School study found that women with severe PMS who practiced meditation twice daily for 15 to 20 minutes experienced a 57% improvement in physical and psychological symptoms.

Light therapy. Light therapy was initially used to treat seasonal affective disorder (SAD), a depressive illness that strikes as the days shorten in winter. Now researchers at the University of California at San Diego have found that exposing PMS patients to bright light every day in the week before menstruation significantly decreases depression. The link between SAD and PMS isn't understood, but it's possible that abnormalities in melatonin, a light-sensitive hormone that helps set the body's internal clock, is a factor in both.

Hormonal treatments. If conservative measures fail, medication may be the next step.

NO

Carol Tavris

THE MYTH OF PMS

Just when you thought it was safe to be a woman, it's back: renewed belief in "raging hormones" and the unruly female body.

Everywhere we turn today—in medical studies, courtroom decisions, workplace reports—we are hearing that the normal changes of women's bodies are a disease, a handicap and the root of emotional woes and practical havoc. "Premenstrual Syndrome" is even being blamed for slowing down the national economy. A physician writing in *The Wall Street Journal* estimated that "the illness costs U.S. industry eight percent of its total wage bill." Another newspaper reported that "PMS-related absenteeism is estimated to have cost industry $5 billion ... not counting women who are working but who aren't functioning as well because of PMS." Some self-help books advise women to turn to routine tasks at "that time of the month" and leave the really hard thinking to later.

Why does all the hoopla about PMS put a cramp in women's style? Because we are left to draw the conclusions that:

- Up to half of all women are sick every month.
- Nearly all of us are sick sometimes.
- How fortunate we are that men are running things!

First, let's sort the myth from the fact: During a woman's menstrual cycle, some physical changes typically occur. It's normal for premenstrual women to have some aches and pains, to have tender breasts, to gain a few pounds (because of temporary water retention) or to crave food (because of increased metabolism as the body prepares the uterine lining).

A small percentage of women report having particularly painful physical and emotional symptoms associated with menstruation: Some describe severe, Jekyll-and-Hyde personality changes that recur cyclically. A larger percentage of women describe mood changes, notably depression and irritability. But what biomedical researchers have done is taken a set of bodily changes that are normal over the menstrual cycle, packaged them into a premenstrual syndrome, and sold them back to women as a *disorder* that needs treatment and attention. Most of the media, many researchers and women themselves now confuse a condition that is abnormal and occurs in *few* women with something that is normal for all women.

Because researchers themselves don't agree on who is suffering what, estimates of the prevalence of the "syndrome" range from 5 percent (women who are severely incapacitated) to a whopping 95 percent—women who will experience, as one article put it, "one or more PMS symptoms sometime in their lives."

Such "checklists" of symptoms often include every possible feeling and problem a person could have—from joint pain, forgetfulness, lethargy, nausea and weight gain to cravings for chocolate, and anxiety about work. Some even list mutually contradictory choices, such as "less interested in sex" *and* "more interested in sex." With so many symptoms covering such a broad spectrum of the human experience, who *wouldn't* have PMS?

NO PROBLEM, NO PROFITS

How did we get to this point? And how did women manage before they knew they had a disorder?

The real mover and shaker on behalf of PMS was British physician Katharina Dalton, M.D., who wrote articles in the 1950s on the "dangers" of menstruation. Dr. Dalton and a colleague coined the term *premenstrual syndrome,* and in 1964 she published a book with the same title. The term stuck, and in the decades that followed, premenstrual syndrome became an increasingly hot research topic.

Mary Brown Parlee, Ph.D., a psychologist at the City University of New York, who has been conducting menstrual-cycle research for many years, observes that increasingly, the big money and

grants began to go *not* to psychologists who were studying normal menstrual cycles, but to biomedical researchers who were looking into menstruation as a disease or a physiological abnormality best studied with the most cutting-edge weapons in the medical arsenal.

This move toward the "medicalization" of PMS, Parlee observes, was—and is—actively supported by drug companies, which stand to make a great deal of money if every menstruating woman would take a few pills every month. It's in the drug companies' interest, she adds, if physicians and the public confuse the small minority of women who have severe premenstrual symptoms with the majority who have normal, undrug-worthy cycles.

And PMS "cures" are a thriving business. Nationwide, nutritionists, psychologists, nurses, doctors and writers are promoting books, tapes and seminars. Physicians are setting up PMS medical groups, some funded by drug companies, for the specific treatment of premenstrual syndrome.

With all these clinicians engaged in treatment and all these years of studies trying to document the existence of this alleged disorder, you might think that researchers would have some idea at this point of what causes it . . . and what cures it. Think again. Numerous theories—that PMS is caused by abnormally high (or low) hormones, low magnesium, high sodium, abnormal thyroids, a deficiency of prostaglandins, steroid fluctuations and on and on—have been advanced, but have not panned out. Indeed, no biological marker has been found that distinguishes women who have severe premenstrual symptoms from those who do not.

Nor has any drug or vitamin been found to be effective in "curing" PMS. Progesterone suppositories and vitamin B-6 supplements, two commonly recommended treatments, work no better than placebos, carefully controlled studies show. (Moreover, megadoses of B-6 carry significant risks, such as nerve damage, for some individuals.)

In fact, in most of the double-blind treatment studies—where neither the woman nor her doctor knows whether she is getting an active drug or a placebo—upward of 60 to 70 percent of the women given a sugar pill report improvement in their symptoms.

FUZZY SCIENCE

So where did the "proof" of such a widespread disorder come from? At first, from studies in which women themselves recall their own mood changes over the course of the month... retrospectively. As a result, many will tell you that they become depressed, weepy, irritable and moody just before menstruation, when, in fact, they did not. Many women "remember" symptoms that did not occur, and forget changes that occurred at other times in their cycles.

When researchers ask people to keep daily mood and symptom diaries for a couple of months, it turns out that women —like men—vary widely over a 35-day span. Some women have no symptoms at all, some do tend to become irritable and grouchy premenstrually, but others are grumpiest midcycle. And many women report feeling *better* before their periods are about to start, describing a "burst of creativity" and higher energy levels—yet few studies of "PMS checklists" have ever included this cheery possibility.

In one fascinating study, two groups of women and a comparable group of men filled out daily inventories of their moods and physical symptoms. Half of the women were aware that menstrual-cycle changes were a focus of the study, and half were unaware. During the premenstrual phase of their cycles, the "aware" women reported a significantly higher level of negative moods and uncomfortable physical changes, such as headaches and muscle tension, and fewer positive feelings, than did either the "unaware" women or the men in the study. The "unaware" women and the men did not differ from each other in the number of mood changes they had.

Why is that? The *belief* in PMS makes it far more likely that a woman will notice some symptoms and ignore others at different times of the month. Expecting bodily changes to occur can make us more sensitive to them. Conversely, distracting influences can override our awareness of changes. Add to this widespread public support for the idea that women are at the mercy of their hormones once a month and women have a convenient cue for any sour mood or slip-up they experience. ("Aha, so that's why I was so grumpy/clumsy/short-tempered Tuesday—I was about to get my period.")

The truth is, a woman's mood swings may have less to do with her "time of month" than with her "time of the week." As several studies have shown, if you want to predict when a woman will feel happiest, you do better to know when it's a Saturday or Sunday than when she is ovulating. Women's positive moods—and men's—in fact peak on the weekends!

THE *REAL* REASON WE SHOULD FEEL IRRITABLE

Do hormones ultimately have anything to do with abilities and behavior? The answer is important. We *should* be worried if the premenstrual workers of America are costing the economy billions of dollars. We *should* be worried if premenstrual college students are flubbing their exams in great numbers. And we *should* be worried if growing numbers of premenstrual females are crashing their cars or murdering their lovers.

But the fact is, there is no evidence to support such dire concerns. Instead, numerous studies have confirmed that women manage their households, thoughts, offices, families and factories at any phase of their cycle. Hysterical headlines notwithstanding, hormonal changes in women have never been reliably linked to behavioral problems or intellectual deficiencies. Psychologist Sharon Golub, Ph.D., of the College of New Rochelle in New York, who reviewed almost 50 years of research on the issue, concluded emphatically, "The menstrual cycle has no consistent demonstrable effect on cognitive tasks, work or academic performance."

What's more, people use biology to explain only certain kinds of actions and emotions: namely, negative ones. No one ever says, "It wasn't my fault that I contributed a thousand dollars to that shelter for the homeless—my hormones make me feel generous once a month."

Finally, all the talk about the biochemical origins of mood changes conveniently overlooks the content of those moods. Maybe the real question is not why some women become irritable before menstruation, but why they aren't angry the *rest* of the month, and why they (and others) are so quick to dismiss their irritations as only being symptoms of menstruation.

It's enough to make me grumpy. I must be premenstrual.

CHALLENGE QUESTIONS

Is Premenstrual Syndrome a Medical Disorder?

1. How do you explain the wide range of opinions about premenstrual syndrome (PMS) despite hundreds of studies?

2. Wartik quotes endocrinologist Jerilynn Prior as acknowledging that the symptoms of PMS are real. But Dr. Prior indicates that they should not be labeled as an illness, stating, "It's one of the many ways by which we've medicalized women's experience." How do you interpret this comment? Do you agree with it? Why, or why not?

3. What are the economic implications of recognizing PMS as a medical condition requiring treatment? For example, consider Tavris's statement that "the big money and grants [go to] biomedical researchers ... looking into menstruation as a disease or a physiological abnormality."

4. If you were to create a comparison chart of the pros and cons of recognizing PMS as a medical condition, what factors would you list under each heading?

5. Imagine you are on a jury for a case involving a woman accused of killing her husband. As her defense she has cited PMS, saying it "made me do it." What kind of expert testimony would you need to hear before you could give credence to her defense?

ISSUE 5

Is Schizophrenia a Disease?

YES: Eve C. Johnstone, from "A Concept of Schizophrenia," *Journal of Mental Health* (vol. 2, 1993)

NO: Theodore R. Sarbin, from "Toward the Obsolescence of the Schizophrenia Hypothesis," *The Journal of Mind and Behavior* (vol. 11, nos. 3 and 4, 1990)

ISSUE SUMMARY

YES: Psychiatrist Eve C. Johnstone contends that schizophrenia is a biological disease, both in the sense of a medical syndrome and in the sense of a physical lesion.

NO: Theodore R. Sarbin, noted researcher and psychologist, argues that schizophrenia is a social construct developed by scientists and practitioners to make sense of a variety of behaviors.

The condition known as "schizophrenia" has been a puzzle ever since it was first labeled. Considered a "thought disorder" or a type of "psychosis," its symptoms typically include hallucinations, delusions, and a general lack of perception about what is real or actual. Why do people act and think this way? What causes schizophrenia?

Until about the fourth century B.C., schizophrenics were thought to be the victims of demons that required exorcising. It was then that the Greek physician Hippocrates suggested a medical model of abnormality, a model that has dominated the understanding of schizophrenia until the present. The medical model assumes that schizophrenics have some kind of "badness" in them. Recently, the medical model has attempted to locate this badness—this disease—in the properties (or physiology) of the body.

A historical and a modern reaction to this dominant disease model has been termed "social constructionism." Social constructionists have traditionally called attention to the "social" elements of schizophrenia. That is, schizophrenia is not merely an objective condition; it is a moral judgment, based upon the ethics of the society in which the judgment occurs. In some cultures, schizophrenics are seen as especially close to God or exceptionally enlightened. Because this is a different social construction of schizophrenia (i.e., it is not bad), there is no need to find its physiological "cause." Although physiological differences between "normals" and "schizophrenics" occur, it is not known whether these differences are the cause of the schizophrenics' behavior or the result of ethical judgments and societal treatment as a consequence of such judgments.

Psychiatrist Eve C. Johnstone supports the former explanation. She carefully examines the notion of "disease" in the medical sense and finds that the concept of schizophrenia fits it in two major respects. First, Johnstone cites evidence to show that the symptoms of schizophrenia form a "syndrome picture" with a characteristic outcome. Second, she attempts to demonstrate that the disorder is based on a physical condition. Johnstone concludes that even if the disease concept is false, the medical model of schizophrenia still has practical value to patients and clinicians.

In contrast, Theodore R. Sarbin finds little of value in the medical model of schizophrenia; he considers the disease "construction" to be no longer tenable. Sarbin describes how this disease notion originated from its social and historic origins, implying that schizophrenia is not an objective thing but a cultural invention. He also attempts to demonstrate that there is no valid biological or psychological distinction between schizophrenics and normals. According to Sarbin, eight decades of research has shown that such distinctions produce an unacceptable number of misdiagnoses, and this research has also failed to differentiate schizophrenic problems from other, more normal problems.

POINT	COUNTERPOINT
• The scientific evidence is sufficient to conclude that schizophrenia is a biological disease.	• Decades of research have failed to produce a reliable distinction between schizophrenia and normalcy.
• The symptoms of schizophrenia form a syndrome picture that has a characteristic outcome.	• The symptoms of schizophrenia originate from social and moral judgments, not from the disease itself.
• Schizophrenics cannot help that they have this disease.	• To make a pattern of behavior such as schizophrenia into a disease is to make a person into an object.
• The medical model of schizophrenia has practical value for patients.	• When behaviors and thoughts are "modeled" medically, it means that *all* our thoughts and behaviors are not chosen but determined.

YES
Eve C. Johnstone

A CONCEPT OF SCHIZOPHRENIA

SCHIZOPHRENIA AS A DISEASE

It is twenty-seven years since as a medical student I saw my first schizophrenic patient. She was about my own age. I remember her name, her face, her perplexity and fear. Her mother was interviewed for the benefit of the students and she described her bewilderment and grief over the inexplicable change in her daughter, who had previously functioned effectively, working successfully in the local textile industry.

I was given to understand that really nothing was known about the cause of this condition, although it was certainly sometimes familial, that the pathogenesis was not understood at all, that although the treatment was relatively successful in the short term, it was entirely empirical and there was no understanding of its mechanism. I was told that in the longer term treatment was not successful, that relapse was usual and most patients suffered a general deterioration of function and could not work, make social relationships or achieve independence.

In the West of Scotland among the deprived individuals who formed the majority of the patients in the big infirmaries, rheumatic heart disease was still common enough for there to be several affected patients in every medical ward that I saw, cases of chronic bronchitis, emphysema and respiratory failure packed the wards every winter, tuberculosis was not yet a disease of the past, and as now cancers and cardiovascular disease were very common. Like many of the idealistic medical students that I now teach, I was fascinated by serious illness and I wanted to look after people who were really very ill, to the best standard possible. To me, at that time, schizophrenia was the worst disease that I had ever seen. It seemed to come from nowhere to strike the young, affect them with bizarre, frightening and non-understandable symptoms, to progressively blunt their abilities and warp their personalities and probably forever destroy their promise and potential. No-one knew why, and not a great deal could be done about it—certainly not about the loss of potential. I could identify all too readily with that situation and could imagine no worse fate.

Research did not seem to be being performed in the way that it was in other specialties. This was, of course, in the 1960s. 'The Divided Self' had been published only a few years before by the Glaswegian psychiatrist Dr. R. D. Laing, and his later work 'Sanity, Madness and the Family' had just reached the shelves. Ideas that schizophrenia was in some way the result of flawed interpersonal interactions within the patients's family and home were widely discussed. I found the acceptance of such ideas very hard to understand, although then, as now, I found that some of the descriptions of the patients' symptomatology and suffering that appear in 'The Divided Self' very perceptive.

At that time I did not appreciate the lack of experimental support that there was for these ideas, and of course they have not stood the test of time, but I could not understand how it could be believed that imperfect interactions that could not really be defined could possibly have such devastating and lasting effects upon some people, when others in the same family were not affected and when there was evidence all around us in that vibrant but often deprived and sometimes violent city, that people could and did triumph over interpersonal difficulties of every kind.

To his credit, the then Professor of Psychiatry in Glasgow, Professor T. Ferguson Rodger, who had at one time been Dr. R. D. Laing's Head of Department, taught his students that although the work of Laing & Esterson was very popular and that Ronnie Laing was in many ways gifted and wrote in a very compelling style, schizophrenia was a disease. I remember him saying, "schizophrenia is a disease like multiple sclerosis or cancer. We do not know its cause, but it will be found one day". I agreed with him then and essentially I agree with him now, although I have given a good deal more thought to the issue than I had when I first accepted the idea.

As a student and in my early years as a psychiatrist, I believed wholeheartedly that in my own lifetime I would see the unravelling of the principal elements of the causation of schizophrenia. After so many years I should perhaps have more sense, but in fact I believe it still, although I would have to concede that the odds I would suggest to a bookmaker are not quite so overwhelming as they would have been at one time. When I was told and readily accepted that schizophrenia was a disease, that concept was not defined. I came across these issues when I was being taught to be a doctor by other doctors, and of course as Kendell pointed out in 1975 in his book, 'The Role of Diagnosis in Psychiatry', most doctors give little thought to the meaning of concepts of illness and disease, and tend to take it for granted that their meaning is self-evident and unambiguous. This is far from the case, and an adequate definition that globally covers the situation of all disorders that physicians would regard as diseases is hard to find. Disease may be defined in various ways (Kendell, 1975); as suffering, by the presence of a lesion, as an imperfection, or indeed it may be defined statistically as in Scadding's (1967) definition, 'the sum of the abnormal phenomena displayed by a group of living organisms in association with a specified common characteristic or set of characteristics by which they differ from the norm for their species in such a way as to place them at a biological disadvantage'. It is not difficult to advance the view that in these terms schizophrenia is a disease, but this is not really what I mean when I express that opinion.

Part of the difficulty about defining what we mean by disease as a general concept is our need to find an all-embracing definition. The concept becomes clearer when individual diseases are considered, because we can then see that there is no consistent defining characteristic. Tuberculosis and syphilis are defined by their bacteriological cause, ulcerative colitis and tumors are defined by histology, porphyria is defined by biochemistry and prion disease by molecular biology, but some other conditions, for example migraine and most psychiatric disorders, are defined as a constellation of symptoms with a characteristic course (i.e. to resolve, to remit or to persist).

This uncertainty, as Kendell (1975) points out, relates to the historical development of our concepts of disease. In the ancient world, symptoms and signs, e.g. fever, asthma, rashes, joint pains, were themselves regarded as diseases to be studied separately, and it was really only with Sydenham's work in the 17th century that the idea of disease as a syndrome and constellation of symptoms having a characteristic prognosis became established (Sydenham, 1696). With the increasing popularity of post-mortem examination in the 19th century, disease became defined by pathological findings rather than by the clinical picture, and later technological development has allowed diseases to be defined in bacteriological, biochemical and molecular biological terms. As these new methods of definition of disease have developed, the older ones have persisted to some extent, so that any medical textbook will list diseases defined in terms of varied concepts which may have little or no relationship to one another.

The principal model of disease in psychiatry is still the syndrome model —i.e. a cluster of symptoms and signs which are associated with a characteristic course over time—and that is partly, but not entirely, what was meant by the idea of schizophrenia as a disease, as it was first discussed with me in the 1960s. While the disorder was regarded as a cluster of symptoms and signs with a characteristic course, part of the idea of its being a disease came from the view that it was like other diseases that we as doctors were familiar with; i.e. like them, although originally defined as a syndrome, it would eventually be found to have a biological cause, be that demonstrated by biochemical, histological or some yet undiscovered means. Furthermore, in accepting the idea of schizophrenia as a disease, we were essentially rejecting the concept of the disorder as a response to imperfect interpersonal interactions within the patient's family. Therefore in terms of the classification of concepts of disease described by Kendell (1975) the concept that was being put forward was a combination of disease as a syndrome and disease as a lesion.

The development of morbid anatomy and histology in the 19th century and later physiology and biochemistry showed that many diseases defined as syndromes were in fact associated with identifiable lesions. This led to the view that the demonstration of such an identifiable lesion was the defining characteristic of disease. There are many problems with this clear-cut and initially appealing view, and as far as much of psychiatry is concerned, there is the very considerable problem that no physical basis has been defined for most of the major syndromes. For some psychiatrists this has not seemed to be the overwhelming difficulty that one might expect. Emil Kraepelin, who defined dementia praecox (1896) (which came to be known as schizophrenia) on the basis of the characteristic course and outcome of a cluster of symptoms and signs, stated that this was a disorder in which if "every detail" were known a specific anatomical pathology with a specific aetiology would be found. Kurt Schneider (1950) saw no difficulty in accepting the idea that the word illness should only be used in situations in which 'some actual morbid change' or 'defective structure' was present in the body. In this context he stated that he did not regard either neurotic states or personality disorders as illness, but simply as 'abnormal varieties of sane mental life'. He still, however, considered schizophrenia and manic-depressive psychosis as illness, along with organic and toxic psychoses, on the basis of the assumption that in time they would prove to have an "underlying morbid physical condition." ...

DEFINING THE SYNDROME

Since the time the concept of dementia praecox, later known as schizophrenia, was first defined, there has a times been controversy about the symptoms and signs which formed the syndrome. In defining dementia praecox, Kraepelin had drawn together catatonia as described by Kahlbaum (1874), hebephrenia described by Hecker (1871) and his own dementia paranoides, and regarded them as manifestations of the same disorder of which he considered delusions, hallucinations and catatonic features to be important characteristics. In 1911 Eugen

Bleuler published his 'Dementia Praecox or the Group of Schizophrenias.' He considered that he was developing Kraepelin's concept, but in fact changed it substantially. Bleuler was influenced by psychoanalytic schools of thought and saw schizophrenia in terms different from the neuropathological ones envisaged by Kraepelin. His term schizophrenia, meaning split mind, was intended to describe a loosening of the association between the different functions of the mind so that thoughts became disconnected and coordination between emotional, cognitive and volitional processes became poor. He considered thought disorder, affective disturbance, autism and ambivalence to be the fundamental symptoms of schizophrenia, and that the more clear-cut phenomena of hallucinations, delusions and catatonic features emphasised by Kraepelin were secondary phenomena. Bleuler's ideas became influential in some centres, particularly in the United States, but Kraepelin's concept of dementia praecox, although that name was no longer used, never lost its domination in many European countries.

The lack of common ground between these two concepts was illustrated by the findings of the US-UK diagnostic project (Cooper et al, 1972). In this comparative study, 250 consecutive admissions between the ages of 20 and 59 were studied in New York and London. Information was obtained from patients and their relatives by structured interviews and a diagnosis using nomenclature from the International Classification of Disease (ICD) (WHO, 1967) was assigned to each patient. The project diagnoses obtained in this way were compared with the diagnoses given independently to the same patients by the hospital staff. In the New

York series 61.5% of the patients were given a hospital diagnosis of schizophrenia, whereas in the London series the proportion was 33.9%. However, in terms of the project diagnoses the percentages were 29.2 and 35.1, i.e. clearly similar. By contrast, 31.5% of the London sample received a hospital diagnosis of manic-depressive disorder, but only 5.2% of the New York sample were given such a diagnosis. Clearly therefore, the concept of schizophrenia in New York at that time was wider than that employed in London. These findings and others encouraged the formulation of operational rules for defining schizophrenia; examples of these are the St. Louis criteria (Feighner et al, 1972) and DSM III R (American Psychiatric Association, 1987).

It is obvious that schizophrenia defined according to the very different concepts used in New York and London might well have different characteristic courses. Problems of definition for diagnosis are not the only issue here, as outcome may also be difficult to define. Stephens (1978) has pointed out that outcome should include at least four areas of function: severity of symptomatology, duration of hospitalization after diagnostic evaluation, employment, and social function. While this is so, studies where this is done (and there are relatively few) are difficult to compare because of variability of clinical practices, employment possibilities, and social circumstances....

The introduction of operational definitions of schizophrenia has clarified the syndrome picture of the disorder, but it adds an additional problem to outcome studies. This is the fact that the St. Louis criteria and DSM III both include a six-month period without return to the previous level of function as an obligatory criterion of diagnosis. As far as most of medicine is concerned, there is no better predictor of what will happen in the future as examination of what has happened, and an illness which has been associated with six months of impaired function of whatever kind is relatively likely to be associated with impairment in the future. The fact that a substantial proportion of people with schizophrenia defined by the St. Louis (Feighner et al, 1972) criteria showed a course of remission and relapse, continuing symptomatology, and social impairments occurred in a substantial proportion of patients—be this judged in long-stay in-patients (Owens & Johnstone, 1980) or in those discharged to the community (Johnstone et al, 1981; Johnstone, 1984; 1991)—does not fully answer the question of whether the syndrome of schizophrenia has a characteristic outcome. This issue is better dealt with by studies that have used diagnostic definitions of schizophrenia which do not include an element of chronicity. The Present State Examination (PSE) (Wing et al, 1974) is a system of diagnostic categorisation which relies upon the features of the mental state detected at a detailed standardized interview. It is conducted in conjunction with a computer programme, CATEGO, which relies substantially upon the presence of Schneider's (1957) first rank symptoms in the diagnosis of schizophrenia. The PSE categorisation can be reliably used in diverse countries and cultures, and was employed in the International Pilot Study of Schizophrenia (WHO, 1975). In that study patients with a schizophrenic categorisation had a poorer outcome than a small group of non-schizophrenic patients in the same investigation. Some studies in which I have been involved are relevant to these issues. The Northwick Park Study of First

Episodes of Schizophrenia (Johnstone et al, 1986) used PSE criteria to identify cases of first episode schizophrenia. Four hundred and sixty-two patients were assessed over a period of 28 months and 253 were considered to have first episodes of schizophrenia. Most of the PSEs were conducted by my former colleague Dr. Fiona Macmillan, although I did some of them, and I do not think that Dr. Macmillan would object to my saying that they were conducted in circumstances that were sometimes less than ideal, on patients who were often unable to cooperate fully and were sometimes suspicious of interviewers that they had only just met.

I suspected when this study was designed that our criteria for first schizophrenic episode, referring clinician's diagnosis of at least possible schizophrenia, categorisation within S (schizophrenia), P (paranoid) or O (other non-affective) categories on application of the CATEGO programme to the PSE (Wing et al, 1974) profiles in patients requiring admission for at least one week with no prior history of psychosis or possible psychosis, and the absence of organic disease, might include patients with brief psychotic episodes who would do well. In fact this was not so. Outcome at two years in terms of relapse, employment, marriage and child care was far from reassuring, and only 13 of 253 cases made educational, occupational or social achievements. Thus the clusters of symptoms fulfilling the PSE (Wing et al, 1974) concept of schizophrenia did indeed appear to predict a characteristically poor outcome, even when the symptoms were detected under less than ideal circumstances. The first episodes study only concerned patients with schizophrenia and the outcome is classed as poor in comparison with the patients' premorbid

function and expectations of the function of well people in the same circumstances, rather than as compared with any group of patients with a different mental illness. This issue was addressed in the follow-up phase of the Northwick Park 'Functional' Psychosis Study (Johnstone et al, 1992). This investigation addresses the relationship between classification within the broad category of functional psychosis and outcome two and a half years later. We examined the outcome in social, clinical and cognitive terms of a cohort of over 200 psychotic patients who were not selected by diagnosis within the broad category of functional psychosis (Johnstone et al, 1991). We considered whether or not outcome in these terms could appropriately be used as a validation of the specific diagnostic categories of schizophrenia, affective disorder and schizoaffective psychosis as derived by the later application of the diagnostic systems of DSM III (American Psychiatric Association, 1980) and the PSE/CATEGO (Wing et al, 1974). The deterioration in occupational and hospital careers demonstrated at follow-up were worse in patients with diagnostic classifications of schizophrenia; and positive and negative features were also worse in patients with a classification of schizophrenia (Johnstone et al, 1992). Although no differences in cognitive test performance were found between the groups based upon diagnostic classification, there was no outcome variable in which cases classed as affective achieved a worse score than cases classed as schizophrenic, and there were several clinical and historical measures which showed a significantly worse outcome for schizophrenic patients. This study therefore provides strong support for the view that the symptoms and signs regarded as typical of schizophrenia form a syndrome picture which has a characteristic outcome.

BIOLOGICAL CONSIDERATIONS

I shall now consider the evidence that there is 'an underlying morbid physical condition', i.e. a biological basis, to schizophrenia. This may conveniently be considered under the headings listed in Table 1.

(1) It has long been known that there is a familial predisposition to schizophrenia. This, of course, suggests that there is a genetic factor in the production of the disorder, but the possibility of shared environment has also to be considered. The matter was elegantly dealt with by the adoption studies of Kety and colleagues (1975), who found high rates of schizophrenia in the biological relatives of schizophrenics who had been adopted away at birth and high rates of the later development of schizophrenia in children of schizophrenic mothers who had been adopted away at birth. This clear genetic predispostion to schizophrenia and the development of molecular genetic techniques are the basis of the intensive genetic studies of schizophrenia which are currently being undertaken.

(2) Certain organic diseases which could not result from any of the social or environmental disadvantages of the disorder occur in association with schizophrenia more often than would be expected by chance (Davison & Bagley, 1969). The disorders are varied and the main common thread between them is that they tend to involve the temporal lobe of the brain, although this is by no means always so. In the great majority of schizophrenic patients no underlying organic disease is found. One of the few studies in which a defined cohort of

Table 1
Areas of Evidence for the Biological Basis of Schizophrenia

1. Familial tendency of the condition
2. Occurrence of schizophrenia-like psychoses
3. Mechanism of the antipsychotic effect of neuroleptics
4. Miscellaneous effects relating to perinatal events
5. Structural brain changes
6. Changes in functional imaging related to neuropsychological performance

patients was examined was carried out in connection with the Northwick Park Study of First Episodes of Schizophrenia (Johnstone, Macmillan & Crow, 1987); this showed underlying organic disease of at least possible aetiological significance in 15 of 268 cases. This frequency of about 6% is in keeping with what other work there is. The tantalising possibility that other organic cases are missed is obvious, but in this cohort no additional relevant illnesses are known to have become evident over the next five years.

(3) In 1952 Delay and Deniker introduced chlorpromazine for the treatment of schizophrenia. This discovery of a new class of drugs which relieved the fundamental psychotic symptoms of schizophrenia was a significant advance, and indeed it revolutionised the management of the disorder. A very substantial research effort was subsequently devoted to understanding how phenothiazines and other anti-schizophrenic drugs act upon the brain. This effort was motivated by the idea that such knowledge might not only lead to a more rational basis for the development of new drugs, but also perhaps give some clue to the nature of the abnormalities which underlie schizophrenic illness. On the one

hand this field of endeavour has been a great success, and it is widely accepted that the mechanism of action of typical anti-schizophrenic drugs is blockade of D, dopamine receptors, but on the other hand the effects of these drugs are seen in all psychotic illnesses, so that they are not specific to schizophrenia. And there is no good evidence of abnormality in dopamine function in schizophrenia. Thus in spite of high hopes at times in the last 15 years, study of the mechanism of action of antipsychotic agents has not provided compelling evidence about the biological basis of schizophrenia. The recent demonstration of additional dopamine receptors, together with the efficacy of 'atypical' antipsychotics has raised hopes that these drugs may derive their antipsychotic effects from actions upon D_3, D_4 or D_5 receptors and that this may provide valuable evidence of the mechanisms underlying schizophrenia. At present this is speculation (Johnstone, 1993).

(4) There is a well documented tendency for individuals who later develop schizophrenia to have been born in the winter months of the year (Hare & Walter, 1978; Hafner et al, 1987). This suggests the possibility that some seasonal variable, possibly infective or dietary, acting before or around the time of birth, may be relevant. Recent evidence that second generation Afro-Caribbean immigrants to the United Kingdom have a substantial increase in the incidence of schizophrenia as compared to the indigenous population, might be interpreted in a similar way. Thus the mothers of such patients might have lacked immunity to some relevant infection and contracted it when they arrived in Britain. Perhaps because of these findings there has been recent interest in pre- or perinatal factors such as birth injury (Murray, Lewis & Revely, 1985) or maternal influenza in pregnancy (O'Callaghan et al, 1991). I was involved with colleagues (Done et al, 1991) in a study which identified and obtained details concerning all individuals in the National Child Development Study (Shepherd, P.M.) who came to require inpatient psychiatric care. The frequency of perinatal and birth complications in various diagnostic groups was compared with that of the total sample. There was no significant increase in perinatal events in schizophrenia, but there was in certain other psychoses of early onset, and some of the patients may well turn out to have schizophrenia in the end. The only specific association with schizophrenia was that the mothers of babies who later developed schizophrenia were of significantly lower weight than other mothers. These results, like so very many findings in schizophrenia research, are not clearcut. It looks unlikely that perinatal events account for the majority of schizophrenia, but they could perhaps account for some of it.

(5) The morbid anatomy of schizophrenia was studied in Kraepelin's time (Kraepelin, 1919), but this early work was conducted when histological techniques were in their infancy and the need to control for fixation and staining artefacts was not appreciated. It is therefore not surprising that these findings were not confirmed by later workers, and in 1976 Corsellis felt forced to conclude that present histological methods are not adequate to demonstrate any convincing structural substrate for the subtle and often reversible mental aberrations that go to make up the 'functional' psychoses. Nonetheless, in that same year, my colleagues and I, using computed tomography (CT) detected

a significant enlargement of the lateral ventricles in a group of patients with chronic schizophrenia (Johnstone et al, 1976). This result has been widely but not invariably replicated, and it has stimulated further work among post-mortem material (Bogerts, Meertes & Schonfeldt-Bausch, 1985; Jellinger, 1985; Jakob & Beckman, 1986; Bruton et al, 1990). Although the findings of the studies are not entirely consistent, there is increasing evidence of smaller lighter brains and abnormalities of neuronal architecture in schizophrenia.

(6) Our CT scan study (Johnstone et al, 1976) showed not only that the lateral ventricles of the schizophrenics were enlarged, but that the degree of this enlargement was significantly related to the degree of cognitive impairment. Poor performance on cognitive tests in schizophrenia had long been noted, following Bleuler's (1911) early writings; however, the view held sway that in spite of their *performance* deficits the cognitive *abilities* of schizophrenic patients did not decline. It was believed that patients did not do the tests well—did not seem to know their own age, their date of birth, or occasionally even their own name— because of lack of volition rather than lack of ability. The idea was that through lack of interest and drive the patients did not try to do the tests, but that if this veil of apathy could be lifted the abilities that lay behind it could be discovered, unimpaired. However, once the poor performance could be related to structural changes, the idea of preserved abilities behind a veil became less credible and extensive studies of cognitive ability in schizophrenia have shown that in a proportion of patients with schizophrenia cognitive impairments are definite and may be severe and crippling (Frith, 1992). The cognitive neuropsychology of schizophrenia has been increasingly widely studied (Frith, 1992) and the introduction of functional imaging has made it possible to relate neuropsychological performance to measures of cerebral blood flow and metabolism (Berman & Weinberger, 1990; Frith et al, 1991; Berman et al, 1993). Again, the findings are not entirely consistent and they do not in themselves demonstrate a clear biological basis, but if the results in all of the areas described are taken together, it appears that while these findings do not amount to proof, the evidence is sufficient to persuade me that schizophrenia is almost certainly a biological disease, that we must continue to seek its causes, and indeed that these will be found.

NO

TOWARD THE OBSOLESCENCE OF THE
SCHIZOPHRENIA HYPOTHESIS

Any effort to criticize or clarify the concept of schizophrenia must begin from the position that "schizophrenia" is a hypothetical construct. Notwithstanding the use of the term to denote a firm diagnostic entity by most textbook writers and clinical practitioners, investigators by the hundreds are still trying to establish the empirical validity of the construct. The output of published and unpublished research directed toward establishing empirical validity has been enormous, yet schizophrenia remains an unconfirmed hypothesis. A great deal of the research is directed to the task of breaking out of the circular reasoning in which "schizophrenia" appears on both sides of a causality equation: unwanted behaviors are taken to be symptoms of schizophrenia; schizophrenia is the cause of unwanted behaviors.

Historical accounts of psychiatry and psychology make clear that the core hypothesis—schizophrenia as a disease entity—continues to serve as an implicit guide to the construction of current versions of the schizophrenia concept. The schizophrenia construction continues to be employed in spite of the well-documented fact that it has been submitted to repeated empirical tests and has been found wanting. My thesis is that decades of research have not provided determinate findings that justify continuing the use of schizophrenia-nonschizophrenia as an independent variable. Having voiced this claim, I quickly add that my judgment of the failure of the schizophrenia hypothesis is in no way a disclaimer to the observation that some people, under some conditions, engage in conduct that others might identify as mad, insane, bizarre, foolish, irrational, psychotic, deluded, inept, unwanted, absurd, or plain crazy.

The focus of my paper is that schizophrenia is a construction put forth by nineteenth century physicians and elaborated within an epistemological context that supported the notion that unwanted conduct was caused by disease processes. Historical forces in the nineteenth century influenced doctors to regard perplexing conduct as the outcome of a subtle brain disease. The opacity of the term "schizophrenia" directed scientists and practitioners to employ a prototype when writing their own definitions or when labelling putative

From Theodore R. Sarbin, "Toward the Obsolescence of the Schizophrenia Hypothesis," *The Journal of Mind and Behavior,* vol. 11, nos. 3 and 4 (1990), pp. 259–261, 264–269, 273–280. Copyright © 1990 by The Institute of Mind and Behavior. Reprinted by permission. Notes and references omitted.

patients. The contemporary construction of schizophrenia is consistent with the prototype of a person with an infectious brain disease. The crude diagnostic efforts of the late nineteenth and early twentieth centuries failed to differentiate patients with organic brain disease from patients employing atypical conduct to solve their identity and existential problems. Because so many diagnosed schizophrenics did not fit the specifications of the prototype, some authorities, notably Eugen Bleuler, suggested the employment of the plural, "the schizophrenias." This stratagem has not been productive, but has preserved schizophrenia as a sacred emblem of psychiatry when experiments have yielded indeterminate results. "The schizophrenias" and its modern equivalent "schizophrenia spectrum disorders" have also been employed to increase the size of an experimental sample in order to achieve statistical significance. Such miscellaneous categories do little more than supply Greek or Latin labels to formalize the lay concept that "people can be crazy in different ways and for different causes or reasons."

Nearly 50 years ago, when I had my first encounters with hospitalized patients, I was confronted with the official lore that schizophrenia was a disease. I did not accept, however, the official lore without reservation. Day to day interactions with inmates of a mental hospital influenced me to be tentative about adopting the prevailing doctrine. In the course of working with men and women who had been diagnosed as schizophrenic by appropriately-qualified psychiatrists, I became aware of the multifarious actions that were interpreted as "presenting symptoms"—actions that family members or employers could not readily assimilate into their constructions of acceptable conduct.

My first patient was a middle-aged women who held the belief that agents of a foreign power were conspiring to kidnap her; the second was a man who believed that his neighbor was directing magnetic rays to the nails in his shoes so that walking was a great effort; a third was a 40 year-old man who argued with an absent opponent about metaphysical propositions; a fourth inmate behaved as if he had lost all power of speech; a fifth would not leave his room, even for meals, afraid that he would be the object of massive microbial invasions; a sixth, a seminary student, claimed to be a saint of the thirteenth century; a seventh, a retired baker, held friendly conversations in the privacy of his room with two long-dead religious figures....

In most cases, these actions were so specific to the individual's life story that it was difficult for me to accept the explanation that some brain anomaly could account for the heterogeneity. The notion of a common cause for such an assortment of human actions can be entertained only if, in Procrustean fashion, we reduce the interesting array of polymorphous actions to a small number of categories, for example, delusions, flattened affect, and hallucinations, and further, if we arbitrarily redefine the categories as "symptoms" of a still-to-be-discovered disease entity. Such a redefinition obliterates the specificity, the individuality, and the problem-solving features of each person's conduct. Further, the acceptance of the redefinition renders irrelevant the search for intentions and meanings behind perplexing interpersonal acts....

SEARCH STRATEGIES

... My preliminary excursions called for a more systematic analysis of the published literature. Professor James Mancuso joined me in a project to review every research article on schizophrenia published in the *Journal of Abnormal Psychology* for the 20-year period beginning in 1959 (Sarbin and Mancuso, 1980).... We found 374 reports of experiments designed to illuminate the concept of schizophrenia. By any standard, the published research on schizophrenia during the 20-year period represented a prodigious effort. It is abundantly clear that in the period under review, students of deviant conduct focused on the central problem: to identify a reliable diagnostic marker, psychological or somatic, that would replace subjective (and fallible) diagnosis. The discovery of such a marker would establish the long sought-for validity for the postulated entity, schizophrenia.

In nearly all the studies, schizophrenia/nonschizophrenia was the independent variable. To accomplish their mission, investigators compared the *average* responses of "schizophrenics" on experimental tasks with the *average* responses of persons who were not so diagnosed. It is no exaggeration to say that the experimental tasks devised by creative investigators numbered in the hundreds. All were constructed for the purpose of rigorously testing miniature hypotheses, the origins of which were linked to the postulate that schizophrenia was an identifiable mental disease or disorder. The choice of these variables was influenced by the lore of schizophrenia, beliefs that could be traced to Kraepelin's and Bleuler's claims that schizophrenics were cognitively or linguistically flawed;

perceptually inefficient; affectively dysfunctional; and psychophysiologically impaired. The experimental hypotheses were formulated from the expectation that whatever the task, the schizophrenics would perform poorly when compared with the performance of a control group. The range and variety of the experimental tasks suggests that the formulators of these experimental hypotheses shared the conviction that "schizophrenics" were persons who were basically flawed, that the putative disease affected all somatic and psychological systems.

Mancuso and I analyzed 374 studies on several dimensions. We drew a number of conclusions, among them, that the criteria for selecting subjects were less than satisfactory. The unreliability for psychiatric diagnosis notwithstanding, the experimenters were satisfied to accept diagnoses made by "two staff psychiatrists," "by a psychiatrist and a psychologist," "by consensus in diagnostic staff conference," etc. It is unknown to what extent the diagnosticians employed the *Diagaostic and Statistical Manual-II*, although it is likely that the lore contained in the *Manual* provided the diagnostic criteria. The dependent variables were assessed with great precision, sometimes to two decimal places. In contrast, the independent variable, schizophrenia/nonschizophrenia, was assessed either by the subjective and fallible judgments of clinicians, or by a vote taken in a diagnostic staff conference....

About 80 percent of the studies reported that schizophrenics performed poorly when compared to control subjects. Variability in performance was the rule. Although the published studies reported mean differences between groups as statistically significant, the differences were small. In those studies where it was possible to reconstruct distributions, it was immediately clear that the performances of the schizophrenic samples and the normal samples overlapped considerably. An examination of a number of such distributions points to an unmistakable conclusion: that most schizophrenics cannot be differentiated from most normals on a wide variety of experimental tasks. If one were to employ the dependent variable as a marker for schizophrenia in a new sample, the increase in diagnostic accuracy would be infinitesimal.

That so many studies showed small mean differences has been taken to mean that the schizophrenia hypothesis has earned a modicum of credibility. The degree of credibility dissolves when we consider a number of hidden variables that could account for the observed differences. A large number of reports noted that the schizophrenic subjects were on neuroleptic medication. It is appropriate to ask whether the small mean differences could be accounted for by the drugged status of the experimental subjects and the non-drugged status of the controls. Other hidden variables are socioeconomic status and education. At least since 1855, it has been noted that the diagnosis of insanity (later dementia praecox and schizophrenia) has been employed primarily as a diagnosis for poor people (Dohrenwend, 1990). Many of the experimental tasks called for cognitive skills. The mean difference in performance on such tasks could well be related to cognitive skills, a correlate of education and socioeconomic status. Some experimenters noted the difficulty in recruiting control subjects whose educational level matched the low levels of schizophrenic samples, in many instances, about tenth grade.

Not assessed in these studies were the effects of patienthood. At the time the hospitalized patients were recruited to be subjects, they had been the objects of legal, medical, nursing, and in some cases, police procedures, not to mention mental hospital routines and their effects on personal identity. As mentioned before, only cooperative, i.e., docile, patients were recruited. It would be instructive to investigate to what degree docility influences the subjects' approach to experimental tasks.

Any of the hidden variables could account for the small mean differences observed in experimental studies. One conclusion is paramount: the 30 years of psychological research covered in our analyses has produced no marker that would establish the validity of the schizophrenia disorder. The argument could be made that psychological variables are too crude to identify the disease process. Biochemical, neurological, and anatomical studies, some would argue (e.g., Meehl, 1989), are more likely to reveal the ultimate marker for schizophrenia. However, reported findings employing somatic dependent variables follow the same pattern as for psychological studies. Variation is the rule. For example, one variable of interest for those who would locate the seat of schizophrenia in the brain is the size of the hemispheric ventricles. Several studies employed computer tomography to measure the size of the ventricles. Homogenizing the results of measurement, they found that the schizophrenic group had larger ventricles than the controls. The degree of variation, however, was such as to preclude using the ventricular size as a diagnostic instrument (Nasrallah, Jacoby, McCalley-Whitters, and Kuperman, 1982; Weinberger, Torrey, Neophytides, and Wyatt, 1979). Another set of investigators, presumably employing a more refined method for measuring the scans, reported no differences between schizophrenics and controls (Jernigan, Zatz, Moses, and Berger, 1982a, 1982b). Another hypothesis, disarray of pyramidal cells in the hippocampus, was advanced by several researchers as a potential marker for schizophrenia. Christison, Casanova, Weinberger, Rawlings, and Kleinman (1989) conducted precise measurements on brains stored in the Yakovlev collection. They found no differences in hippocampal measurements when the brains of schizophrenics were compared to the brains of controls.

It is important to note the high degree of variability in biomedical and psychological measurements. To isolate the elusive marker, investigators must discover indicators that cluster near the mean for the experimental sample and at the same time do not overlap with the control sample or with other presumed diagnostic entities. None of the studies we reviewed met this requirement.

SCHIZOPHRENIA AS DISEASE: A SOCIAL CONSTRUCTION

The prevailing mechanistic framework directs practitioners to perceive crazy behavior as caused ultimately by anatomical or biochemical anomalies. An alternative framework is available, one not dependent on the notion that human beings are passive objects at the mercy of biochemical forces. The starting point in this framework is the observation that candidates for the diagnosis of schizophrenia are seldom people who seek out doctors for the relief of pain or discomfort. Rather, they are persons who undergo a prediagnostic phase in

which moral judgments are made on their nonconforming or perplexing actions by family members, employers, police officers, or neighbors. In the absence of reliable tests to demonstrate that the unwanted conduct is caused by anatomical or biochemical distortions, diagnosticians unwittingly join in the moral enterprise. They confirm the initial prediagnostic judgment that the deviant behavior belongs to a class of behaviors that are unwanted. After appropriate rituals, diagnosticians can confirm the moral verdict and encode it with a proper medical term, schizophrenia.

The foregoing remarks are preliminary to my argument that schizophrenia is a social construction initially put forth as a hypothesis by medical scientists and practitioners. A social construction is an organized set of beliefs that has the potential to guide action. The construction is communicated and elaborated by means of linguistic and rhetorical symbols. The categories are vicariously received, passed on from generation to generation through symbolic action. Like any construction, the schizophrenia hypothesis serves certain purposes and not others. A pivotal purpose for schizophrenia is diagnosis—professional practice requires diagnosis before treatment can be rationally prescribed. It is important to remind ourselves that any social construction can be abandoned when alternate constructions are put forth that receive symbolic and rhetorical support from scientific and political communities.

To find the origin of the schizophrenia construction, one must refer to historical sources. Because of space limitations, a full historical account is not possible. Instead I point to some pertinent observations. Ellard (1987), an Australian psychiatrist, has contributed a provocative argument under the title "Did Schizophrenia Exist Before the Eighteenth Century?" Ellard's historical analysis begins from a skeptical posture, namely, to "reflect on the question whether or not there has ever been an entity of any kind at all that stands behind the word, 'schizophrenia', and if so, what its true nature might be" (p. 306). Citing well-known authorities, Ellard points to significant changes in the description of schizophrenia over the past 50 or 60 years. He cites the common observation that contemporary clinicians seldom encounter patients who fit the prototype advanced by Kraepelin and Bleuler. If the nosological criteria for schizophrenia changed so radically in a half-century, is it not conceivable that the criteria changed significantly in the half-century before Kraepelin and Bleuler?—and in the half-century before that? Ellard makes clear that schizophrenia is a construction of medical scientists that is historically-bound.

As a point of departure, Ellard takes the construction and eventual abandonment of the nineteenth century diagnosis, masturbatory psychosis. Medical orthodoxy posited a psychosis characterized by restlessness, silliness, intellectual deterioration, and inappropriate affect. The entrenched belief in the association between biological activities and crazy behavior nurtured the idea of masturbatory insanity well into the twentieth century. Although at one time professionally acceptable, it was ultimately abandoned as an empty if not counterproductive hypothesis.

Employing the vaguely-defined "thought disorder" as the criterion of schizophrenia, Ellard searched the literature for evidence of cases noted by physicians and historians. His reading of case histories and medical records led to the conclusion that insanities involving "thought disorders" were identified in the eighteenth and nineteenth centuries, but such cases were exceedingly rare in the seventeenth century. It remains for future historians to identify the social, political, and professional conditions that brought about the creation of a diagnosis centered on ambiguously-defined "thought disorder." ...

Intrinsic and Extrinsic Support for the Disease Construction

Despite its failure when examined by empirical methods, the social construction of schizophrenia has persisted. Its persistence is a function of the support it has received. Two classes of support can be identified: support intrinsic to the biomedical model; and support extrinsic to the model in the form of social practices and unarticulated beliefs.

Biological research has served as intrinsic support for the schizophrenia construction. I need but mention the names of hypotheses that have been subjected to laboratory and clinical testing: taraxein, CPK (creatine phosphokinase), serotonin, and dopamine, among others. The composite impact of all this research activity is that an entity exists, waiting for refined methods and high technology to identify the causal morphological, neuro-transmission, or biochemical factor.... [C]ountless studies have not identified the disease entity. Nevertheless, the profession and the public have interpreted the sustained research activity by responsible scientists as evidence that the schizophrenia construction is a tenable one.

Guided by the mechanistic paradigm (that behavior is *caused* by antecedent physico-chemical conditions) and operating within the medical variant of that paradigm (that the causes of atypical conduct are to be found in disease entities), research scientists employed a number of broad categories as the defining criteria of schizophrenia. Such categories as cognitive slippage, anhedonia, social withdrawal, ambivalence, thought disorder, loosening of associations, delusions, inappropriate affect, and hallucinations, among others, have been employed for classifying the observed or reported conduct of persons brought to diagnosticians by concerned relatives or by forensic or social agencies. The diagnostic process involved locating the putative patient's conduct in one or more of these broad categories, and then inferring the diagnosis of schizophrenia. Thus, immediate and remote origins of the *meanings* of an individual's atypical conduct become irrelevant to the objective of the diagnosis. A scientist interested in the *person* would have little to go on from reading research reports. Readers of these reports are frustrated if they search for connections between a particular instance of unwanted conduct—the presumed basis for the diagnosis—and some dependent variable assessed after a diagnosis has been made. No causal link can be postulated to account, for example, for a schizophrenic patient's anomalous brain scan and his specific claims to having daily conversations with St. Augustine.

Typically, journal articles provide statements of statistically significant associations between such variables and *diagnoses,* not between such variables and *conduct.* Since heterogeneous acts are lumped together into homogenized diagnoses, experimental results cannot provide information that would allow inferences about the relation between the experimental variable and specific behav-

iors. The conventional publication style facilitates the illusory conclusion that a cause, or partial cause, of schizophrenia has been discovered. Because distributions of the dependent variable are not usually published, the reader cannot calculate the proportions of false positives and false negatives that would be generated if the dependent variable were to be used as a diagnostic instrument. Not reporting the proportion of cases contrary to the hypothesis, like the employment of diagnoses as the independent variable, facilitates the belief that some enduring property of schizophrenia has been isolated....

In addition to direct biological research, the genetic transmission hypothesis has been advanced to support the construction of schizophrenia. Highly visible scientists have reported a heritability factor for schizophrenia. Wide publicity, both within the profession and outside, has been given to studies of twins and to studies of children of schizophrenics who were reared by adoptive parents (see, for example, Gottesman and Shields, 1972; Kety, Rosenthal, Wender, and Shulsinger, 1968; Kety, Rosenthal, Wender, Shulsinger, and Jacobsen, 1975). Current textbooks cite these investigations as revealed truth, but the extensive critiques of the studies are seldom noted. That the reported studies are riddled with methodological, statistical and interpretational errors has been repeatedly demonstrated (see especially, Abrams and Taylor, 1983; Benjamin, 1976; Kringlen and Cramer, 1989; Lewontin, Kamin, and Rose, 1984; Lidz, 1990; Lidz and Blatt, 1983; Lidz, Blatt, and Cook, 1981; Marshall, 1986; Sarbin and Mancuso, 1980). The extent of these criticisms suggests that establishing the validity of "schizophrenia" should have had logical priority over the identification of its genetic features.

My aim is not to rehash the arguments pro and con of the heredity thesis, rather to show that the wide publicity given genetic studies has served as additional support to maintain the schizophrenia construction. My thesis holds for genetic research as it does for psychological and biological research: that no firm ontological basis has been established for schizophrenia. In the absence of determinate criteria, investigators direct their efforts toward discovering intergenerational similarities—not of identifiable behavior but of *diagnosis*, a far cry from the subject matter of behavior genetics in which intergenerational similarities of *behavior* are studied.

In addition to intrinsic supports, it is possible to identify a number of extrinsic supports that help explain the tenacity of the schizophrenia construction. Although constructions that are congruent with the concurrent scientific paradigm may appear self-supporting, they are in great measure sustained by forces external to the scientific enterprise.

A vast bureaucratic network at federal, state, and local levels legitimizes biochemical conceptions of deviant conduct, including schizophrenia. Federal agencies that control research grants advocate studies the aim of which is the understanding and ultimately the control of "the dread disease" schizophrenia....

In addition to bureaucratic advocacy, in recent decades the pharmaceutical industry has been instrumental in furthering the schizophrenia doctrine. Pharmaceutical companies support countless research enterprises in which medications are clinically tested on patients, many of whom are diagnosed as schizophrenic. The psychiatric journals are to a great extent subsidized by pharmaceutical advertising, such advertising being directed to physicians who are legally empowered to prescribe medications.

The implicit power of bureaucracy and the commercial goals of pharmaceutical companies would be minimal if the schizophrenia messages fell on deaf ears. A readiness to believe the schizophrenia story follows from the unwitting acceptance of an ideology—a network of historically-conditioned premises....

One strand in the texture of the schizophrenia ideology is the creation of the mental hospital institution. The transformation of the asylum to a mental hospital, in the context of preserving order, paved the way for regarding inmates as objects. The hospital and its medical climate were legitimated through legislative acts and judicial rulings. The courts, usually acting on the advice of physicians, granted almost unlimited power to physicians to employ their skills and their paradigms in the interest of protecting society. Because of culturally-enscripted roles for physicians and patients, once the physician made the diagnosis, the patient became a figure in an altered social narrative. The power of physicians relative to patients created a condition in which physicians could distance themselves from patients—a necessary precondition for the draconian surgical and medical treatments mentioned previously....

A parallel premise is that "certain types of people are more dangerous than other types of people" (Sarbin and Mancuso, 1980). The origins of the connection between being schizophrenic and being dangerous are obscure. Several strands in the fabric of this premise can be identified, among them, the Calvinistic equation of being poor and being damned, and the attribution "dangerous classes" to the powerless poor. "Dangerous to self or other" remains as a criterion for commitment in most jurisdictions.

The overrepresentation of poor people in the class "schizophrenics" has been repeatedly documented. In addition, Pavkov, Lewis, and Lyons (1989) have shown that being black and coming to the attention of mental health professionals is predictive of a diagnosis of schizophrenia.... Landrine (1989) has concluded on the basis of research evidence that the social role of poor people is a stereotype in the epistemic structure of middle-class diagnosticians. The linguistic performances and social interactions of poor people are of the same quality as the performances of men and women diagnosed as schizophrenics, particular of the "negative type" (Andreasen, 1982), those social failures who have adopted a strategy of minimal action.

With the renewed emphasis on the Kraepelinian construction, interest in studying the relations between socioeconomic status (SES) and psychiatric diagnoses has declined. This decline in interest is not due to any change in the demographics. Schizophrenia is primarily a diagnosis for poor people. The advent of neo-Kraepelinian models, especially the diathesis-stress construction, turned attention to genetics research and to the study of stress. But SES has not figured prominently in stress research. Dohrenwend (1990), a leading epidemiologist, has noted that "... relations between SES or social class and psychiatric disorders have provided the most challenging cues to the role of adversity in the development of psychiatric disorders. The problem remains what it has always been: how to unlock the riddle that low SES

can be either a cause or a consequence of psychopathology" (p. 45). The adversity thesis might be illuminated through an examination of the observation that the outcome of "schizophrenia" varies with economic and social conditions (Warner, 1985). Landrine's research, cited above, adds to the puzzle another dimension: lower class stereotypes held by middle class diagnosticians....

CONCLUSION

To recapitulate: my thesis is that schizophrenia is a social construction, generated to deal with people whose conduct was not acceptable to more powerful others. During the heyday of nineteenth century science, the construction was guided by metaphors drawn from mechanistic biology. Physicians formulated their theories and practices from constructions that grew out of developing knowledge in anatomy, chemistry and physiology. The construction has an ideological cast —its proponents were blind to the possibilities that the absurdities exhibited by mental hospital patients were efforts at sense-making. Instead proponents followed the tenets of mechanistic science: that social misconduct, like rashes, fevers, aches, pains, and other somatic conditions, was caused by disease processes. Reliable and sustained empirical evidence—a cardinal requirement of mechanistic science—has not been put forth to validate the schizophrenia hypothesis. Despite the absence of empirical support, the schizophrenia construction continues its tenacious hold on theory and practice.

My recommendation is that we banish schizophrenia to the musty historical archives where other previously-valued scientific constructions are stored, among them, phlogiston, the luminiferous ether, the geocentric view of the universe, and closer to home, monomania, neurasthenia, masturbatory insanity, lycanthropy, demon possession, and mopishness.

I emphasize that I am not recommending formulating a new descriptive term to replace schizophrenia. It is too late for that. The referents for schizophrenia are too diverse, confounded, changing, and ambiguous (Bentall, Jackson, and Pilgrim, 1988; Carpenter and Kirkpatrick, 1988). The fact that two persons (or 200) who exhibit no absurdities in common may be tagged with the same label demonstrates the emptiness of the concept.

Abandoning the schizophrenia hypothesis, however, will not solve the societal and interpersonal problems generated when persons engage in absurd, nonconforming, perplexing conduct. The first step in solving such problems calls for critical examination of the societal and political systems that support the failing biomedical paradigm. Such examination would be instrumental in replacing the mechanistic world view with a framework that would regard persons as agents trying to solve existential and identity problems....

Understanding the interpersonal or existential themes in the stories of troubled persons is hampered when we rely on the customary vocabulary of pathology: toxins, tumors, traumata, dysfunctional traits, or defective genes. Understanding is more likely to be facilitated if we follow the lead of poets, dramatists, and biographers, and focus on the language of social relationships.

CHALLENGE QUESTIONS

Is Schizophrenia a Disease?

1. What would a social constructionist's view of schizophrenia imply for psychological diagnosis? for psychotherapy?

2. What would a medical model (disease) view of schizophrenia imply for psychological diagnosis? for psychotherapy?

3. If, according to the social constructionist, the diagnosis of schizophrenia is to some degree an ethical or moral judgment, and if our ethics depend upon our particular culture, does this mean that *any* cultural ethic is acceptable? What implications does this *relativity* of ethic have for diagnosis and psychotherapy?

4. Why does Sarbin say that physiological differences between normals and schizophrenics do not necessarily support a disease conception?

5. What would a social constructionist say about Johnstone's reliance on the scientific method? Could the scientific method itself be a social construction of some type? Why, or why not?

ISSUE 6

Is the Gulf War Syndrome Real?

YES: Dennis Bernstein and Thea Kelley, from "The Gulf War Comes Home: Sickness Spreads, But the Pentagon Denies All," *The Progressive* (March 1995)

NO: Michael Fumento, from "What Gulf War Syndrome?" *The American Spectator* (May 1995)

ISSUE SUMMARY

YES: Journalists Dennis Bernstein and Thea Kelley claim that there are some four dozen disabling, sometimes life-threatening medical problems related to environmental and chemical exposure affecting thousands of soldiers who fought in the Persian Gulf War.

NO: Michael Fumento, a science and economics reporter, argues that medical experts have not found any evidence to support the existence of a syndrome related to the war and that the illnesses and symptoms suffered by Gulf War veterans are more likely caused by stress and other natural causes.

Since Operation Desert Storm—the 1991 international effort to drive invading Iraqi forces out of Kuwait—more than 45,000 veterans out of the approximately 650,000 troops who served in the Persian Gulf War have complained of symptoms that have collectively become known as the Gulf War Syndrome. These symptoms include rashes, fatigue, headaches, vision problems, infections, joint and bone pain, birth defects in babies conceived after the war, and cancer.

The syndrome has been compared to the afflictions suffered by veterans of the Vietnam War. During that conflict, the defoliant Agent Orange was released over the jungles. Agent Orange contained dioxin as a contaminant, a substance that is toxic to humans and animals. Numerous studies have linked dioxin exposure to skin rashes, nervous system disorders, muscle aches, digestive problems, and certain cancers. Despite these studies, it took the Department of Veterans Affairs 10 years of debate before it finally connected Agent Orange to the similar health concerns suffered by Vietnam War veterans.

Unlike the health problems of the Vietnam veterans, the causes of the Gulf War veterans' varied symptoms are less clear. A number of entities are currently searching for an explanation. The American Legion claims that toxins from a long list of possible environmental origins—including fumes from burning oil wells and landfills, contact with hydrocarbons, pesticides sprayed over military vehicles, poor sanitary conditions, local parasites, inoculations, and insect bites—may be to blame. The U.S. government is exploring other causes, such as the drug *pyridostigmine bromide*, an experimental pharmaceutical issued to soldiers to protect them against a possible nerve gas attack. The drug (as yet not approved for general use) was administered under a special waiver from the Food and Drug Administration. It was to be distributed with the informed consent of soldiers after the Department of Defense conducted its own research. Troops ordered to take the drug were reportedly never warned about its possible side effects, such as memory loss and respiratory problems. In addition, research on the drug was conducted only on men, so the drug's effects on women were unknown.

Another explanation being proposed is that veterans' health problems are the result of exposure to depleted uranium. Uranium was used to coat some artillery shells and tanks to protect them from enemy fire. However, on impact, depleted uranium releases radioactive particles of a related compound. The government claims that a relatively small number of personnel were exposed to this material and that none of them have shown any adverse symptoms. Nevertheless, the dangers of depleted uranium exposure have become a major issue among U.S. veteran groups as well as among war veterans in Britain.

Despite widespread reports of health problems among Gulf War veterans, the Department of Veterans Affairs and the Pentagon insist that the symptoms are either psychological or due to chance. Major-General Ronald Blanck, commander of the Walter Reed Army Medical Center in Washington, D.C., in addressing Congress said, "Extensive evaluation and thorough epidemiological investigations have failed to show any commonality of exposure or unifying diagnosis to explain these symptoms." Many politicians, however, are fighting back and have vowed not to allow the Gulf War Syndrome to become another Vietnam-style denial by the government.

In the following selections, Dennis Bernstein and Thea Kelley argue that although the Pentagon denies it, exposure to environmental and toxic substances in the Persian Gulf is responsible for illnesses experienced by thousands of veterans and their families. Michael Fumento argues that the many illnesses suffered by Gulf War veterans have been attributed to the so-called syndrome without sufficient evidence. He blames veterans' health complaints on post-traumatic stress disorders rather than on exposure to environmental contaminants, and he faults the media for contributing to the hysteria.

YES

Dennis Bernstein and Thea Kelley

THE GULF WAR COMES HOME: SICKNESS SPREADS, BUT THE PENTAGON DENIES ALL

The Persian Gulf War is not over. It drags on in the lives of tens of thousands of Gulf War veterans. Gulf War Syndrome, or Desert Fever as it is often called in Britain, is a set of some four dozen disabling, sometimes life-threatening medical conditions that afflict thousands of soldiers who fought in the war, as well as their offspring, their spouses, and medical professionals who treated them.

The symptoms suggest exposure to medical, chemical, or biological warfare agents, but the Pentagon denies such exposure occurred and claims it can't identify any common link among those who suffer from Gulf War Syndrome. Don Riegle, the recently retired Senator from Michigan who held hearings on the subject beginning in the fall of 1992, doesn't buy it. He believes the Pentagon may be engaged in a massive cover-up of this serious health problem.

The scale of the problem is enormous. More than 29,000 veterans in the United States with symptoms of Gulf War Syndrome have signed onto the Veterans Administration's Persian Gulf War Registry, 9,000 more have registered separately with the Pentagon, and the Pentagon's list is growing by 1,000 veterans a month.

"These are horrendous statistics that show the true scale of this problem," said Riegle last October when he released his final report on Gulf War Syndrome. Riegle condemned "the heartlessness and irresponsibility of a military bureaucracy that gives every sign of wanting to protect itself more than the health and well-being of our servicemen and women who actually go and fight our wars. To my mind, there is no more serious crime than an official military cover-up of facts that could prevent more effective diagnosis and treatment of sick U.S. veterans."

Birth defects are one of the most alarming problems associated with Gulf War Syndrome. One National Guard unit from Waynesboro, Mississippi, reported that of fifteen children con- ceived by veterans after the war, thirteen had birth defects. An informal survey of 600 afflicted veterans conducted by Senator Don Riegle's Banking, Housing, and Urban Affairs Committee last fall found that 65 percent of their babies were afflicted with dozens of medical problems, including severe birth defects.

Another disturbing phenomenon is the apparent transmission of the syndrome from soldiers to their family members. Riegle's study found that 77 percent of the wives of these veterans were also ill, as well as 25 percent of the children conceived before the war.

Riegle believes the Pentagon knows that U.S. veterans were exposed to chemical or biological weapons in the Gulf War. "The evidence available continues to mount that exposure to biological and chemical weapons is one cause of these illnesses," Riegle said. "I have evidence that despite repeated automatic denials by the Department of Defense, chemical weapons [were] found in the war." Riegle added that "laboratory findings from gas masks" showed the presence of biological warfare materials "that cause illnesses similar to Gulf War Syndrome."

The cover-up is not limited to the U.S. Government, however. Britain's Ministry of Defense is also being less than forthcoming. It has "a policy of denying Desert Fever for fear of big compensation claims," the British newspaper *Today* reported on October 10. A British Defense spokesperson told the paper, "We have no evidence that this illness exists." More than 1,000 out of the 43,000 British troops who served in the Persian Gulf have cited symptoms of Gulf War Syndrome.

＊　＊　＊

At 3 A.M. on January 19, 1991, Petty Officer Sterling Symms of the Naval Reserve Construction Battalion in Saudi Arabia awakened to a "real bad explosion" overhead. Alarms went off and everybody started running toward their bunkers, Symms said. A strong smell of ammonia pervaded the air. Symms said his eyes burned and his skin was stinging before he could don protective gear. Since that time, he has experienced fatigue, sore joints, running nose, a chronic severe rash, open sores, and strep infections. Symms and other soldiers described several such chemical attacks to Riegle's committee in May 1994.

One of the men interviewed by the committee who requested anonymity wrote home to his mother about the attack: "I can deal with getting shot at, because even if I got hit, I can be put back together—a missile, I can even accept that. But gas scares the hell out of me. . . . I know they detected a cloud of dusty mustard gas because I was there with them, but today everyone denies it. I was there when they radioed the other camps north of us and warned them of the cloud."

Front-line officers assured their troops that it was not a chemical attack, that what they heard was a sonic boom. "Members of Symms's unit were given orders not to discuss the incident," says Senator Riegle's report dated May 25, 1994.

Former U.S. Army Sergeant Randall L. Vallee served in the Persian Gulf as an advance scout. Vallee told Congress back in 1992 that he was convinced Iraqi Scud missiles were armed with chemical or biological warfare agents. "I was in numerous Scud missile attacks when I was in Dhahran," says Vallee. "It seemed like every time I was back there we'd come under fire."

Vallee has been afflicted by at least a half dozen serious medical conditions that started shortly after the Scud attacks. He had been in "perfect health" before his Gulf War service. Vallee supported what scores of veterans have already told Congress: that after every Scud attack, hundreds of alarms signaling chemical and biological attacks would sound, to the point where they were routinely shut off and reset as a matter of course.

Vallee and other members of his detail questioned their superiors about the alarms and about the presence of chemical-warfare agents in the Gulf. "After the whole ordeal was over, we asked about it and they said, 'No, the alarms are just acting that way because they're sensitive.' They gave us stories like, 'Oh, it's because of supersonic aircraft' or 'sand in the alarms.' There was always a story as to why the alarms sounded."

Last August, Vallee received a phone call from the Pentagon's Lieutenant Colonel Vicki Merriman, an aide to the Deputy Assistant Secretary of Defense for Chemical and Biological Matters.

"She asked me about my health and my family," says Vallee. But after some small talk, "the colonel's attitude turned from one of being concerned about my well-being to an interrogator trying to talk me out of my own experiences. She started using tactics of doubt regarding my statements. She said in regard to chemical and biological agents that there was absolutely no way that any soldiers in the Gulf were exposed to anything. Her exact words were, 'The only ones whining about problems are American troops, why aren't any of our allies?' And that was her exact word, 'whining.'"

* * *

British Gulf war vet Richard Turnball was surprised to hear Lieutenant Colonel Merriman's suggestion that only U.S. vets complained of Gulf War Syndrome. Turnball, who lives just outside Liverpool, served eighteen years in the British Royal Air Force. During the war against Iraq, Turnball built nuclear, biological, and chemical shelters, and instructed British troops in use of chemical monitoring and protective clothing. Turnball was based in Dhahran, Saudi Arabia.

Turnball is convinced there was widespread use of chemical-warfare agents. "People got sick in the chest and eyes, they got infections and skin rashes," he says. "One lad had his whole body covered with spots from head to toe" soon after a Scud attack that Turnball is convinced was chemical in nature.

"Within seconds of the warhead landing on January 20, every chemical-agent monitoring device in the area was blasting the alarm. We were put into the highest alert for twenty minutes," says Turnball, "and then we were told it was a false alarm caused by the fuel from aircraft taking off."

Corporal Turnball carried out two residual-vapor-detection tests for chemical and biological agents on January 20, shortly after the Scud hit "and both were positive," he says. Field supervisors dismissed the test results, claiming that jet fuel set off the indicators. Turnball was skeptical. "We tried on umpteen occasions, when aircraft were taking off in mass numbers," he says. "We stood on the side of the runway closer to the area where the aircraft were taking off, we carried out tests, and we got no readings."

At one point, Turnball says, he was warned to drop the case, and that if he kept it up he might be subject to secrecy laws under which he could be imprisoned. "I've had a very, very senior officer friend of mine ring me up and say, 'Richie, back off, you're kicking over a can of worms.' "

Before he went to war, Turnball said, he was in top condition, worked out every day, and was an avid scuba diver. Since his return, he has had twenty-four separate chest infections, and he has been forced to give up scuba diving because he "can't take the pressure below a few feet." Turnball can no longer run or swim or even take long walks. He said he has been put on steroids and uses two inhalers to help ease serious respiratory complications.

Turnball says the allies "used us as guinea pigs for new drugs" and chemical-weapons testing. He believes "probably both" chemical warfare agents and experimental drugs are responsible for his illness. "I feel we were subject to a chemical attack that affected us," he says. "As a serviceman, I can accept that, it's my job. But I believe more damage was done due to experimentation by our government. Many people got sick after taking some of the drugs. I came down with a high fever, I was sweating excessively. I actually stopped breathing a couple of times."

After three years of illness and fighting with the defense ministry, Turnball is still amazed by the denials that come out of the various bureaucracies. "We were always told that there was a 99.999 percent possibility of a chemical attack. We were expecting it. That was in our intelligence briefings. 'Inevitable' was the word used. And now they deny it."

* * *

Dr. Vivian Lane has never been to the Persian Gulf and is not a wife or mother of a Gulf War vet. The forty-three-year-old former squadron leader and former chief medical officer at the Royal Air Force base in Stafford, England, said she became seriously ill after treating a half dozen "very sick" British soldiers upon their return from the Persian Gulf. Dr. Lane says she was forced to move in with her elderly parents after she could no longer care for herself. Her parents, now in their eighties, are sick and suffering from lesions "very similar" to the ones she is suffering from, she says. "Nobody in this country can tell us why or what they are."

From December 1990 through June 1991 Dr. Lane treated at least six veterans who had the syndrome. Since that time, the aviation medical specialist, a former athlete, has been in great pain. She remembers waking up at four o'clock in the morning "with a terrific, excruciating, crushing type of chest pain and abdominal pain. When I got to the toilet, I didn't know whether to sit on it or stand over it. It just got worse from there. I managed somehow to get myself down to the medical center on base. All I remember was the excruciating chest pains. Next thing I know, I'm in intensive care. My parents had been brought to my bedside because everyone thought I was going to die. They didn't know what was wrong with me."

Dr. Lane offers a different angle on the hundreds of inoculations the soldiers were given before they left for the Persian Gulf. The protective shots were issued by the fistful, says Lane, and it's a wonder more people didn't have serious reactions. "With the amount we were banging into them, I'm surprised we didn't have more people falling over. We were attacking both arms, both buttocks, and their legs to get it all into them all at once. I think anybody with that amount of injections being shoved into them all within a couple of minutes of each other, would not feel terribly well."

Dr. Lane is one of several hundred former British soldiers suing the Ministry of Defense for medical redress. She says she is not holding her breath for results, though. "Frankly, I don't mean to be nasty, but I think they've bitten off more than they can chew."

Corporal Terry Walker was in the Persian Gulf from January to April 1991. Walker was a driver for the British Army's Fourth Armoured Brigade, First Armoured Division in Saudi Arabia. He has been sick ever since. He says his whole family suffers from Gulf War Syndrome.

In a recent interview, Walker described what he, too, believes was the Iraqi chemical Scud attack on January 20. "I was at the docks at Al-Jubayl about 2:30 in the morning," he said. "There was a couple of mighty bangs above our heads and suddenly all the chemical alarms went off and there were soldiers just running around in sheer panic, running around trying to get on their chemical suits." He says an "ammonia-like smell" filled the air after the sirens went off.

Walker, who had trouble getting his gas mask on, became ill soon after the Scuds hit. "I was feeling the burning sensation under the chin, around the back of the head as well. And ever since I've come back from the Gulf I've been ill." Walker suffers from chest infections, rashes, and headaches. Many of the people he served with were also sick after the attack, he says.

"As soon as the bangs happened, all these alarms went off and it was obvious that there was a chemical attack," says Walker, "but our superiors told us it was the jet fighters flying over with the sonic booms, and that it was also the fumes from the jets that set the alarms off."

"The thing is," says Walker, "they never went off before. The planes were flying day in and day out, and the alarms never went off at all, and on January 20, for about a ten-mile, fifteen-mile radius, these alarms went off."

Walker, who has since left the military, is furious with the military establishment in his country for "covering up what happened and the real risks" that would be faced by allied forces. "When they sent us out to fight the war, we expected them to look after us. Instead, when we came back they just tried to cover it up. They said there was nothing wrong at all because the general public would go against them if they found out about the exposures to chemical and biological warfare and how it gets into your whole family."

It is his family's illnesses that he objects to the most. "We knew there was a risk of being killed," he says, "but we didn't know that we would come back from the war so ill, and that our families would be getting sick, too. The wife has been ill since I've come back."

Walker's wife has had chronic abdominal pain and has been hospitalized at least seven times in the last three years. "She's been cut open twice but they couldn't find what was wrong," says Walker. The Walkers are extremely troubled about the health of their six-week-old child who has been plagued with a cold and respiratory problems "from day one."

* * *

Canadian legislator John O'Reilly recently raised the issue of Gulf War Syndrome in the House of Commons. O'Reilly asked the Defense Minister's Parliamentary Secretary, Fred Mifflin, what the government was doing to assist "deserving Canadians" who have been ill after serving in the Persian Gulf. Mifflin responded that the veterans had been cared for by Defense Department doctors and were experiencing "no difficulty whatsoever."

If Mifflin had spoken to Canadian Navy Lieutenant Louise Richard, he might have thought twice before painting such a rosy picture. Lieutenant Richard is an active-duty medical officer stationed at the National Defense Medical Center in Ottawa, the largest military hospital in Canada. Lieutenant Richard volunteered for service in the Persian Gulf as an operating-room nurse. She treated Americans, Britons, and Iraqi prisoners of war.

After eight years of commended service, Richard will be discharged from the Canadian Navy in September because of severe illness. She suffers from many of the same medical conditions afflicting some two dozen veterans interviewed for this article: severe respiratory problems, short-term memory loss, bronchitis, asthma, and pneumonia.

When Richard began to make a ruckus over her war-related illness and threatened to take it to the media, she ran into a stone wall of official denials and intimidation. "They've basically threatened me and said, 'It's all in your head, it's bullshit, don't go forward with it in the media.'" Richard says the threat from her medical superiors, whom she refuses to name for fear of further retribution, ran the gamut of intimidations. "It was the whole thing," says Richard, "your career, your pension—you know, the package."

She's frustrated at the lack of attention to the problem in Canada. "There doesn't seem to be anything happening since we're back," she says. "There's no research, no follow-up, there's nothing going on to help us." She said that she knows of many people in her position who have chosen to remain silent. "People fear to disclose anything because they don't want to ruin their pension or their career or whatever," she says. "I'm angry, because we were valued individuals when we were sent there, and now we're back, and we're not valued individuals at all. We're basically treated like mushrooms in a dark room."

* * *

Dr. Saleh Al-Harbi is an immunologist in Kuwait's Ministry of Public Health, and director of the immunogenetics unit of Kuwait University Medical Center. He says many people in Kuwait and Iran are suffering from what appear to be illnesses involving exposure to chemical and biological warfare agents.

"After the war we were getting diseases, respiratory diseases and unknown blood diseases such as leukemia, but not the typical kind, and for unknown reasons," he says. He is currently investigating with U.S. researchers the underlying causes of the medical conditions that have been plaguing Kuwaitis since the war. "Birth-related problems increased dramatically after liberation," he says, "and those kinds of cases have been reported to me."

He, too, is under pressure to keep a lid on his findings and concerns. "The authorities here are also standing with the Europeans' and Americans' point of view, but we believe that this is something political. I'm independent in mentioning this, and hopefully I will not get any threats from the superiors regarding this matter. They don't want the bad news and rumors to go around."

Dr. Al-Harbi characterizes the syndrome as a form of multiple chemical sensitivity, an explanation that is gaining favor in the United States as well.

Senator Riegle's report says that British and U.S. Army specialists, using sophisticated detection devices, made at least twenty tests that were positive for the presence of chemical-warfare agents. According to his report, "The Kuwaiti, U.S., and British governments all received reports on the discovery and recovery of bulk chemical agents."

Riegle's report also confirms than the alarms used in the war to warn troops of the presence of chemical warfare agents sounded thousands of times. In some cases, the report says, the alarms were sounding so frequently that they were simply turned off.

"The Defense Department told us at a hearing that they were all false alarms," says a former Riegle aide. "There were 14,000 of those chemical-alarm-monitoring units used during the war, and they're telling us that every time they went off, on all 14,000, they were false alarms. That's a little hard to believe."

According to a letter from Riegle to Veterans Affairs Secretary Jesse Brown, eighteen chemical, twelve biological, and four nuclear facilities in Iraq were bombed by the U.S.-led allied forces. Debris from the bombings was dispersed upwards into upper atmospheric currents, as shown by a U.S. satellite videotape obtained by Congress.

The Veterans Administration has only recently admitted that there is a problem with some "mystery illness" afflicting vets and their families. But the Pentagon denies there is any connection to chemical or biological warfare exposures.

In a May 25, 1994, "Memorandum for Persian Gulf Veterans," Defense Secretary William Perry and Joint Chiefs Chairman John Shalikashvili wrote:

"There have been reports in the press of the possibility that some of you were exposed to chemical or biological weapons agents. There is no information, classified or unclassified, that indicated that chemical or biological weapons were used in the Persian Gulf."

On June 23, 1994, the Defense Department's science board reported the results of an investigation into chemical and biological exposures in the Persian Gulf War. According to the report, "there is no evidence that either chemical or biological warfare was deployed at any level, or that there was any exposure of U.S. service members to chemical or biological warfare agents."

* * *

On December 13, 1994, the Pentagon released a report that says there was no single cause for Gulf War Syndrome. Veterans' groups were highly critical of this report. "It is more lies by the Pentagon to confuse and cover up the real causes of Gulf War Syndrome," says Major Richard Haines, president of Gulf Veterans International. In January, the Institute of Medicine of the National Academy of Sciences released a report critical of the Pentagon's research on Gulf War Syndrome.

Pentagon spokesman Dennis Boxx still maintains "we do not have any indication at this point that these things are transmittable to children or spouses."

Such declarations are consistent with the official British Ministry of Defense line. According to a July 14, 1994, letter from the Chemical and Biological Defense Establishment to the Pentagon's Lieutenant Colonel Vicki Merriman, "there was no evidence of any chemical warfare agent being present" in the Persian Gulf.

Ironically, when Senator Riegle first approached officials at the Department of Defense about veterans' possible exposures to chemical and biological warfare agents in the Persian Gulf, he was told by Walter Reed Army Medical Center commander Major General Ronald Blank that the issue was not even explored because "military intelligence maintained that such exposures never occurred."

While the Pentagon has refused to admit that chemical and biological warfare agents were present during the Gulf War, Senator Riegle stated on October 8, 1994, that "these Department of Defense explanations are inconsistent with the facts as related by the soldiers who were present, and with official government documents prepared by those who were present, and with experts who have examined the facts."

According to official Pentagon documents, at least eight members of the U.S. military who served in the Persian Gulf, in fact, received letters of commendation for locating and identifying chemical-warfare agents during the war. Army Captain Michael Johnson was awarded the Meritorious Service medal for overseeing the "positive identification of a suspected chemical agent." The certificate that accompanied Private First Class Allen Fisher's bronze star medal stated that his discoveries were the "first confirmed detection of chemical-agent contamination in the theater of operation."

In a memorandum dated January 4, 1994, to "Director, CATD," Captain Johnson of the Nuclear Biological and Chemical Branch of the Army wrote to his superiors: "Recent headlines have aroused considerable interest in the possible exposure of coalition forces to Iraqi chemical agents. Much of this interest is the result of health problems by Gulf War veterans that indicated exposure to chemical agents. Although no government officials have confirmed use, there is a high likelihood that some coalition forces experienced exposure to chemical agents."

Captain Johnson stated that he believed "coalition soldiers did experience exposure to Iraqi chemical agents." Johnson, who was commander of the 54th Chemical Troop, had cited in his report an example of a British soldier who was exposed. According to Johnson, "the soldier had an immediate reaction to the liquid contact. The soldier was in extreme pain and was going into shock." Captain Johnson first notified his superiors of his concerns in August 1991.

"This official dissembling and effort to obscure the facts are a continuation of Defense Department tactics," said Riegle in a written statement accompanying his October report. "The serious question remains as to why we were not provided with an official report dating from the time of the incident by the Department of Defense."

"If you look at the symptoms associated with biological and chemical contamination," says a former aide to Senator Riegle, "you'll see the same symptoms that are present in these veterans to varying degrees. The common denominator in all their illnesses is the breaking down of their immune system just as AIDS [acquired immunodeficiency syndrome] does, making them sicker and sicker as the days and years go by, and eventually incapacitating and killing some of them. And it's somehow being passed along to other people. We were getting hundreds of calls from people saying, 'He brought home this duffel bag, and we opened it up, and my eyes and hands started burning, and now I'm sick. What's wrong? What's happened?' "

NO

Michael Fumento

WHAT GULF WAR SYNDROME?

It has become a ritual by now. Each morning they inspect their skin, study their gums, feel their neck and armpits for swollen lymph nodes. When they cough, when their joints ache a bit, when they itch or whenever anything doesn't seem quite right with their bodies, they panic—and for good reason. Having stood down the fifth-largest military in the world, the men and women who served our country in the Persian Gulf are being told their fate will be forever linked to that line they guarded in the sand. For they are at risk of suffering one of the most insidious afflictions of the late twentieth century —Gulf War Syndrome.

Or so they've been told by over 500 newspaper and magazine stories, and a slew of television shows ranging from "20/20" to "Nightline" to "60 Minutes." No fewer than three respected men's magazines have featured the story, with such titles as GQ's "Cover-Up: U.S. Victims of the Gulf War." What vets haven't been told is the source of their fear may lie a bit closer to home than the windswept deserts of the Middle East.

That which is called Gulf War Syndrome comprises ailments diagnosed in some of the almost 700,000 men and women assigned to the Gulf region in 1990 and 1991. More than 50,000 vets have now signed on to the Persian Gulf Registry. While some of these vets say they are perfectly healthy and simply want to be monitored, the majority have joined the registry because they believe they may be suffering from the alleged syndrome.

BURNING SEMEN

According to Rep. Lane Evans (D-Ill.), "The commonality of experiences that [Gulf War veterans] have faced seem to be fairly convincing that they are suffering serious problems...." Likewise, CNN titled one of its interview segments "Gulf War Veterans Complain of Common Symptoms."

Yet their symptoms are anything but similar. They include, among others: aching muscles, aching joints, abdominal pain, facial pain, chest pain, blood clots, flushing, night sweats, blurry vision, photosensitivity, jaundice, bruising, shaking, vomiting, fevers, sinus growths, irritability, fatigue, swollen lymph nodes, weight loss, weight gain, loss of appetite, heartburn, nausea, bad breath, hair loss, graying hair, rashes, sore throat, heart disease, diverticulitis and other intestinal disorders, kidney stones, a growth in the eye, tingling and itching sensations, sore gums, cough, cancer, diarrhea with and without bleeding, constipation, testicular pain, epididymitis, unspecified swelling, memory loss, dizziness, inability to concentrate, choking sensation, depression, lightheadedness, hot and cold flashes, labored breathing, sneezing, sensitive teeth and other dental problems, neurological disorders, nasal congestion, bronchitis, leg cramps, twitching, hemorrhoids, thyroid problems, welts, rectal and vaginal bleeding, colon polyps, increased urination, a "bulging disk" in the neck, hypertension, blood in urine, insomnia, headaches, and "a foot fungus that will not go away."

The symptom list reads like the index of a medical self-help book. Veterans have even blamed the syndrome for their having contracted malaria, herpes, and tuberculosis, diseases heretofore thought to have been spread by mosquitoes, sexual intercourse, and coughing. Many symptoms are highly subjective, such as "lumps under the skin" or "thick saliva." Readers or viewers of news reports don't know this, however, because whenever they see or hear a list of symptoms it's rarely more than about five items long, implying the syndrome spectrum is fairly small.

Yet the definition of the syndrome has been widened even beyond Gulf vets to include their wives and children. In addition to suffering most of the illnesses of their husbands, these women also claim to suffer yeast infections, menstrual cramps, and irregular periods, while the children's attributed ills include earaches and rashes, among others. Some wives and girlfriends of vets have even complained that their men's semen burned their skin, rather like the blood of the creatures in the *Alien* films.

* * *

If the definition of this syndrome is murky, the cause is hardly more clear. Theories as to the specific cause or causes of the illnesses have ranged from the use of depleted uranium in American shells to fumes from burning oil fires. A 1994 Centers for Disease Control (CDC) study found that while firefighters did have increased exposure to certain toxics from the burning wells, personnel in nearby Kuwait City had essentially the same exposure as persons living in the United States. Yet few American soldiers were even as close as Kuwait City. Likewise, a National Institutes of Health report issued in April 1994 made short order of the uranium theory, noting among other things that the use of the material was highly localized.

At a hearing on May 6, 1994, Sen. John D. Rockefeller IV (D-W.Va.), then-chairman of the Senate Veterans' Affairs Committee, implicated the drug Pyridostigmine bromide, which had been given Gulf troops as "pretreatment" for nerve agent poisoning. But a National Institutes of Health (NIH) report released on June 22, 1994, noted this drug has been used by some patients for decades—in doses of up to 6,000 milligrams a day—with "no significant long-term effects. By contrast, the troops received a mere thirty milligrams for up to three weeks."

Nonetheless, Rockefeller continues to hammer at Pyridostigmine bromide as being the syndrome's most likely cause, which says something about the even less likely causes. On a December "Nightline" broadcast focusing on the offspring of Gulf War vets, Rockefeller went on to claim that the drug causes birth defects in Gulf vet offspring. But no birth defects have been associated with women who used the drug before or during pregnancy, much less with the more tenuous exposure of the male.

GAS PAINS

The most chilling theory, and the one to which the media has given the most credence, was suggested by the USA Today headline, "Trail of Symptoms Suggests Chem-arms." Chemical weapons were the focus of a 160-page report from the Senate Banking Committee. Don Riegle (D-Mich.), then-chairman of the committee, had been among the minority who voted against the resolution authorizing President George Bush to take military action against Iraq—as were four of the most vocal congressmen on the issue of Gulf War Syndrome.

The Riegle report includes testimony from a number of vets who appear convinced that they were exposed to chemical weapons and believe they are now suffering as a result. The media reported statements such as the one by a fellow who told USA Today, "I know in my heart I was gassed."

But chemical weapons experts such as Dr. George Koelle, professor emeritus at the University of Pennsylvania and a former chemical warfare specialist for the military during World War II, have pointed out that if the men were really exposed to such weapons, they would darned well know it. Koelle says, "None [of the Gulf War vets] exhibit symptoms characteristic of either blistering agents like mustard or organo-phosphates, those types of agents which would be primarily in use."

Koelle's experience with chemical warfare victims from World War II indicates that, as he put it, "Blistering agents or mustard leave very little in the way of residual effects. Acute effects, yes, even fatal ones, but lasting effects are not characteristic." He recalls that during the Second World War he tried recruiting into a study chemical-weapons victims who were still suffering from the attack but couldn't find any. Further, he notes, this was the case with soldiers who had suffered massive acute exposure, much less soldiers who by their own statements could not have received a high dosage.

He is also aghast that chemical weapons could be blamed, as they are in the Banking Committee report, for illnesses in family members of exposed persons; only a contagion could accomplish this, he notes.

In a "60 Minutes" segment on Gulf War Syndrome broadcast on March 12, reporter Ed Bradley, who six years earlier began the Alar apple scare, suggested that the veterans' symptoms could have been the result of poisoning by sarin. Sarin is a nerve agent the Germans developed before World War II but never deployed. Eight days later, the world was horrified to find out what the real symptoms of sarin poisoning are when terrorists planted the gas aboard several Tokyo subway cars. Passengers fainted, vomited, and went into convulsions. Over 5,000 needed immediate hospitalization, and eight died within hours.

This is what chemical weapons do; they incapacitate an enemy. Conversely, vets who have now become convinced they suffered gas attacks in the Gulf say that at the time they had symptoms no more serious than tingling on the back of the neck or dry mouth or perhaps a burning sensation in the lungs. In contrast with the thousands of Japanese subway riders, no U.S. soldier in the Gulf was ever hospitalized or incapacitated by any unseen weapon.

* * *

Admitting as much was Dr. Charles Jackson of the Tuskegee VA Medical Center in Huntsville Alabama. Jackson brought great publicity to the issue of Gulf War Syndrome in 1993 by using the syndrome, and exposure to chemical-biological warfare, as a diagnosis for numerous ailing members of a Naval Reserve Seabee unit. "But suppose they'd developed something that was insidious so they didn't need to incapacitate in the field," he told *USA Today*, "something that would get you when you got home." For a guy as wily as Saddam Hussein has proved to be, inventing a chemical weapon that didn't even begin working until years after the war was lost would be pretty stupid indeed.

Neither the NIH report, nor another produced by the Department of Defense in June—by a task force chaired by Nobel prize winner Dr. Joshua Lederberg of Rockefeller University—was able to pinpoint a specific cause for the mysterious syndrome. A third report, released in December by the Defense Department's Comprehensive Clinical Evaluation Program, declared, "There is no clinical evidence for a single or unique agent causing a 'Gulf War Syndrome.'" Rather, it said, "unexplained illnesses reported by Persian Gulf veterans are not a single disease or apparent syndrome, but rather multiple illnesses with overlapping symptoms and causes."

An Institute of Medicine report released in January criticized the government's efforts to study the problem and reach scientific conclusions. It then made the seemingly bizarre recommendation that Vice President Al Gore be in charge of coordinating the Gulf War Syndrome research effort. Gore has no scientific or medical background. But even the Institute of Medicine panel said it couldn't find evidence to support the argument that chemical weapons and medicine dispensed to vets were the chief causes of the syndrome.

THE EXPERTS AGREE

If these various reports could find no syndrome, how to explain all those sick men, with their sick wives and sick children?

Lost in the rush to find the most quotable or pathetic victim is the notion that everybody occasionally becomes ill. Says Edward Young, former chief of staff at the Houston VA Medical Center, one of the three centers set up to investigate ailments among Gulf War vets, "We're talking about people who have multiple complaints. And if you go out on the street in any city in this country, you'll find people who have exactly the same things, and they've never been to the Gulf."

An early Army study of seventy-nine Indiana reservists who served in the Gulf and complained of a variety of symptoms found "no objective evidence for an outbreak of disease." It said, "Problems and symptoms like those found here would be expected to occur throughout the Reserve forces which deployed."

A wider, on-going VA study has compared over 7,000 Gulf War veterans with 7,000 veterans who had served elsewhere during the same period. While the controls are not scientifically matched and the results have not been prepared in proper form for publication, there seems to be no difference in illnesses. As Lederberg observes, "You can't even take numbers as we have seen them and draw the conclusion that anybody's sicker from serving in the Gulf than comparable people elsewhere," though he adds that doesn't necessarily "mean it isn't true."

* * *

One advocacy group that opposed the Gulf War deployment, the Military Family Support Network of Fort Bragg, North Carolina, has attributed both miscarriages and birth defects to exposures in the Gulf. But a combined study of pregnancies at several bases found the miscarriages of Gulf vets' wives to be at the same level as that population had before deployment to the Gulf. This was about half the civilian rate.

Yet in a December 1994 "Nightline" broadcast focusing on the children of Gulf War vets, the show's reporter made the alarming claim, "In Waynesville, Mississippi, thirteen of fifteen babies born to returning members of a National Guard Unit were reported to have severe and often rare health problems."

Reported, yes—but without substantiation. The Mississippi Department of Health investigated the alleged cluster and found that of fifty-four births to returning Guardsmen in that state, there were three major defects, with two to four expected in a group that size. They also found four minor defects, with three to five expected. There were no more premature or low birth-weight children than would be expected.

A larger study of 620 pregnancies at Robins Air Force Base in Georgia also found defects and miscarriages among Gulf vets' children to be at or below normal levels. In the Persian Gulf Registry of veterans, the reported rates of miscarriage are below that of the general population.

THE REAL CAUSE

The thing unspoken in the Gulf syndrome allegations is that somehow the vets, their wives, and their offspring are supposed to be immune to illness. If they are not, then the illness must be from exposure to something in the Gulf. The fallacy employed is the one universally used to show causation where none is otherwise apparent. It is the bulwark of scare-of-the-weekism, as in "My wife began using a cellular phone and then developed a brain tumor, therefore the phone caused the tumor."

Does all this mean that, for all categories of illness, Gulf vets, their wives, and offspring have no more problems than other people? Not at all. Gulf veterans show extraordinarily high rates of post-traumatic stress, and they also suffer disproportionately from drug and alcohol dependency.

But with a few exceptions, the vast number of symptoms attributed to Gulf War Syndrome can be brought on by stress. While the Allies ultimately won a quick, lopsided victory, the soldiers had no idea that would be the case. What they did know was that, in facing Saddam Hussein's Iraq, they were threatened by horrible weapons which no American had faced since World War I.

A further stressor for many was the quick transformation from civilian to combatant—as was the case with reservists and National Guardsmen. The Indiana reservist study concluded that, to the extent there were abnormalities, they appeared to be related to the stress of being ripped quickly out of civilian life and being sent to a war zone, and then a few months later being thrust back into civilian life. This may explain why reservists and National Guardsmen are far more likely to complain of Gulf War-related ills than are active duty soldiers.

* * *

Massive illness brought on by stress among veterans is nothing new. Stephen E. Straus, of the National Institute of Allergies and Infectious Diseases, told *Science News,* "There is a spectrum of this illness that is seen with all military adventures." Civil War veterans had undiagnosable symptoms, including fatigue, breathlessness, and gastrointestinal symptoms. In World War I, some 60,000 British troops were found to suffer from a mysterious "effort syndrome," a problem that recurred in World War II. Similar phenomena have been called variously "soldier's heart," "neurasthenia," "combat fatigue," "shell shock," or the Vietnam-era "post-traumatic stress disorder." But a major difference between then and now is that now there is a mass media to publicize the claims.

Indeed, the closest Gulf War Syndrome comes to having a prime cause may be the American media. The study of the seventy-nine Indiana reservists found that many of the symptoms appeared to arise in response to reports of other people being sick. "When we have media reports of a particular symptom that hasn't been reported before," said Army spokeswoman Virginia Stephanakis, "suddenly by God we'll get plenty of those."

Hillary Clinton surely understands the power of the media in this regard. Since her health-care reform setback, she has adopted Gulf War Syndrome as a personal cause and pledged to do whatever she could to bring more attention to the plight of the ailing Gulf vets. The *Washington Post* reported that the first lady "has become the Clinton administration point-person on the Gulf War Syndrome issue." In March, her husband announced he was forming a special panel of physicians, scientists, veterans, and unspecified "others" to investigate the mystery ailment. Even the mainstream media found the president's announcement a bit much, with several newspapers referring to Clinton's act, combined with an effort to prevent trimming the Veterans' Affairs budget, as a move to "outflank his GOP rivals on veterans' issues."

There are plenty of veterans' issues at play. Under the enacted legislation, veterans can receive anywhere from $89 to $1,823 a month, depending on the extent of their alleged disabilities. To qualify, they must have been symptomatic at least six months and be found to suffer fatigue, skin problems, headaches, muscle pains, joint pains, nerve disorders, neuropsychological problems, respiratory problems, sleep disturbances, stomach problems, heart problems, and menstrual disorders that began during or within two years after the war and lasted at least six months.

Other vets may simply have succumbed to the lure of litigation. Some 2,000 of them have joined a $1 billion lawsuit against both American and foreign companies, alleging that these companies gave Iraq the chemicals needed to produce the weapons that they claim caused their illnesses.

HYSTERIA, BUT NO LAUGHING MATTER

There's no reason to think, however, that most of those vets who say they are sick from exposure in the Gulf are not sincere. Indeed, most may be truly sick. As Dr. Dimitrios Trichopoulos, the head of the Department of Epidemiology at the Harvard School of Public Health, explains it, when many people hear they should be ill, they become ill—the flip side, as it were, of the placebo effect. "If you keep telling people they should be sick, of course they believe it," Trichopoulos says.

Phantom epidemics in which many people fall ill upon hearing they may have been exposed to something harmful are not uncommon. Two years ago, more than 2,000 children in and around Cairo fell suddenly ill in an epidemic of fainting that some blamed on chemical and biological agents. The "epidemic" proved to be only psychological.

In 1986, reports of hundreds of girls in the Israeli-occupied West Bank hospitalized with symptoms of nausea, dizziness, headaches, abdominal pains, and fatigue sparked an international incident. At least one newspaper blamed the maladies on nerve gas; others pointed to a pesticide. Ultimately, medical investigators found nothing to blame for the epidemic other than mass hysteria. U.S. schools are also occasionally swept by such hysterias.

The illnesses attributed to Gulf War Syndrome also seem to have a peculiar way of targeting Americans. Although there are some ill Canadian, British, and Australian troops, as of last year no more than a few dozen of the 42,000 British troops who served in the war reported any kind of mysterious illness.

The British Surgeon General has denied that any "medical condition exists that is peculiar to those who served in the Gulf conflict."

Brian McMahon, who was Trichopolous's predecessor as head of the Department of Epidemiology at the Harvard School of Public Health and is now professor emeritus at the school, says, "We've been through this before. We saw this broad array of symptoms with PCBs in Michigan. When you get such an array with the only thing in common being exposure," he said, you're seeing psychosomatic illness. "People are looking at clouds and trying to see faces instead of looking at data," he said.

Still, some veterans—and their terrified wives—are truly suffering. Stress-related illness is "a devastating problem with physical consequences," says Dr. Barry Rumack, a toxicology expert and clinical professor at the University of Colorado School of Medicine. "It's just not anything chemical."

WEIRD SCIENCE

Unfortunately, with rare exceptions, scientific evidence, statistical data, and mundane explanations have lost out to exotic theories, lobbyists' demands, politicians' polemics, and numerous unsubstantiated anecdotes. The Banking Committee report found no room for discussions of background rates of illness, yet it devoted seventeen pages to personal testimonies. These are emotional, sad and compelling anecdotes—but they're anecdotes just the same.

Naval Reserve Seabee Nick Roberts is one of the Seabees diagnosed under the auspices of Dr. Charles Jackson. Roberts suffers from lymphoma, a cancer of the lymph glands. In November 1993, he told a congressional panel that of the thirty-three members in his military reserve unit, ten have been diagnosed with the same illness. He also held up a list of what he said were 173 cancer-stricken Gulf veterans. The media promptly reported his testimony. Yet a Persian Gulf Registry update five months later showed only eight lymphomas out of all Gulf vets in America, with thirty-eight cancers of all types. This cancer rate was about fifty percent *below* that of the comparison non-Gulf veterans, although the control group was not scientifically matched.

Lymphomas are thought to usually develop decades after their instigation (although with AIDS patients who have suffered almost a complete collapse of their immune system, this can be shortened to a few years). What may be the most celebrated case of Gulf War Syndrome—and the only one with death widely attributed to it—is that of lymphoma victim Michael Adcock. But Army spokeswoman Stephanakis said Adcock had just arrived in Saudi Arabia when he was diagnosed with his first symptom. "He [Adcock] had rectal bleeding six days after arriving and the family blamed it on the Gulf," she said skeptically.

"Beyond a shadow of a doubt, I believe Michael died of multiple chemical exposure," Adcock's mother told the *Washington Times* in May 1993. She cited exposure to oil well fires, paint used to insulate vehicles from chemical weapons exposure, and lead in the diesel fuel used in lanterns and heaters as probable causes for her son's lymphoma. Six months later, in congressional testimony, she was convinced the cause was a chemical weapon released in a Scud missile explosion—which authorities said was actually a sonic boom—the day before her son's rectal bleeding began.

No reporter or congressman dared suggest it was more probable that Adcock's cancer was merely one of the almost 50,000 lymphomas diagnosed that year. No one dared consider the possibility that Mrs. Adcock's statements were one woman's sad effort to cope with the unexpected loss of a child. Surely much of why the coverage of Gulf War Syndrome has been so lopsidedly unskeptical is that to do otherwise is to be branded a rotten human being, not unlike those who, a decade earlier, questioned what proved to be the outrageous estimates of missing and kidnapped children.

THE REAL COVER-UP

Just ask the Houston VA center's Edward Young. In an interview with the *Birmingham Daily News*, he said he had seen enough alleged victims of the disease to be convinced there wasn't one. "It really rankles me when people stand up and call it 'Persian Gulf Syndrome,'" said a clearly frustrated Young. "To honor this thing with some name is ridiculous." Although he later asked that his comments not be printed, the American Legion, the chief lobbying group for the syndrome, got wind of them and complained to the VA, which unceremoniously yanked Young from his position. The VA cited his lack of compassion.

The CBS program "Eye to Eye with Connie Chung" originally expressed great interest in doing a show debunking the alleged syndrome, or at least telling both sides of the story. Producer Mary Raffalli collected a great deal of information on the subject and said the show would definitely be done. But it wasn't

—according to Susan Zirinski, a CBS producer, the program at the time was understaffed and the piece seemed time-sensitive, although she now concedes it was not.

Some syndrome proponents, however, are willing to concede that science is not on their side. Last year, after Congress passed legislation providing compensation without a clear definition of the ailment, Veterans' Affairs Secretary Jesse Brown admitted, "This legislation is revolutionary. We have never before provided payment for something we're not even certain exists." Jay Rockefeller, asked if there was a definite connection between Gulf War service and defective offspring, said, "If you were to ask as a human being, I would have to say absolutely. If you were to ask me as a scientist, I would have to say we cannot yet prove there is a link." Seen any non-human scientists lately? Rockefeller was saying the problem with scientists is they insist on using science to draw conclusions. And the science here, as he admits in his own way, does not support his position.

*   *   *

Nor will it ever, which may be what those "others" to be appointed to President Clinton's panel are all about. As Mary R. Stout, then-national president of Vietnam Veterans of America, once testified before a congressional panel:

> I guess, to sum up all of what this means to us and what it means to ... veterans, is that if we must now presume that the scientific community cannot be trusted —and in some cases obviously—we are assuming that—a political decision must be made on this issue to provide compensation to veterans.

The year was 1990 and the issue wasn't Gulf War Syndrome but the defoliant Agent Orange, and the vets in question were from Vietnam. Study after study found that, other than stress, there was no difference in levels of illness between soldiers who could have been exposed to the herbicide and those who were not, and that many convinced they'd been exposed clearly hadn't been. The scientific community thus became untrustworthy and was overridden by the political "community." The case of the Gulf War Syndrome is currently following a similar course.

Where does this leave the vets? Dr. Russell Tarver, who led the Mississippi National Guard birth-defect investigation, strayed from his data during an interview just long enough to offer an opinion. "I think it's unconscionable to frighten people out of reproducing unless you have some good data to support that contention," he said. "I think you're committing a crime against those veterans."

CHALLENGE QUESTIONS
Is the Gulf War Syndrome Real?

1. Consider the emotional stories presented by Bernstein and Kelley. What reported events and conditions would you suggest deserved further investigation? Explain your choices.

2. How might reading Bernstein and Kelley's selection affect a Gulf War veteran who is ill? Explain.

3. According to Fumento, veterans claiming to be suffering from Gulf War Syndrome report a wide variety of symptoms. Does this in itself negate the argument supporting the reality of Gulf War Syndrome? Why, or why not?

4. Fumento argues that media attention may be the primary cause of Gulf War Syndrome. What support does he give for his position? Answer his argument from the opposing point of view, that is, that media attention has helped to disseminate the truth about Gulf War Syndrome.

On the Internet . . .

http://www.dushkin.com

www.Yahoo.com: Health: Mental Health

This is Yahoo's index site for mental health, with access to 1,032 other sites and indices. The focus of these sites include addiction and recovery, diseases and conditions, and suicide. *http://www.yahoo.com/ Health/Mental_Health/*

Sex Laws

This is a launching site for an international journey through sexual mores and practices. It can be used as a database for both ethical and cultural relativism. *http://laws.home.ml.org/*

Bulimia Nervosa Research, Re: Diagnosis

This site offers summaries on over 140 articles on the diagnosis of bulimia. It is provided by Internet Mental Health, a free encyclopedia of mental health information whose goal is to promote improved understanding, diagnosis, and treatment of mental illness throughout the world. *http://www. mentalhealth.com/dis-rs1/p24-et02.html*

PART 3

Developmental and Health-Related Disorders

The balance between people's individual rights and freedoms and society's right to place limits on these freedoms is frequently debated. Do parents have an absolute right to raise their children as they see fit, or should society place limits on how parents can treat their children? Do pregnant women have an absolute right to govern their own bodies, or should society require pregnant women to modify their behavior when necessary to protect their fetuses? Should people be allowed to engage in whatever sexual practices bring them pleasure as long as they are not hurting anyone, or does society have a right to label certain practices as unacceptable?

Often these debates are fueled by research findings in abnormal psychology. The same research can be interpreted quite differently by different people, however.

■ Do Physically Punished Children Become Violent Adults?

■ Is Yo-Yo Dieting Dangerous?

■ Should Drug Use by Pregnant Women Be Considered Child Abuse?

■ Is Sex Addiction a Myth?

ISSUE 7

Do Physically Punished Children Become Violent Adults?

YES: Murray A. Straus, from "Discipline and Deviance: Physical Punishment of Children and Violence and Other Crime in Adulthood," *Social Problems* (May 1991)

NO: Joan McCord, from "Questioning the Value of Punishment," *Social Problems* (May 1991)

ISSUE SUMMARY

YES: Murray A. Straus, a social science researcher, finds a relationship between the physical punishment that young children receive and the violent acts that they commit during their teenage and adult years.

NO: Joan McCord, a professor of criminal justice, concludes that children who are rejected and neglected, not those who are physically punished, become the most violent adults.

Using physical means to punish children (e.g., spanking or slapping) is a time-honored and, some would say, infamous tradition. Even ancient biblical texts warn of "sparing the rod and spoiling the child."

Interestingly, 1994 was one of the first years on record in which a survey (commissioned by the National Committee for the Prevention of Child Abuse) indicated that a majority of parents reported *not* physically punishing their children. Why have parents begun to question physical punishment? Many of us have "survived" such punishment, but is it actually "good" for us? Does it help or hinder a child's development? Do many parents go too far, and are many children unalterably damaged by a switch or a paddle? What role do such practices play in child abuse?

These and many other questions are currently being considered by psychologists. Unfortunately, the experts seem to differ almost as much as parenting traditions and practices. Some psychologists, such as James Dobson in his book *Dare to Discipline* (Bantam Books, 1982), favor the use of punishment such as spanking, as long as parenting also includes encouragement and affection. In contrast, child development professionals Lee Salk and T. Berry Brazelton contend that physical punishment is not appropriate for behavior problems. Physical punishment, they argue, has too many negative, long-term consequences, including leading the children to become violent.

This is the position taken by Murray A. Straus in the following selection. Straus describes an explanatory model for understanding how violence begets violence—his Cultural Spillover Theory. This theory holds that violence in one sphere of life engenders violence in other spheres, regardless of how "legitimate" that violence is. In other words, even though the spanking of children is itself lawful, the fact that it is violent inevitably increases the probability of other types of violence, including those of the unlawful variety. As evidence for his theory, Straus cites correlational studies that indicate that the more an adult experienced physical punishment as a child, the higher the probability that he or she will assault his or her spouse.

Joan McCord, in opposition, asserts that the correlational nature of such evidence allows for all types of explanations. McCord emphasizes that any negative life experience can lead to crime and violence, not just physical punishment. Parental neglect of children is also highly associated with violent crime as well as physical abuse. McCord offers an alternative explanation, which she terms Construct Theory. This theory suggests that discipline, including nonphysical punishment and even the use of rewards, teaches children to focus on their own pains and pleasures, and thus teaches them to be egocentric. This egocentricity, or concern primarily for one's self, means that the welfare of others is secondary, increasing the probability that violence toward others will occur.

POINT	COUNTERPOINT
• Adults who were physically punished as children engaged in more violent crime and property crime.	• Children who were physically punished *and* given parental affection were less likely to become criminals.
• The more physical punishment experienced as a child, the higher the probability of assaulting a spouse as an adult.	• Neglect and sexual abuse were in fact more likely than physical abuse to lead to violence.
• "Legitimate violence" tends to spill over to illegitimate violence and other crimes.	• The children of criminals are likely to be criminals themselves because of a variety of factors.
• Use of physical punishment is associated with an increased risk of child abuse.	• Poor socialization, not punishment per se, contributes to inappropriate behavior.

YES
Murray A. Straus

DISCIPLINE AND DEVIANCE: PHYSICAL PUNISHMENT OF CHILDREN AND VIOLENCE AND OTHER CRIME IN ADULTHOOD

In this paper I present a theoretical model intended to aid research on physical punishment of children and its consequences. The model focuses primarily on the hypothesis that while physical punishment by parents or teachers may produce conformity in the immediate situation, in the long run it tends to *increase* the probability of deviance, including delinquency in adolescence and wife-beating, child abuse, and crime outside the family (such as robbery, assault, and homicide) as an adult. This hypothesis involves considerable irony since the intent of physical punishment is to increase socially *conforming* rather than deviant behavior. As shown below, almost all parents and a majority of teachers believe that physical punishment is an appropriate and effective form of discipline....

DEFINITIONS

Physical Punishment
Exploring such issues as the legitimacy of physical punishment requires some definition of terms. Physical punishment is a legally permissible physical attack on children. The most common forms are spanking, slapping, grabbing, and shoving a child "roughly"—with more force than is needed to move the child. Hitting a child with an object is also legally permissible and widespread (Wauchope and Straus 1990). Parents in the United States and most countries have a legal right to carry out these acts, as do teachers in most U.S. states and most nations; whereas, the same act is a criminal assault if carried out by someone not in a custodial relationship to the child.

The section on "General Justification" of violence in the Texas Penal Code, for example (9.61, West Publishing Company 1983), declares that the use of force, but not deadly force, against a child younger than 18 years is justified

From Murray A. Straus, "Discipline and Deviance: Physical Punishment of Children and Violence and Other Crime in Adulthood," *Social Problems*, vol. 38, no. 2 (May 1991), pp. 134–144, 147–149. Copyright © 1991 by The Society for the Study of Social Problems. Reprinted by permission. References and some notes omitted.

(1) when the actor is the child's parent or step-parent or is acting in *loco parentis* to the child, and (2) when and to the degree that the actor reasonably believes that force is necessary to discipline the child or to safeguard or promote welfare.

The New Hampshire Criminal Code (627.6:I, Equity Publishing 1985) similarly declares that "A parent, guardian, or other person responsible for the general care and welfare of a minor is justified in using force against such a minor when and to the extent that he reasonably believes it necessary to prevent or punish such a minor's misconduct." Both these statutes cover parents and teachers, and neither sets any limit except "not deadly."

Is Physical Punishment Violence?

Since the concept of violence is used in this paper as often as physical punishment, it also needs to be defined. Though the lack of a standard definition or consensus on its meaning results in considerable confusion, the following definition makes clear the conceptual framework of this paper, even though it will not be accepted by all readers: *Violence* is an act carried out with the intention, or perceived intention, of causing physical pain or injury to another person.

This definition and alternative definitions are examined in detail in Gelles and Straus (1979). As defined, violence is synonymous with the term "physical aggression" as used in social psychology (Bandura 1973; Berkowitz 1962). This definition overlaps with but is not the same as the legal concept of "assault." The overlap occurs because the definition of assault, like the definition of violence, refers to an *act*, regardless of whether injury occurred as a result of that act. However, the concept of assault is more narrow than that of violence because not all acts of violence are crimes, including acts of self-defense and physical punishment of children. Some violent acts are required by law—for example, capital punishment.[1]

The fact that physical punishment is legal is not inconsistent with the definition of violence just given, since, as noted, there are many types of legal violence. An examination of the definition shows that physical punishment of children fits every element of the definition of violence given. Thus, from a theoretical perspective, physical punishment and capital punishment are similar, despite the vast difference in level of severity.

PHYSICAL PUNISHMENT OF CHILDREN AS THE PRIMORDIAL VIOLENCE

Incidence of Physical Punishment by Parents

Ninety-nine percent of the mothers in the classic study of *Patterns of Child Rearing* (Sears, Maccoby, and Levin 1957) used physical punishment as defined above on at least some occasions, and 95 percent of students in a community college sample reported having experienced physical punishment at some point (Bryan and Freed 1982).... [T]he National Family Violence Surveys (Straus 1983; Wauchope and Straus 1990), studies of large and nationally representative samples of American children conducted in 1975 and 1985... found that almost all parents in the United States use physical punishment with young children—over 90 percent of parents of children age 3 and 4. A remarkable correspondence exists between the results of these four surveys in the near universality with which physical punishment was used on children age 2 to 6; and also between the two national surveys in showing that physical punishment was still being used on one out of three children at age 15.

Despite the widespread use of physical punishment, there is nontheless considerable variation—more than enough to enable empirical study of the correlates of physical punishment. First, we see that the percentage of people experiencing physical punishment drops off rapidly with age so that by age 13 there are nearly equal numbers of children who are and who are not punished. Second, at each age, there is enormous variation in how often a specific child experiences physical punishment (Wauchope and Straus 1990).

Incidence of Physical Punishment in Schools

In 1989 all but eleven states permitted physical punishment of children by school employees. A 1978–79 national survey of schools found an annual incidence of 2.5 instances of physical punishment per 100 children. Only five states reported no instances of physical punishment (calculated from Hyman 1990: Appendix B). These figures are probably best interpreted as "lower bound" estimates, and the reported absence of physical punishment in five states must also be regarded with some caution.

A THEORETICAL MODEL

In the light of the above incidence rates and the previously listed reasons for the importance of research on physical punishment, a framework is needed to help stimulate and guide research. This section presents such a framework in the form of a causal model. The model was created on the basis of previous theoretical and empirical research.

Cultural Spillover Theory

An important component of the theoretical model to be presented is what I have called "Cultural Spillover Theory" (Baron and Straus 1987; Baron, Straus, and Jaffee 1988; Straus 1985), which holds that violence in one sphere of life tends to engender violence in other spheres, and that *this carry-over process transcends the bounds between legitimate and criminal use of force.* Thus, the more a society uses force to secure socially desirable ends (for example, to maintain order in schools, to deter criminals, or to defend itself from foreign enemies) the greater the tendency for those engaged in illegitimate behavior to also use force to attain their own ends.

Cultural Spillover Theory was formulated as a macro-sociological theory to explain society-to-society differences in violence rates, such as the huge differences between societies in the incidence of murder and rape. My colleagues and I tested this theory using a 12 indicator index to measure the extent to which violence was used for socially legitimate purposes ranging from physical punishment of children to capital punishment of criminals. We found that the higher the score of a state on the Legitimate Violence Index, the higher the rate of criminal violence such as rape (Baron and Straus 1987, 1989; Baron, Straus, and Jaffee 1988) and murder (Baron and Straus 1988).

We must also understand the individual-level processes which underlie the macro-level relationship. These can be illustrated by considering the hypothesis that use of physical punishment by teachers tends to increase the rate of violence by children in schools. The individual level aspect of this hypothesis is based on two assumptions: (1) that children often mistreat other children, (2) that teachers are important role models. Therefore, if children frequently misbehave toward other children, and if teachers who serve as role models use violence to correct misbehavior, a larger proportion of children will use violence to deal with other children whom they perceive as having mistreated them than would be the case if teachers did not provide a model of hitting wrongdoers.

The Cultural Spillover Theory overlaps with the "Brutalization" Theory of capital punishment (Bowers 1984; Hawkins 1989), and the "Cultural Legitimation" Theory of homicide (Archer and Gartner 1984). All three of these theories can be considered a variant of what Farrell and Swigert (1988:295) identify as "social and cultural support" theories of crime, including the Differential Association Theory, the Delinquent Subculture Theory, and the Social Learning Theory. Each of these theories seeks to show that crime is not just a reflection of individual deviance (as in psycho-pathology theories of crime) or the absence of social control (as in Social-Disorganization Theory). Rather, crime is also engendered by social integration into groups which share norms and values that support behavior which the rest of society considers to be criminal. Thus, the processes which produce criminal behavior are structurally parallel to the processes which produce conforming behavior, but the cultural content differs.[2]

The Model

The theoretical model diagramed in Figure 1 depicts the causes and consequences of physical punishment and suggests salient issues for empirical investigation. It is a "system model" because it assumes that the use of physical punishment is a function of other characteristics of the society and its members and that physical punishment in turn influences the society and its members....

Each of the blocks in Figure 1 should also have arrows between the elements within each block; except for Block II at the center of the model, they were omitted to provide a clear picture. The arrows within Box II posit a mutually reinforcing relationship between physical punishment in the schools and by parents. It seems highly plausible that a society which approves of parents hitting children will also tend to approve of teachers doing the same, and that when physical punishment is used in the schools, it encourages parents to also hit children....

ANTECEDENTS OF PHYSICAL PUNISHMENT BY PARENTS

Block I at the left of the model identifies characteristics of the society, of the schools, of families, and of individual parents which are hypothesized to influence the extent to which physical punishment is used. This list is far from exhaustive, as are the hypotheses to be tested. Both are intended only to illustrate some of the many factors which might influence use of physical punishment.[3]

Societal Norms

Physical punishment is deeply rooted in Euro-American religious and legal traditions (Foucault 1979; Greven 1990). It would be difficult to find someone who could not recite the biblical phrase "spare the rod and spoil the child." The common law of every American state permits parents to use physical punishment. These are not mere vestiges of ancient but

Figure 1

System Model of Causes and Consequences of Physical Punishment

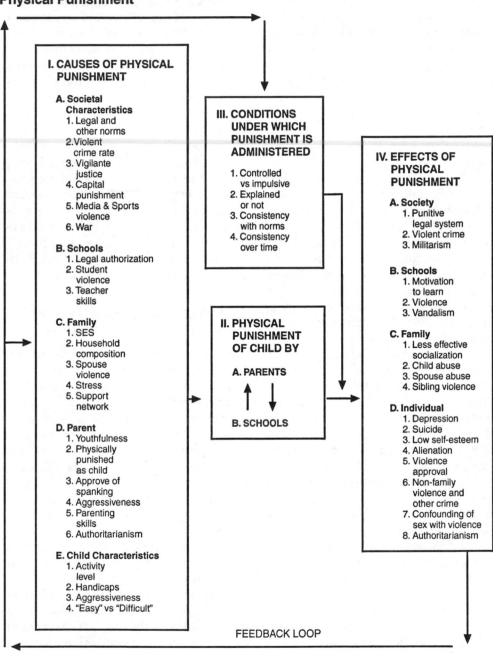

I. CAUSES OF PHYSICAL PUNISHMENT

A. Societal Characteristics
1. Legal and other norms
2. Violent crime rate
3. Vigilante justice
4. Capital punishment
5. Media & Sports violence
6. War

B. Schools
1. Legal authorization
2. Student violence
3. Teacher skills

C. Family
1. SES
2. Household composition
3. Spouse violence
4. Stress
5. Support network

D. Parent
1. Youthfulness
2. Physically punished as child
3. Approve of spanking
4. Aggressiveness
5. Parenting skills
6. Authoritarianism

E. Child Characteristics
1. Activity level
2. Handicaps
3. Aggressiveness
4. "Easy" vs "Difficult"

III. CONDITIONS UNDER WHICH PUNISHMENT IS ADMINISTERED
1. Controlled vs impulsive
2. Explained or not
3. Consistency with norms
4. Consistency over time

II. PHYSICAL PUNISHMENT OF CHILD BY

A. PARENTS

B. SCHOOLS

IV. EFFECTS OF PHYSICAL PUNISHMENT

A. Society
1. Punitive legal system
2. Violent crime
3. Militarism

B. Schools
1. Motivation to learn
2. Violence
3. Vandalism

C. Family
1. Less effective socialization
2. Child abuse
3. Spouse abuse
4. Sibling violence

D. Individual
1. Depression
2. Suicide
3. Low self-esteem
4. Alienation
5. Violence approval
6. Non-family violence and other crime
7. Confounding of sex with violence
8. Authoritarianism

FEEDBACK LOOP

no longer honored principles. In addition to defining and criminalizing "child abuse," the child abuse legislation which swept through all 50 states in the late 1960s often reaffirmed cultural support for physical punishment by declaring that nothing in the statute should be construed as interfering with the rights of parents to use physical punishment. There is a certain irony to this legislation because, as will be suggested below, use of physical punishment is associated with an *increased* risk of "child abuse."[4]

Approval of physical punishment.
Attitude surveys have repeatedly demonstrated high approval of physical punishment. Ninety percent of the parents in the 1975 National Family Violence Survey expressed at least some degree of approval of physical punishment (Straus, Gelles, and Steinmetz 1980:55). Other studies report similar percentages. For example, a 1986 NORC national survey found that 84 percent agreed or strongly agreed that "It is sometimes necessary to discipline a child with a *good, hard spanking* (italics added). Moreover, this approval does not apply only to small children. The New Hampshire Child Abuse Survey (described in the Methodological Appendix and in Moore and Straus 1987) found that less than half of the parents interviewed (47 percent) strongly disagree with the statement "Parents have a right to slap their teenage children who talk back to them." When asked whether "Spanking children helps them to be better people when they grow up," only one out of six disagreed (16.7 percent).

Approval of hitting and actual hitting.
There is evidence that, as hypothesized by the path going from Block I.D2 of the theoretical model to Block II.A, parents who approve of physical punishment do it more often. Parents who approve of slapping a teenager who talks back reported hitting their teenager an average of 1.38 times during the year, about four times more often than the average of .33 for the parents who did not approve. For younger children, the frequency of physical punishment was much greater (an average of 4.9 times for preschool children and 2.9 times for 6-12 year old children), but the relationship between approval and actual hitting was almost identical.

Role Modeling
The path in Figure 1 from I.D2 to II.A, and from II.A to IV.C2 is based on the assumption that children learn by example, and we have seen that over 90 percent of parents provide examples of physical punishment. However, as noted above, there is a great deal of variation in how long physical punishment continues to be used and in the frequency with which it is used. This variation made it possible to test the hypothesis that the more a person experienced physical punishment, the more likely such persons are to use physical punishment on their own children. ...

EFFECTS OF PHYSICAL PUNISHMENT BY PARENTS

Block IV on the right side of Figure 1 illustrates the hypothesized effects of physical punishment on individuals, schools, families, and the society. The empirical analyses to be reported are all derived from the proposition that the "legitimate violence" of physical punishment tends to spill over to illegitimate violence and other crime. If subsequent research supports these effects, the next step will be research to identify the processes which produce them.

Physical Punishment and Physical Abuse

The basic tenant of Cultural Spillover Theory—that legitimate violence tends to increase the probability of criminal violence—is represented by the path going from II.A (physical punishment by parents) to IV.C2 (physical abuse by parents).

Analysis of the New Hampshire Child Abuse Survey (Moore and Straus 1987) shows that parents who believe in physical punishment not only hit more often, but they more often go beyond ordinary physical punishment and assault the child in ways which carry a greater risk of injury to the child such as punching and kicking. Specifically, parents who approved of physical punishment had a child abuse rate of 99 per 1,000, which is four times the rate for parents who did not approve of physical punishment (28 per 1,000).

Assaults on Siblings and Spouses

From the 1975 National Family Violence Survey (Straus 1983), we know that children who were physically punished during the year of that survey have almost three times the rate of severely and repeatedly assaulting a sibling three or more times during the year. Though it is likely that many of these children were physically punished precisely because of hitting a sibling, it is also clear that the physical punishment did not serve to reduce the level of assaults to the rate for children who were not physically punished.

Similarly, findings from the 1975 National Family Violence Survey (Straus 1983) clearly show that for both men

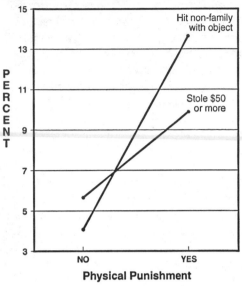

Figure 2

Juvenile Assault and Theft Rate by Physical Punishment

and women the more physical punishment a respondent experienced as a child, the higher the probability of assaulting a *spouse* during the year of the survey. These findings are consistent with the hypothesized path from Box II.A to IV.C3.

Physical Punishment and Street Crime

The theoretical model predicts that ordinary physical punishment increases the probability of "street crime" (path from Box II.A to IV.D.4). Evidence consistent with that hypothesis is presented in Figure 2 for juveniles and Figures 3 and 4 for adults.

The juvenile crime data are from a 1972 survey of 385 college students (Straus 1973, 1974, 1985) who completed a questionnaire referring to events when they were high school seniors. The questionnaire included an early version of the Conflict Tactics Scales and also a self-report delinquency scale. Figure 2

Figure 3
Non-Family Assaults of Adults by Physical Punishment as a Teen

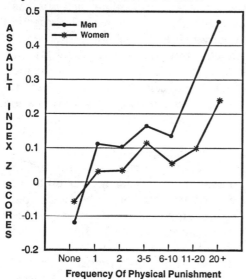

Frequency Of Physical Punishment

vestigation 1985). Consequently, despite the low rate, we examined the relationship of arrests to physical punishment experienced during the teenage years. Although the differences overall are statistically significant (F = 3.75, p < .001), the graph does not show the expected difference between those who were and were not hit as a teen. Instead, only respondents who were hit extremely often (eleven or more times during the year) had the predicted higher arrest rates. It is possible that these erratic results occur because the base rate for arrests is so low. A statistical analysis based on a characteristic which occurs in such a small percentage of the population is subject to random fluctuations unless the sample is much larger than even the 6,002 in the 1985 survey....

shows that significantly more children who were physically punished engaged in both violent crime and property crime.

The findings on crime by adults were obtained by an analysis of covariance of the 1985 National Family Violence Survey sample, controlling for socioeconomic status. Figure 3 shows that the more physical punishment experienced by the respondent as a child, the higher the proportion who as adults reported acts of physical aggression *outside the family* in the year covered by this survey. This relationship is highly significant after controlling for SES. The results are parallel when physical punishment by the father is the independent variable.

Although the arrest rate of respondents in the 1985 National Family Violence Survey was very low (1.1 percent or 1,100 per 100,000 population), this is very close to the 1,148 per 100,000 rate for the entire U.S. population (Federal Bureau of In-

SUMMARY AND CONCLUSIONS

This paper formulated a theoretical model of the links between physical punishment of children and crime and also presented preliminary empirical tests of some of the paths in the model. Although the empirical findings are almost entirely consistent with the theory, they use data which cannot prove the theory because they do not establish the causal direction. Nevertheless, the fact that so many analyses which could have falsified the theory did not strengthens the case for the basic proposition of the theory: that although physical punishment may produce short term conformity, over the longer run it probably also creates or exacerbates deviance.

The Causal Direction Problem
The causal direction problem can be illustrated at the macro level by the correlation between laws authorizing

Figure 4
Arrests Per 1,000 by Physical Punishment as a Teen

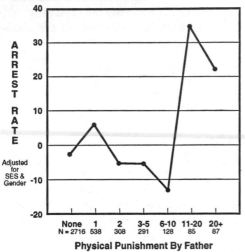

Physical Punishment By Father

physical punishment in schools and the homicide rate. It is likely that at least part of this relationship occurs because both physical punishment and crime are reflections of an underlying violent social climate. When crime and violence flourish, even ordinarily law-abiding citizens get caught up in that milieu. When crime rates are high, citizens tend to demand "getting tough" with criminals, including capital punishment and laws such as those recently enacted in Colorado and other states. These laws added protection of property to self-defense as a circumstance under which a citizen could use "deadly force." The question from the perspective of Cultural Spillover Theory is whether such laws, once in effect, tend to legitimize violence and, therefore, further increase rather than reduce violent crime.

The causal direction problem in the individual-level findings is even more obvious because it is virtually certain that part of the linkage between phys-

ical punishment and crime occurs because "bad" children are hit, and these same bad children go on to have a higher rate of criminal activity than other children.[5] However, the question is not whether misbehaving children are spanked but whether spanking for misbehavior, despite immediate compliance, tends to have longer term negative effects. Research by Nagaraja (1984), Patterson (1982), and Patterson and Bank (1987) suggests that this is the case. This research found an escalating feedback loop which is triggered by attempts to use physical punishment or verbal aggression to control deviant behavior of the child. These processes together with the hypothesized legitimation of violence are modeled in Figure 5.

It should be noted that physical punishment usually does not set in motion the deviation amplifying process just discussed, at least not to the extent that it produces seriously deviant behavior. We must understand the circumstances or branching processes which produce these different outcomes. The variables identified in Box III of Figure 1 ("Conditions Under Which Punishment is Administered") and by the diagonal path in Figure 5, are likely to be crucial for understanding this process. Three examples can illustrate this process. (1) If physical punishment is administered "spontaneously" and as a means of relieving tension, as advocated by a number of child care "experts" (e.g., Ralph 1989), it may increase the risk of producing a person who as an adult will be explosively violent, as compared to physical punishment is administered under more controlled circumstances. The latter is assumed to provide a model of controlled use of force. (2) If physical punishment is accompanied by verbal assaults, it may

Figure 5
Process Model of Effects of Corporal Punishment

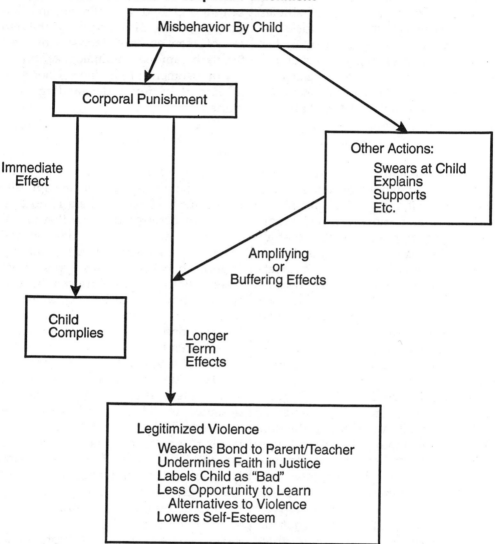

increase the risk of damage to the child's self-esteem compared to physical punishment administered in the context of a supportive relationship. (3) If physical punishment is administered along with reasoned explanations, the correlation between physical punishment and child's aggressiveness may be reduced.

A study by Larzelere (1986) found such a reduction, but also found that despite the lowered relationship, a statistically significant relationship remains.

Research Implications
Both the overall theoretical model (Figure 1) and the micro-process model (Figure

5) can only be adequately investigated with longitudinal and experimental data. There are already examples of studies at the macro-level which meet these criteria, including the research of Archer and Gartner (1984) on the effects of war on the homicide rate and research on the "brutalization" effect of executions (Bowers 1984; Hawkins 1989). At the individual level, McCord's follow up of the Cambridge-Somerville Youth Study (1988) sample illustrates what can be done with a longitudinal design. As for experiments, it would be unethical to randomly assign groups of parents to "spanking" and "no spanking" conditions. However, the fact that almost all parents do spank makes a number of experiments possible because the treatment can be in the form of helping parents use alternatives to spanking. One example would be an interrupted time series using volunteer parents. Another example would be a randomized field trial of a "no-spanking" parent education program.

There are hundreds of research questions that spring from the theoretical model presented in this paper. The process of transforming that model into meaningful research can be aided if criminologists and family violence researchers collaborate more than in the past to seek a full accounting of the links between physical punishment and crime outside the family. There are no serious structural or theoretical barriers to discourage such mutually informed work, but there is a set of beliefs that continues to define "family violence" in ways which inhibit research on physical punishment. Among family violence researchers, but especially those concerned with wife-beating, there has been a reluctance, and sometimes even condemnation, of considering ordinary physical punishment as part of the same continuum as wife-beating and child abuse (Breines and Gordon 1983: 505, 511). Spanking children is not seen as "real family violence." Similarly, among criminologists, physical punishment of children is not seen as important for understanding "real crime."

The theory developed in this paper and the research evidence so far available on that theory support the opposite formulation. However, there is no contradiction between the idea that all violence has something in common and the idea that there are important differences between various types of violence. Both propositions can be correct, and both approaches are needed for research on this complex phenomenon. Whether one focuses on the common elements in all violence or on the unique aspects of a certain type of violence depends on the purpose of the study. Research intended to inform interventions designed to aid "battered women" or "abused children," or to deter "wife-beating" or "street crime" must focus on the specific situation of those specific types of victims and offenders (Straus 1990c). However, for research intended to inform programs of "primary prevention" (Caplan 1974; Cowen 1984) of violent crime such as wife beating and homicide, it is essential to understand the social structural and social psychological process by which violence becomes an integral part of both legitimate and criminal behavior. The theoretical model presented in this paper suggests that the almost universal use of physical punishment in child rearing is part of the process.

NOTES

1. This brief discussion shows that the fact of a physical assault having taken place is not sufficient for understanding violence. Several other dimensions also need to be considered. It is also important that each of these other dimensions be measured separately so that their causes and consequences and joint effects can be investigated. Other dimensions include the seriousness of the assault (ranging from a slap to shooting), whether a physical injury was produced (from none to death), the motivation (from a concern for a person's safety, as when a child is spanked for going into the street, to hostility so intense that the death of the person is desired), and whether the act of violence is normatively legitimate (as in the case of slapping a child) or illegitimate (as in the case of slapping a spouse), and which set of norms are applicable (legal, ethnic or class norms, couple norms, etc.). See Gelles and Straus (1979) for further analyses of these issues.

2. There are a number of other theories relevant to the issues discussed in this paper. The larger theoretical task will be to integrate Cultural Spillover Theory and the theories just listed with theories such as Control Theory (Hirshi 1969), Labeling Theory (Scheff 1966; Straus 1973), Social Learning Theory (Bandura 1973; Berkowitz 1962; Eron, Walder, and Lefkowitz 1971; Gelles and Straus 1979; McCord 1988), and a variety of personality mediated theories. Although space limitations required deletion of my initial attempts to specify some of the interrelationships, the concluding theoretical discussion is a small step in that direction. I argue that physical punishment might bring about changes in personality, such as lowered self-esteem or increased powerlessness and alienation. These personality variables can, by themselves, serve as "risk factors" for violence. At the empirical level, it will require a "competing theories" research design and triangulation via several different types of research to adequately investigate these issues.

3. Moreover, due to space limitations, I will only discuss the paths for which I carried out empirical tests. However, since a reader of an earlier draft of the paper questioned the hypothesized paths and feedback loop running from use of corporal punishment back to low teacher and parental skill (I.C3 and I.D5), the reasoning needs to be summarized: It is simply that to the extent parents and teachers use corporal punishment as a means of inducing appropriate behavior, they get less practice in using other means of inducing appropriate behavior and, therefore, do not enhance their skills in those techniques, thus further increasing the probability of using corporal punishment.

4. A study of the reasons for including reaffirmation of corporal punishment in the child abuse legislation might provide important insights on American attitudes about children and violence. Such a study could be undertaken by analysis of the proceedings of state legislatures. For the moment, I would like to suggest two scenarios, both of which may have been operating. The first reason is that both spring from a concern about the welfare of children, and specifically the idea that children need to be protected from abuse but also need "strong discipline" (including physical punishment "when necessary") if they are to become responsible law-abiding citizens. The second reason is that the combination reflects a political compromise which the advocates of "child protection" needed to make in order to have the legislation pass. However, these two reasons overlap to a certain extent because conservative members of the legislatures who needed to be placated favor physical punishment because they deeply believe it is in the best interests of children.

5. I emphasize "a higher *rate*" because most "bad" children, regardless of whether they have been physically punished, do not become criminals. The theory put forth in this paper does not assert that corporal punishment is a necessary and sufficient cause of violence and other crime. On the contrary, crime is a multiply determined phenomenon, and corporal punishment is assumed to be only one of these many causes. Consequently, many individuals who have not been assaulted as children engage in crime, just as many who have been assaulted by teachers or parents avoid criminal acts.

NO

Joan McCord

QUESTIONING THE VALUE
OF PUNISHMENT

The author critically examines and rejects the claim that physical punishments lead to aggression through the acceptance of norms of violence. She proposes an alternate theory to account for how children acquire norms and why they become violent. The proposed Construct Theory explains why abused, neglected, and rejected children—as well as those who are punished—tend to become anti-social.

"Spare the rod and spoil the child," many have argued. "No," say others, as they refer to evidence that physical punishment leads to, rather than prevents, violent behavior. Yet only a few, it seems, have whispered that we should question the value of every type of punishment, including psychological punishments and deprivation of privileges as well as physical punishments.

When attention has been focused only on physical punishment, critics typically note that such discipline provides a model for the use of force, thereby teaching people to use force. Murray Straus, for example, argues that corporal punishment contributes to a cycle of violence that includes violent crime, child abuse, spouse abuse, non-violent crimes, ineffective family socialization, and ineffective schooling. Straus accounts for correlations between the use of physical punishment, on the one hand, and antisocial or dysfunctional behaviors on the other by means of Cultural Spillover Theory. This theory is an amalgam of explanations that consider behavior to be learned through imitation of models and adoption of norms supported by groups with whom an individual associates. In this view, individuals come to accept the use of violence—and to be violent—because they see violence as legitimated through its use by role models, and they generalize the behavioral norm to include illegitimate uses of violence.

While Straus is correct that physical punishments tend to increase aggression and criminal behavior, I believe he takes too narrow a view about the mechanisms that account for the relationships. My conclusion is grounded in evidence from longitudinal studies about the transmission of violence from

From Joan McCord, "Questioning the Value of Punishment," *Social Problems*, vol. 38, no. 2 (May 1991), pp. 167–176. Copyright © 1991 by The Society for the Study of Social Problems. Reprinted by permission.

one generation to the next. I offer a competing theory, one that merges evidence from experimental studies designed by psychologists to understand the conditions under which children learn and that considers critical issues related to the learning of language. The competing theory, which I call the Construct Theory, suggests how the same mechanism that links physical punishment to aggression can be triggered by nonphysical punishments and neglect. Before turning to the competing theory, I present empirical evidence that physical punishment leads to aggression and criminal behavior and then show that the Cultural Spillover Theory inadequately explains the relationship.

PROBLEMS WITH THE CULTURAL SPILLOVER EXPLANATION

Much of the research to which Straus refers in his analysis of the relationship between physical punishment and misbehavior is cross-sectional. With such data, as Straus acknowledges, one cannot determine whether punishments were a cause or an effect of the behavior. Three longitudinal studies that measured discipline prior to the age serious antisocial behavior began, however, suggest temporal priority for punitive discipline. Comparing children whose parents depended on physical punishments with those whose parents did not in Finland (Pulkkinen 1983), Great Britain (Farrington 1978), and in the United States (McCord 1988), researchers found that those whose parents used harsh physical punishments had greater probabilities for subsequently committing serious crimes. Longitudinal studies of victims of child abuse, too, suggest that violence tends to increase the probability that victims will commit serious crimes (McCord 1983; Widom 1989).

The theory of Cultural Spillover, like similar theories that attempt to explain pockets of violence, postulates acceptance of norms exhibited by the subculture using violence. Although longitudinal studies suggest that violence in the family precedes violence in society, they contain data incongruent with a theory that explains the causal mechanism as socialization into norms that legitimize violence.

One incongruence is revealed in my study of long-term effects of child abuse in which I compared abused sons with neglected and rejected and loved sons (McCord 1983). The classifications were based on biweekly observations in the homes when the boys were between the ages of 8 and 16 years and living in high-crime areas. Records of major (FBI Index) crime convictions were collected thirty years after the study ended. Twenty-three percent of those reared in loving families and 39 percent of those reared in abusing families had been convicted; but the conviction rate was 35 percent for the neglected and 53 percent for the rejected boys. That is, the data show almost as much violence produced from neglect as from abuse, and greater violence from rejection without abuse than from abuse. Because neglect and rejection typically lead to socialization failure, these results raise doubts that acceptance of norms of violence account for transmission of violence. It would be an anomaly if the very conditions that undermine acceptance of other types of norms promoted norms of violence.

One might argue that Cultural Spillover Theory accounts for violence among the abused and some other theory accounts for violence among neglected and rejected children. Yet neglect and rejection have enough in common with abuse to suggest that a more parsimonious account would be desirable. Furthermore, as will be shown, when neglect is combined with abuse, the result is not increased violence as one would expect were there different causes involved.

My data from the Cambridge-Somerville Youth Study records permitted further checks on the Cultural Spillover Theory. The data include parental criminal records as well as coded descriptions of family life between 1939 and 1945. Sons' criminal records had, as noted, been collected in 1978, when the sons were middle-aged. Among the 130 families containing two natural parents, 22 included a father who had been convicted for an Index crime. Fifty-five percent (12) of their sons were convicted for an Index crime. In comparison, twenty-five percent (27) of the 108 sons of noncriminal men had been convicted ($X^2_{(1)}$ = 7.60, P = .006). The criminal fathers were more likely to use physical punishment: 73 percent compared with 48 percent ($X^2_{(1)}$ = 4.43, P = .035). Further, the combined impact of a criminal father using physical punishment appeared to be particularly criminogenic.

These data support the view that use of physical punishment increases the likelihood that sons of criminals will be criminals. Cultural Spillover Theory suggests that the increase comes about because sons adopt the norms displayed through physical punishments. If the theory were correct, then the transmission of norms of violence should be particularly effective under conditions that promote acceptance of other types of norms as well. The evidence, however, gives another picture.

Many studies have shown that warmth or affection facilitates acceptance of social norms (e.g., Austin 1978; Bandura and Huston 1961; Bandura and Walters 1963; Baumrind 1978; Bender 1947; Bowlby 1940; Glueck and Glueck 1950; Goldfarb 1945; Hirschi 1969; Liska and Reed 1985; Maccoby 1980; McCord 1979; Olson, Bates, and Bayles 1990; Patterson 1976). Parental affection for the child should increase concordance if a similar mechanism for acceptance of norms accounts for a connection between parents' and children's aggression. To test this hypothesis, the 130 families were divided into three groups: those not using physical punishment, those using physical punishment and also expressing affection for the child, and those using physical punishment and not expressing affection for the child.

The data show that parental affection did not increase acceptance of norms of violence, but the opposite. For individuals reared with physical punishment, those whose parents were affectionate were *less* likely to become criminals. This result does not easily fit an assumption that normative acquisition accounts for the violence.

Another inconsistency is apparent in a longitudinal study that at first glance might appear to support the Cultural Spillover Theory. Widom (1989) retraced children reported to have been victims of abuse or neglect prior to the age of 11. Using records from elementary schools and hospitals at birth, Widom was able to match 667 of 908 children on sex, race, and age with children not known to have been either abused or neglected. Widom's analyses, based either on aggregate data combining abuse with neglect or matched and unmatched cases, have led her to conclude that violence breeds violence.

I reanalyzed her data (Widom 1990) to differentiate effects of neglect from effects of violence.

The matched pairs were divided into those in which the child had experienced sexual abuse (85 females, 15 males), neglect but not physical abuse (205 females, 254 males), physical abuse but not neglect (14 females, 35 males), and both physical abuse and neglect (29 females, 30 males). Assuming that acceptance of a norm of violence accounts for the high rates of crime that Widom found to follow abuse, crime would be considerably more prevalent among those who had been physically abused than among those who had been neglected but not abused.

Using Widom's codes of the individuals' criminal records, I compared each case with the matched control to see which had the worse criminal record. If both had been convicted of at least one crime, the one convicted for more crimes was counted as being worse.

The data show that neglect is about as criminogenic as sexual abuse and physical abuse. Moreover, the combined effects of neglect and abuse are not worse than those of either alone as would be expected if each had separate causal impact. Comparisons of cases and controls for crimes of violence (e.g., assault, murder, attempted murder) produced similar results.

These comparisons again suggest that continuity in violence among abusing families has been mistakenly attributed to transmission of norms of violence. Among males, neglect and sexual abuse were in fact more likely than physical abuse to lead to violence. Yet if transmission of social norms accounts for violence, physical abuse should create more. The reanalysis of these data suggest that one ought to search for a common cause, for something shared by neglect and abuse that might lead to violence.

In sum, violence seems to beget violence, but studies of child abuse and of family socialization undermine the argument that violence begets violence *through acceptance of family (subcultural) norms of violence*. Because neglect, rejection, and physical abuse result in similarly high rates of crime, it seems appropriate to search for a cause in terms of what they have in common.

A sound understanding of the way children learn can explain why physical abuse, neglect, and rejection lead to antisocial behavior. Below I develop such an understanding to show that a norm of self-interest, rather than a norm of violence, underlies the education shared by those who are rejected, neglected, and abused. It is the norm of self-interest that leads to violence in some circumstances.

UNDERMINING SOME ASSUMPTIONS

Side stepping the issue of how infants learn, many psychologists have simply assumed that babies are completely self-centered. In contrast, the evidence shows that how much children care about their own pleasures and pains and what they will consider pleasurable and painful is largely a function of the way are taught.

It may, for instance, be tempting to believe that an infant "instinctively" cries for food, to be held, or to have dirty diapers removed, but evidence points to large contributions from experience. In a study of neonates, Thoman, Korner, and Benson-Williams (1977) randomly assigned primiparous healthy newborns to conditions in which one third were held when they awakened. As anticipated by the authors, the babies who were held spent more time with their eyes open and cried less vigorously while being held; unexpectedly, however, they spent more time crying during non-stimulus periods. The babies had been equated for pretrial behaviors, so the authors suggest that the infants had come to associate their crying with being picked up during the 48 hour training period.

In another study also showing that neonates learn from their environments, Riese (1990) compared 47 pairs of monozygotic twins, 39 pairs of dizygotic twins of the same sex, and 72 pairs of dizygotic twins of the opposite sex. Using standardized tests for irritability, resistance to soothing, activity level when awake, activity level when asleep, reactivity to a cold disk on the thigh and to a pin prick, and response to cuddling, she found significant correlations for the dizygotic twins (both same and opposite sex), indicating shared environmental influences, but no significantly larger correlations among the monozygotic pairs. Riese concluded that "environment appears to account for most of the known variance for the neonatal temperament variables" (1236).

Just as neonates can learn to cry in order to be picked up, children learn what to consider painful. Variability in recognizing sensations as painful has been dramatically evidenced through studies of institutionalized infants, who received serious injuries without seeming to notice (Goldfarb 1958). During the period of observation, one child caught her hand in the door, injuring a finger so severely that it turned blue; yet the child did not cry or otherwise indicate pain. Another child sat on a radiator too hot for the teacher to touch. Observed injuries also included a child who was cutting the palm of his own hand with sharp

scissors and another who had removed from her cornea a steel splinter that had been imbedded for two days without any report of pain. All the children, however, gave pain responses to a pin prick, dispelling the hypotheses that they had a higher than normal threshold for pain. Goldfarb reasonably concluded: "The perception of pain and the reaction to pain-arousing stimuli are episodes far more complex than is implied in the concept of pure, unencumbered sensation" (1945: 780–781).

Often, children show no signs of pain after a fall until adults show that they expect a "pained" response. Studies with college students that feeling pain is influenced by pain exhibited by models (Craig and Theiss 1971), role playing as calm or upset (Kopel and Arkowitz 1974), and feedback from one's own responsive behavior (Bandler, Madaras, and Bem 1968). My personal experience and reports from students suggest that children whose mothers do not respond to their cuts with anxious concern do not exhibit such pain-behavior as crying when they fall.

Not only do children learn what is painful, but they attach pleasure to circumstances intended to result in pain. Solomon (1980) demonstrated that over a range of behaviors, pain-giving consequences acquire positive value through repetition (see Shipley 1987; Aronson, Carlsmith, and Darley 1963; Walster, Aronson, and Brown 1966). Studies showing that children learn to repeat behaviors that result in "reinforcement" through negative attention demonstrate that expectations are only one basis for the attraction of "pain-giving" stimuli (Gallimore, Tharp, and Kemp 1969; Witte and Grossman 1971).

Children also learn without extrinsic reinforcement. Curious about why so many young children appeared to increase their aggressiveness in experimental situations, Siegel and Kohn (1959) measured aggression both with and without an adult in the room. Only when adults were present did escalation occur. The authors drew the sensible conclusion that young children assume that what is not forbidden is permitted.

The egocentric motivational assumption that underlies classic theories of socialization has been subjected to a series of criticism, most notably by Butler (1726) and Hume (1960 [1777]). These authors pointed out that the plausibility of the egocentric assumption rests on circular reasoning. The fact that a voluntary action must be motivated is confused with an assumption that voluntary actions must be motivated by desire to benefit from them. Often the only evidence for self-interest is the occurrence of the act for which a motive is being sought.

Raising further questions about the assumption of egocentrism in children, some studies indicate that altruistic behavior is not always egoistic behavior in disguise (Batson et al. 1988; Grusec and Skubiski 1970). In fact, altruistic behavior turns up at very young ages (Rheingold and Emery 1986; Zahn-Waxler and Radke-Yarrow 1982; Zahn-Waxler et al. 1988) suggesting that even babies are not exclusively interested in themselves.

The prevalent view that children require punishment in order to learn socialized behavior rests on three erroneous assumptions. The first two—that children are motivated by self-interest and that what gives them pain is "fixed"—have been shown to lack support in empirical research. The third—that unless there are punishments rules have no power—

is addressed in my proposal of Construct Theory.

AN ALTERNATIVE: CONSTRUCT THEORY

Construct Theory states that children learn what to do and what to believe in the process of learning how to use language. In simplest form, Construct Theory claims that children learn by constructing categories organized by the structure of the language in their culture. These categories can be identified by descriptions, much as one might identify a file, for example, "accounting," "things to do," "birthdays," "Parsons, T.," "true." Some categories are collections of objects, but others are actions that can be identified by such descriptions as "to be done" or "to be believed" or "to be doubted."

Learning a language requires learning more than concepts. Children learn not only what to count as tables and chairs, cars and trucks, but also what to count as painful or pleasant, undesirable or desirable, and worth avoiding or pursuing. In learning labels, in learning how to name and to re-identify objects, children are constructing classifications. The classification systems they develop will permeate what they notice and how they act as well as what they say.

Construct Theory explains the fact that different people consider similar events to have different affective characteristics —for example, as undesirable and desirable—because individuals construct different classifications of the events. This theory can account for relations between knowledge and action that have led many theorists to conjure "pro-attitudes" as the means by which some knowledge sometimes changes behavior (e.g.,

Kenny 1963; Milligan 1980; Müller 1979; Nowell-Smith 1954). According to Construct Theory, those reasons that move one to action are classified as "reasons worth acting upon"; no special entity need also be attached to them.[1] Construct Theory also explains how language can be learned and how people can communicate, for it shows the way in which meanings can be made public through the categories that are constructed.[2]

Learning a language involves learning to formulate sentences as well as learning how to use words. At its most fundamental level, sentences involve stringing together what logicians call "predicates" (which can be thought of as classes) and functional relations among them. Perhaps no component of a sentence is so critical to understanding how punishment works as the connective "if... then," for on this connective punishments rely. This connective also gives linguistic expression to what the neonates described above learned when they cried and were picked up (if I cry, then I will be picked up), what an infant learns by pushing a ball (if I push, then it will roll), and what the child learns when discovering natural consequences in the physical world.

Both natural and artificial contingencies provide information to the child who is learning about consequences. When a child is credibly threatened with punishment, the information conveyed extends beyond the intended message that the child ought not do something. A punishment is designed to give pain. Unless the chosen event is thought by the punisher to be painful, it would not be selected as a means for controlling the child's behavior. What is selected as a punishment, then, shows what the punisher thinks to be painful.[3]

A child also perceives the intention of the punisher to give pain (and may attempt to thwart the intention by saying such things as "I didn't like the dessert anyway" or "There's nothing good on TV anyhow"). So the use of punishment shows the child that the punisher is willing to hurt the threatened or punished child. This knowledge may decrease the child's desire to be with the punisher or to care how the punisher feels, thereby reducing the socializing agent's influence.

An interesting study illustrated another feature of punishment: it conveys information about what (according to the punisher) is valuable, thus potentially enhancing the value of the forbidden. Aronson and Carlsmith (1963) asked preschool children, individually, to compare five toys until they established stable transitive preferences. The experimenter then said he had to leave the room for a few minutes and placed on a table the toy ranked second-favorite by the child. The child was told not to play with that toy but that playing with the others was permissible. Half of the 44 children were randomly assigned to each of two conditions. In the "mild threat" condition, the experimenter said he would be annoyed if the child played with the forbidden toy. In the "severe threat" condition, the experimenter said that if the child played with the forbidden toy, the experimenter would be very angry and would take all the toys and never come back. The experimenter left the child for 10 minutes. Approximately 45 days later, the children were again asked to rank the five toys. For this ranking, 4 of the children from the mild threat condition ranked the forbidden toy as a favorite whereas 14 of those in the severe threat condition regarded the forbidden toy as the favorite. Conversely, 8 of those who were merely told that the experimenter would be annoyed had decreased their preference for the forbidden toy whereas none of the children who were threatened with punishment had they played with the toy decreased their preference for it.

In a near replication, Lepper (1973) found that, two weeks later, children from his stronger threat condition were more likely to cheat in a game. There are two explanations for this. Lepper explained the findings by suggesting that the children who resisted with severe threat reasoned: "I am the sort of person who would break the rules except for the fact that I would be punished." In contrast, according to this self-referential theory, the children under mild threat defined themselves as the sorts of people who generally conform to rules and requests.

I suggest an alternative explanation: The different exposures in the experiment taught the children something about the world and about other people—not primarily something about themselves. The more severe threats taught the children that they ought to orient their behavior around estimates of consequences *to themselves*. In the process of assessing their self-interests, the children looked for attractive features of that which had been forbidden. The "mild threat" condition in both experiments, however, implied only that the child should be concerned about how the experimenter might feel.

Punishments are invoked only when rules are disobeyed, so that telling a child about rules in conjunction with information about punishments for infractions informs a child that he or she has a choice: obey, or disobey-and-accept-the-consequences named as punishment.

Negative correlations between a parent's use of punishments and insistence that rules be followed were so strong in their study of misbehavior that Patterson, Dishion, and Bank (1984) could not use both measures in their model. Believing that punishments were more important, they dropped the follow-through measure. The data, however, show equally that a parent who insists that rules be followed need not use punishments to socialize children.

It might be tempting to argue that rewards circumvent the unwanted effects of punishment as a means for teaching norms. That would be a mistake. Although using rewards does not hazard rejection of the purveyor, rewarding shares many of the characteristics of punishing. Rewards as well as punishments employ the "if... then" relationship. Laboratory studies have demonstrated, as predicted from the Construct Theory, that contingent reinforcements sometimes interfere with the discovery of general rules (Schwartz 1982). Studies have demonstrated, also as predicted from Construct Theory, that incentives larger than necessary to produce an activity sometimes result in devaluation of the activity being rewarded (Greene and Lepper 1974; Lepper, Greene, and Nisbett 1973; Lepper et al. 1982; Ross 1975; Ross, Karniol, and Rothstein 1976).

Like those involved in punishments, contingencies that use rewards convey more information than intended when a socializing agent uses them to convince a child to do something. A reward is designed to be attractive, so rewards contain information about what the rewarder believes to be valuable. When a reward is clearly a benefit to the person being promised the reward, rewarding teaches the child to value his or her own benefit.[4]

In addition to learning that whatever requires reward is probably considered unpleasant, children. learn that the reward is something considered valuable by the reward-giver. That children *learn* to perceive rewards as valuable has been demonstrated in the laboratory (Lepper et al. 1982). Children were told a story about a mother giving her child two supposed foods; children in the study were asked which the child in the story would prefer: "hupe" or "hule." Children in the experimental group were told that the mother explained to her child that (s)he could have one ("hupe" or "hule" for different children) if (s)he ate the other. In this condition, the contingent relation led the children to suppose that the second food was a reward for eating the first. The children overwhelmingly thought the second food would be preferred—and gave grounds for the choice in terms of its tasting better. The experiment showed that the continguent relation, rather than the order of presentation, influenced preference because children in the control condition who were told only that the child's mother gave the child first one and then the other food either refused to make a choice or gave no reason for a selection (which they equally distributed between the two). In other experiments with preschool children, play objects have been manipulated similarly, showing that an activity that is arbitrarily selected as the one to be rewarded will be "discounted" whereas the arbitrarily selected inducement gains value (e.g., Lepper et al. 1982; Boggiano and Main 1986). These studies show that children learn what to value as well as how to act from perceiving the ways in which rewards are used.[5]

The Construct Theory explains why punishments tend to increase the attraction of activities punished—and why extrinsic rewards tend to reduce the value of activities rewarded. The categorizing that children learn as they learn sentences in a language can be schematically represented by formal logic. When children become aware of the logical equivalence between the conditional (if x then y) and the disjuctive (either not-x or y), they learn that *rewards and punishments weaken the force of a rule by introducing choices.* If rewards are designed to give pleasure to the child and punishments are designed to give the child pain, then their use teaches children that they ought to value their own pleasure and to attempt to reduce their own pain.

CONCLUSION

Rewards and punishments are used to manipulate others. They often result in short-term gains, but their use teaches children to look for personal benefits. Like rewards and punishments, neglect and rejection teach egocentrism. Children brought up among adults who do not attend to their well-being are given no grounds for learning to consider the welfare of others.

Using punishment seems particularly short-sighted. Punishments may increase the attraction of forbidden acts. They also risk desensitizing children both to their own pains and to the pains of others (Cline, Croft, and Courrier 1973; Pearl 1987; Thomas et al. 1977). Although severe penalties may force compliance in specific instances, the behavior being punished is actually more likely to occur at a time or place when opportunities for detection are reduced (Bandura and Walters 1959).

No increase in punishment or in reward can guarantee that children will make the choices adults wish them to make. Several studies show, however, that children are more likely to want to do what an adult wishes if the adult generally does as the child desires. In one study, randomly selected mothers of preschoolers were trained to respond to their children's requests and to avoid directing them during a specified period of time each day for one week. Their children complied with more of the mother's standardized requests in the laboratory than the comparison group of children whose mothers used contingency training (Papal and Maccoby 1985). The results are mirrored in a natural setting with the discovery that children reared at pre-school age in a consensual environment were among the most likely to value autonomy, intellectual activity, and independence as well as to have high educational aspirations ten years later (Harrington, Block, and Block 1987).

In another study, mothers and children were observed at home for three months when the children were between 9 and 12 months in age. Mothers were rated for their sensitivity to their babies, a rating based on their perceived ability to see things from the baby's perspective, positive feelings expressed toward the baby, and adaptations favoring the baby's arrangements of his or her own behavior. Discipline was rated for verbal commands as well as for frequency of any physical interventions. The baby's compliance was a simple measure of the proportion of verbal commands the baby obeyed without further action by the mother. Compliance turned out to be practically unrelated to discipline, although it was strongly related to the mother's responsiveness. The authors note: "The findings suggest that a disposition toward obedience emerges in a responsive, accommodating social environment without extensive training, discipline or other massive attempts to shape the infant's course of development" (Stayton, Hogan, and Ainsworth 1971:1065).

Punishments—nonphysical as well as physical—teach children to focus on their own pains and pleasures in deciding how to act. If parents and teachers were to substitute non-physical punishments for physical ones, they might avoid teaching children to hit, punch, and kick; yet, they would nevertheless perpetuate the idea that giving pain is a legitimate way to exercise power. If the substitute for physical punishment were to be non-physical punishments, the consequences could be no less undermining of compassion and social interests.

Children do not require punishments if their teachers will guide them consistently, and they do not require rewards if intrinsic values of what they ought to do are made apparent to them. I am not suggesting that a child will be constantly obedient or agree completely with the values of those who do not punish. No techniques will guarantee a clone. Rather, I do suggest that children can be taught to follow reasonable rules and to be considerate—and that the probabilities for their learning these things are directly related to the use of reason in teaching them and to the consideration they see in their surroundings.

Straus turns a spotlight on physical punishment, suggesting that by using violence to educate, adults legitimize the use of violence. I paint a broader canvas, suggesting that by using rewards and punishments to educate, adults establish self-interest as the legitimate grounds for choice.

NOTES

1. This interpretation of language provides a modification of the Aristotelian notion that action is the conclusion of a practical syllogism; it adds a proviso that the syllogism must correctly represent the classification system of the actor, and then "straightway action follows." The interpretation also reflects the Humean claim that reason alone cannot account for action. It does so by including motivational classifications as separate from purely descriptive classifications.

2. Wittgenstein (1958) demonstrated the implausibility of accounting for language through private identification of meanings.

3. Thus, there is the irony that when teachers use school work, parents use performing chores, and both use being by oneself as punishments, they are likely to create distaste for learning, doing chores, and being alone.

4. One could, of course, reward a child by permitting some action beneficial to others or by permitting the child a new challenge.

5. The phenomenon is well enough known to have produced several theories, ranging from balance theory (Heider 1946) and Theory of Cognitive Dissonance (Festinger 1957) to Psycholoical Reactance (Brehm 1966; Brehm and Brehm 1981). None to my knowledge has tied the phenomenon with language.

REFERENCES

Aronson, Elliot, and J. Merrill Carlsmith 1963 "Effect of the severity of threat on the devaluation of forbidden behavior." Journal of Abnormal and Social Psychology 66:584–588.

Aronson, Elliot, J. Merrill Carlsmith, and John M. Darley 1963 "The effects of expectancy on volunteering for an unpleasant experience." Journal of Abnormal and Social Psychology 6:220–224.

Austin, Roy L. 1978 "Race, father-absence, and female delinquency." Criminology 15:487–504.

Bandler, Richard J., George R. Madaras, and Daryl J. Bem 1968 "Self-observation as a source of pain perception." Journal of Personality and Social Psychology 9:205–209.

Bandura, Albert and Aletha C. Huston 1961 "Identification as a process of incidental learning." Journal of Abnormal and Social Psychology 63:311–318.

Bandura, Albert and Richard H. Walters 1959 Adolescent Aggression. New York: Ronald. 1963 Social Learning and Personality Development. New York: Holt, Rinehart, and Winston.

Batson, C. Daniel, Janine L. Dyck, J. Randall Brandt, Judy G. Batson, Anne L. Powell, M. Rosalie McMaster, and Cari Griffitt 1988 "Five studies testing two new egoistic alternatives to the empathy-altruism hypothesis." Journal of Personality and Social Psychology 55:52–77.

Baumrind, Diana 1978 "Parental disciplinary patterns and social competence in children." Youth and Society 9:239–276.

Bender, Loretta 1947 "Psychopathic behavior disorders in children." In Handbook of Correctional Psychology, ed. R. Lindner and R. Seliger, 360–377. New York: Philosophical Library.

Boggiano, Ann K., and Deborah S. Main 1986 "Enhancing children's interest in activities used as rewards: The bonus effect." Journal of Personality and Social Psychology 31:1116–1126.

Bowlby, John 1940 "The influence of early environment on neurosis and neurotic character." International Journal of Psychoanalysis 21:154–178.

Brehm, Jack W. 1940 A Theory of Psychological Reactance. New York: Academic Press.

CHALLENGE QUESTIONS

Do Physically Punished Children Become Violent Adults?

1. How would you manage your own children's behavior? Would you use punishment, rewards, or neither? Why?

2. Why do you think parents elect to use physical punishment in their child-rearing practices?

3. What other research in developmental psychology is relevant to this issue? Cite the research and describe how it pertains to the issue.

4. McCord argues that the people who only (or primarily) care for themselves are more prone to violence. How would McCord advocate that parents raise their children?

5. How would you characterize McCord's main criticism of Straus's Cultural Spillover Theory? How does McCord's own theory account for her criticism of Straus's theory?

ISSUE 8

Is Yo-Yo Dieting Dangerous?

YES: Frances M. Berg, from *Health Risks of Weight Loss*, 3rd ed. (*Healthy Weight Journal*, 1995)

NO: National Task Force on the Prevention and Treatment of Obesity, from "Weight Cycling," *Journal of the American Medical Association* (October 19, 1994)

ISSUE SUMMARY

YES: Nutritionist Frances M. Berg contends that yo-yo dieting, or weight cycling, is associated with an elevated risk of physical and mental health problems and that it increases the risk of regaining lost weight.

NO: The National Task Force on the Prevention and Treatment of Obesity maintains that there is no convincing evidence that weight cycling has any major effects on heart disease risk, the effectiveness of future diets, increased percentage of body fat, or metabolism.

Dieting has become a way of life for many people; close to 50 million Americans are currently dieting. But most will not lose as much weight as they want, and most will not keep off the weight they have lost. So why are so many Americans dieting?

Obesity has become widespread in the United States: 30 percent of the population is considered obese, up from 25 percent 10 years ago. Obesity has been linked with increased risks for certain diseases, including diabetes, heart disease, and some cancers. In addition, there are social and economic implications related to obesity. Many contend that overweight people are less likely to marry, earn less money, and are less likely to be accepted to elite colleges. As a result, more and more people are dieting.

It has been shown that most diets fail. Often, after lost weight is regained, dieters start over again and end up caught in a repeated lose/gain cycle known as "yo-yo dieting" or "weight cycling." Yo-yo dieting is considered by experts to be more dangerous than actually being overweight, and many urge overweight individuals to stop dieting and accept themselves as they are. Some theories as to why yo-yo dieting may be unsafe are that yo-yo dieting lowers metabolic rate, or the rate at which calories are burned; that yo-yo dieting increases the percentage of stored fat and reduces lean muscle tissue; that a lowered metabolic rate and an increase in fat stores can make subsequent dieting more difficult; and that yo-yo dieting may increase one's desire for fatty foods.

Frequent dieting has also been linked with psychological concerns. Some studies have reported a lower level of life satisfaction among weight cyclers. There is also some evidence that frequent dieting may predispose an individual to disordered eating, including binge eating, or compulsive overeating. Research also indicates that among all dieters, both obese and of normal weight, anxiety, depression, and stress are associated with the up-and-down weight cycling that accompanies frequent dieting. These studies conclude that those who maintain a stable weight are better off psychologically, regardless of what they weigh.

Researchers have discerned a relationship between yo-yo dieting and an increased risk of heart disease based on findings from the Framingham Heart Study, a 30-year analysis of weight fluctuations in over 3,000 adults. The study indicated that weight gain or loss in a short period of time increases the risk of a person's dying from heart disease.

Since evidence suggests that most diets fail and that many actually increase the risk of subsequent failure in dieting, is it safer to remain overweight than to try to lose weight? Recent research shows that it *is* more dangerous to remain overweight than to try to lose extra pounds. On the other hand, there is no evidence that *all* diets fail. Some people do lose and maintain weight, although the numbers and dieting methods are unclear. There are also important medical benefits associated with even modest weight loss, including improvements in blood pressure, blood fats (cholesterol), and blood sugar control.

In the following selections, Frances M. Berg asserts that dieting, especially yo-yo dieting, is more dangerous than being overweight. She maintains that people with a history of weight cycling have shown increased stress levels—even those who gained and lost as little as five pounds. The National Task Force on the Prevention and Treatment of Obesity argues that among obese individuals, the benefits of even moderate weight loss are significantly greater than any risks associated with dieting.

YES

Frances M. Berg

WEIGHT CYCLING

The possible risks of repeated bouts of losing and regaining weight, called weight cycling or yo-yo dieting, have gained wide attention in the public press. And for good reason: if weight cycling is harmful and is the almost inevitable result of weight loss, then perhaps weight loss itself is harmful and weight loss an inappropriate goal even for large patients, placing more importance on prevention.

This possibility has major implications for the $30 to $50 billion weight loss industry and for the focus of health care in the United States.

Weight cycling has been under intense investigation at several institutions in the U.S. and other countries since 1986, following studies that suggested losing weight on a very low calorie diet and regaining that weight made subsequent weight loss more difficult.

However, research has shown inconsistent results on several issues. This has led some researchers to conclude weight cycling is not important. Others believe the variables have not yet been found which affect weight cycling changes—perhaps certain subgroups are more likely to be affected, or individuals are more vulnerable at times in their lives, such as during pregnancy.

The Diet and Health report of the National Academy of Sciences notes the possible detrimental effects of weight cycling. Similarly, the Surgeon General's Report on Nutrition and Health recommends that "the health consequences of repeated cycles of weight loss and gain" be given "special priority," and a poll of obesity experts lists weight cycling as one of the key causes of obesity.

There is little doubt that weight cycling is extremely prevalent in the U.S. Sixty to 80 million people are trying to lose weight, and most of those who lose weight apparently regain it fairly quickly.

In a review of weight cycling research, Kelly Brownell and Judith Rodin cite a six-year study which tracked the weight of 153 middle-aged adults and found the women lost an average of 27 pounds and gained 31 pounds during the six years. The men lost and gained an average of more than 22 pounds. For the women, this was a gain of 21 percent of their initial body weight, and a loss of 19 percent. For the men it was about 12 percent lost and gained.

Another study tracked 332 overweight persons and found the vast majority either lost or gained significant amounts of weight.

Weight cycling research focuses on two major issues:

1. Is weight cycling associated with increased risk to physical or mental health?
2. Does weight cycling make weight management more difficult by invoking survival mechanisms?

Major concerns have been raised that cycles of weight variability increase risk factors and the risk of mortality, especially cardiovascular deaths. Other concerns are that weight cycling may lower metabolic rate, decrease the ability to lose weight, increase the body's fat-to-lean ratio and waist-hip ratio, and increase the appetite for dietary fat.

CYCLING MAY THREATEN HEART

Research consistently shows an increase in mortality from all causes and from coronary heart disease with weight cycling.

Weight cycling is associated with greater risks for coronary heart disease and other severe health problems in a major study published recently in the *New England Journal of Medicine* by L. Lissner and colleagues.

The findings are based on a 32-year analysis of weight fluctuations in 3,130 men and women in the Framingham Heart Study.

Individuals with a high weight variability—many weight changes or large changes—were 25 to 100 percent more likely to be victims of heart disease and premature death than those whose weight remained stable. They had increased total mortality, and increased mortality and morbidity due to coronary heart disease.

The relative risk for a high degree of weight variability compared with 1.0 for a low degree of variability is as follows:

Men

Total mortality 1.30

Mortality due to CHD 1.48

Morbidity due to CHD 1.48

Morbidity due to cancer 1.04

Women

Total mortality 1.27

Mortality due to CHD 1.47

Morbidity due to CHD 1.42

Morbidity due to cancer 1.16

These results seemed to hold true regardless of the individual's initial weight, long-term weight trend and/or cardiovascular risk factors such as blood pressure, cholesterol level, glucose tolerance, smoking and physical activity.

Even though nearly 50 percent of women who diet are not overweight, the researchers note, the weight cycling risks are seen at all weight categories, whether thin or obese.

The degree of weight variability was evaluated in relation to total mortality, mortality from coronary heart disease, morbidity due to coronary heart disease and morbidity due to cancer. Risks were considerably increased for all except cancer, which did not differ significantly.

When age groups were considered separately, weight fluctuation was most strongly associated with adverse health outcomes in the youngest group (age 30 to 40). This is also the group seen as most likely to diet.

The researchers found that a person's weight at age 25 makes an important contribution to whether there will be great variability.

Both men and women gained weight at an average rate of .11 kg per square meter per year.

Researchers from Goteborg, Sweden, and Boston University are involved in the current study. They cite their research in Sweden which found large fluctuations in body weight, measured at three intervals, was associated with heart disease in men and total mortality in both men and women.

In an effort to control for weight changes that may have been caused by illness, diseases and deaths for the first four years were excluded. This study does not distinguish between several weight changes and a single large weight change.

The researchers say weight cycling may account for the observed increase in deaths in these ways:

1. Factors that influence coronary risk (such as cholesterol levels) may change with fluctuating weight and end up worse than before.
2. The amount and distribution of body fat as weight is lost and regained may change. During weight loss, a person loses both fat and lean body mass, but may regain mostly fat. This fat tends to settle in the abdomen, a location linked to increased heart disease risk.
3. People may increasingly prefer high-fat diets when they lose and re-gain weight. Studies have shown that weight-cycling laboratory animals tend to eat more fat.

In view of their findings, they suggest it may be important to look at public health implications of current weight loss practices. They note that about half of American women and one-fourth of men are dieting at any one time, with many of these efforts unsuccessful. Weight is commonly regained and the cycle repeated.

Kelly Brownell, PhD, a psychologist and weight specialist at Yale University involved in the study, says the harmful effects of weight cycling may be equal to the risks of remaining obese.

"The pressure in this society to be thin at all costs may be exacting a serious toll," Brownell says. The study's findings indicate that weight cycling is "potentially a very serious public health issue" because it affects such large numbers of people.

"It may be equally bad to lose the same five pounds 10 times as to lose 50 pounds and regain it once," he said.

The relative risk of increased risk with weight fluctuation is in the range of 1.25 to 2.00, which is similar to the risk attributed to obesity and to several of the cardiovascular risk factors, say Brownell and Rodin. Thus, determining weight cycling effects is an important question.

HARVARD ALUMS RISK DISEASE BY "ALWAYS" DIETING

Men risk heart disease, hypertension and diabetes by 'always' dieting, regardless of their weight, according to the Harvard Alumni studies reported by Steven N. Blair, an epidemiologist at the Cooper Institute for Aerobics Research in Dallas.

"One of the fundamental tenets of the weight loss industry is if you get people to eat less, they'll lose weight. And if they lose weight, they'll be better off. And there is no evidence to support either one," Blair said at the American Heart Association's annual epidemiology meeting in March 1994.

Earlier, Blair reported higher mortality with weight loss among the Harvard alumni. His latest report investigates non-fatal disease in 12,025 men, average age 67. The men who said they were always dieting had a heart disease rate of 23.2 percent, compared to 10.6 for those who "never" dieted. Their rates for hypertension were 38.3 percent, compared with 23.4 percent for the group who never dieted, and for diabetes 14.6 percent, compared with 3 percent.

Among men who dieted part of the time—"often," "sometimes," or "rarely"—the more they dieted, the higher their rates of disease. These findings held true even among the leanest group of men, and were basically unchanged by weight gain, physical activity, smoking or alcohol intake.

In addition to reporting dieting frequency, the men identified their shape variation at six points through life, total pounds lost, and the number of times they had lost 5, 10, 20 and 30 or more pounds.

In view of his findings, Blair advises people to keep a stable weight and avoid either weight gain or weight loss.

BONE LOSS WITH WEIGHT LOSS

Several studies of large population bases show higher mortality rates with weight loss, causing researchers to puzzle over the possible mechanisms whereby weight loss could cause long-term harm, even though it seems beneficial in reducing obesity-related risk factors in short-term studies.

One possible mechanism may be the bone mineral loss which accompanies weight loss. Weight cycling may increase this loss.

Mineral content in women's bones diminishes with weight loss, even when adequate nutrition and aerobic exercise are present. These findings from the USDA Human Research Center in Grand Forks, N.D., support clues which may explain recent findings in federal studies of potentially higher mortality with weight loss. The Grand Forks Center tested 14 women, age 21–38, in a five-month residential program using dual energy x-ray absorptiometry (DXA) to assess bone mineral status and soft tissue composition. The women lost 8.1 kg on a moderate nutrient-adequate diet with an aerobic exercise program. Both bone mineral content and bone mineral density decreased (36 g and .01 g/cm2 respectively).

Similar results were found at the Osteoporosis Research Centre in Copenhagen, Denmark. Using the DXA method, the study reports 51 obese patients averaged a 5.9 percent loss of total body bone mineral/TBBM during 15 weeks. One patient, who lost 45 kg, lost 754 g bone mineral in nine months. Greater mineral loss was reported in legs than arms. Postmenopausal women who did not get estrogen replacement tended to lose more bone mineral. Bone mineral loss correlated with body fat loss, not with fat-free mass loss, so that as more fat was lost, more mineral was lost as well.

When patients maintained their weight loss, they lost no more bone. If they regained, bone was regained as well. The Danish researchers concluded this level of bone loss was normal for weight loss in obese persons. They suggest an initiating factor in bone loss may be having less weight bearing on the bones.

WEIGHT CYCLING DROPS METABOLISM FOR WRESTLERS

Weight cycling is practiced with single-minded dedication by many high school and college athletes in the sport of wrestling.

Not only must the elite wrestler be talented, fit and superbly trained, but usually he is also actively engaged in weight reduction, even in the lower weight classes of 103 and 112 pounds.

The weight-cycling wrestler commonly loses 10 or more pounds in a few days to make weigh-ins for a match or tournament. He regains this weight quickly, and repeats the cycle many times throughout the wrestling season. Severe water deprivation and dehydration are often a part of his fasting episodes.

Long term effects of such strenuous weight loss efforts on the young wrestler are unknown.

Cold intolerance, weakness, and inability to concentrate are frequently reported. Other reported effects include changes in electrolyte balance, testosterone levels, nutritional status, renal function, thermal regulation, body composition and strength.

Growth and development may be delayed during one of the most active growth periods of a young man's life. The possibility of developing long-lasting eating disorders has been suggested.

FOOD EFFICIENCY

Metabolic effects of this severe weight cycling may cause an increase in food efficiency, and make losing more difficult.

Recent research with high school wrestlers on loss-and-gain cycles gives evidence of a lowered metabolism, as reported in the *Journal of the American Medical Association.*

The wrestlers were attending summer camp at the University of Iowa. It was several months after their last competitive match, and their weight had returned to normal.

The group of 27 wrestlers who cycled their weight were found to have significantly lower resting metabolic rate per unit of lean body mass than those defined as noncyclers.

Weight cyclers were defined as those who:

1. Cut weight 10 or more times during wrestling season.
2. Lost 4.5 kg or more weekly.
3. Reported they cut weight often or always.

(box continued on next page)

Noncyclers

1. Cut weight less than 5 times during the season.
2. Lost no more than 1.4 kg weekly.
3. Reported they cut weight sometimes, rarely or never.

Noncyclers were matched for age, weight, height, surface area, lean body mass, and percent body fat.

The cyclers competed farther below their natural off-season weight than did the noncyclers.

Results showed a significant difference in resting metabolic rate between the cyclers and noncyclers. The difference in resting energy expenditure was 14 percent. Oxygen consumption differed significantly. No differences were shown in respiratory quotient, oral temperature, pulse or blood pressure.

STUDIES NEEDED

The researchers suggest weight cycling was a likely cause of lower metabolic rates, although they grant it is possible that low metabolism came first and even made the severe cycling necessary, as wrestlers with low energy requirements could have had more difficulty controlling weight. They recommended longitudinal studies be conducted to assess any health changes resulting from weight restriction and fluctuation.

Although the body fat for both groups of wrestlers in this study is similar, an increase of fat over lean has been noted during fast weight regain, and a redistribution of fat is suggested as possible. Research is cited that shows increased preference for fat in the diet among weight cycling female rats.

The researchers speculate there may be psychological implications of repeated weight cycling, including frustration over the increasing difficulty in losing weight, which could lead to unhealthy methods of weight loss.

The high school or college wrestler differs from the typical weight cycler in the general population in that he is young, male, physically active, well-muscled, with low body fat. His diet and binge cycle is relatively short, usually lasting about three months a year for perhaps three to six years.

Psychologically, as a successful athlete, he is likely to have high self-esteem and strong social support.

Strong statements against excessive weight loss and the fluid and food deprivation practices often used by wrestlers have been issued by the American College of Sports Medicine and the American Medical Association.

Hank Lukaski, director of the Grand Forks Center, says people have the potential to regain some bone loss when they regain weight. But it is unknown whether bone mineral content and bone density are fully or only partially restored, or whether bone quality is as good as before, or how essential trace elements are affected. Further, the effect on bone quality of repeated bouts of weight loss and regain are unknown, Lukaski says.

WEIGHT CYCLING INCREASES STRESS

People with a history of weight cycling showed greater pathologic characteristics than those with stable weights, independent of weight, in recent research by John Foreyt, PhD, of Baylor College of Medicine, Houston, TX, and colleagues at Yale and the University of Nevada. The researchers suggest that weight cycling may be causal to the mental distress and pathology they found.

Men and women whose weight fluctuated up or down, as little as five pounds in a year, reported lower feelings of well-being, more out-of-control eating, and higher stress levels than people whose weight was stable in this study. And this was true regardless of their body weight.

The researchers say they did not expect such a large number of significant findings with the tight five-pound categories: "Psychologically, such small shifts in weight in both normal weight and obese individuals may be very important."

In obese women, weight maintenance was associated with fewer significant negative life stressors.

Weight fluctuation was strongly associated with negative psychological effects in both normal weight and obese individuals. Weight change and obesity were also associated with a poorer psychological score.

The researchers studied 497 adults, stratified into five age groups, 25 normal weight and 25 obese in each age and sex category.

The subjects were assessed twice with the Brownell Weight Cycling Questionnaire, which measures current dieting, weight satisfaction, abnormal eating patterns and body image. They reported on health, weight fluctuation, feelings of well-being and depression, stressful life events, and eating self-efficacy (ability to control urges to overeat in high-risk situations). Their weight was assessed over one year to classify them, through a weight change of 5 pounds or more, as maintainers, gainers or losers.

The researchers suggest that attempts at weight loss may be stressful for various reasons, including the self-denial required, the disruption of routine, and a concern about failure. Repeated failures to control weight may reduce one's feeling of self-efficacy, and add to feelings of depression.

"Once inappropriate dieting is initiated, regardless of body weight, fluctuations and increasing obesity may follow," says their report. They cite research that shows that among obese individuals, more than half fluctuate up or down 12 pounds over intervals of 1 to 5 years.

While the researchers suggest that weight change likely causes these adverse effects, they grant the reverse is possible—psychological distress may cause weight change. They recommend further research on assessing and treating weight fluctuation for individuals of all weights.

Weight cycling appears consistently linked to increased psychopathology, lower life satisfaction, more disturbed eating in general, and perhaps increased risk for binge eating in the research, Brownell and Rodin report.

They cite research by Everson and Matthews that found lower levels of life satisfaction related to increased weight cycling in women, but not men. A study of a large sample of runners found weight cycling associated with higher levels of disturbed eating practices. Other studies show repeated or chronic dieting may predispose an individual to disordered eating, including binge eating. One study showed restrained eating (dieting) to be a stronger predictor of weight fluctuation than body weight itself.

FINDINGS STIR CONTROVERSY

The recent findings are likely to be controversial and to further fuel the weight cycling debate among scientists, says Claude Bouchard, PhD, of Laval University, Quebec, in an editorial in the same issue of the *New England Journal of Medicine* as the Lissner study.

Bouchard notes that a recent review of 18 studies of weight cycling in rodents, by Hill and Reed, found no clear evidence that weight cycling makes future weight loss harder and weight gain easier.

They found no evidence that weight cycling increases total body fat or central adiposity, increases subsequent caloric intake, increases food efficiency, decreases energy expenditure, or increases blood pressure, insulin resistance, or cholesterol levels. However, Bouchard suggests there may be a preference for dietary fat in refeeding and that the observed risks could result from higher fat intake.

Rat studies may not provide the weight cycling information needed for humans and, given that human studies are difficult to design, this may be why weight cycling studies give such confusing and conflicting results, says Carolyn Berdanier, PhD, a researcher at the University of Georgia.

Berdanier says rats and mice differ from humans in several important ways. Most critically to weight cycling research, they continue to grow in length throughout their lives. This growth is expensive in calories, and affects the degree of body fat storage, keeping them leaner.

NO

National Task Force on the
Prevention and Treatment
of Obesity

WEIGHT CYCLING

Weight cycling refers to the repeated loss and regain of weight. When weight cycling is caused by repeated attempts at weight loss, it is popularly known as "yo-yo dieting." Regrettably, with currently available dietary treatments for obesity, many people who lose weight will later regain it. Repeated bouts of weight loss and regain are distressing both to patients and their caregivers, making the search for ways to prevent the development of obesity and for more effective means of long-term maintenance of utmost importance. Much attention has been focused by both the lay press and professional literature on possible physiological and psychological hazards of weight cycling. Standard texts of nutrition and dietetics now present the detrimental effects of weight cycling as established fact. Some have suggested that remaining obese may be preferable to undergoing repeated failed attempts at permanently reducing body weight. The purpose of this article is to address concerns about the effects of weight cycling and to provide guidance on the risk-to-benefit ratio of attempts at weight loss, given current scientific knowledge.

METHODS

Original reports were obtained through MEDLINE and psychological abstracts searches for 1966 through 1994 on weight cycling, yo-yo dieting, and weight fluctuation, supplemented by a manual search of bibliographies. Forty-three English-language articles that evaluated the effects of weight change or weight cycling on humans or animals were reviewed in depth. Studies of human subjects were emphasized. Cited studies were reviewed by experts in the fields of nutrition, obesity, and epidemiology to evaluate study design and the validity of the authors' conclusions based on the published data....

DEFINING WEIGHT CYCLING

Much of the confusion about the effects of weight cycling and the inconsistencies in the outcomes of studies attempting to clarify its effects can be traced to the lack of a standardized definition for weight cycling. At its simplest, the definition of a single weight cycle may seem intuitively obvious: a loss followed by a gain (or vice versa). However, the multiple factors involved in both the definition and measurement of weight cycling are formidable, particularly when the clinically important variables are not yet known. Such confusion is reflected in the multiple definitions of weight cycling found in both cross-sectional and prospective studies seeking to determine metabolic and psychological effects of weight cycling and in observational population-based studies with a primary goal of determining mortality. Although the term "cycling" suggests a more regular pattern of weight change than the more general term "fluctuation," the two are often used interchangeably.

Providing a clinically relevant measure for weight cycling encompasses many components. How many cycles are involved? Is a loss followed by a gain similar in effect to a gain followed by a loss? What is the magnitude of weight change in each cycle? Are several small cycles more or less detrimental than one or two large cycles? What about the duration of each weight cycle? Is a loss that is maintained for 1 year and then regained of greater or less benefit than one that is only maintained for 6 months? Do any detrimental effects of weight cycling on health come about only years after the cycling occurs, or are adverse effects more likely soon after the weight change occurs? Is the effect of a cycle caused by intentional weight change the same or different from a cycle that occurs unintentionally? In which populations (if any) does cycling exert its deleterious effects—in women, in men, in normal-weight vs obese individuals, in ethnic minorities? Despite the numerous studies of weight cycling available, these fundamental questions remain unanswered.

Even such basic information as the normal degree of weight fluctuation during short periods in nonclinical populations is currently unknown. For example, among nine normal-weight women who were recruited as "noncyclers" for an observational study on the basis of self-reports of "rarely or never" dieting and stable weight within 2.3 kg during 5 years, four women experienced weight fluctuations of more than 2.3 kg once or twice during the course of three measurements during 1 year. In a retrospective chart review of 332 overweight adults in a general medical population, Williamson and Levy found significant weight fluctuation. Of all subjects, 34% lost weight (mean, 5.3 kg; SD, 4.8 kg) and 66% gained weight (mean, 5.7 kg; SD, 4.8 kg) between two visits 1 to 5 years apart. Studies to determine the prevalence, magnitude, and frequency of weight fluctuation in the general population are therefore needed. Cutter et al have recently critically analyzed the multiple issues involved in the definition of weight cycling and have proposed that the number of weight cycles be used as the primary measure, using an arbitrary minimal threshold (eg, 2.3 kg [5 lb]) as a cycle (G. R. Cutter et al, unpublished data, 1994). Currently, however, no single definition of weight cycling can be endorsed, and studies should attempt to measure multiple components of weight change with the aim of further clarifying clinically important components.

CONCERNS ABOUT WEIGHT CYCLING

Most concerns about the adverse effects of weight cycling fall into three major areas: the effects on metabolism and weight loss, on morbidity and mortality, and on psychological well-being.

Influence of Weight Cycling on Metabolism

There have been numerous studies that have examined the effects of repeated loss and regain of weight on metabolism and body composition. In 1986, Brownell et al reported that weight-cycled rats showed an increased food efficiency and that weight cycling made weight loss harder and weight regain easier. The authors hypothesized that animals may regain more body fat in relation to lean body mass during each weight cycle, leading to progressive increases in body fat content relative to total weight. Reed and Hill critically reviewed the published literature on weight cycling in rodents and concluded that the existing data did not support the hypothesis that weight cycling promoted obesity, increased body fat, or had permanent effects on metabolism. In fact, the majority of available data suggest that weight cycling in animals does not independently affect any parameter of energy balance (food intake, body composition, or energy expenditure). For example, although it is commonly contended that weight cycling in animals reduces fat-free mass and increases body fat over time, most investigators have reported that weight cycling does not increase body fat or relative adiposity compared with controls. Although the few reports of adverse metabolic effects of weight cycling have been widely quoted both in the lay press and scientific literature, Reed and Hill have described limitations in many of these studies, including choice of control groups, paradigms for producing weight cycling, and effects of gender and aging. They concluded that most, if not all, claims of adverse effects due to weight cycling were not based on strong experimental evidence.

The implication of reports of possible detrimental effects of weight cycling in animals prompted research on the problem in humans. These studies included small prospective trials that evaluated metabolic effects of weight loss in obese women, as well as studies in persons repeating a weight loss program. In one widely cited study, 57 individuals repeating a very low-calorie diet program had a significantly lower rate of weight loss during their second attempt. However, there was a great deal of intersubject variability in time (68 to 2860 days) and in percentage of weight regained (5% to 440%) between diets. Intervening factors, such as changes in body composition with age, make interpretation of the results difficult. In addition, although the authors made attempts to study only adherent patients, differences in compliance to the dietary regimen, particularly among outpatients, may have been a factor in their findings. Smith and Wing found that subjects had significantly worse dietary adherence when repeating a very low-calorie diet program.

Furthermore, other studies have found no relationship between the number of previously reported weight loss cycles and the efficacy of weight loss. Although one study showed that weight-cycling wrestlers had a lower resting metabolic rate than noncycling wrestlers, the cross-sectional nature of this study makes it unclear whether cycling reduced the metabolic rate or whether those whose baseline energy expenditure was low gained weight easily and therefore needed to engage more frequently in efforts to reduce their body weight. Other cross-sectional and prospective studies have not found differences in energy efficiency between cyclers and noncyclers among athletes, nonobese women, or obese women when adjusted for differences in weight and/or lean body mass. Although Manore et al found that cyclical dieters had a lower energy expenditure (per kilogram of body weight) during exercise than weight-stable controls, their weight-cycling subjects were both significantly heavier and fatter than controls, making appropriate comparisons difficult. Lissner et al studied the relationship between weight cycling and metabolic rate in 846 men participating in the Baltimore Study of Aging. They found no evidence that body weight fluctuation was associated with depression in basal metabolic rate; in fact, individuals with the highest variability in body weight had the smallest decreases in metabolic rate over time, whether adjusted for body surface area or for lean body mass.

In addition, neither body composition (percentage of fat vs nonfat tissue) nor body fat distribution appears to be adversely affected by history of weight cycling in humans, independent of body mass index (BMI) (calculated by dividing the weight in kilograms by the square of height in meters). Prentice et al found no detrimental effects on lean body mass as a result of "natural" annual weight cycling in a population of Gambian men. Prospective and cross-sectional studies have generally failed to find differences in body composition between weight cyclers and noncyclers among the obese, those of normal weight, or wrestlers who frequently cycle to "make weight."

Paradoxically, McCargar et al found that the percentage of body fat during three test periods 6 months apart was more stable in cycling than in noncycling normal-weight women.

Because visceral adipose tissue deposition is associated with a variety of adverse health outcomes, the effect of weight cycling on visceral fat deposition is clinically relevant. In a cross-sectional study, Rodin et al found a higher waist-to-hip ratio, often used as a surrogate marker for increased visceral fat deposition, among "high" as compared with "low" weight-cycling women. However, BMI, which is known to be correlated with waist-to-hip ratio, was not adequately controlled for in this study. Lissner et al found an association between body weight variability and increased ratio of subscapular-to-triceps skinfold thickness, suggesting that fluctuators might have greater increases in truncal adiposity. However, the absence of an increased waist-to-hip ratio suggested that the truncal fat deposition they observed did not appear to favor upper vs lower body obesity. In a study of weight-cycling wrestlers, the fat lost during peak season was found to be preferentially lost from the trunk compared with noncycling controls, although no differences existed between groups by off-season. Other studies have found no difference in body fat distribution between weight cyclers vs noncyclers. Anthropometric measures, such as skinfold measurements and body circumferences, do not differentiate between visceral and subcutaneous abdominal fat depots, in contrast with computed tomography and magnetic resonance imaging. When visceral fat measured via magnetic resonance imaging in 14 cycling vs 14 noncycling nonobese and mildly obese women, no difference in visceral adipose tissue deposition existed between groups, although subcutaneous adipose tissue deposition was slightly greater in cyclers. Similar results were observed in a prospective study of obese men and women who underwent one cycle of weight loss and regain during the course of a year.

In summary, the majority of studies did not find a higher prevalence of unfavorable body fat distribution among weight cyclers, and there was no evidence that weight cycling led to increased visceral adipose tissue deposition. In a review of the literature on weight cycling in humans, Wing concluded that most studies showed no adverse effects of weight cycling on body composition, resting metabolic rate, body fat distribution, or future successful weight loss, and subsequently published studies tend to support this conclusion.

Influence of Weight Cycling on Morbidity and Mortality

The potential effects of weight cycling on long-term morbidity and mortality are of greater concern. A number of large population-based observational studies have shown increased risks of variations in body weight for all-cause and cardiovascular mortality, whereas two smaller studies showed no such effect. In some of these studies, variation in weight appeared to be associated with increased mortality, even after control for coronary heart disease risk factors and preexisting disease that might influence weight. In addition to weight cycling, weight loss over time has been found to be associated with increased mortality, even when care has been taken to exclude for smoking and preexisting illness.

These observational studies, however, have several limitations. Only one of these studies attempted to distinguish intentional from unintentional weight loss. In that study, a history of voluntary dieting, although associated with a higher coefficient of variation of body weight, did not predict mortality. None of these studies controlled for variability in body composition and fat distribution, which are known to influence both morbidity and mortality. In addition, the myriad ways in which weight cycling was defined in these studies makes between-study comparisons difficult. For example, use of the coefficient of variation of weight may not be the best means to determine cycling, because this measure is more sensitive to single large changes in weight, rather than frequent small changes. As previously discussed, it is unknown if differences in frequency of weight cycling or amount of weight change per cycle influences outcome. Other potential causes of weight change, such as depression, which significantly affects weight change during long-term follow-up, have rarely been assessed. In fact, general psychological well-being appears to be associated with weight stability rather than weight gain or loss, although assumptions cannot be made about causality.

Finally, mechanisms by which weight cycling might affect mortality in humans remain unexplained. Although studies of changes in cardiovascular risk factors in animals with weight cycling have yielded inconsistent results, human studies have not demonstrated any mechanism by which weight cycling increases risk of cardiovascular disease. In a study of 202 obese men and women, Jeffery et al found no evidence that a history of weight cycling worsened cardiovascular risk factors. Similarly, the majority of cross-sectional and prospective studies have not demonstrated associations between weight cycling and increases in blood pressure, fasting blood levels of glucose or insulin, impaired glucose tolerance measured by oral glucose tolerance test or glycohemoglobin, dyslipidemias or alterations in fat metabolism including fat cell size, basal or stimulated lipolysis, and lipoprotein lipase activity. Schotte et al found no association between weight cycling and glycemic control in 327 men with non–insulin-dependent diabetes mellitus, although differences in the need for hypoglycemic medications may have obscured differences in metabolic control. Holbrook and colleagues, in a study of older adults, found that both self-reported weight gain and weight fluctuation between ages 40 and 60 years were associated with an elevated relative risk (RR) for diabetes mellitus, as evaluated by oral glucose tolerance test. However, a history of dieting to control weight during this time was not associated with increased risk for diabetes. One study did find an association between body weight variability and decreased glucose tolerance after an oral glucose tolerance test, but the magnitude of the increase in plasma glucose (1 mg/dL [0.05 mmol/L] for every 1-kg deviation about the slope) was only about half the size of the effect of 1-kg weight gain per year on glucose tolerance. Although concerns have been raised about the possibility of weight cycling leading to increased fat consumption, the majority of studies in humans have not shown an association between weight cycling and fat preference or fat consumption.

The majority of subjects in population-based observational studies were either nonobese or only mildly obese (BMI<30). If weight cycling has deleterious effects on health, such effects may be limited to those who are not obese. Blair and associates, in an analysis of data from the Multiple Risk Factor Intervention Trial, found that the increased mortality associated with body weight variability was limited primarily to men in the lowest tertile for BMI (<26.08). Similarly, in a study that examined the effects of weight loss on morbidity and mortality, Pamuk and colleagues found that the increase in RR for mortality with weight loss was primarily limited to those in the bottom two tertiles for weight (BMI <29). Among women in the top tertile for weight, all-cause mortality was elevated only among those losing more than 15% of their total body weight. Among men, RR for death was not increased with any degree of weight loss. Moderate weight loss (5% to 14% of initial body weight) was actually associated with reduced cardiovascular mortality among men in the highest tertile for weight. In addition, the proportion of individuals reporting intentional weight loss is greater in obese than in lean individuals. Therefore, weight cycling and weight loss may have both differing causes and effects in obese and nonobese individuals, and caution should be taken in applying the findings of population-based studies to obese patients. The National Institutes of Health Technology Assessment Conference statement on methods for voluntary weight loss and control advised that the data on long-term adverse health consequences of weight cycling, while provocative, were not sufficiently conclusive to dictate clinical practice. This recommendation appears to be appropriate until better data become available.

Psychological Effects of Weight Cycling

Repeated failed attempts at permanent weight loss are obviously distressing. Anecdotes abound regarding the negative effects of such failures on mood and self-esteem. Unfortunately, few well-controlled studies have assessed the impact of weight cycling on psychological functioning. Those that have are generally cross-sectional and cannot distinguish between negative effects of weight cycling and preexisting psychological factors that may predispose individuals to repeatedly lose and regain weight. Currently, scientifically valid data on the psychological effects of weight cycling are not available. Determination of the psychological impact of weight cycling requires further study.

HEALTH RISKS OF OBESITY

In contrast to weight cycling, obesity is associated with increased risks of morbidity and mortality. Furthermore, the biological bases of the increased risk have been well described. Both cross-sectional and cohort studies have shown strong associations between obesity and hyperlipidemia, hypertension, and hyperinsulinemia, leading to an increased prevalence of coronary artery disease and non–insulin-dependent diabetes mellitus. Studies have also clearly documented the amelioration of these conditions with modest weight loss. Certain types of cancer, degenerative joint disease, sleep apnea, gout, and gallbladder disease are also more prevalent with increasing obesity. The economic cost attributable to obesity-related illness has been estimated to exceed $39 billion yearly. The elevations in RR for these conditions are particularly striking in younger adults. One study found that the presence of obesity in adolescent males was associated with increased mortality as long as 50 years later, independent of adult weight. Not all individuals with a given weight or degree of obesity have the same risk for medical complications. Prognostic factors, including gender, amount and location of excess body fat, family history, and the presence of risk factors such as hyperlipidemia, play a role in determining an individual's risk of obesity-related conditions. Evaluation of such risk should determine whether weight loss treatment is medically necessary, as well as the type and intensity of any intervention.

RECOMMENDATIONS FOR FUTURE STUDIES ON WEIGHT CYCLING

Unfortunately, designing studies to correct for the deficiencies identified in this article is exceedingly difficult. For example, even if the issue of voluntary weight loss were to be addressed, not all confounding variables could be adequately controlled. With 40% of all women and 25% of all men in the United States reporting attempts to lose weight at a single point in time, who are the individuals who actually change their weight? Those who consider themselves "chronic" dieters or always on a diet are not necessarily those who lose weight. Unsuspected illness, psychological dysfunction, or deterioration in a known medical condition may contribute to weight change, even in those already attempting weight loss. A randomized, controlled long-term trial weight loss or weight cycling vs weight stability or gain would be extraordinarily complex in design, as well as prohibitively expensive. Thus, innovative approaches to the use of available databases and small-scale clinical studies are needed to determine answers to this important but difficult question.

Descriptive, population-based studies to determine the natural history of weight fluctuation and patterns of weight change in the general population may help to better define the normative level of weight fluctuation and aid the development of a clinically useful definition of weight cycling. Studies examining health risks of weight cycling in obese populations are also needed, particularly because there is some evidence that any adverse effects of weight cycling may be blunted in those at the greatest medical risk for obesity. Animal and human studies that might elucidate putative mechanisms for adverse effects of weight cycling (such as change in fatty acid profile of various tissues would be useful. The roles of physical activity, smoking, stress, and alcohol intake in creating weight cycles also deserve further study.

CONCLUSIONS

Based on the currently available data, we conclude the following:

- There is no convincing evidence that weight cycling in humans has adverse effects on body composition, energy expenditure, risk factors for cardiovas-

cular disease, or the effectiveness of future efforts at weight loss.

- The currently available evidence regarding increased morbidity and mortality with variation in body weight is not sufficiently compelling to override the potential benefits of moderate weight loss in significantly obese patients. Therefore, obese individuals should not allow concerns about hazards of weight cycling to deter them from efforts to control their body weight.

- Determination of the psychological impact of weight cycling requires further investigation.

- Individuals who are not obese and who have no risk factors for obesity-related illness should not undertake weight loss efforts, but should focus on the prevention of weight gain by increasing physical activity and consuming a healthful diet as recommended by the *Dietary Guidelines for Americans*.

- Although conclusive data regarding long-term health effects of weight cycling are lacking, obese individuals who undertake weight loss efforts should be ready to commit to lifelong changes in their behavioral patterns, diet, and physical activity.

CHALLENGE QUESTIONS
Is Yo-Yo Dieting Dangerous?

1. What assumptions did you have about dieting before you encountered this issue? How did the arguments on either side of the issue affect your thinking?

2. Given the "confusing and conflicting results" of weight-cycling studies, how would you advise someone who has tried many diets to balance the health risks against his or her desire to be thin? What factors most influenced your decision?

3. Berg appears to attribute yo-yo dieting to societal pressures to be thin. Respond to this theory from the point of view of the National Task Force.

4. How do you explain the vast differences among the conclusions about dieting? What subjective factors might influence the interpretation of something as easily measurable as weight?

5. Use the data and conditions described in the National Task Force report to create an advisory (similar to those for alcohol and tobacco products) for people considering or following a diet plan.

ISSUE 9

Should Drug Use by Pregnant Women Be Considered Child Abuse?

YES: Paul A. Logli, from "Drugs in the Womb: The Newest Battlefield in the War on Drugs," *Criminal Justice Ethics* (Winter/Spring 1990)

NO: Maureen A. Norton-Hawk, from "How Social Policies Make Matters Worse: The Case of Maternal Substance Abuse," *Journal of Drug Issues* (Summer 1994)

ISSUE SUMMARY

YES: Paul A. Logli, an Illinois prosecuting attorney, argues that it is the government's duty to enforce children's right to begin life with healthy, drug-free minds and bodies. Logli believes that pregnant women who use drugs should be prosecuted because they may harm the life of their unborn children.

NO: Social worker Maureen A. Norton-Hawk contends that prosecuting women who use drugs during pregnancy will lead to fewer women seeking prenatal care. Norton-Hawk acknowledges that drug use during pregnancy can have devastating effects on newborns, but she argues that there is more opportunity to help pregnant addicts and their babies if they can come for prenatal care and drug treatment without fearing prosecution.

The effects that drugs have on a fetus can be mild and temporary or severe and permanent, depending on the extent of drug use by the mother, the type of substance used, and the stage of fetal development at the time the drug crosses the placental barrier and enters the bloodstream of the fetus. In recent years, there has been a dramatic increase in the number of drug-exposed babies born in the United States, and medical experts are beginning to understand the health consequences that these children face. Both illegal and legal drugs, such as cocaine, crack, marijuana, alcohol, and nicotine, are responsible for increasing incidents of premature births, congenital abnormalities, fetal alcohol syndrome, mental retardation, and other serious birth defects. The exposure of the fetus to these substances and the long-term involuntary physical, intellectual, and emotional effects are disturbing. In addition, the medical, social, and economic costs to treat and care for babies who are exposed to or become addicted to drugs while in utero (in the uterus) warrant serious concern.

In recent years, attempts have been made to establish laws that would allow the incarceration of drug-using pregnant women on the basis of "fetal abuse."

Some cases have been successfully prosecuted: mothers have been denied custody of their infants until they enter appropriate treatment programs, and criminal charges have been brought against mothers whose children were born with drug-related complications. The underlying presumption is that the unborn fetus should be afforded protection against the harmful actions of another person, specifically the use of harmful drugs by the mother.

Those who profess that prosecuting pregnant women who use drugs is necessary insist that the health and welfare of the unborn child is the highest priority. They contend that the possibility that these women will avoid obtaining health care for themselves or their babies because they fear punishment does not absolve the state from the responsibility of protecting the babies. They also argue that criminalizing these acts is imperative to protect fetuses or newborns who cannot protect themselves. It is the duty of the legal system to deter pregnant women from engaging in future criminal drug use and to protect the best interests of infants.

Others maintain that drug use and dependency by pregnant women is a medical problem, not a criminal one. Many pregnant women seek treatment, but they often find that rehabilitation programs are limited or unavailable. Shortages of openings in chemical dependency programs may keep a prospective client waiting for months, during which time she will most likely continue to use the drugs to which she is addicted and prolong her fetus's drug exposure. Many low-income women do not receive drug treatment and adequate prenatal care due to financial constraints. And women who fear criminal prosecution because of their drug use may simply avoid prenatal care altogether.

Some suggest that medical intervention, drug prevention, and education is needed for pregnant drug users instead of prosecution. Prosecution, some contend, drives women who need medical attention away from the very help they and their babies need. Others respond that prosecuting pregnant women who use drugs will help identify those who need attention, at which point adequate medical and social welfare services can be provided to treat and protect the mother and child.

In the following selections, Paul A. Logi, arguing for the prosecution of pregnant drug users, contends that it is the state's responsibility to protect the unborn and the newborn because they are least able to protect themselves. He charges that it is the prosecutor's responsibility to deter future criminal drug use by mothers who violate the rights of their potential newborns to have an opportunity for a healthy and normal life. Maureen A. Norton-Hawk insists that prosecuting pregnant drug users is counterproductive to improving the quality of infant and maternal health. The threat of arrest and incarceration will decrease the likelihood that pregnant drug users will seek out adequate prenatal care.

YES

Paul A. Logli

DRUGS IN THE WOMB: THE NEWEST BATTLEFIELD IN THE WAR ON DRUGS

INTRODUCTION

The reported incidence of drug-related births has risen dramatically over the last several years. The legal system and, in particular, local prosecutors have attempted to properly respond to the suffering, death, and economic costs which result from a pregnant woman's use of drugs. The ensuing debate has raised serious constitutional and practical issues which are far from resolution.

Prosecutors have achieved mixed results in using current criminal and juvenile statutes as a basis for legal action intended to prosecute mothers and protect children. As a result, state and federal legislators have begun the difficult task of drafting appropriate laws to deal with the problem, while at the same time acknowledging the concerns of medical authorities, child protection groups, and advocates for individual rights.

THE PROBLEM

The plight of "cocaine babies," children addicted at birth to narcotic substances or otherwise affected by maternal drug use during pregnancy, has prompted prosecutors in some jurisdictions to bring criminal charges against drug-abusing mothers. Not only have these prosecutions generated heated debates both inside and outside of the nation's courtrooms, but they have also expanded the war on drugs to a controversial new battlefield—the mother's womb.

A 1988 survey of hospitals conducted by Dr. Ira Chasnoff, Associate Professor of Northwestern University Medical School and President of the National Association for Perinatal Addiction Research and Education (NAPARE) indicated that as many as 375,000 infants may be affected by maternal cocaine use during pregnancy each year. Chasnoff's survey included 36 hospitals across the country and showed incidence rates ranging from 1 percent to 27 percent. It also indicated that the problem was not restricted to urban populations

From Paul A. Logli, "Drugs in the Womb: The Newest Battlefield in the War on Drugs," *Criminal Justice Ethics*, vol. 9, no. 1 (Winter/Spring 1990), pp. 23–39. Copyright © 1990 by *Criminal Justice Ethics*. Reprinted by permission of The Institute for Criminal Justice Ethics, 899 Tenth Avenue, New York, NY 10019. Notes omitted.

or particular racial or socio-economic groups. More recently a study at Hutzel Hospital in Detroit's inner city found that 42.7 percent of its newborn babies were exposed to drugs while in their mothers' wombs.

The effects of maternal use of cocaine and other drugs during pregnancy on the mother and her newborn child have by now been well-documented and will not be repeated here. The effects are severe and can cause numerous threats to the short-term health of the child. In a few cases it can even result in death.

Medical authorities have just begun to evaluate the long-term effects of cocaine exposure on children as they grow older. Early findings show that many of these infants show serious difficulties in relating and reacting to adults and environments, as well as in organizing creative play, and they appear similar to mildly autistic or personality-disordered children.

The human costs related to the pain, suffering, and deaths resulting from maternal cocaine use during pregnancy are simply incalculable. In economic terms, the typical intensive-care costs for treating babies exposed to drugs range from $7,500 to $31,000. In some cases medical bills go as high as $150,000.

The costs grow enormously as more and more hospitals encounter the problem of "boarder babies"—those children literally abandoned at the hospital by an addicted mother, and left to be cared for by the nursing staff. Future costs to society for simply educating a generation of drug-affected children can only be the object of speculation. It is clear, however, that besides pain, suffering, and death the economic costs to society of drug use by pregnant women is presently enormous and is certainly growing larger.

THE PROSECUTOR'S RESPONSE

It is against this backdrop and fueled by the evergrowing emphasis on an aggressively waged war on drugs that prosecutors have begun a number of actions against women who have given birth to drug-affected children. A review of at least two cases will illustrate the potential success or failure of attempts to use existing statutes.

People v. Melanie Green On February 4, 1989, at a Rockford, Illinois hospital, two-day-old Bianca Green lost her brief struggle for life. At the time of Bianca's birth both she and her mother, twenty-four-year-old Melanie Green, tested positive for the presence of cocaine in their systems.

Pathologists in Rockford and Madison, Wisconsin, indicated that the death of the baby was the result of a prenatal injury related to cocaine used by the mother during the pregnancy. They asserted that maternal cocaine use had caused the placenta to prematurely rupture, which deprived the fetus of oxygen before and during delivery. As a result of oxygen deprivation, the child's brain began to swell and she eventually died.

After an investigation by the Rockford Police Department and the State of Illinois Department of Children and Family Services, prosecutors allowed a criminal complaint to be filed on May 9, 1989, charging Melanie Green with the offenses of Involuntary Manslaughter and Delivery of a Controlled Substance.

On May 25, 1989, testimony was presented to the Winnebago County Grand Jury by prosecutors seeking a formal indictment. The Grand Jury, however, declined to indict Green on either charge. Since Grand Jury proceedings in the State of Illinois are secret, as are the jurors' deliberations and votes, the reason for the decision of the Grand Jury in this case is determined more by conjecture than any direct knowledge. Prosecutors involved in the presentation observed that the jurors exhibited a certain amount of sympathy for the young woman who had been brought before the Grand Jury at the jurors' request. It is also likely that the jurors were uncomfortable with the use of statutes that were not intended to be used in these circumstances.

It would also be difficult to disregard the fact that, after the criminal complaints were announced on May 9th and prior to the Grand Jury deliberations of May 25th, a national debate had ensued revolving around the charges brought in Rockford, Illinois, and their implications for the ever-increasing problem of women who use drugs during pregnancy.

People v. Jennifer Clarise Johnson On July 13, 1989, a Seminole County, Florida judge found Jennifer Johnson guilty of delivery of a controlled substance to a child. The judge found that delivery, for purposes of the statute, occurred through the umbilical cord after the birth of the child and before the cord was severed. Jeff Deen, the Assistant State's Attorney who prosecuted the case, has since pointed out that Johnson, age 23, had previously given birth to three other cocaine-affected babies, and in this case was arrested at a crack house. "We needed to make sure this woman does not give birth to another cocaine baby."

Johnson was sentenced to fifteen years of probation including strict supervision, drug treatment, random drug testing, educational and vocational training, and an intensive prenatal care program if she ever became pregnant again.

SUPPORT FOR THE PROSECUTION OF MATERNAL DRUG ABUSE

Both cases reported above relied on a single important fact as a basis for the prosecution of the drug-abusing mother: that the child was born alive and exhibited the consequences of prenatal injury.

In the Melanie Green case, Illinois prosecutors relied on the "born alive" rule set out earlier in *People v. Bolar*. In *Bolar* the defendant was convicted of the offense of reckless homicide. The case involved an accident between a car driven by the defendant, who was found to be drunk, and another automobile containing a pregnant woman. As a result, the woman delivered her baby by emergency caesarean section within hours of the collision. Although the newborn child exhibited only a few heart beats and lived for approximately two minutes, the court found that the child was born alive and was therefore a person for purposes of the criminal statutes of the State of Illinois.

The Florida prosecution relied on a live birth in an entirely different fashion. The prosecutor argued in that case that the delivery of the controlled substance occurred after the live birth via the umbilical cord and prior to the cutting of the cord. Thus, it was argued, that the delivery of the controlled substance occurred not to a fetus but to a person who enjoyed the protection of the criminal code of the State of Florida.

Further support for the State's role in protecting the health of newborns even against prenatal injury is found in the statutes which provide protection for the fetus. These statutes proscribe actions by a person, usually other than the mother, which either intentionally or recklessly harm or kill a fetus. In other words, even in the absence of a live birth, most states afford protection to the unborn fetus against the harmful actions of another person. Arguably, the same protection should be afforded the infant against intentional harmful actions by a drug-abusing mother.

The state also receives support for a position in favor of the protection of the health of a newborn from a number of non-criminal cases. A line of civil cases in several states would appear to stand for the principle that a child has a right to begin life with a sound mind and body, and a person who interferes with that right may be subject to civil liability. In two cases decided within months of each other, the Supreme Court of Michigan upheld two actions for recovery of damages that were caused by the infliction of prenatal injury. In *Womack v. Buckhorn* the court upheld an action on behalf of an eight-year-old surviving child for prenatal brain injuries apparently suffered during the fourth month of the pregnancy in an automobile accident. The court adopted with approval the reasoning of a New Jersey Supreme Court decision and "recognized that a child has a legal right to begin life with a sound mind and body." Similarly, in *O'Neill v. Morse* the court found that a cause of action was allowed for prenatal injuries that caused the death of an eight-month-old viable fetus.

Illinois courts have allowed civil recovery on behalf of an infant for a negligently administered blood transfusion given to the mother prior to conception which resulted in damage to the child at birth. However, the same Illinois court would not extend a similar cause of action for prebirth injuries as between a child and

its own mother. The court, however, went on to say that a right to such a cause of action could be statutorily enacted by the Legislature.

Additional support for the state's role in protecting the health of newborns is found in the principles annunciated in recent decisions of the United States Supreme Court. The often cited case of *Roe v. Wade* set out that although a woman's right of privacy is broad enough to cover the abortion decision, the right is not absolute and is subject to limitations, "and that at some point the state's interest as to protection of health, medical standards and prenatal life, becomes dominant."

More recently, in the case of *Webster v. Reproductive Health Services*, the court expanded the state's interest in protecting potential human life by setting aside viability as a rigid line that had previously allowed state regulation only after viability had been shown but prohibited it before viability. The court goes on to say that the "fundamental right" to abortion as described in *Roe* is now accorded the lesser status of a "liberty interest." Such language surely supports a prosecutor's argument that the state's compelling interest in potential human life would allow the criminalization of acts which if committed by a pregnant woman can damage not just a viable fetus but eventually a born-alive infant. It follows that, once a pregnant woman has abandoned her right to abort and has decided to carry the fetus to term, society can well impose a duty on the mother to insure that the fetus is born as healthy as possible.

A further argument in support of the state's interest in prosecuting women who engage in conduct which is damaging to the health of a newborn child is especially compelling in regard to maternal drug use during pregnancy. Simply put, there is no fundamental right or even a liberty interest in the use of psycho-active drugs. A perceived right of privacy has never formed an absolute barrier against state prosecutions of those who use or possess narcotics. Certainly no exception can be made simply because the person using drugs happens to be pregnant.

Critics of the prosecutor's role argue that any statute that would punish mothers who create a substantial risk of harm to their fetus will run afoul of constitutional requirements, including prohibitions on vagueness, guarantees of liberty and privacy, and rights of due process and equal protection....

In spite of such criticism, the state's role in protecting those citizens who are least able to protect themselves, namely the newborn, mandates an aggressive posture. Much of the criticism of prosecutorial efforts is based on speculation as to the consequences of prosecution and ignores the basic tenet of criminal law that prosecutions deter the prosecuted and others from committing additional crimes. To assume that it will only drive persons further underground is to somehow argue that certain prosecutions of crime will only force perpetrators to make even more aggressive efforts to escape apprehension, thus making arrest and prosecution unadvisable. Neither could this be accepted as an argument justifying even the weakening of criminal sanctions....

The concern that pregnant addicts will avoid obtaining health care for themselves or their infants because of the fear of prosecution cannot justify the absence of state action to protect the newborn. If the state were to accept such reasoning, then existing child abuse laws would have to be reconsidered since

they might deter parents from obtaining medical care for physically or sexually abused children. That argument has not been accepted as a valid reason for abolishing child abuse laws or for not prosecuting child abusers....

The far better policy is for the state to acknowledge its responsibility not only to provide a deterrant to criminal and destructive behavior by pregnant addicts but also to provide adequate opportunities for those who might seek help to discontinue their addiction. Prosecution has a role in its ability to deter future criminal behavior and to protect the best interests of the child. The medical and social welfare establishment must assume an even greater responsibility to encourage legislators to provide adequate funding and facilities so that no pregnant woman who is addicted to drugs will be denied the opportunity to seek appropriate prenatal care and treatment for her addiction.

ONE STATE'S RESPONSE

The Legislature of the State of Illinois at the urging of local prosecutors moved quickly to amend its juvenile court act in order to provide protection to those children born drug-affected. Previously, Illinois law provided that a court could assume jurisdiction over addicted minors or a minor who is generally declared neglected or abused.

Effective January 1, 1990, the juvenile court act was amended to expand the definition of a neglected or abused minor....

those who are neglected include... any newborn infant whose blood or urine contains any amount of a controlled substance....

The purpose of the new statute is to make it easier for the court to assert jurisdiction over a newborn infant born drug-affected. The state is not required to show either the addiction of the child or harmful effects on the child in order to remove the child from a drug-abusing mother. Used in this context, prosecutors can work with the mother in a rather coercive atmosphere to encourage her to enter into drug rehabilitation and, upon the successful completion of the program, be reunited with her child.

Additional legislation before the Illinois Legislature is House Bill 2835 sponsored by Representatives John Hallock (R-Rockford) and Edolo "Zeke" Giorgi (D-Rockford). This bill represents the first attempt to specifically address the prosecution of drug-abusing pregnant women....

The statute provides for a class 4 felony disposition upon conviction. A class 4 felony is a probationable felony which can also result in a term of imprisonment from one to three years.

Subsequent paragraphs set out certain defenses available to the accused.

It shall not be a violation of this section if a woman knowingly or intentionally uses a narcotic or dangerous drug in the first twelve weeks of pregnancy and: 1. She has no knowledge that she is pregnant; or 2. Subsequently, within the first twelve weeks of pregnancy, undergoes medical treatment for substance abuse or treatment or rehabilitation in a program or facility approved by the Illinois Department of Alcoholism and Substance Abuse, and thereafter discontinues any further use of drugs or narcotics as previously set forth.

... A woman, under this statute, could not be prosecuted for self-reporting her addiction in the early stages of the pregnancy. Nor could she be prosecuted under this statute if, even during the subsequent stages of the pregnancy, she discontinued her drug use to the extent that no drugs were present in her system or the baby's system at the time of birth. The statute, as drafted, is clearly intended to allow prosecutors to invoke the criminal statutes in the most serious of cases.

CONCLUSION

Local prosecutors have a legitimate role in responding to the increasing problem of drug-abusing pregnant women and their drug-affected children. Eliminating the pain, suffering and death resulting from drug exposure in newborns must be a prosecutor's priority. However, the use of existing statutes to address the problem may meet with limited success since they are burdened with numerous constitutional problems dealing with original intent, notice, vagueness, and due process.

The juvenile courts may offer perhaps the best initial response in working to protect the interests of a surviving child. However, in order to address more serious cases, legislative efforts may be required to provide new statutes that will specifically address the problem and hopefully deter future criminal conduct which deprives children of their important right to a healthy and normal birth.

The long-term solution does not rest with the prosecutor alone. Society, including the medical and social welfare establishment, must be more responsive in providing readily accessible prenatal care and treatment alternatives for pregnant addicts. In the short term however, prosecutors must be prepared to play a vital role in protecting children and deterring women from engaging in conduct which will harm the newborn child. If prosecutors fail to respond, then they are simply closing the doors of the criminal justice system to those persons, the newborn, who are least able to open the doors for themselves.

NO

Maureen A. Norton-Hawk

HOW SOCIAL POLICIES MAKE MATTERS WORSE: THE CASE OF MATERNAL SUBSTANCE ABUSE

This article addresses the issue of maternal substance abuse and the consequences of our current punitive approach. The article initially presents information that defines the scope of the problem and then offers case illustrations of the court's attempt to deal with women who use drugs and alcohol when pregnant. The article then focuses on characteristic of interventions that have the potential for bringing about a deterioration of the problem of maternal substance abuse.

In an attempt to address maternal substance abuse evolving social policy is relying on the criminal justice system. In fact since 1987 there have been more than 160 criminal prosecutions against women for their drug or alcohol use during pregnancy (Paltrow 1992). However, the prosecution of these women fails to rectify the problem of substance-abusing pregnant women and, in fact, this policy exacerbates the problem of drug and alcohol use during pregnancy.

Each year approximately 739,200 women use one or more illegal drugs during pregnancy (Gomby and Shiono 1991). Calculations by the National Association for Perinatal Addiction Research and Education (NAPARE) indicate that maternal drug use annually affects 375,000 newborns (Chasnoff 1989). Studies have indicated that a relationship exists between the use of various illicit drugs and lower birth weight and smaller head circumference, irritability, neurobehavioral dysfunction, sudden infant death syndrome (Zuckerman 1991), negative responses to multiple stimuli (Howard and Beckwith) 1989), and a potential for malformation of developing systems (Zuckerman 1991). It is important to note that while there exists a correlation between illicit drug use and physiological/psychological problems in newborns, neither causality nor a complete understanding of the potential harm of specific substances has been established. This difficulty in confirming a direct link between drug use and drug effect in pregnant addicts is due in part to the involvement of other extraneous variables such as the lack of prenatal care (Kronstadt

1991), poor maternal health, inadequate maternal nutrition, and polydrug use (Zuckerman 1991).

These physiological/psychological effects on newborns, if accurate, can result in dramatic social and medical costs. The General Accounting Office (1990) found that in one hospital the median cost for the medical care of a newborn was $4,100 higher for drug-exposed infants with the cost rising as high as $135,000 for a drug-exposed, premature infant needing intensive care for several months (Halfon 1989). The cost climbs as we confront the problem of boarder babies—those children abandoned in the hospital at birth. Foster care for one of these children is estimated to be $6,000 annually (General Accounting Office 1990). For a group of nine thousand identified as crack-exposed infants, the Office of the Inspector General (1990) estimated that the total cost of hospital and foster care for this group until the age of five will approximate $500 million.

Prenatal exposure to illicit substances is hardly the only concern. Five to ten percent of pregnant women continue to drink heavily (Balisy 1987) resulting in Fetal Alcohol Syndrome (FAS). Estimates of the incidence of FAS is 1 to 3 cases per 1,000 live births (Abel and Sokol 1987) or nearly 5,000 newborns annually (Office of the Inspector General 1990). Fetal Alcohol Syndrome is marked by dysfunction of the central nervous system, prenatal and postnatal growth deficiency, and facial malformations (Warren 1987; Abel 1984) and is the third leading cause of birth defects associated with mental retardation (Office of the Inspector General 1990). In 1980, the estimated cost for medical, educational and custodial services for children born with Fetal Alcohol Syndrome or Fetal Alcohol Effect in the United States was $2.7 billion (Balisy 1987).

In an attempt to grapple with the physiological, social and economic costs of drug and alcohol use during pregnancy, twenty-six states have prosecuted these women on charges of child abuse/neglect, contributing to the delinquency of a minor, causing dependency, child endangerment, drug possession, assault with a deadly weapon, manslaughter, homicide, vehicular homicide and delivering a controlled substance to a minor (Paltrow 1992). Though the rhetoric implies that the goal of these prosecutions is to protect the child and increase infant health, prosecution of pregnant addicts will not protect the child, more will this policy increase the likelihood of infant health. Rather than the creation of a social policy that effectively remedies a social problem, what has emerged is a regressive intervention—an intervention that makes the original aim of the policy less attainable or cause a deterioration of the social problem one wanted to ameliorate (Sieber 1981:10).

An example of such a failed intervention is the effect of the decision of the U.S. Supreme Court in *Brown v. Board of Education*, which held that separate schools are inherently unequal. Courts mandated that segregated schools be integrated. To comply with the Court's order, Boston, as in other areas of the country, imposed a system of busing students (Lukas 1986).

Social Problem   **Goal**
Unequal Education   Integration

Intervention
Busing

The result of this social intervention was the flight of whites to the suburbs or the placement of their children in private schools as a means of avoiding, at all costs, the court-mandated busing. This "white flight" caused an even more segregated school system as the number of white students in the system dropped from 67,028 in 1967 to 11,555 in 1992 (Canellos 1993), thus making the goal of integration less attainable and making the problem of inequitable education more pronounced.

We can apply this framework of regressive interventions to maternal substance abuse.

Social Problem	Goal
Substance Abuse by Pregnant Women	Decrease Drug Use/Insure Infant Health

Intervention
Prosecution

Most Americans would agree that ingestion of illicit substances by pregnant women is a social concern and many would argue that punitive sanctions need to be applied. According to a popular magazine poll, 46% favored criminal penalties for prenatal substance abuse (*Glamour* 1988). Problematic as such popular surveys are, this poll may indicate that, at least for a portion of the population, the pervasive ideology is that prosecution and indictment of maternal substance abusers will decrease their drug use thus increase the likelihood of infant health.

But does the prosecution of pregnant substance abusers insure the health of their newborns? Brenda Vaughan, a Washington, D.C. resident who was originally arrested for writing bad checks, tested positive for cocaine and was sent to jail until the date her baby was due to protect her fetus. The judge stated:

> I'm going to keep her locked up until the baby is born because she's tested positive for cocaine. She's apparently an addictive personality, and I'll be darned if I'm going to have a baby born that way (Cassen Moss 1988:20).

While incarcerated, Ms. Vaughn received no drug treatment, was allowed to detoxify with no medical supervision, received only spotty prenatal care (Smith 1990), and lost weight because of improper nutrition (Cassen Moss 1988)—hardly an environment that would insure the health of the newborn.

Does the prosecution of pregnant addicts increase the likelihood that pregnant substance abusers will avail themselves of available drug treatment thus preventing potential harm to the fetus? In May 1989, Melanie Green was indicted on charges of manslaughter and delivery of a controlled substance to a minor after the purported drug induced death of her newborn. The publicity surrounding this arrest impeded efforts to get women to seek and remain in prenatal care and drug treatment. The Prenatal Center for Chemical Dependence at Northwestern University received numerous calls from women who were frightened that they would also be arrested. These women, who up until that time had been receiving prenatal care at the facility, wanted to stop seeing the doctors rather than risk possible prosecution (Chasnoff 1990). Thus, we can see the regressive nature of such interventions.

The question now becomes what are the dynamics of regressive interventions. How can a social policy actually make the goal of the intervention less attainable or cause a deterioration in the original social problem? To deal with these questions one needs to understand the notion of a conversion mechanism. A conversion mechanism is a feature or characteristic of an intervention or social policy that interacts with the environment and results in a regressive intervention. At least six types of conversion mechanisms have been suggested: functional imbalance (an overemphasis on a specific goal), exploitation (the exploitation of the intervention by the target population), goal displacement (the goal of efficiency overshadows the goal of effectiveness), provocation (the stirring up of emotions), derogatory classification (consequences of labeling), and placation (interventions that are primarily a means of placating certain groups in the society) (Sieber 1981). We will now examine each of these conversion mechanisms and illustrate how a punitive approach to pregnant drug users fail to deal with the two key goals of eliminating substance abuse during pregnancy and protecting the fetus and newborn.

CONVERSION MECHANISMS

Functional Imbalance
Social policies can have regressive effects when there is such an emphasis on a specific goal rather than other facets of the social problem. For example, the Nixon administration's War on Drugs concentrated on drug supply from Mexico. While the United States' policy was successful in diminishing the flow of marijuana across our southern borders, not only did other countries replace Mexico as our prime supplier, but domestic production increased. Thus, the intervention undertaken, to eliminate drugs at their source, while successful in one area, may

have actually made the overall problem more pronounced by failing to address the "demand" side of the drug problem (Goode 1989).

The emphasis in addressing the problem of maternal substance abuse through prosecution of these women focuses on punishment and incarceration. By concentrating almost exclusively on retribution, needs and issues that are created by this position are overlooked. There exists little consideration for the fact that there are few treatment facilities that deal with pregnant drug abusers and fewer jails and prisons that can adequately deal with an expectant mother.

In one case brought by Prisoners with Children, the plaintiff delivered her baby on the floor of the Kern County Jail in Bakersfield, California (Cassen Moss 1988).

> Pregnant women in jail are routinely subject to conditions that are hazardous to fetal health such as gross overcrowding, 24-hour lock-up with no access to exercise or fresh air, exposure to tuberculosis, measles, and hepatitis, and a generally filthy and unsanitary environment (Cole 1990:2667).

In the prison system health care officials warn that prisons are extremely deficient in the resources needed to accommodate pregnant women (Barry 1989). Thus, the fetus may be in as much danger, if not more, from the intervention.

Exploitation
Another aspect of social policies that may bring about regressive effects is the potential for exploitation by the target group. In other words, the group that is the target of the social policy uses an intervention, not for its intended purposes, but for personal benefit. Pregnant

women who are prosecuted and incarcerated for their drug use may have little desire to stop using drugs and drugs are probably as, if not more, available in jails. Brenda Vaughan, during her incarceration, reported that on a couple of occasions she had the opportunity to use drugs (Cassen Mass 1988). So by incarcerating these women they are being placed in an environment where their drug use can continue and potentially accelerate. Not only may the women have as great or even greater accessibility to drugs but, because of contact with a diverse inmate subculture, they may also have the opportunity to experiment with different drugs and may make drug connections in jail that can endure long after release. Thus, the potential for greater abuse of drugs by women who are reluctant to stop using is inherent in the design of this punitive approach making resolution of the problem less likely.

Goal Displacement
A regressive intervention can result when the benefits of providing an efficient and inexpensive method in dealing with a problem takes precedent over the policy's efficacy. For example, in addressing marijuana use, spraying the plant with paraquat—a toxic herbicide—may seem like an efficient strategy to deter use of the drug. However, this strategy, because it does not change patterns of use, may be less than effective in improving the health of marijuana users, decreasing social and medical costs of drug use, or decreasing the demand for the drug from other sources.

Likewise, the policy that deals with maternal substance abusers through indictments and prosecution may appear to be, at first glance, the most efficient strategy to decrease use if one assumes that

fear of legal consequences can deter one from use. "What people like about doing it this way (incarceration) is it doesn't cost any money. You don't have to raise taxes. You just have to bring down a couple of indictments" (Kennedy 1989:1).

The question still remains is the incarceration of maternal substance abusers effective in reducing their drug use. Or is our punitive social policy simply a response that gives the picture that something is being done about the problem but a policy that never really addresses the underlying issues that are the basis of continued maternal substance abuse? The women who are prosecuted are overwhelmingly low-income, single women, primarily women of color who are dependent on public facilities for their care. Incarceration leaves unaddressed the possible roots of the problem: poverty, unemployment, and lack of educational and vocational opportunities (Smith 1990).

Additionally, pregnant women are seldom welcome in treatment programs. Pregnant and addicted women were refused admission to 54% of seventy-eight treatment programs surveyed in New York City. Sixty-seven percent of the programs denied treatment to pregnant addicts on Medicaid and addicted specifically to crack (Chavkin 1989). Treatment facilities justify exclusion of pregnant women arguing that their program may be unable to adequately care for the women during detoxification, may be ill equipped to provide prenatal care, and may lack the appropriate facilities and expertise to provide newborn and child care services (Kumpfer 1991). Rather than allocate moneys for social programs and treatment or instead of demanding legislation mandating treatment facilities accept pregnant addicts, the method that appears the most efficient is prosecution and incarceration.

> The focus on maternal behavior allows the government to appear to be concerned about babies without having to spend the money, change any priorities or challenge any vested interest (Pollitt 1990:410).

Provocation

Social policies have the potential to provoke a counterproductive emotional response in the group targeted by this intervention. If the practice of indictments and prosecution of maternal substance abusers continues, pregnant mothers who use drugs may refrain from any form of prenatal care thus increasing the risk to the child (Pollitt 1990).

Further, when the social policy is perceived as illegitimate, this intervention can engender anger and defiance, not just on an individual level, but also on a collective scale (Sieber 1981:119). Numerous groups have come forth to protest the prosecution of pregnant women. Paltrow, of the American Civil Liberties Union, contends that government intrusion in pregnant women's lives in unconstitutional and violates the fundamental right to privacy (Kennedy 1989). The indictment of a Waltham woman for motor vehicle homicide after an accident where the woman was driving under the influence of alcohol and where her unborn child was killed, resulted in an outcry among advocates of women's rights. Eight groups filed an *amicus* brief. Though the goal of these groups may in fact be to protect the woman's legal rights, the focus on constitutional and legal issues detracts from some resolution of the original problem—to reduce substance abuse among pregnant women. People may become so embroiled in the controversy over women's rights that the social/medical problems confronting pregnant substance abusers and their infants becomes a secondary consideration. That is one protects rights but still offers no solution.

Additionally, subcultures may engage in certain illicit behavior primarily to symbolize their rejection of dominant group motives. Drug use among minorities may symbolize a rejection of the dominant middle-class values of health and abstinence. If this is the case, focusing on addicted babies may simply be a way of perpetrating the symbolic function of drug-using behavior.

Derogatory Classification

Derogatory classification is the regressive effect of some interventions where the societal label imposed on an individual "may induce a change in the expectations of others, as well as a change in self-perception" (Sieber 1981:141). This process can be examined within the context of deviance amplification.

Once a behavior is defined and accepted as deviant, the tendency of the society's nondeviant members is to isolate the individuals who fit the deviant definition. With the separation from the larger population those defined as meeting the criteria for inclusion into the deviant group, not only cease to have information regarding normal behavior and acceptable norms, but will in fact develop a value system that supports and enhances continued deviant behavior (Wilkins 1965).

This may well be the case with the pregnant substance abuser. The pregnant addict fails to conform exclusively to any one existing deviant category for she is not simply a substance abuser nor solely a negligent parent. Placement in the special classification of pregnant drug abuser relegates the woman to the periphery of society where she will have less contact with mainstream society and its norms, where she will have access to deviant group norms that explain, rationalize, and justify her substance abuse thus decreasing the likelihood of substantive change in her drug-abusing behavior.

Placation

Placation is a characteristic of a social policy where the goal of the intervention is one of "placating certain parties whose support is considered necessary" (Sieber 1981:165). An example of this process is the eventual support by the Reagan administration for the proposed legislation introduced by Mothers Against Drunk Driving (MADD). MADD is a group of individuals who had been negatively affected by a drunk driver and who, as a group, demanded legislative action—not against the liquor companies, but against those individuals who chose to drink and drive. In particular this group supported, and had overwhelming congressional approval for, federal legislation that would force states to increase the drinking age to twenty-one. President Reagan, who favored federal noninterference in state matters, was reluctant to sign any such legislation. Under pressure from his advisors who informed the president that he could not afford to oppose such legislation, Reagan signed the bill. Though it appears that Reagan conceded an issue to popular and political pressure, however, he effectively placated a large and vocal segment of the population (Reinarman 1988). Thus, while MADD was successful and certainly placated, larger issues with potentially greater ramifications, such as the role of alcohol as a potentially harmful drug, were not addressed. Further, this legislative action, while potentially ineffective, gave the appearance to the general public that steps were being taken to resolve drunk driving thus allaying public concern.

This same process of placating certain groups, and at the same time scarcely addressing and possibly exacerbating the problem of maternal substance abuse, may be best examined on a macro or societal level and can be understood within the framework of our current drug policy. Since the 1960s, the U.S. government has been waging a war on drugs (Czajkoski 1990) with questionable and variable results. Even if we are not winning the war, a war on drugs, as in any war, may serve a number of useful control purposes. For example, during a war the general population is often willing to accept an abridgment of civil liberties and a subordination of the individual. This type of abridgment would never be accepted by the general public in more stable times. Today in the name of the War on Drugs and zero tolerance the general population appears willing to accept random drug screens—what seems to many a clear violation of self-incrimination and privacy rights.

In such a war mentality the pregnant substance abuser is branded as the enemy, and is exposed and sanctioned. Through this punishment the illusion that the battle is being won is perpetuated and as a result the public is placated by war victories. Furthermore, by punishing these drug-abusing expectant mothers, usually members of poor and disenfranchised groups (National Association for Perinatal Addiction Research and Education 1992), we are focusing on a group whose political power is minimal. The likelihood of protest of the current punitive policy or consideration of violations of civil rights are minimized. In terms of placation the punishment of pregnant substance abusers shows something is being done about the drug problem, even if nothing is being accomplished; satisfies the public; and avoids addressing central problems in the social system such as poverty, unemployment, and lack of education that may in fact exacerbate the drug problem.

CONCLUSION

Certainly we are dealing, in the case of pregnant substance abusers, with a very special population. Exactly what we should do seems at times problematic. What is clear, as we have shown, is what we should not do. Evidence indicates that time and time again, whether we are dealing with desegregation of schools, fighting the war on drugs, or confronting the issue of poverty, certain features of our social policies bring about a deterioration of the problem that we desire to ameliorate. This use of counterproductive social policies is certainly the case in the prosecution of alcohol- and drug-abusing pregnant women.

What we need to do now is to reexamine the policy of arresting, indicting and incarcerating pregnant substance abusers and offer some alternatives that would be more productive in dealing with the pregnant addict. If we really want to try to insure the health of infants born to alcohol- and drug-abusing mothers, rather than arrest these women, an approach that may place a woman in an environment counterproductive to infant and maternal health, we should insist instead on screening and channeling high-risk expectant mothers into appropriate social services. These services could in-

clude AFDC, WIC, Medicaid, prenatal and health care agencies, family planning services, and drug and alcohol treatment. The earlier assistance is offered the more likely this intervention can be of value to both mother and child.

Rather than arresting, indicting and incarcerating pregnant substance abusers —a practice that increases the likelihood a woman will not access prenatal care and decreases the likelihood of infant health—we need to increase appropriations for drug and alcohol treatment facilities that are geared toward substance-abusing expectant mothers. These long-term facilities, in addition to confronting the woman's drug-using behavior, would offer detoxification, prenatal care, and infant and child care services. These neonatal and pediatric services could include treatment for drug-affected babies. Experts contend that cocaine-affected babies can be greatly improved with therapy and other special attention. Dr. Chasnoff of NAPARE estimates that 300,000 children have suffered some damage due to the expectant mother's cocaine use, but that less than 10% receive treatment (Treaster 1993).

Rather than arrest, indict and incarcerate the woman who uses drugs or alcohol when pregnant—a policy that labels then marginalizes these women and decreases the likelihood of their wholesale participation in society—we should focus on policies that may change addictive behavior. Clearly the war on drugs, while increasing the prison population, has done little to affect addiction. Certainly fear has not stopped women who are pregnant from drug use. The $7.4 billion allocated by the previous administration to enforce compliance with existing drug laws (Corn 1990) might better be used for education and treatment. A policy that offers hope may well draw more women than our current regressive policy.

REFERENCES

Abel, E. 1984. *FAS and FAE*. New York: Plenum Press.

Abel, E. and R. J. Sokol. 1987. Incidence of Fetal Alcohol Syndrome and economic impact of FAS-related anomalies. *Drug and Alcohol Dependence* 19:51–70.

Balisy, S. S. 1987. Maternal substance abuse: The need to provide legal protection for the fetus. *Southern California Law Review* 60:1209–38.

Barry, E. 1989. Pregnant prisoners. *Harvard Women's Law Journal* 12:199–200.

Cannellos, P. 1993. Walk to schools sought anew. *Boston Globe* 29 January.

Cassen Moss, D. 1988. Pregnant? Go directly to jail. *American Bar Association Journal* November 1:20.

Chasnoff, I. J. 1989. Drug use and women: Establishing a standard of care. *Annals of New York Academy of Sciences* 562:2008–10.

Chasnoff, I. J. 1990. Testimony. The President's National Drug Abuse Strategy before the Subcommittee on Health and Environment of the U.S. House of Representatives Committee on Energy and Commerce. 30 April.

Chavkin, W. 1990. Drug addiction and pregnancy: Policy crossroads. *American Journal of Public Health* 80:483–7.

Cole, H. M. 1990. Legal interventions during pregnancy. *Journal American Medical Association* 264:2667.

Corn, D. 1990. Justice's war on drug treatment. *The Nation* 14 May 250:659–62.

Czajkoski, E. H. 1990. Drugs and the warlike administration of justice. *Journal of Drug Issues* 20(1): 125–130.

General Accounting Office. 1990. Drug exposed infants: A generation at risk. (GAO/HRS-90-138). June.

Glamour. 1988. This is what you thought: 46% say prenatal abuse should be a criminal offense. 86:109.

Gomby, D. S. and P. H. Shiono. 1991. Estimating the number of drug exposed infants. *Future of Children* 1(1): 17–25.

Goode, E. 1989. *Drugs in American society*. New York: A. A. Knopf.

Halfon, N. 1989. Testimony Born hooked: Confronting the impact of perinatal substance abuse.

The Select Committee on Children, Youth, and Families. U.S. House of Representatives. 27 April.

Howard, J. and L. Beckwith. 1989. The development of young children of substance-abusing parents: Insights from seven years of intervention and research. *Zero to Three*. 1(5):8–12.

Kennedy, J. 1989. Uncertainties surround infant cocaine case. *Boston Globe*. 23 August.

Kronstadt, D. 1991. Complex developmental issues of prenatal drug exposure. *Future of Children* 1(1):36–49.

Kumpfer, K. L. 1991. Treatment programs for drug abusing women. *Future of Children* 1(1):51–60.

Lukas, J. A. 1986. *Common ground*. New York: Vintage Books.

National Association for Perinatal Addiction Research and Education 1992. Epidemiological study of the prevalence of alcohol and other drug use among pregnant and parturient women in Illinois.

Office of the Inspector General. 1990. Getting straight: Overcoming treatment barriers for addicted women and their children. Fact sheet. U.S. House of Representatives. 23 April. Hearing Select Committee on Children, Youth, and Families.

Paltrow, L. 1992. Criminal prosecutions against pregnant women. National update and overview. Reproductive Freedom Project, American Civil Liberties Union Foundation. April.

Pollitt, K. 1990. Fetal rights—A new assault on feminism. *The Nation* 26 March: 409–18.

Reinarman, C. 1988. The social construction of an alcohol problem. *Theory and Society* 17:91–120.

Seiber, S. 1981. *Fatal remedies*. New York: Plenum Press.

Smith, B. V. 1990. Testimony. Law and policy affecting addicted women and their children. Hearing Select Committee on Children, Youth and Families. U.S. House of Representatives. 17 May.

Treaster, J. B. 1993. For children of cocaine fresh reasons for hope. *New York Times*, 16 February.

Warren, K. 1987. Alcohol and birth defects: FAS and related disorders. *National Institute on Alcohol Abuse and Alcoholism* vii.

Wilkins, L. 1965. The deviance amplifying system. In *Social deviance*, ed. Farrell and Swigert, 182–4.

Zuckerman, B. 1991. Drug exposed infants: Understanding the medical risk. *Future of Children* 1(1):26–35.

CHALLENGE QUESTIONS

Should Drug Use by Pregnant Women Be Considered Child Abuse?

1. If protecting the fetus is the main concern in prosecuting a pregnant woman who takes drugs, how would you suggest the law treat such a woman?

2. How should the issue of the original intent of a law affect prosecutions for abuse of a fetus? Why?

3. Imagine that you are a prosecutor about to try a case against a woman who is accused of child abuse because she took drugs during pregnancy. Are you satisfied that her conviction would protect the fetus? Why, or why not?

4. Norton-Hawk's argument against prosecuting drug-using mothers appears also to argue against social interventions for societal problems. Apply her criticisms to a similar societal problem, such as teenage smoking. Do they alter or support your opinions about government efforts to control tobacco? Explain your thinking.

ISSUE 10

Is Sex Addiction a Myth?

YES: William A. Henkin, from "The Myth of Sexual Addiction," *Journal of Gender Studies* (Spring 1991)

NO: Patrick J. Carnes, from *Don't Call It Love: Recovery from Sexual Addiction* (Bantam Books, 1991)

ISSUE SUMMARY

YES: Psychotherapist William A. Henkin asserts that there is no such thing as an addiction to sex. The concept of sexual addiction, he argues, is part of antisexual obsessions in our culture, and belief in sexual addiction poses a real danger to people's civil liberties.

NO: Patrick J. Carnes, a sex therapist, argues that a significant number of people have identified themselves as sexual addicts—persons with unstoppable, repetitive behavior patterns that are destructive to the addict and to his or her family. Sexual addicts, Carnes claims, experience the same kind of neurochemical dependency that other addicts, such as alcoholics, compulsive gamblers, and compulsive overeaters, do.

The way we define or label a particular behavior greatly affects the way people react to it. When a society labels a particular behavior, like masturbation or oral sex, as an unnatural act and the result of a narcissistic, unstable mental disorder, we "know" that people who engage in these behaviors have a psychological disorder that requires treatment by psychologists, psychiatrists, and psychotherapists. If we define the behavior as a moral disorder or a sin, we "know" that the person needs redemption, absolution, and some kind of spiritual or moral counseling.

In recent years, our society has wavered about whether to define alcoholism and substance abuse as compulsive behaviors, addictions, or diseases. If they are diseases, then medical insurance may pay for treatment. A similar effort has been made to classify sexual behaviors that have patterns of pathology and compulsivity similar to those of alcoholism and other addictions. If the *Diagnostic and Statistical Manual of Mental Disorders (DSM-III-R)*, the handbook of psychiatrists, does *not* list "sexual addiction" or "obsessive-compulsive sexual behavior" as a psychosexual disorder, insurance companies may not pay for treatment.

More recently, some therapists have borrowed the label *addiction* from alcohol and substance abuse and applied it to behavior that the patient, the therapist, or society labels "promiscuous."

The debate over whether sexually compulsive behavior is an addiction or a psychosexual, obsessive-compulsive behavior disorder may sound like a quibble over words. But words, especially definitions, can be extremely powerful. Witness the major social changes that occurred when feminists in the early 1970s redefined *rape* as "an act of rage, power, and the need for control" instead of "a sexual act," as it was commonly defined before 1970. Redefining *rape* changed the treatment of both the rapist and the victim. How we define *promiscuous* or whether we label a particular case of promiscuous sex an "obsessive-compulsive psychosexual condition" or an "addiction" will have a definite impact on how we view and treat persons who exhibit this behavior.

In the following selections, William A. Henkin dismisses the concept of sexual addiction as a myth created for the profit of certain therapists who want to control the way other people think about erotic acts and their sexual behavior. Patrick J. Carnes maintains that compulsive, uncontrollable, self-destructive patterns of sexual behavior constitute an addiction that requires treatment.

YES

William A. Henkin

THE MYTH OF SEXUAL ADDICTION

Failure is an opportunity.
If you blame someone else,
there is no end to the blame.

Therefore the Master
fulfills her own obligations
and corrects her own mistakes.
She does what she needs to do
and demands nothing of others.

—Tao te Ching

SEX

However natural and innate the physiology of sex acts might be, the way their practice is seen in humans depends as well on cultural norms. Nearly 20 years ago, anthropologist Donald Marshall wrote that on the Polynesian island of Mangaia, "there is no social contact between the sexes, no rendezvous that does not lead directly to coitus—copulation is the only imaginable outcome of heterosexual contact." From childhood on, he reported, Mangaians were trained to enjoy sex and to assure sexual pleasure to their partners.

At about the same time, an entirely different perspective on sex was provided by John C. Messenger, who studied an Irish island he called Inis Beag. There, not just partnered sex, but *any* kind of sexual expression "such as masturbation, mutual exploration of bodies, use of either standard or slang words relating to sex, and open urination and defecation—is severely punished by word or deed."

As Havelock Ellis demonstrated nearly a century ago, social comparisons need not take us to remote islands. Concerning modesty, for instance, Louis XI was greeted upon his first entry into France by three naked women representing Sirens; they "were greatly admired by the public." Similar welcomes were accorded royalty elsewhere in Europe in the 15th and 16th centuries. In 18th century France and Prussia, members of royalty and the intelligentsia alike often welcomed to their homes the lovers of their wives and husbands, men and women bathed nude together in Russia, and women bared their chests in Italy's warm summers. As Edward Brecher has pointed out, nude bathing was common on some of England's popular beaches well into Victoria's 19th century.

We cannot reasonable understand sex or sexuality without recognizing the extent to which sexual mores express the specific sociology of a particular people in a particular time and place. While a Mangaian youth might regard one [sexual encounter] a night, every night, as sexual poverty, her Inis Beag counterpart might equally regard one [sexual encounter] a month as sinful, or at least pathological.

Closer to home, in 1952, when the American Psychiatric Association published the first *Diagnostic and Statistical Manual of Mental Disorders* (DSM), homosexuality, promiscuous sexual activity, fellatio, cunnilingus, and masturbation were all officially designated mental illnesses. By 1980, 28 years later, the *DSM-III*, third edition, included none of these ailments. If Kinsey, Hunt, and Hite can be believed, the behaviors had not changed, of course; human judgments had. And human judgment is what the vogue for sexual addiction is all about.

ADDICTION

According to the *Oxford English Dictionary*, the word "addiction" derives from Roman law and originally meant a formal surrender by sentence of a judge. Over time, the word came to mean devotion to a habit, place, person, or idea, or the pursuit of some interest. Since it implied a preference, inclination, or penchant, people were said to be addicted to reading, art, their trades, melancholy, virginity, or thoughts of the next life, as well as to wealth, strong drink, and the devil. Addiction as such was not considered a bad thing, although one person might disapprove of what another was addicted *to*.

During the 20th century psychiatrists adopted addiction and made it specific to biochemistry. The *Psychiatric Glossary* of the American Psychiatric Association defines addiction as:

> Dependence on a chemical substance to the extent that a physiologic need is established. This [need] manifests itself as withdrawal symptoms... when the substance is removed.

The *Psychiatric Glossary* cross-references addiction to drug dependence, which it defines as:

> Habituation to, abuse of, and/or addiction to a chemical substance.... The term thus includes not only the addiction (which emphasizes physiologic dependence), but also drug abuse (where the pathologic craving for drugs seems unrelated to physical dependence).

The glossary offers as examples of the drugs upon which a person might become dependent:

> alcohol; opiates; synthetic analgesics with morphine-like effects; barbiturates; other hypnotics, sedatives, and some anti-anxiety agents; cocaine, psychostimulants; marijuana; and psychotomimetic drugs.

By the time the psychiatric establishment appropriated addiction and relegated it to a state of chemical dependence, the idea that devotion to or interest in books, politics, or money could be addicting had lost its currency. Though people do periodically attempt to "cure" themselves of habits such as nailbiting and leaving closet doors ajar, the only sorts of nonchemical dependencies modern doctors seriously endeavor to treat are better thought of as compulsions. According to the *Psychiatric Glossary*, a compulsion is:

> an insistent, repetitive, intrusive, and unwanted urge to perform an act that is contrary to one's ordinary wishes or standards. Since it serves as a defensive substitute for still more unacceptable unconscious ideas and wishes, failure to perform the compulsive act leads to overt anxiety. Compulsions are obsessions that are still felt as impulses.

The large importance of the small semantic distinction I am making lies in the difference between a condition and a behavior. A condition such as addiction describes the way one *is*, however temporarily; a behavior, which one may or may not perform compulsively, is something one *does*. Many kinds of psychotherapy treat compulsive behaviors, but apart from hypnosis and the grosser forms of behavior modification, no strictly medical or psychological program has ever clearly demonstrated success in treating addictions.

Stanton Peele, author of *Love and Addiction*, has pointed out that "self-cure can work, and depending on someone else to cure you usually does not." Inpatient rehabilitation facilities, recognizing what combination of efforts can enhance success in treating addiction, have made self-help concepts the core of their programs. The understandings that underlie all these self-help approaches

began to take shape in 1935, when Bill W. met Dr. Bob and the seeds of a fellowship were sown that soon became known as Alcoholics Anonymous, or AA for short.

CLOSE ENCOUNTERS OF THE ANONYMOUS KIND

Friends, if you are not and never have been a problem drinker; if you have never even known someone who was a problem drinker; nonetheless, AA had probably touched your life. And it is increasingly likely that the part of your life AA has touched has to do with your sexuality.

Twelve-step programs like AA help addicts recover in part because they provide external systems that specifically support people in staying away from their chemicals of obligation while the physical addiction fades and they develop the internal resources they need to cope with their psychological dependence or habituation. Though chewing gum instead of smoking does not provide the group support of people sharing a problem and a goal in common, it does provide a similarly alternative habit into which an addict can channel some of his or her craving during withdrawal.

Gum and groups have been pejoratively described as crutches for people who cannot resolve their habits on their own, but using a crutch to support a fragile freedom from an addiction may be as critical as using a crutch to support the body's weight while a broken leg bone heals. After all, the addict is wrestling with chemical dependence and its concomitant withdrawal symptoms. Suddenly, removing the addictive substance can provoke sweats, tremors, convulsions, hallucinations, and even death. Whatever can reduce that strain, short of giving in to the addiction itself, can help the addict struggle free. Group support is one such valuable aid.

Freedom from chemical dependency and the kindness of strangers may not be the end, however. "Addicts may switch not only from one chemical substance to another, but from a chemical to a social 'high,'" says Stanton Peele, and in any kind of self-cure, the "key word is self: taking charge of your own problem."

If your own problem is not based in biochemistry or genetics, as chemical dependency seems at least in part to be, then what is restrained by participation in an Anonymous addicts group may not be a habit at all. It may be, instead, exactly what is supposed to emerge after the addiction has been overcome: your self, and along with it the concomitant freedom to take charge of your problem.

Participation in almost any support group has the potential to alter a person's behavior. Peer pressure, the insights afforded by other people's autobiographies, and the pleasures of belonging all conspire to bring a person into line with the edicts of the group he or she has chosen.

In recent years, programs based on AA's precepts have been devised for people who feel dependent not only on chemicals, but on just about every kind of foible that could ail a human mind or body, including, of course, sex.

The problem with sex addict groups is that they conspire to identify as addictions behavior patterns that may be compulsions and may be no more than shame responses to presumptions of social pressure. In either case, peer pressure, insights, and the pleasures of belonging encourage people to relinquish hope of achieving the kind of mastery over themselves, and control over their own free choices, that they joined those groups in order to discover.

THE MYTH OF SEXUAL ADDICTION

In a 1986 presentation to the American Psychological Association, Martin P. Levine and Richard R. Troiden addressed "the newly discovered 'conditions' of sexual addiction and sexual compulsion from the sociological perspective of symbolic interactionism." In the revision of their paper, published in the *Journal of Sex Research*, they demonstrate that the definitions are conceptually flawed and that the criteria for these "conditions" are subjective and value laden. There is nothing inherently pathological in the conduct that is labeled sexually compulsive or addictive. Rather than referring to actual clinical entities, sexual addiction and compulsion refer to learned patterns of behavior that are stigmatized by dominant institutions.

In the United States, the authors observe, three distinct sexual scripts or erotic codes coexist; since the ideals that underlie them are mutually exclusive, the codes are in competition. For that reason it is not even a person's sexual behavior, but rather the prevailing script that determines whether "a behavior is labeled as a psychosexual disorder or as sexually normal."

Levine and Troden call the three sexual scripts they discuss procreative, relational, and recreational. The first holds that

> sexual expression is dirty, sinful, and wrong except when it occurs in marriage and for reproductive purposes. ...

Casual sex and frequent sexual intercourse are defined as pathological conditions.

The relational script, on the other hand,

regards sexual activity as a means of expressing and reinforcing emotional and psychological intimacy.... Any act is appropriate in the relational context, provided that both partners mutually approve.

The recreational script

perceives mutual pleasure as the chief purpose of sexual activity, [and] endorses sexual contacts between mutually interested partners, even if they are total strangers, and permits them to engage in any agreed-upon act that enhances sensual pleasure....

These three scripts have different definitions of control over erotic conduct. The procreative code views any nonmarital or nonprocreative sexuality as indicating a lack of sexual control; the relational code regards nonrelational sex as indicating a lack of sexual control, whereas issues of control are irrelevant in recreational scripts, which define only nonconsensual sex as deviant.

According to Levine and Troiden, the procreative ethic was this nation's primary erotic code at midcentury, when psychiatrists described such nonprocreative erotic acts as masturbation, homosexuality, and oral sex as evidence of mental disorders. Once reproductive sex lost its holy patina, relational and recreational scripts gained ascendance; and in the 1960s and 1970s, large numbers of Americans "came to view nonmarital sex, mate swapping, one-night stands, homosexuality and the use of pornography as viable sexual options."

By 1980, in fact, not only had masturbation, oral sex, and homosexuality disappeared from the DSM; at the same time, therapists discovered a whole new collection of sexual pathologies, including pre-mature ejaculation, failure to achieve orgasm, fear of sex, and low levels of sexual desire. Whereas in 1952 Americans were considered sick for wanting too much sex, by 1980 they were sick for wanting too little. Once again, to specific nature of each behavior had not changed; people who wanted [sex] a lot still wanted [sex] a lot; people who were bored by sex remained bored by sex. What had changed was the sexual script—the human judgment—favored by the people who dominated social thinking in those years.

In the 1980s sexual revisionism set in with a vengeance. Herpes, hepatitis and AIDS; the rise of radical religious and social movements; and, perhaps, the inevitable return swing of the cultural pendulum: Any or all might be blamed or credited for the shift. But if the procreative script shared preeminence with the relational script, the recreational script was out in any case.

Soon, self-help groups founded on the same premises and steps that made AA successful appeared to help people conquer this whole new battery of nominal disabilities. As antisex became a hot topic in the dailies, some sex-negative groups assumed the Anonymous mantle. They espoused heterosexual monogamy with a kind of holy zeal and sought to recast mate-swapping, cruising, and other recently popular behaviors as disorders that required therapy—or as addictions best served by self-help groups.

But wait—however pumped up some people get on their fantasies or hormones, sexual behavior is still not a substance, nor does the unsatisfied need for sexual expression provoke withdrawal symptoms. Sexual behavior is a highly charged facet of human experience, however, that affects and is affected by biochemical changes in the body and brain that are associated with emotions. Consequently, sexual behavior also has a history of frightening some people so badly that rather than labor to understand it, they seek to suppress it in themselves as well as in others.

Throughout the centuries people have rationalized their sexual fears, and hidden their resulting bigotry behind the skirts of bureaucratic religions, legal proscriptions, and pseudoscientific authority. To 18th-century Western physicians, masturbation was a well-known cause of insanity; to their 19th-century counterparts, it was clear that women had few sexual desires. So, as the 20th century draws to a close, an increasing number of psychologists seem to know that human beings can be addicted to their own erotic behaviors.

Now, whether the subject is masturbation, flashing, or rape—or eating, jogging, or watching television, for that matter—any behavior can be done compulsively. While I do not wish to imply that child molesters and rapists are free of pressing problems, I object to denominating those problems as addictions.

First of all, to do so is to raise the value of a transitory social ideology above the variety of ongoing human experience; second, it offers a simplistic explanation for an issue that deserves detailed attention. At one end of the psychological spectrum, compulsions may reflect a person's shame or guilt for having feelings—in this case for having sexual feelings specifically—at all. At the other end they may represent a single facet of a complex character disorder.

Perhaps the pathology that does not change with the winds of social reformation lies in the need some people have to meddle in other people's affairs. As Levine and Troiden write, there is noth-

ing intrinsically pathological in the behaviors the *DSM* defines as psychosexual disorders, whether the definitions are taken from the category that prevailed in 1952, the category that prevailed in 1980, or the category that prevails in the revised *DSM-III-R* today.

Instead, sexual behaviors

are defined as pathological only because they violate prevailing erotic norms. Rather than referring to actual clinical entities, psychosexual disorders denote forms of stigmatized erotic conduct. In this sense they are value judgments cloaked as pseudoscientific diagnosis. By inventing and treating these "conditions," that is, by "medicalizing" morality, mental health professionals and sexologists pathologize non-normative sexual practices; they function as social control agents, enforcing conformity to culturally hegemonic erotic standards....

As used currently, the terms "sexual addiction" and "sexual compulsion" employ prevailing cultural standards as the basis for determining erotic control or deviance.

THE DEATH OF SEX

The man who put sex addiction on the map is psychologist Patrick Carnes. In the preface to his book *Out of the Shadows*, originally published in 1983 as *The Sexual Addiction*, Carnes explains how the book grew out of a paper he wrote in 1976, based on his experiences treating sex offenders for two years.

Although he reports that his paper was influential and circulated widely, he refrained from publishing his work for several reasons: Not everyone he regarded as a sex addict was a sex offender; he did not yet have adequate data to support his belief that sexual acting out could constitute an addiction; and there was no network of programs in place—no Sex Addicts Anonymous, Sex and Love Addicts Anonymous, Sexoholics Anonymous, or the like—to help people troubled by their alternative sexual urges. "Most of all," however, Carnes explains, "I was afraid of the public reaction, which is always unpredictable in sexual matters. In short, it was an idea whose time had not come."

Indeed, in 1976 American society was still in the throes of a recreational sex script. By 1983, though we were not ready to resurrect the procreational scripts promulgated by foes of abortion, homosexuality, and extramarital intercourse, at least the time *had* come for a change. Before a relational script could dominate the scene, however, the ruling recreational scripts had to be overthrown. In the fine tradition of American clinical psychiatry, the simples way to overthrow those scripts was to medicalize the behaviors that defined them.

No one person can redefine entries for so Biblical an opus as the *Diagnostic and Statistical Manual of Mental Disorders*. So far, each revision has required a huge committee and more than a decade of debate. But one influential person can spearhead a movement that redefines a social ideal, and can thereby profoundly alter the context in which a *DSM* committee sits.

Carnes and his followers attribute addiction to behavior. This revisionist judgment is not written in stone, and it is not written in biochemistry, but it may be written in a future *DSM*, as oral sex and masturbation were in *DSM*s of the not-so-distant past.

Carnes does not claim that every person who engages in any behavior represented in his schema is a sex addict

in need of rehabilitation. As he writes, "behavior by itself does not make an addict." It is Carnes' contention that "addicts are people who cannot stop their behavior which is crippling them and those around them," and that, by implication, behaviors that are damaging and out of the actor's control are addictions.

The script Carnes would put in place lays the ground for a social ideology that dictates which erotic pleasures you may take tonight and which you had best foreswear; and if you do not like the limits of that tolerance, Carnes warns, your discomfort or rebellion itself suggests that you may be the new sex addict on your block.

ADDICTION TO THE MYTH

Perhaps we should start to contemplate the meaning of our society's "addiction" to addiction terminology. Psychological health is advanced through increased awareness of personal responsibility for one's feelings, thoughts, beliefs, and behaviors. By couching sexual behavior in terms of addiction, the psychological meaning of a person's erotic experience is diminished and his or her personal responsibility for that experience is demeaned.

On an individual basis, the lack of personal responsibility that is thus encouraged, formalized by organizational structures, and given credence by professional caregivers with a great deal to gain by identifying a whole new bailiwick of illness, encourages people who are distressed or confused by their sexuality to think of themselves as impotent in the face of their own problems.

Socially, rapists and other sexually abusive individuals are provided with a sanctioned legal defense for their dangerous practices—"I couldn't help it, I'm an addict"—while people who read erotic literature or watch erotic theater are stigmatized for their harmless ones. Thus, the safety, psychological health, and civil liberties of us all are jeopardized by a cultural ideal that encourages both the suppression and the repression not only of people's behaviors but of their thoughts and feelings as well, in private and in public, in the names of social service and our own good.

If we accept the idea of sex addiction we give up the rights to our own erotic processes. If we relinquish the rights to suffer our own pains and ignominies, we give away the rights to learn from them and to grow into increasingly responsible adult human beings. And as history shows, if we do not embrace our own responsibilities, others will readily do so for us.

Laws are already in place regarding sexual activities that clearly have victims; activities, in brief, that are nonconsen-sual. Whether those laws are adequate, whether they are appropriately enforced, and whether their enforcement is or can be effective are all questions beyond the purview of this essay. Here, the question boils down to whether the food is to be blamed if I overeat.

After 20 years of relative freedom, it has once again become the vogue to legislate morality and to usurp individuals rights, sexual and otherwise. But it is precisely those processes by which sexual freedom among consenting adults is denied that the life of one person and the life of a whole society is suppressed, because it is precisely those processes that infantilize a person and a people; first by relieving them of hard choices, next by withholding their responsibilities for making those choices, and finally by taking away their power to make them altogether.

This is why the debate about sexual addiction is not a debate about whether sex is good or not. It is a debate about who shall determine which of us shall be free.

NO

THE SIGNS OF ADDICTION

- A woman uses a vibrator so intensely she burns herself and has to go to the emergency room.
- A thirty-one-year-old man, married and the father of three small children, has been having sex with men in "hot johns" since he was seventeen. He got married to stop. He went through treatment for alcoholism to stop. Now he has AIDS. So does his wife. They are both dying.
- The priest has a thousand-dollar-a-week prostitution habit. His only way to support the habit is to steal from the parish he serves.
- Their children and friends knew. But his wife was in the dark until she discovered three volumes carefully annotating his sexual encounters with fifteen hundred women.
- A thirty-eight-year-old dentist is furious about his wife's sexual unavailability. He secretly drugs her to have sex with her.
- A thirty-five-year-old schoolteacher is stunned as she watches *Looking for Mr. Goodbar* and recognizes that it fits her life with frightening accuracy.
- A thirty-three-year-old woman leaves her toddlers alone while she goes off to meet her lovers.
- A sixty-six-year-old man is arrested for the third time for stealing lingerie.
- A minister is confronted by the bishop, who has heard about his affairs with parishioners.
- A corporate technical guru has been the subject of seven sexual harassment complaints in two years. Now there is one from a major customer.
- A youth leader has sex with yet another boy. He plans suicide if ever discovered.

The signs of addiction. Some would say these cases are matters of sexual excess or bad judgment or accidents. Others would dismiss them as bizarre or perverted, part of the ragged edge of life. In reality, they represent a much more serious problem: a life-threatening obsession with sex. These situations involved people whose lives were dominated by a pattern of out-of-control sex. Such people are sex addicts. They have experiences that others don't have, at least not in the same way or to the same extent. The patterns of their lives signify the presence of an illness we are just beginning to understand.

We are surrounded by the signs of sex addiction yet still resist its reality. We can accept that people can be sick with alcoholism or can destroy themselves with gambling or food—but not sex. There are some who see the problem clearly but hesitate to call it an addiction. They choose words like "compulsive" or "hypersexual"—yet they have absolutely no problem calling compulsive gambling an addiction. Why is there so much resistance to recognizing the clear signs of sexual addiction? The answer resides in the central role sex plays in all of our lives.

1. *Sex is essential.* Sex is key to the survival of our species, and some of our richest cultural symbols relate to the meaning and beauty of sex. Our songs and literature testify that some of our best moments as human beings are sexual. The first statement made about every one of us is a sexual statement: It's a boy! It's a girl! Our sex —male or female—is a fundamental definition of who we are and strongly influences how we live out our lives.

2. *Sex is powerful.* People in passion will murder, betray, and exploit others. Sex sells products from cologne and cars to newspapers and talk shows. Sex changes our mood and relieves tension. From migraine headaches to arthritis, medical research tells us, sex can be a significant force in healing. But most important, sex for many becomes a bonding force; it sustains relationships through some of our most significant and difficult moments.

3. *Sex is frightening.* Current estimates suggest that one out of ten men will commit date rape and that one million women will be raped this year, over half of them by someone they know. Over forty million American adults were abused sexually as children. Each day an average of three thousand teenage girls in the United States become pregnant. Our fears of sexual excess emerge in religious teachings, legislative action, and zoning ordinances, which together express an unwritten cultural code suggesting that sex is dirty and bad. Most adults can confirm that this is the cultural judgment by recalling myths told them as children to prevent sexual play. Our fear of sexual excess serves as a sad counterpoint to our own profound fears and self-doubts about our sexual adequacy. The irony, of course, is that performance anxiety and sexual exploitation are driven by some of the same fear-based sexual assumptions rooted in our culture.

… On the basis of our research and clinical experience, there are ten signs that indicate the presence of sexual addiction:

1. A pattern of out-of-control behavior
2. Severe consequences due to sexual behavior
3. Inability to stop despite adverse consequences
4. Persistent pursuit of self-destructive or high-risk behavior
5. Ongoing desire or effort to limit sexual behavior
6. Sexual obsession and fantasy as a primary coping strategy
7. Increasing amounts of sexual experience because the current level of activity is no longer sufficient

8. Severe mood changes around sexual activity
9. Inordinate amounts of time spent in obtaining sex, being sexual, or recovering from sexual experience
10. Neglect of important social, occupational, or recreational activities because of sexual behavior....

WHEN IS SOMEONE A SEX ADDICT?

No one sign is proof that sex addiction is present. But... usually many of the signs are present concurrently. Taken together, they form a pattern revealing the underlying illness. Sometimes people focus on specific behaviors. As one reporter put it, "How many affairs do you have to have before you are a sex addict?" The question parallels asking how many drinks it takes to be an alcoholic or how many bets to be a compulsive gambler. The answer is not one of quantity but rather of pattern. For example, drinking ceases to be social and becomes problematic and then addictive as out-of-control behavior becomes the norm in the alcoholic's life. The same standards apply in sex addiction.

Important barriers exist to our acknowledging the signs of sex as an addiction. In our culture, we find it difficult to talk about sex in a straightforward, serious fashion without sensationalizing, making jokes, or somehow discrediting the value of the discussion. Also we fear what would happen if a part of our population was out of control sexually. Perhaps most important remains our persistent view of sex as always a matter of self-control or choice. In that sense there is a direct parallel with concepts of alcoholism in the forties and fifties. Alcoholism was perceived as a problem of character and not as an illness that afflicted millions. Now we know that alcoholism is often transmitted across generations. In the stories that follow we shall also see examples of generation after generation of out-of-control, destructive sexual behavior.

Sexism and sexual stereotypes also affect our acceptance of sexual addiction. The cultural expectation that "boys will be boys" obscures sexual addiction with popular notions of sexual conquest and the good life. In contrast, women addicts report that one of their greatest obstacles to getting help was not being believed because women are perceived as the guardians of morality and not prone to sexually excessive behavior. In earlier times it was also deemed to be manly to be able to control one's liquor. Many men had trouble admitting they had a problem with alcohol because of how they perceived manhood. Women, on the other hand, were not supposed to have a problem with drinking. It took years before there was wide acceptance of women alcoholics in the health care system. Our cultural stereotypes prevent us from seeing that people are in desperate trouble.

HOW CAN IT BE AN ADDICTION WHEN NO DRUG IS INVOLVED?

People ask how sex can be an addiction. It is not like a drug or alcohol which is foreign to the body. For professionals in addictionology (the science of addiction), this is familiar territory, already traversed in the areas of compulsive gambling and compulsive eating. We have learned that addictive obsession can exist in whatever generates significant mood alteration, whether it be the self-nurturing of food, the excitement of gambling, or the arousal of seduction. One of the more destructive parts of sex addiction is that you literally carry your own source of supply.

By focusing on external chemicals like alcohol, we have missed the significance of being able to get high on our own brain chemicals. We find that compulsive gamblers, for example, have abnormally low beta-endorphin levels. Like alcoholics who experience an opiate deficiency, they manufacture a state of excitement to make up for the deficit. Prolonged use alters these individuals' brain chemistry until they "require" the excitement in order to feel "normal." Similarly, Harvey Milkman and Stanley Sunderwirth summarize research on sexuality in their book *Craving for Ecstasy: The Consciousness and Chemistry of Escape:*

> It is becoming more evident that orgasm is not so much a function of the genitals as it is of the brain. As early as the sixteenth century it was known that opium ingestion decreased sexual activity and in some cases could cause impotence. Opiates occupy endorphin receptor sites on the presynaptic terminals of neurons in the central nervous system. In this way opiates mimic the pain-killing and the euphoric effects of our own endorphins. The inference is obvious: endorphins (and the limbic system) must somehow be involved in the ecstasy of sexual activity and orgasm.

> The relationship between endorphins and orgasms was demonstrated by a group of neuroscientists who showed that the level of endorphins in the blood of hamsters increased dramatically after several ejaculations. This finding would account for the well-known decrease of pain during and after sex.... The rush of endorphins into the central nervous system could also explain the euphoria usually experienced immediately following orgasm and loss of romantic interest just after sex.

Beyond the pleasurability of love, there also exists the "rush" or intoxication experience during the attraction stage of new love. Dorothy Tennov described the pursuit of this experience as "limerance"—the state in which one finds oneself romantically compelled. Michael Liebowitz describes the compulsive pursuit of this condition as "hysteroid dysphoria"—a "common pattern of repeated intense romantic involvements." In Liebowitz's book *The Chemistry of Love,* he underlines the importance in romantic attraction of the peptide called phenylethylamine, or PEA.

According to Liebowitz, PEA is critical to the chemistry of courtship. Its molecular structure parallels that of amphetamines and creates a high-arousal state. The mood-altering effect of PEA is immediate but short-lived. Its intense impact tapers off as the romance gets past the initial "limerance" stage to the bonding of the long-term attachment phase of love. The impact also may be affected by context. For example, monkeys injected with concentrations of PEA demonstrated hypersexual or supererotic behavior—but only in the presence of other monkeys. So the psychobiological connection is crucial. For PEA to result in excessive sexuality in primates, the object of affection has to be present.

Considerable evidence also indicates that PEA and sexual arousal are highly affected by the presence of fear, risk, and danger. For instance, PEA concentrations have been measured as extremely high in connection with divorce court trials. Experiments with attraction have shown that fear serves as an important escalator of desire. For example, in one study students were interviewed by an attractive interviewer. Those who were (falsely) told they might receive an electric shock rated the interviewer more attractive than those who were not given this "warning."

Two important contexts must be considered to put PEA research in perspective. First, PEA is probably but one of many brain chemicals that exist in the chemistry of sexuality and love. Of the over three hundred chemicals involved in the chemistry of the brain, we have a working understanding of only about sixty. Breakthroughs in neuroscience are occurring almost daily, but we still have much to learn. Some experts like Milkman and Sunderwirth, as well as Liebowitz, speculate that designer drugs that go by street names like "Ecstasy" and "Love" have molecular constructions that will serve as models for expanding our knowledge base. For now, the isolation of PEA is but one significant contribution to our ongoing quest for knowledge.

The second context is that PEA research fits with other efforts to link danger or fear to addiction. Skydiving, shoplifting, and gambling share the emotions of high risk. Pioneering work in the risk-taking personality has been done by Marvin Zuckerman, whose research on the biological basis of sensation seeking amplifies what is occurring in the neuroscience of addiction. Many studies he underlines show the existence of low levels of monoamine oxidase (MAO) as a biological factor in seeking high risk; MAO is an enzyme that regulates the neurotransmissions of arousal in the brain. In compulsive gambling, we are already able to link alterations of brain chemistry with different levels of risk. Perhaps we will be able to do the same for sex.

Some people object to breaking down love and sex into chemical components, believing that such analysis takes the magic away. However, it is now commonplace to talk of the neurochemistry of stress reactions. Almost everybody can describe a Type A personality: the hard-driving, goal-oriented, high-risk individual. Few of us would have difficulty understanding the role of adrenaline and its impact on the heart. Yet we are reluctant to accept the same kind of analysis of love and sexuality. The reality of neuroscience exists. We will all become neurochemists to some degree as the emerging science helps us to understand our behavior. Neurochemistry does not invalidate anything we know about addiction. It simply helps us to understand the mechanisms of what addicts have been telling us about for years.

Over and over in our survey we heard addicts talk about their sexuality as a potent drug. Mark, [a] physician sex addict..., really became clear about this when he was told that masturbation was part of his problem. On learning that he would have to stop masturbating, he reacted strongly: "I said that's impossible. Nothing's wrong with it—I'm a physician, there's nothing wrong with masturbation. Then I realized masturbation had been my trouble all my life. That was my drug. From that moment on I worked my AA approach on my masturbation. One day at a time I stopped masturbating, and as soon as I stopped masturbating, my life started getting better."

Almost immediately Mark was able to see how sex was like a drug for him.

One day I walked into the hospital. Someone had died and two people started crying. I walked down the hall and all of a sudden I started to weep.

Spontaneous weeping. I believe that all that masturbating I did in college and medical school kept me going. It helped me numb an enormous amount of feeling. When my father died and when my brother died, even though it's against our religion I immediately had sex with my wife. She knew if there was any way to get me calmed down if I was upset, it was to have sex with me.

Similarly, Peter described the pain and anguish when he stopped his sexual bingeing:

I can remember many, many, many times during withdrawal when I was crying and howling like a wounded animal in my condominium and I was lying prostrate on the floor in the living room pounding my fist into the carpeting and I would call someone up—usually my sponsor, but I would call other people, too. They would pick up the phone and say hello, and I would just start bawling. Bawling uncontrollably. Those people loved me unconditionally. After the numbness wore off I started to have a lot of feelings come up, as so many people do, feelings of rage, anger, hysteria at times. . . . I realized what I was grieving for was that life as I had known it up until then was dying. I would no longer be able to do the things I had been doing in order to get the anesthesia I was so desperately looking for. That was a very mournful period for me.

To suggest that addiction can involve only chemicals external to the body is to dismiss the sex addict's reality. Such misperception also overlooks a rapidly expanding body of scientific literature.

SEX AND THE OTHER ADDICTIONS

One common scenario is that of the recovering alcoholic who finds that his sexual behavior increases dramatically. He may even discover that he rationalized earlier excessive sexual behavior as a result of the drinking. When his drinking stops, his sexual behavior not only continues but escalates. Many individuals have entered recovery from sex addiction by first committing to a program of recovery for chemical dependency.

People who experience dual dependencies like chemicals and sex often make this striking observation: chemical abuse is easier to stop than sexual addiction. They point to several factors explaining why this is so. First, sex addicts often begin sexually compulsive behavior early in life. Compulsive sex . . . can start in childhood. So a thirty-year-old addict who started abusing chemicals at the age of seventeen may have been using sex to cope since he was five. In fact, many sex addicts in our survey talked of using chemicals as a way to kill pain they felt about their sexuality. Second, unlike an alcoholic, who can avoid alcohol, a sex addict carries the source of supply within. A more difficult recovery is one of the prices of getting high on one's brain chemistry.

Ironically, one of the cofounders of Alcoholics Anonymous clearly struggled with this pattern: the venerable Bill Wilson found his sexual behavior a source of great pain. Pulitzer Prize–winning author Nan Robertson describes this story in detail in her book *Getting Better: Inside Alcoholics Anonymous*:

Wilson's marriage to Lois Burnham in 1918 lasted until his death at the age of seventy-five in 1971. She believed in him fiercely and tended his flame. Yet, particularly during his sober decades in A.A. in the forties, fifties and sixties, Bill Wilson was a compulsive womanizer. His flirtations and his adulterous behavior filled him with guilt, according to old-timers close to him, but he continued to stray off the reservation. His last and most serious love affair, with a woman at A.A. headquarters in New York, began when he was in his sixties. She was important to him until the end of his life.

There are those whose rigidity about alcoholism precludes their accepting addictions beyond alcohol. The tragic truth is that the patterns of dual dependency recovery may have existed from the very beginnings of AA.

Nor are dual addictions limited to sex and chemicals. We have noted the role of eating disorders, compulsive "busyness," and other addictive behaviors. In our survey, less than 17 percent of respondents reported only sexual addiction. Dual addictions included:

Chemical dependency	42 percent
Eating disorder	38 percent
Compulsive working	28 percent
Compulsive spending	26 percent
Compulsive gambling	5 percent

For many sexual addicts, these multiple out-of-control paths exacerbate feelings of powerlessness.

Two recovering addicts, Kevin and Sue, were asked at a regional conference about the interactions among addictions. Specifically, they were asked, "If a sex addict is also an alcoholic, how can sexual performance occur when we know that alcohol is a depressant and inhibits sexual performance?" Their articulate responses echo the findings of our survey.

Kevin

Most of us began our sexual addiction at an early age; in my case, age eight with masturbation. My first drunk was age sixteen. I used alcohol, not only to feel good, but it also medicated my fear and pain of my "sinful" acting out, having been raised in a strict Catholic family. I used enough alcohol to feel good and to give me the courage to "chase" for sexual partners, and at the same time to remove "morality" issues. Later on I found amphetamine that would enhance my acting out so that I could go for hours in my sex addiction while the alcohol kept me from thinking about what I was doing. I also was an addiction binger and addiction trader so that I could satisfy my craving needs through food, work... anything to feel normal.

Because of threats from my wife, I went to AA and found relief from alcohol but still felt I was leaving half of me outside the doors of AA for my secret addiction. I was convinced it was a result of being an alcoholic. I then decided that my problem was overeating and went to OA. My acting out decreased only to find it rage again. I now faced it without alcohol or food and found the pain of this addiction was killing me after having been exposed to the principles of the 12 Step programs. I also felt this was a "character defect" as shown in the 4th Step of AA. I finally found a 12 Step program for sexual addiction. Since then I've found out my use of food with sex is a common story.

I would lose weight to be physically attractive to gain sex partners and when I would binge out, I would get into my self-hatred, loathing myself. I used food to not only medicate myself, but gained weight in order to be non-attractive to others. When I got tired of that, I would repeat the cycle over and over again... a lust machine to eating machine and vice versa.

Susan

I did much of the same thing, except, as a woman, I was deeper "under the gun" because of society's pressure to have the "perfect" shape along with the burden of being mankind's guardian and caretaker of morality. Overweight men can get by easier, attracting more partners than women can who are heavy. We women tend to suffer bulimia more than men which is a major clue that we were sexually abused as children and suffer from sexual addiction. Many eating disorder units do not even address these issues. I also agree with Kevin regarding the use of alcohol, cocaine and amphetamines, that to the sex addict, at least perceptually, does greatly enhance the pleasure of sex addiction. Why not cocaine and sex for the best synergism of sensual pleasure? Those who insist that the pharmacology of these drugs have the opposite effect do not understand sex addiction.

If the role of multiple addictions is not understood, the pattern of sex addiction is likely to be ignored.

THE DENIAL OF AN ILLNESS

People can admit that sex addiction exists but still deny its impact. One way to do that is to argue that "sex addiction exists, but it is exceedingly rare." Professionals who have expressed this opinion have been hard pressed to explain the growth of twelve step groups like Sexaholics Anonymous, Sex Addicts Anonymous, Sex and Love Addicts Anonymous, and Sexual Compulsives Anonymous. Most major cities and many rural areas have active, growing programs. They are not advertised; they get their members from referral services or therapists or by word of mouth. Esti-mates by the various fellowships indicate that over two thousand groups meet every week and that the number is growing exponentially.

As we found with alcoholism, it is easy to identify the skid row drunk in the last stages of hitting bottom. Yet, there are many whose lives are in profound disarray because of their drinking who can nevertheless maintain appearances. From the outside, things look fine or even great. The same is true of sex addiction. Until we understand how hidden sex addiction can be and yet thrive, we will continue to see it as a rare illness, affecting other people, not ourselves or those we know and love.

Another way to deny the illness is to say "sexual addiction may be widespread but it is not serious." One of the common jokes about sex addiction is that "if you are going to have an addiction, this is the one to have." The perception is that you cannot hurt yourself by too much sex. Suicide, unwanted pregnancies, family disintegration, violence, dramatic health care costs, and child abuse —all consequences of sex addiction—can be denied. But as a culture we will have to come to terms with another illness we are just beginning to understand: AIDS.

Shortly before this chapter was completed, one of the members of our research team died suddenly of AIDS. He was a recovering sex addict who was one of the gentlest of souls and a good friend to have. He worked extremely hard and excelled at solving problems with research in the real world.... We miss him very much.

When you experience losses like this, it is hard to hear jokes about sex addiction. This is not to say that funny things never happen. They sure do. Rather, it is that, as when you truly understand racism or ageism or sexism, some jokes cease to be funny. They become a commentary on our cultural denial and our collective ability to ignore human suffering.

As Nietzsche said, we give things power when we deny their existence. So it is important to proceed with our anatomy of this addiction. It is essential to understand the inner workings of this illness and all that it touches before we explore the transformation of recovery.

CHALLENGE QUESTIONS

Is Sex Addiction a Myth?

1. How might the confusion of moral and therapeutic terminology affect the argument over whether or not there is such a thing as sex addiction?

2. If sexual behavior can be considered an addiction, should a sexually abusive individual be able to use this as a legal defense?

3. What do you feel is Henkin's strongest argument supporting his belief that sex addiction is a myth? Why?

4. How do you think Carnes might explain Henkin's resistance to the reality of sex addiction?

5. Given that the meaning of the term *addiction* has changed over time, how would you redefine it to meet the criteria for sex addiction established by Carnes?

On the Internet . . .

http://www.dushkin.com

Health Reform Links
This is the most complete launching site on the issue of health care reform available on the Web. Every conceivable approach is lavished with many informative and thought-provoking links. *http://ccme-mac4.bsd.uchicago.edu/ccmedocs/Reform*

Guide to Women's Health Issues
This is an effective launching site for gender issues in health care. *http://www.coil.com/~tsegal/womens_health.html*

PART 4

The Methods, Ethics, and Policy of Abnormal Psychology

As researchers and clinicians, psychologists are often drawn into conflicts and debates between different groups in society and between individuals. Psychologists try to use their best judgment, based on their clinical experience and the research literature, to inform these debates. But the available research is often incomplete or flawed. A host of factors also can bias the interpretation of research and clinical experience.

In the meantime, society—including lawmakers, bureaucrats administering the laws, and judges and juries in courtrooms—must make decisions that can greatly influence the resources, opportunities, and freedoms made available to individual members of the society. Are the outcomes always in the best interest of these individuals?

■ Does Health Care Delivery and Research Benefit Men at the Expense of Women?

■ Are Memories of Sex Abuse Always Real?

ISSUE 11

Does Health Care Delivery and Research Benefit Men at the Expense of Women?

YES: Leslie Laurence and Beth Weinhouse, from *Outrageous Practices: The Alarming Truth About How Medicine Mistreats Women* (Fawcett Columbine, 1994)

NO: Andrew G. Kadar, from "The Sex-Bias Myth in Medicine," *The Atlantic Monthly* (August 1994)

ISSUE SUMMARY

YES: Health and medical reporters Leslie Laurence and Beth Weinhouse claim that women have been excluded from most research on new drugs, medical treatments, and surgical techniques that are routinely offered to men.

NO: Physician Andrew G. Kadar argues that women actually receive more medical care and benefit more from medical research than do men, which explains why women generally live longer than men.

In 1989 Harvard University reported that taking an aspirin tablet every other day could prevent heart disease based on a study involving 22,000 male physicians. The findings were generalized to include both men and women, and the final reports claimed that aspirin, which helps prevent blood clotting, would be useful to all adults. Dr. Suzanne Oparil, president of the American Heart Association, however, believes that aspirin might not be beneficial to women because they have generally faster rates of blood clotting than men.

Why weren't women included in the Harvard aspirin study or in other research that might help prevent their premature deaths or disabilities? The answer goes back to 1975, when the National Commission for the Protection of Human Subjects of Biomedical and Behavioral Research issued guidelines limiting research on pregnant women. This ban on using women stemmed from fears following the thalidomide crisis in the late 1950s. Thalidomide, a sedative and antinausea drug that was used to help treat morning sickness during early pregnancy, was responsible for many children being born with deformities after their mothers used the drug while they were pregnant. Two years after this incident the Food and Drug Administration (FDA) published recommendations that all women of "childbearing potential" be excluded from early phases of drug trials to avoid any damage to fetuses.

By the mid-1980s many women began to question the FDA-mandated exclusion of women from drug trials. In 1985 the National Institutes of Health

(NIH) issued a statement urging researchers to include women in their studies. In 1990 it was reported, however, that women were still not included in major federally funded clinical studies and that the NIH was not enforcing its policy of including women.

Things began to change, beginning with the 1991 launching of the *Women's Health Initiative*, a 14-year study of women's health. And in 1993 the FDA lifted its ban on using women in drug trials. Although there has been obvious progress, claims are still being made that women and men are not treated equally regarding medical care and research. Many argue that women are being shortchanged with regard to research on heart disease and AIDS and that they are also twice as likely *not* to be tested for lung cancer as men, even though lung cancer is the leading cancer killer of women.

A relatively recent concern pertains to AIDS and HIV-related conditions. In particular, AIDS research has a proportionately higher number of men participating in drug and other scientific trials. Additionally, though AIDS is a major killer of women, especially in urban areas, the official definition of AIDS has until recently excluded HIV-related conditions that were specific to females. What is known about HIV and AIDS seems to have been acquired from research on men only.

Despite concerns that health care and research in the United States benefit men at the expense of women, there is ample evidence to the contrary: Department of Health and Human Services studies show that women see their physicians more frequently, have more surgery, and are admitted to hospitals more often than men. Currently, two out of three medical dollars are spent by women. A 1981 study conducted at the University of California at San Diego reviewed over 40,000 patient office visits and found that the health care men and women received was similar over two-thirds of the time. When the care differed, it was women who were given more lab tests, drug prescriptions, and return appointments.

Women have also benefitted from medical research involving high-tech procedures. Laparoscopic surgery and ultrasound are two advanced techniques that were first developed for use on women's bodies (these procedures were later adapted for men). Women's diseases have also been the recipient of research dollars. Breast cancer, the second leading cancer killer of women, has received more funding than any other tumor research. In 1993 the National Cancer Institute spent over $213 million dollars on breast cancer and $51 million dollars on prostate cancer. Although one-third more women die of breast cancer than men of prostate cancer, research into breast cancer received more than four times the funding of prostate cancer research.

In the following selections, Leslie Laurence and Beth Weinhouse argue that women have been short-changed with regard to health care and medical research. Andrew G. Kadar disagrees, claiming that though it is often believed that women do not get the same consideration in medical care and research as men, the truth appears to be exactly the opposite.

YES

Leslie Laurence and
Beth Weinhouse

OUTRAGEOUS PRACTICES: THE ALARMING TRUTH ABOUT HOW MEDICINE MISTREATS WOMEN

There is unfortunately a clear path from the ignorant attitudes about women's bodies prevalent in the last century to the ignorant attitudes that exist today. A century ago physicians removed women's ovaries to treat a variety of unrelated complaints. They believed women's reproductive organs were responsible for almost everything that can and did go wrong with the human body. How much has changed? Recent medical students say that, during anatomy lectures on the female reproductive system, lecturers take pains to describe the female reproductive system as inefficient, badly designed, and prone to problems....

We may be horrified by the "ovariotomies" and "clitoridectomies" of the nineteenth century, but what of the hundreds of thousands of unnecessary hysterectomies being performed today?...

Nearly 550,000 hysterectomies are performed in the United States each year, making hysterectomy one of the most common operations of all. Yet the vast majority of these operations are elective, not lifesaving. When the American College of Obstetricians and Gynecologists recently announced its wish for ob-gyns to become the primary-care physicians for postmenopausal women, one woman doctor retorted, "If they want to do that, they're going to have to leave some organs in first."

How far have we really come from the days when women were told their psychological symptoms were due to physical problems and their reproductive organs were removed as a cure? Today women are frequently told that their very real physical symptoms—chest pains, menstrual problems, endometriosis, gastrointestinal pain—are psychological, and are handed a prescription for antidepressants or tranquilizers.

The medical textbooks of the 1800s may seem laughably ignorant today, but as recently as the 1970s physicians were being taught that morning sickness was caused by a woman's resentment at being a mother, PMS [premenstrual syndrome] was also a psychological disorder, and menopause represented the end of a woman's usefulness in life. And the doctors who were trained with those textbooks are still practicing medicine.

Instead of putting today's inequities in perspective, the examples of past abuses of women serve only to show that we haven't come as far as we thought....

THE RESEARCH GAP

In June 1990, American women got a rude shock. For all the complaints women leveled against the health care system —most having to do with insensitive male doctors and dissatisfaction with gynecological and obstetric care—the majority of women still assumed that at least they were included in America's state-of-the-art medical research. But they were wrong. For at least the past several decades women in this country had been systematically excluded from the vast majority of research to develop new drugs, medical treatments, and surgical techniques.

It was on June 18, 1990, that the government's General Accounting Office (GAO) released its report of an audit of the National Institutes of Health (NIH). The audit found that although NIH had formulated a policy in 1986 for including women as research subjects, little had been done to implement or monitor that policy. In fact, most researchers applying for NIH grants were not even aware that they were supposed to include women, since the NIH grant-application book contained no mention of the policy. Because the 1986 policy urged rather than required attention to gender bias, most institutes, and most researchers, had simply decided to ignore it altogether or pay it only slight heed: "It used to be

enough for a researcher to say, 'Women and minorities will not be excluded from this study,'" explains one woman in NIH's Division of Research Grants. But not excluding women is very different from actively recruiting and including them....

The GAO found that women were being underrepresented in studies of diseases affecting both men and women. In the fifty applications reviewed, one-fifth made no mention of gender and over one-third said the subjects would include both sexes, but did not give percentages. Some all-male studies gave no rationale for their exclusivity. "The [NIH] may win the Nobel Prize, but I'd like to see them get the *Good Housekeeping* seal of approval," said Congresswoman Barbara Mikulski (D-Md.), voicing her hopes that the behemoth medical institution could be made more woman-friendly.

As if medical research were some kind of exclusive male club, some of the biggest and most important medical studies of recent years had failed to enroll a single woman:

- The Baltimore Longitudinal Study, one of the largest studies to examine the natural process of aging, began in 1958 and included no women for its first twenty years because, according to Gene Cohen, then deputy director of the National Institute on Aging (NIA), the facility in which the study was conducted had only one toilet. The study's 1984 report, entitled "Normal Human Aging," contained no data on women. (Currently 40 percent of the participants in this study are women ... although 60 percent of the population over age sixty-five is female.)
- The by-now-infamous Physicians' Health Study, which concluded in 1988

that taking an aspirin a day might reduce the risk of heart disease, included 22,000 men and no women.

- The 1982 Multiple Risk Factor Intervention Trial, known as Mr. Fit, a long-term study of lifestyle factors related to cholesterol and heart disease, included 13,000 men and no women. To this day no definitive answer exists on whether dietary change and exercise can benefit women in preventing heart disease.
- A Harvard School of Public Health study investigating the possible link between caffeine consumption and heart disease involved over 45,000 men and no women.
- Perhaps most unbelievably, a pilot project at Rockefeller University to study how obesity affected breast and uterine cancer was conducted solely on men. Said Congresswoman Olympia Snowe (R-Me.) upon hearing of this study, "Somehow, I find it hard to believe that the male-dominated medical community would tolerate a study of prostate cancer that used only women as research subjects." ...

Protection or Paternalism?

The objection to women's participation in health research that is most difficult to counter is the concern over exposing a fetus to a drug or treatment that might be dangerous, or at least has not been proven safe. Recent history makes it impossible to dismiss these fears. In the 1950s the drug thalidomide, given to European women to combat nausea during pregnancy, caused thousands of children to be born with severe deformities. In this country the drug diethylstilbestrol (DES) was widely prescribed to pregnant women during the 1940s and 1950s to prevent miscarriage, but has led to gynecological cancers and other medical problems in the offspring of the women who took it.

But in their effort to expose the fetus to "zero risk," scientists have shied away from including not just pregnant women in their studies, but any woman who could potentially become pregnant.

Translated into research practice, that meant that no woman between the ages of fifteen and fifty could participate in the earliest stages of new drug research unless she had been surgically sterilized or had a hysterectomy. (And since many studies have an upper age limit of sixty-five, that leaves a narrow window of opportunity for women to participate.) Exceptions were made only in the case of extremely severe or life-threatening illnesses.

While policies to protect unborn children seem to make sense on first reading, upon closer examination they represent protectionism run amok. An increasing number of studies are showing that exposure to chemicals and environmental toxins can affect *sperm*, yet no one is suggesting that men be excluded from research in order to protect their unborn children. When Proscar, a drug used to treat enlarged prostate glands, was found to cause birth defects in the offspring of male animals given the drug, men in the drug trials simply had to sign a consent form saying they would use condoms. Women weren't given the option of using contraception during the trial. By grouping together all women between the ages of fifteen and fifty as potentially pregnant, researchers were implying that women have no control over their reproductive lives. ...

WOMEN'S HEARTS: THE DEADLY DIFFERENCE

Kathy O'Brien (not her real name), a forty-two-year-old smoker, had been experiencing chest pains on and off for about a year. Her father and two of her uncles had died of heart attacks when young. She went to a clinic in the rural area of northwest New Jersey where she lived, and there the local doctors told her she probably had gallstones. When the pain got worse, she went back to the clinic, where they told her she'd have to have a sonogram of her gallbladder. She left without having it done. Instead Kathy went home, collapsed from chest pain, and nearly died. She had suffered a massive heart attack and gone into cardiac arrest. Technically dead, she had to be defibrillated with electrical shocks on the way to the hospital. The following day she was transferred to a larger, teaching hospital, where doctors did an angiogram and found a blockage in a major blood vessel. After bypass surgery she recovered well. But why, wondered the cardiologists at the larger hospital, didn't anyone recognize heart disease in a heavy smoker with chest pain and a serious family history of death from heart attack?

Though it has been the leading cause of death in American women since 1908, heart disease is one of the best-kept secrets of women's health. It wasn't until 1964 that the American Heart Association [AHA] sponsored its first conference on women and heart disease....

The real topic of this conference wasn't women and heart disease, however. It was how women could take care of their *husbands'* hearts. "Hearts and Husbands: The First Women's Conference on Coronary Heart Disease" explained to women the important role they played in keeping their spouses healthy. "The conference was a symposium on how to take care of your *man:* how to feed him and make sure he didn't get heart disease, and how to take care of him if he did," explains Mary Ann Malloy, M.D., a cardiologist at Loyola University Medical Center in Chicago, and head of the AHA's local Women and Heart Disease committee. The conference organizers prepared an educational pamphlet called "Eight Questions Wives Ask." There was no discussion at all of ways for women to recognize their own symptoms or to prevent the disease that was killing more of them than any other, no mention of how women could look after their own heart health. And no one objected, including women, because, for the medical profession and the public, heart disease was an exclusively male problem.

Both physicians and the public still harbor the misconception that women do not suffer from heart disease. Yet many more women die from cardiovascular disease—478,000 in 1993—than from all forms of cancer combined, which are responsible for 237,000 deaths. Although women seem to fear breast cancer more, only one in eight women will develop it (and not all of them will die of it), while one in two will develop cardiovascular disease. And for those who persist in thinking of heart disease as a male province, in 1992 (the most recent statistics available), more women than men died of cardiovascular disease. Among women, 46 percent of all deaths are due to cardiovascular disease; in men it's 40 percent. Because heart disease tends to be an illness of older, postmenopausal women, the incidence of heart disease, and the number of deaths, have been rising as women's life expectancies have increased. "Women didn't die of heart disease when the median age of death was the fifties or sixties," says Nanette K. Wenger, M.D., professor of medicine (cardiology) at Emory University School of Medicine in Atlanta.

Yet despite these ominous numbers, the vast majority of research into coronary artery disease, the type of heart disease that causes most heart attacks, has been done on middle-aged men. "We're very much in an infancy in terms of understanding heart disease in women," says Irma L. Mebane-Sims, Ph.D., an epidemiologist at the National Heart, Lung and Blood Institute. Compared with men's hearts, women's hearts are still largely a mystery. . . .

"IT'S ALL IN YOUR HEAD": MISUNDERSTANDING WOMEN'S COMPLAINTS

Just as the physical diseases of women are poorly understood, so, too, are a panoply of psychosomatic disorders, extremely controversial diagnoses in which emotional distresses are transferred into physical symptoms for which people then seek treatment. Somatization, as this process is known, has existed for centuries and is, to this day, remarkably common: Some 80 percent of healthy adults are believed to have psychogenic symptoms in any given week—for instance a stomachache that coincides with an important deadline or a headache that comes on after a fight with the boss. . . .

Such a dynamic has a great bearing on women: they make up the majority of people suffering from such psychosomatic disorders as chronic fatigue syndrome, fibromyalgia, irritable bowel syndrome, and chronic pelvic pain (which can also be the result of an organic disorder such as endometriosis). The hidden scandal is that there is no shortage of doctors who will treat women's psychogenic complaints as if they're organic in origin, often leading to a chamber of medical horrors, including an array of unnecessary surgeries instead of the treatment women may really need: help in understanding the emotional reasons for their disease.

Of course women are willing participants in their mistreatment. Resisting psychological consultation, they embark on a medical odyssey, dragging their strange array of symptoms from specialist to specialist until they find someone who will give them the one thing they desperately need: a diagnosis. "These are very beleaguered patients," says Nortin Hadler, M.D., a North Carolina rheumatologist with a particular interest in somatization. "The worst thing to happen to any patient is not to be believed. You can't get better if you can't prove you're ill."

The corollary is that, because women suffer from psychosomatic illness disproportionately and express their medical problems in a more open and emotional style compared with men, their complaints frequently *aren't* listened to—even when they're directly related to an organic disease. "The perception among many physicians is that women tend to complain a lot, so you shouldn't pay too much attention to them," says Donna Stewart, head of women's health at Toronto Hospital, a teaching hospital affiliated with the University of Toronto. As a result, many of women's *legitimate* physical ailments are not attended to, sometimes with serious consequences. . . .

WOMEN AND DOCTORS: A TROUBLED RELATIONSHIP

Most women who visit physicians aren't aware of the lack of research into women's health, the difficulties in diagnosing women with cardiac disease, or the discrimination against women in medical school. What they *are* aware of is dissatisfaction with their physicians and with their health care in general. They base these opinions on what goes on in the doctor's office and the respect—or lack of it—they receive there. "The usual experience for a woman going to a gynecologist includes humiliation, depersonalization, even pain, and too seldom does she come away with her needs having been met," asserts gynecologist John M. Smith, M.D., author of *Women and Doctors*. And gynecologists are certainly not the only physicians guilty of this mistreatment.

Marianne J. Legato, M.D., associate director of the Center for Women's Health at Columbia–Presbyterian Medical Center, has toured the country talking with women about their experiences as patients. "The general mood is anger," she says. Women complained to her that their physicians were insensitive, uninterested, rushed, arrogant, and uncommunicative. Because women's health care is fragmented, with women seeing a gynecologist for reproductive health, an internist for a general physical, and other specialists for more specific problems, one woman told her she felt "like a salami, with a slice in every doctor's office in town."

None of this surprises Dr. Legato, who says that medicine is a mirror of the rest of society and its values. "Women, the old, the poor, children, and minority groups as a whole who haven't achieved economic power are taken less seriously and held in less regard ... which kind of leaves the emphasis on white males."

Many physicians interact with their women patients based on a view of the female sex that was already archaic decades ago. "If she's premenopausal, she is dismissed as suffering from PMS; if she's postmenopausal, then she obviously needs hormone replacement therapy; if she's a homemaker, she has too much time on her hands; if she's a business executive, then the pressure of her job is too much for her. She just can't win," writes Isadore Rosenfeld, M.D.

Medical school textbooks from only two decades ago portray women not much differently from the "walking wombs" that physicians treated in the 1800s. In this century gynecologists embraced the idea that hormones were the long-suspected link between the uterus and the brain. This theory led them to believe that a pelvic exam could help diagnose mental problems. Conditions such as painful or irregular periods, excessive morning sickness or labor pain, and infertility became indications that a woman was battling her femininity. One 1947 obstetrics textbook, still on a practicing physician's shelf, introduces a chapter on such pregnancy problems as heartburn, nausea and vomiting, constipation, backache, varicose veins, and hemorrhoids with the sentence "Women with satisfactory self-control and more than average intelligence have fewer complaints than do other women."

Things still hadn't improved by the 1970s. A 1973 study of how women were portrayed in gynecology textbooks found that most textbooks were more concerned with the well-being of a woman's husband than with the woman herself. Wrote the authors, "Women are consistently described as anatomically destined to reproduce, nurture, and keep their husbands happy." A popular 1971 ob-gyn textbook portrayed women as helpless, childlike creatures who couldn't survive sex, pregnancy, delivery, or child raising without their doctors and added, "The traits that compose the core of the female personality are feminine narcissism, masochism, and passivity."

While current textbooks seem generally more sensitive and realistic, the physicians who trained on the older books are still in practice. When *JAMA*, a leading medical journal, ran an article in 1991 about gender disparities in medical care, they received a letter from a physician in Ohio who wrote that perhaps women's "overanxiousness" about their health and their greater use of health services "may be due to temperamental differences in gender-mediated clinical features of depression, which are manifested by women's less active, more ruminative responses that are linked to dysfunction of the right frontal cortex in which the metabolic rate is higher in females." In other words women are more anxious about their health because they are somehow brain-damaged. With doctors like this, no wonder women are unhappy.

Women as Patients

Surveys show that women are more dissatisfied with their physicians than men are. And the dissatisfaction is not necessarily due to the quality of the medical care women receive, but to the lack of communication and respect they perceive in the encounter. In a 1993 Commonwealth Fund survey of twenty-five hundred women and a thousand men on the subject of women's health, women reported greater communication problems with their physicians, and were more likely to change doctors because of their dissatisfaction. One out of four women said she had been "talked down to" or treated like a child by a physician. Nearly one out of five women had been told that a reported medical condition was "all in your head."

The perception nationwide is that doctors and patients just don't understand each other. A study of one thousand complaints from dissatisfied patients at a large Michigan health maintenance organization found that more than 90 percent of the problems involved communication. "The most common complaints had to do with a lack of compassion on the physician's part," says Richard M. Frankel, Ph.D., associate professor of medicine at the University of Rochester School of Medicine and Dentistry. "Patients would complain their physician never looked at them during the entire encounter, made them feel humiliated or used medical jargon that left them confused." ...

"Women are patronized and treated like little girls," says Ann R. Turkel, M.D., assistant clinical professor of psychiatry, Columbia University College of Physicians and Surgeons. "They're even referred to as girls. Male physicians will call female patients by their first names, but they are always called 'Doctor.' They don't do that with men. Women are patted on the head, called 'dear' or 'honey.' And doctors tell them things like, 'Don't you worry your pretty little head about it. That's not for you to worry about; that's for me to worry about.' Then they're surprised when women see these statements and reactions as degrading and insulting." ...

There is also a perception among women that physicians don't take women's time seriously. How else to explain what happened to Roberta, a busy magazine editor who was on a tight deadline schedule the day of her doctor's appointment. "My office was just one city block from the doctor's office, so I called them five minutes before my appointment time to see if the doctor was running on schedule," she recalls. The receptionist assured her he was, so Roberta left her office and arrived at her appointment on time—only to be kept waiting for nearly an hour. "When I finally saw the doctor, I was practically shaking with rage, and my blood pressure was sky high," she says. Even though the doctor apologized and spent a lot of time talking with her after the checkup, Roberta decided to find another doctor.

"I think women are kept waiting longer for an appointment than men are," says Dr. Turkel. "I wouldn't go to a gynecologist who kept me waiting in the waiting room for an hour and a half, but I hear these stories all the time from women patients about their gynecologist's office."

Advice columnist Ann Landers even gave a rare interview to *JAMA* to let physicians know how dissatisfied women are with their doctors. "I can't say too often how angry women are about having to wait in the doctor's office," she said. "And, who do they complain to? The office manager, who is also a woman. Then, when the male doctor finally sees them—an hour later—the woman is so glad to see him that she soft-pedals the inconvenience. She wants to see the doctor as a 'knight in shining armor.' This should change. The doctor's time is no more important than the patient's and, while I can understand special circumstances, I can't understand why a doctor is *always* running late."

Doctors may treat women as if they are inferior patients, but studies show that they are anything but. Women tend to ask more questions—and receive more information because of their inquisitiveness. Women also show more emotion during office visits and are more likely to confide a personal problem that may have a bearing on their health to their physicians. Men, on the other hand, ask fewer questions of their physicians, give less information to the doctor, and display less emotion. During a typical fifteen-minute office visit, women ask an average of six questions. Men don't ask any. . . .

Although physicians should be thrilled to have patients who are interested in their health, ask questions, and volunteer personal information, women's concerns are often dismissed as symptoms of anxiety, their questions brushed aside. In business, successful executives are often seen as having forceful, take-charge personalities, while women with similar attributes are described as aggressive or bitchy. In medicine, male patients seem to describe symptoms, while women complain. Instead of valuing women as active, informed patients, doctors are more likely to prefer patients who don't ask questions, don't interrupt, don't question their judgment, and—perhaps most important—get in and out of the office as quickly as possible. Researchers have actually found that physicians *like* male patients better than female ones, even when factors such as age, education, income, and occupation are controlled for.

Perhaps because of these attitudes, women often feel frustrated when they try to ask questions and receive explanations. One study reported that women received significantly more explanations than men—but not significantly more explaining *time*. Wrote the authors, "It is possible that many of the explanations they received were brief and perfunctory. Or, put differently, the men may have received fewer but fuller explanations than the women." The study also found that women were less likely than men to receive explanations that matched the level of technicality of the questions they asked. Doctors tended to talk down to women when answering their questions....

Miscommunication or Mistreatment?

Far more serious than patronizing attitudes and lack of consideration for women's time are the myths about women patients' complaints that jeopardize women's health care.

"Physician folklore says that women are more demanding patients," says Karen Carlson, M.D., an internist at Massachusetts General Hospital in Boston. "From my experience women are interested in health and prevention, desire to be listed to and treated with respect, want the opportunity to present and explain their agenda, and want their symptoms and concerns taken seriously."

But all too often women's symptoms are not taken seriously because physicians erroneously believe that these symptoms have no physical basis and that women's complaints are simply a sign of their demanding natures.

A 1979 study compared the medical records of fifty-two married couples to see how they had been treated for five common problems: back pain, headache, dizziness, chest pain, and fatigue. "The physicians' workups were significantly more extensive for the men than they were for women," reported the authors. "These data tend to support the argument that male physicians take medical illness more seriously in men than in women."

Another study found that women were shortchanged even in general checkups. Men's visits are more likely to include vision and hearing tests, chest X rays, ECGs, blood tests, rectal examinations, and urinalyses.

Dr. Carlson, speaking to a roomful of women physicians at an annual meeting of the American Medical Women's Association, cited evidence to show that women may actually complain *less* than men. "The myth is that women complain more, but studies show another truth," she says. Carlson cited studies showing that, compared with men, women with colon cancer are more likely to delay care and experience diagnostic delay. That women with chronic joint symptoms and arthritis are less likely to report pain. That women have more severe and frequent colds, but men are more likely to overrate their symptoms. That women delay seeking help for chest pain or symptoms of a heart attack. These studies point to women as being more stoic, yet when they finally do show up in the doctor's office, they are apt to be met with skepticism.

Betsy Murphy (not her real name) had been seeing the same doctor for years. "We had a perfectly fine relationship as long as I just went for my yearly checkups and didn't ask a lot of questions," she recalls. "But then I got my first yeast infection and had to go see him for a prescription—the medicine wasn't available over-the-counter then." Betsy told her doctor what she thought she had—she had talked to enough friends and read enough magazine articles to recognize the distinctive cottage-cheeselike discharge, yeasty odor, and intense itching. "But he ignored me when I told him what I thought was wrong. After he took a culture and examined it under the microscope, he sneeringly said, 'Well, Ms. Murphy, it seems as if your diagnosis is correct.'" Although he diagnosed the problem and prescribed the medication, Betsy left his office feeling insulted and patronized.

At a recent workshop on the patient-physician partnership, an auditorium full of physicians was asked how they would handle a "problem" patient. One of these "problems" was the patient who comes in and announces his or her own diagnosis. The physicians, almost unanimously, ridiculed the patient for daring to speculate what was wrong. They preferred that someone just present a description of symptoms, as specifically and articulately as possible. "It's no help for someone to come to me and say, "I have a cold and I just need some medicine,'" said a participating doctor to a journalist in the audience. "Instead the patient should describe how they feel as specifically as possible. And obviously some people are more articulate and some less; that's where the doctor's skill comes in." In other words, a patient should show up for an appointment and tell the doctor, "I have a stuffy nose and I keep sneezing," and then wait for the doctor, in his infinite wisdom, to pronounce, "You have a cold." For a patient, male or female, who is reasonably certain what is wrong, the suggestion seems ludicrous.

Women's dissatisfaction with their medical care can lead to serious health consequences. They may switch doctors so frequently that they receive no continuity of care. Or they may simply avoid seeing doctors altogether because they find the experience humiliating. When men without a regular source of health care are asked why they don't have one, they tend to reply that they don't need a doctor. But women are more apt to say that they cannot find the right doctor, or that they have recently moved, or that their previous doctor is no longer available. In the Commonwealth Fund poll, 41 percent of women (compared with 27 percent of men) said they had switched doctors in the past because they were dissatisfied. "If you brought your car in to be fixed and the person who fixed it did an okay but not great job, but was nasty, wouldn't you go to another mechanic? The same is true of physicians," says Frankel.

Physicians seem to realize there's a problem, but many of their efforts to remedy it are laughable. One 1993 article in the medical newspaper *American Medical News* advised doctors that if they wanted to make their practice "women-friendly," they should "create an atmosphere similar to that of a living room. This includes the seating, lighting and wall decorations." Yet it's difficult to imagine any woman listing "ugly wallpaper" as a reason for being dissatisfied with her health care. It's not the decor women are complaining about when they complain about doctors' offices.

Ob-gyn John Smith lists padded stirrups and speculum warmers as among the improvements women have gotten their doctors to make since the 1960s. But even those superficial improvements are not enough. What women really want are doctors who will listen to them, talk to them, and treat their medical questions and problems with respect and empathy....

THE FUTURE OF WOMEN'S HEALTH

... Despite helter-skelter improvements in the care of women, the move toward special centers, nurse-run practices, and medical school curricula in women's health suggests a larger trend: the feminization of medicine. More women than ever are entering medical school. By the year 2010 the AMA estimates that one-third of all doctors will be women.... Not surprisingly these women are bringing a feminine, and sometimes feminist, sensibility to the practice of medicine.

"Feminism is about empowering all our patients—men, women, and children —and treating them with respect," says Laura Helfman, M.D., an emergency room doctor in North Carolina. "We're doctors, we're not gods up on high." To Helfman this means taking the opportunity to do "a gentle and warm pelvic exam so I can reeducate the person receiving it that it doesn't have to be awful." To a gynecologist friend of hers it means making sure the patients never have to wait and that they always get to speak with the doctor. To a surgeon friend it means holding the patient's hand in the recovery room....

These practitioners are putting the rest of the health care system on notice. Women, both as physicians and as patients, are primed to transform the way medicine is practiced in this country. And so we celebrate the new female norm: the 60-kilogram woman. She has breasts and a uterus and a heart and lungs and kidneys. But she's much more than that. No longer a metaphor for disease, she's the model for health.... The time is right for a new woman-centered health care movement. It's the least women should demand.

NO

Andrew G. Kadar

THE SEX-BIAS MYTH IN MEDICINE

"When it comes to health-care research and delivery, women can no longer be treated as second-class citizens." So said the President of the United States on October 18, 1993.

He and the First Lady had just hosted a reception for the National Breast Cancer Coalition, an advocacy group, after receiving a petition containing 2.6 million signatures which demanded increased funding for breast-cancer prevention and treatment. While the Clintons met with leaders of the group in the East Room of the White House, a thousand demonstrators rallied across the street in support. The President echoed their call, decrying the neglect of medical care for women.

Two years earlier Bernadine Healy, then the director of the National Institutes of Health [NIH], charged that "women have all too often been treated less than equally in... health care." More recently Representative Pat Schroeder, a co-chair of the Congressional Caucus for Women's Issues, sponsored legislation to "ensure that biomedical research does not once again overlook women and their health." Newspaper articles expressed similar sentiments.

The list of accusations is long and startling. Women's-health-care advocates indict "sex-biased" doctors for stereotyping women as hysterical hypochondriacs, for taking women's complaints less seriously than men's, and for giving them less thorough diagnostic workups. A study conducted at the University of California at San Diego in 1979 concluded that men's complaints of back pain, chest pain, dizziness, fatigue, and headache more often resulted in extensive workups than did similar complaints from women. Hard scientific evidence therefore seemed to confirm women's anecdotal reports.

Men more often than women undergo angiographies and coronary-artery-bypass-graft operations. Even though heart disease is the No. 1 killer of women as well as men, this sophisticated, state-of-the-art technology, critics contend, is selectively denied to women.

The problem is said to be repeated in medical research: women, critics argue, are routinely ignored in favor of men. When the NIH inventoried all the research it had funded in 1987, the money spent on studying diseases unique to women amounted to only 13.5 percent of the total research budget.

Perhaps the most emotionally charged disease for women is breast cancer. If a tumor devastated men on a similar scale, critics say, we would declare a state of national emergency and launch a no-cost-barred Apollo Project–style program to cure it. In the words of Matilda Cuomo, the wife of the governor of New York, "If we can send a woman to the moon, we can surely find a cure for breast cancer." The neglect of breast-cancer research, we have been told, is both sexist and a national disgrace.

Nearly all heart-disease research is said to be conducted on men, with the conclusions blindly generalized to women. In July of 1989 researchers from the Harvard Medical School reported the results of a five-year study on the effects of aspirin in preventing cardiovascular disease in 22,071 male physicians. Thousands of men were studied, but not one woman: women's health, critics charge, was obviously not considered important enough to explore similarly. Here, they say, we have definite, smoking-gun evidence of the neglect of women in medical research —only one example of a widespread, dangerous phenomenon.

Still another difference: pharmaceutical companies make a policy of giving new drugs to men first, while women wait to benefit from the advances. And even then the medicines are often inadequately tested on women.

To remedy all this neglect, we need to devote preferential attention and funds, in the words of the *Journal of the American Medical Women's Association*, to "the greatest resource this country will ever have, namely, the health of its women."

Discrimination on such a large scale cries out for restitution—if the charges are true.

In fact one sex does appear to be favored in the amount of attention devoted to its medical needs. In the United States it is estimated that one sex spends twice as much money on health care as the other does. The NIH also spends twice as much money on research into the diseases specific to one sex as it does on research into those specific to the other, and only one sex has a section of the NIH devoted entirely to the study of disease afflicting it. That sex is not men, however. It is women.

* * *

In the United States women seek out and consequently receive more medical care than men. This is true even if pregnancy-related care is excluded. Department of Health and Human Services surveys show that women visit doctors more often than men, are hospitalized more often, and undergo more operations. Women are more likely than men to visit a doctor for a general physical exam when they are feeling well, and complain of symptoms more often. Thus two out of every three health-care dollars are spent by women.

Quantity, of course, does not guarantee quality. Do women receive second-rate diagnostic workups?

The 1979 San Diego study, which concluded that men's complaints more often led to extensive workups than did women's, used the charts of 104 men and women (fifty-two married couples) as data. This small-scale regional survey prompted a more extensive national review of 46,868 office visits. The results, reported in 1981, were quite different from those of the San Diego study.

In this larger, more representative sample, the care received by men and women was similar about two thirds of the time. When the care was different, women overall received more diagnostic tests and treatment—more lab tests, blood-pressure checks, drug prescriptions, and return appointments.

Several other, small-scale studies have weighed in on both sides of this issue. The San Diego researchers looked at another 200 men and women in 1984, and this time found "no significant differences in the extent and content" of workups. Some women's-health-care advocates have chosen to ignore data from the second San Diego study and the national survey while touting the first study as evidence that doctors, to quote once again from the *Journal of the American Medical Women's Association*, do "not take complaints as seriously" when they come from women: "an example of a double standard influencing diagnostic workups."

When prescribing care for heart disease, doctors consider such factors as age, other medical problems, and the likelihood that the patient will benefit from testing and surgery. Coronary-artery disease afflicts men at a much younger age, killing them three times as often as women until age sixty-five. Younger patients have fewer additional medical problems that preclude aggressive, high-risk procedures. And smaller patients have smaller coronary arteries, which become obstructed more often after surgery. Whereas this is true for both sexes, obviously more women fit into the smaller-patient category. When these differences are factored in, sex divergence in cardiac care begins to fade away.

To the extent that divergence remains, women may be getting better treatment.

At least that was the conclusion of a University of North Carolina/Duke University study that looked at the records of 5,795 patients treated from 1969 to 1984. The most symptomatic and severely diseased men and women were equally likely to be referred for bypass surgery. Among the patients with less-severe disease—the ones to whom surgery offers little or no survival benefit over medical therapy—women were less likely to be scheduled for bypass surgery. This seems proper in light of the greater risk of surgical complications, owing to women's smaller coronary arteries. In fact, the researchers questioned the wisdom of surgery in the less symptomatic men and suggested that "the effect of gender on treatment selection may have led to more appropriate treatment of women."

As for sophisticated, pioneering technology selectively designed for the benefit of one sex, laparoscopic surgery was largely confined to gynecology for more than twenty years. Using viewing and manipulating instruments that can be inserted into the abdomen through keyhole-sized incisions, doctors are able to diagnose and repair, sparing the patient a larger incision and a longer, more painful recuperation. Laparoscopic tubal sterilization, first performed in 1936, became common practice in the late 1960s. Over time the development of more-versatile instruments and of fiber-optic video capability made possible the performance of more-complex operations. The laparoscopic removal of ectopic pregnancy was reported in 1973. Finally, in 1987, the same technology was applied in gallbladder surgery, and men began to enjoy its benefits too.

Years after ultrasound instruments were designed to look inside the uterus, the same technology was adapted to search for tumors in the prostate. Other pioneering developments conceived to improve the health care of women include mammography, bone-density testing for osteoporosis, surgery to alleviate bladder incontinence, hormone therapy to relieve the symptoms of menopause, and a host of procedures, including in vitro fertilization, developed to facilitate impregnation. Perhaps so many new developments occur in women's health care because one branch of medicine and a group of doctors, gynecologists, are explicitly concerned with the health of women. No corresponding group of doctors is dedicated to the care of men.

So women receive more care than men, sometimes receive better care than men, and benefit more than men do from some developing technologies. This hardly looks like proof that women's health is viewed as secondary in importance to men's health.

* * *

The 1987 NIH inventory did indeed find that only 13.5 percent of the NIH research budget was devoted to studying diseases unique to women. But 80 percent of the budget went into research for the benefit of both sexes, including basic research in fields such as genetics and immunology and also research into diseases such as lymphoma, arthritis, and sickle-cell anemia. Both men and women suffer from these ailments, and both sexes served as study subjects. The remaining 6.5 percent of NIH research funds were devoted to afflictions unique to men. Oddly, the women's 13.5 percent has been cited as evidence of neglect. The much smaller men's share of the budget is rarely mentioned in these references.

As for breast cancer, the second most lethal malignancy in females, investiga-

tion in that field has long received more funding from the National Cancer Institute [NCI] than any other tumor research, though lung cancer heads the list of fatal tumors for both sexes. The second most lethal malignancy in males is also a sex-specific tumor: prostate cancer. Last year approximately 46,000 women succumbed to breast cancer and 35,000 men to prostate cancer; the NCI spent $213.7 million on breast-cancer research and $51.1 million on study of the prostate. Thus although about a third more women died of breast cancer than men of prostate cancer, breast-cancer research received more than four times the funding. More than three times as much money per fatality was spent on the women's disease. Breast cancer accounted for 8.8 percent of cancer fatalities in the United States and for 13 percent of the NCI research budget; the corresponding figures for prostate cancer were 6.7 percent of fatalities and three percent of the funding. The spending for breast-cancer research is projected to increase by 23 percent this year, to $262.9 million; prostate-research spending will increase by 7.6 percent, to $55 million.

The female cancers of the cervix and the uterus accounted for 10,100 deaths and $48.5 million in research last year, and ovarian cancer accounted for 13,300 deaths and $32.5 million in research. Thus the research funding for all female-specific cancers is substantially larger per fatality than the funding for prostate cancer.

Is this level of spending on women's health just a recent development, needed to make up for years of prior neglect? The NCI is divided into sections dealing with issues such as cancer biology and diagnosis, prevention and control, etiology, and treatment. Until funding allocations for sex-specific concerns became a political issue, in the mid-1980s, the NCI did not track organ-specific spending data. The earliest information now available was reconstructed retroactively to 1981. Nevertheless, these early data provide a window on spending patterns in the era before political pressure began to intensify for more research on women. Each year from 1981 to 1985 funding for breast-cancer research exceeded funding for prostate cancer by a ratio of roughly five to one. A rational, nonpolitical explanation for this is that breast cancer attacks a larger number of patients, at a younger age. In any event, the data failed to support claims that women were neglected in that era.

Again, most medical research is conducted on diseases that afflict both sexes. Women's-health advocates charge that we collect data from studies of men and then extrapolate to women. A look at the actual data reveals a different reality.

The best-known and most ambitious study of cardiovascular health over time began in the town of Framingham, Massachusetts, in 1948. Researchers started with 2,336 men and 2,873 women aged thirty to sixty-two, and have followed the survivors of this group with biennial physical exams and lab tests for more than forty-five years. In this and many other observational studies women have been well represented.

With respect to the aspirin study, the researchers at Harvard Medical School did not focus exclusively on men. Both sexes were studied nearly concurrently. The men's study was more rigorous, because it was placebo-controlled (that is, some subjects were randomly assigned to receive placebos instead of aspirin); the women's study was based on responses to questionnaires sent to nurses and a review of medical records. The women's study, however, followed nearly four times as many subjects as the men's study (87,678 versus 22,071), and it followed its subjects for a year longer (six versus five) than the men's study did. The results of the men's study were reported in the *New England Journal of Medicine* in July of 1989 and prompted charges of sexism in medical research. The women's-study results were printed in the *Journal of the American Medical Association* in July of 1991, and were generally ignored by the nonmedical press.

Most studies on the prevention of "premature" (occurring in people under age sixty-five) coronary-artery disease have, in fact, been conducted on men. Since middle-aged women have a much lower incidence of this illness than their male counterparts (they provide less than a third as many cases), documenting the preventive effect of a given treatment in these women is much more difficult. More experiments were conducted on men not because women were considered less important but because women suffer less from this disease. Older women do develop coronary disease (albeit at a lower rate than older men), but the experiments were not performed on older men either. At most the data suggest an emphasis on the prevention of disease in younger people.

Incidentally, all clinical breast-cancer research currently funded by the NCI is being conducted on women, even though 300 men a year die of this tumor. Do studies on the prevention of breast cancer with specifically exclude males signify a neglect of men's health? Or should a disease be studied in the group most at risk? Obviously, the coronary-disease research situation and the breast-cancer research situation are not equivalent, but together they do serve to illustrate a point: diseases are most often studied in the highest-risk group, regardless of sex.

What about all the new drug tests that exclude women? Don't they prove the pharmaceutical industry's insensitivity to and disregard for females?

The Food and Drug Administration [FDA] divides human testing of new medicines into three stages. Phase 1 studies are done on a small number of volunteers over a brief period of time, primarily to test safety. Phase 2 studies typically involve a few hundred patients and are designed to look more closely at safety and effectiveness. Phase 3 tests precede approval for commercial release and generally include several thousand patients.

In 1977 the FDA issued guidelines that specifically excluded women with "childbearing potential" from phase 1 and early phase 2 studies; they were to be included in late phase 2 and phase 3 trials in proportion to their expected use of the medication. FDA surveys conducted in 1983 and 1988 showed that the two sexes had been proportionally represented in clinical trials by the time drugs were approved for release.

The 1977 guidelines codified a policy already informally in effect since the thalidomide tragedy shocked the world in 1962. The births of armless or otherwise deformed babies in that era dramatically highlighted the special risks incurred when fertile women ingest drugs. So the policy of excluding such women from the early phases of drug testing arose out of concern, not out of disregard, for them. The policy was changed last year, as a consequence of political protest and recognition that early studies in both sexes might better direct testing.

* * *

Throughout human history from antiquity until the beginning of this century men, on the average, lived slightly longer than women. By 1920 women's life expectancy in the United States was one year greater than men's (54.6 years versus 53.6). After that the gap increased steadily, to 3.5 years in 1930, 4.4 years in 1940, 5.5 in 1950, 6.5 in 1960, and 7.7 in 1970. For the past quarter of a century the gap has remained relatively steady: around seven years. In 1990 the figure was seven years (78.8 versus 71.8).

Thus in the latter part of the twentieth century women live about 10 percent longer than men. A significant part of the reason for this is medical care.

In past centuries complications during childbirth were a major cause of traumatic death in women. Medical advances have dramatically eliminated most of this risk. Infections such as smallpox, cholera, and tuberculosis killed large numbers of men and women at similar ages. The elimination of infection as the dominant cause of death has boosted the prominence of diseases that selectively afflict men earlier in life.

Age-adjusted mortality rates for men are higher for all twelve leading causes of death, including heart disease, stroke, cancer, lung disease (emphysema and pneumonia), liver disease (cirrhosis), suicide, and homicide. We have come to accept women's longer life span as natural, the consequence of their greater biological fitness. Yet this greater fitness never manifested itself in all the millennia of human history that preceded the present era and its medical-care system—the same system that women's-health advocates accuse of neglecting the female sex.

To remedy the alleged neglect, an Office of Research on Women's Health was established by the NIH in 1990. In 1991 the NIH launched its largest epidemiological project ever, the Women's Health Initiative. Costing more than $600 million, this fifteen-year program will study the effects of estrogen therapy, diet, dietary supplements, and exercise on heart disease, breast cancer, colon cancer, osteoporosis, and other diseases in 160,000 postmenopausal women. The study is ambitious in scope and may well result in many advances in the care of older women.

What it will not do is close the "medical gender gap," the difference in the quality of care given the two sexes. The reason is that the gap does not favor men. As we have seen, women receive more medical care and benefit more from medical research. The net result is the most important gap of all: seven years, 10 percent of life.

CHALLENGE QUESTIONS

Does Health Care Delivery and Research Benefit Men at the Expense of Women?

1. Do you feel that the effectiveness of communication between doctor and patient is relevant to this issue? Why, or why not?

2. Laurence and Weinhouse refer to "women's dissatisfaction with their medical care." What, if any, are the dangers of women's perceiving physicians as unresponsive to their needs? What kinds of changes would you recommend in the training of doctors to address this concern?

3. Many former prescription drugs are now available over the counter. There is also a growing interest in "alternative" medicine and nonpharmaceutical treatment. Do you see a connection between these trends and "women's dissatisfaction" with their medical care? Why, or why not?

4. How might having more information about high-risk categories (for example, age and gender) affect the interpretation of data cited on both sides of the issue?

5. What kind of unbiased survey would you prepare to accurately study and evaluate a physician's communication skills? Keep in mind that you would be dealing, at least in part, with patients' subjective opinions.

ISSUE 12

Are Memories of Sex Abuse Always Real?

YES: Ellen Bass and Laura Davis, from *The Courage to Heal: A Guide for Women Survivors of Child Sexual Abuse* (Harper & Row, 1988)

NO: Lee Coleman, from "Creating 'Memories' of Sexual Abuse," *Issues in Child Abuse Accusations* (vol. 4, no. 4, 1992)

ISSUE SUMMARY

YES: Ellen Bass and Laura Davis, both counselors of victims of child sexual abuse, assert that even a faint or vague memory of sexual abuse is prime evidence that sexual abuse has occurred.

NO: Psychiatrist Lee Coleman argues that individual memories of sexual abuse are susceptible to manipulation by laypersons and mental health professionals and that "memories" of sexual abuse that never occurred can be created in therapy.

It is hard to imagine a more heinous crime than sexual abuse. Yet, perhaps surprisingly, it is a crime that often goes unpunished. Frequently, sexual abusers are family members and their victims are children who are too young to protest or to know that they are being violated. This is part of the reason why memories have become so significant to the sexual abuse issue. Often, it is not until the victims become adults that they realize they were abused.

The problem is that the reliability of memory itself has come into question. Some cognitive psychologists have expressed doubt about the accuracy of memories when people are formally questioned (such as on the witness stand). Another issue is whether or not memory is subject to manipulation. People under hypnosis, for example, tend to be susceptible to the hypnotist's suggestions as to what they "should" remember. Do therapists of alleged victims of sexual abuse make similar suggestions? Could these therapists be unconsciously or consciously "shaping" through therapeutic suggestion the memories of the people they treat?

In the following selections, Ellen Bass and Laura Davis argue that memories of sexual abuse and what they identify as symptoms of sexual abuse are sufficient evidence that a person was abused. They provide a list of experiences that, if remembered, indicate that a person was probably abused. They also describe a number of the symptoms that they contend are commonly experienced by those who have been abused. Bass and Davis emphasize that a lack of explicit memories about sexual abuse does not mean that abuse did not occur.

Lee Coleman refutes the claims of those who place faith in all memories of sexual abuse. He argues that people can be led to believe that they were sexually abused when, in fact, they were not. Coleman presents a case to show that so-called recovered memories of sexual abuse can be created in therapy with the encouragement of mental health professionals. He holds that professionals who consider themselves specialists in sexual abuse recovery tend to accept without question that sexual abuse has occurred if a client says it has, to encourage as many memories as possible, and to accept all allegations of sexual abuse as real. Coleman views these professionals as manipulative and often without awareness.

POINT	COUNTERPOINT
• If someone says that they believe they were sexually abused, they probably were.	• People can be made to believe that they have been sexually abused when, in fact, they have not.
• Memories for traumatic events are likely to be repressed, so they must be "helped" to be recovered.	• "Helping" memories to be recovered can unintentionally create them.
• Mental health professionals do not create people's memories for them.	• Mental health professionals sometimes create false memories for their patients.
• Memory is like a videotape that records things exactly as they occur.	• Evidence shows that memory is not infallible and can be distorted and inaccurate.

YES

Ellen Bass and Laura Davis

THE COURAGE TO HEAL

If you have been sexually abused, you are not alone. One out of three girls, and one out of seven boys, are sexually abused by the time they reach the age of eighteen. Sexual abuse happens to children of every class, culture, race, religion, and gender. Children are abused by fathers, stepfathers, uncles, brothers, grandparents, neighbors, family friends, baby-sitters, teachers, strangers, and sometimes by aunts and mothers.[1] Although women do abuse, the vast majority of abusers are heterosexual men.

All sexual abuse is damaging, and the trauma does not end when the abuse stops. If you were abused as a child, you are probably experiencing long-term effects that interfere with your day-to-day functioning.

However, it is possible to heal. It is even possible to thrive. Thriving means more than just an alleviation of symptoms, more than band-aids, more than functioning adequately. Thriving means enjoying a feeling of wholeness, satisfaction in your life and work, genuine love and trust in your relationships, pleasure in your body.

Until now, much of the literature on child sexual abuse has documented the ravages of abuse, talking extensively about "the tragedy of ruined lives," but little about recovery. This [reading] is about recovery—what it takes, what it feels like, how it can transform your life.

People say "time heals all wounds," and it's true to a certain extent. Time will dull some of the pain, but deep healing doesn't happen unless you consciously choose it. Healing from child sexual abuse takes years of commitment and dedication. But if you are willing to work hard, if you are determined to make lasting changes in your life, if you are able to find good resources and skilled support, you can not only heal but thrive. We believe in miracles and hard work.

HOW CAN I KNOW IF I WAS A VICTIM OF
CHILD SEXUAL ABUSE?

When you were a young child or teenager, were you:

• Touched in sexual areas?

Excerpted from Ellen Bass and Laura Davis, *The Courage to Heal: A Guide for Women Survivors of Child Sexual Abuse* (Harper & Row, 1988), pp. 20–22, 70–83. Copyright © 1988 by Ellen Bass and Laura Davis. Reprinted by permission of HarperCollins Publishers, Inc.

- Shown sexual movies or forced to listen to sexual talk?
- Made to pose for seductive or sexual photographs?
- Subjected to unnecessary medical treatments?
- Forced to perform oral sex on an adult or sibling?
- Raped or otherwise penetrated?
- Fondled, kissed, or held in a way that made you uncomfortable?
- Forced to take part in ritualized abuse in which you were physically or sexually tortured?
- Made to watch sexual acts or look at sexual parts?
- Bathed in a way that felt intrusive to you?
- Objectified and ridiculed about your body?
- Encouraged or goaded into sex you didn't really want?
- Told all you were good for was sex?
- Involved in child prostitution or pornography?[2]

If you are unable to remember any specific instances like the ones mentioned above but still have a feeling that something abusive happened to you, it probably did....

Children often cope with abuse by forgetting it ever happened. As a result, you may have no conscious memory of being abused. You may have forgotten large chunks of your childhood. Yet there are things you do remember. When you are touched in a certain way, you feel nauseated. Certain words or facial expressions scare you. You know you never liked your mother to touch you. You slept with your clothes on in junior high school. You were taken to the doctor repeatedly for vaginal infections.

You may think you don't have memories, but often as you begin to talk about what you do remember, there emerges a constellation of feelings, reactions, and recollections that add up to substantial information. To say "I was abused," you don't need the kind of recall that would stand up in a court of law.

Often the knowledge that you were abused starts with a tiny feeling, an intuition. It's important to trust that inner voice and work from there. Assume your feelings are valid. So far, no one we've talked to thought she might have been abused, and then later discovered that she hadn't been. The progression always goes the other way, from suspicion to confirmation. If you think you were abused and your life shows the symptoms, then you were....

* * *

I've looked the memories in the face and smelled their breath. They can't hurt me anymore.

For many survivors, remembering is the first step in healing. To begin with, you may have to remember that you *were* abused at all. Second come specific memories.... The third kind of remembering is the recovery of the feelings you had at the time the abuse took place. Many women have always remembered the physical details of what happened but have forgotten the emotions that went with it. One survivor explained, "I could rattle off the facts of my abuse like a grocery list, but remembering the fear and terror and pain was another matter entirely."

Remembering is different for every survivor. If, as a young woman, you turned your abuser in to the police and testified against him in court, there's not much chance you forgot. Likewise, if you had to raise your abuser's child, or abort it, you've probably always remembered. Or the abuse may have been so present in the daily texture of your life that there was no way to forget.

One woman who'd kept a vivid image of what had happened to her said she sometimes wished she *had* forgotten: "I wish I could have gotten shock treatments like my mother. She had forgotten huge segments of her life, and I used to envy her." On the other hand, this woman said she was glad she'd always known just how bad things were: "At least I knew why I was weird! Knowing what had happened allowed me to work on the damn problem."

You may not have forgotten entirely, but coped by having selective memories.

I always knew that we had an incestuous relationship. I remember the first time I heard the word "incest," when I was seventeen. I hadn't known there was a word for it. I always remembered my father grabbing my breasts and kissing me.

I told my therapist, "I remember every miserable thing that happened to me." It seemed like I remembered so much, how could there be more? I didn't remember anything *but* abuse. But I didn't remember being raped, even though I knew I had been. I categorically told my therapist, "I don't want to remember being raped." We talked about the fact that I didn't want to remember that for months. Yet I knew my father had been my first lover.

There is no right or wrong when it comes to remembering. You may have multiple memories. Or you may just have one. Years of abuse are sometimes telescoped into a single recollection. When you begin to remember, you might have new images every day for weeks on end. Or you may experience your memories in clumps, three or four of them coming in a matter of days, then not again for months. Sometimes survivors remember one abuser, or a specific kind of abuse, only to remember, years later, a second abuser or a different form of abuse.

There are many women who show signs of having been abused without having any memories. You may have only a vague feeling that something happened but be unable to remember what it was. There are reasons for this, and to understand them, we have to first look at the way early memories are stored.

ABOUT MEMORIES

The process of storing memories is complex. We store different experiences in the right and left halves of our brain. The left brain stores sequential, logical, language-oriented experience; the right stores perceptual, spatial experiences. When we try to retrieve right-brain information through left-brain techniques, such as logic and language, we sometimes hit a blank. There are some experiences that we are simply not going to remember in an orderly, precise way.

If you were abused when you were preverbal, or just as you were learning to talk, you had no way of making sense of what was happening to you. Babies don't know the difference between touching someone's penis and touching someone's leg. If a penis is put in their mouth, they will suck it, much as they would a breast or a bottle. Young children are aware of sensations but cannot come up with a name or a concept—like "sexual abuse" —for what is being done to them.

Another thing that makes remembering difficult is the simple fact that you are trying to remember details of something that happened a long time ago. If you ask friends who weren't abused, you will find that most of them also don't remember a great number of details from their childhood. It is even more difficult to remember the times when we were hurt, humiliated, or otherwise violated.

If the abuse happened only once, or if it was an abuse that is hard to name (inappropriate boundaries, lewd looks, subtler forms of abuse), it can be even harder to remember. For others, the constancy of the abuse prevents detailed naming. As one survivor put it, "Do you remember every time you sat down to eat? What you had for dinner the Tuesday you turned six? I remember the flavor. It was a constant, like eating. It was always there."

WHAT REMEMBERING IS LIKE

Recovering occluded memories (those blocked from the surface) is not like remembering with the conscious mind. Often the memories are vague and dreamlike, as if they're being seen from far away.

The actual rape memories for me are like from the end of a tunnel. That's because I literally left my body at the scene. So I remember it from that perspective—there's some physical distance between me and what's going on. Those memories aren't as sharp in focus. It's like they happened in another dimension.

Other times, memories come in bits and pieces.

I'd be driving home from my therapist's office, and I'd start having flashes

of things—just segments, like bloody sheets, or taking a bath, or throwing away my nightgown. For a long time, I remembered all the things around being raped, but not the rape itself.

If memories come to you in fragments, you may find it hard to place them in any kind of chronological order. You may not know exactly when the abuse began, how old you were, or when and why it stopped. The process of understanding the fragments is a lot like putting together a jigsaw puzzle or being a detective.

Part of me felt like I was on the trail of a murder mystery, and I was going to solve it. I really enjoyed following all the clues. "Okay, I was looking at the clock. It was mid-afternoon. Why was it mid-afternoon? Where could my mother have been? Oh, I bet she was at..." Tracing down the clues to find out exactly what had happened was actually fun.

Ella is a survivor who remembered in snatches. To make sense of her memories, she began to examine some of her own strange ways of coping. She started to analyze certain compulsive behaviors, like staring at the light fixture whenever she was making love:

I'd be making love and would think, "Why would somebody lay here, when they're supposed to be having a pleasurable experience, and concentrate on a light fixture?" I remember every single lighting fixture in every single house we ever lived in! Why have I always been so obsessed with light under doors, and the interruption of light? That's a crazy thing for an adult woman to be obsessive about—that someone walks past and cracks the light. What's that about?

What it was about was watching to see if her father's footsteps stopped outside her door at night. If they stopped, that meant he'd come in and molest her. Once Ella started to pay attention to these kinds of details, the memories started to fit in place.

Flashbacks

In a flashback, you reexperience the original abuse. Flashbacks may be accompanied by the feelings you felt at the time, or they may be stark and detached, like watching a movie about somebody else's life.

Frequently flashbacks are visual: "I saw this penis coming toward me," or "I couldn't see his face, just the big black belt he always wore." First-time visual memories can be very dramatic:

My husband was beginning to initiate some lovemaking. I had a flash in my mind. The closest way I can describe it is that it was much like viewing slides in a slide show, when the slide goes by too fast, but slow enough to give you some part of the image. It was someone jamming their fingers up my vagina. It was very vivid, and enough of the feelings came sneaking in that I knew it wasn't a fantasy. There was an element of it that made me stop and take notice. I lay there and let it replay a couple of times.

I felt confused. I was aware that it was something that happened to me. I even had a recollection of the pain. I scrambled around in my mind for an explanation. "Was that a rough lover I had?" Immediately I knew that wasn't the case. So I went back into the flash again. Each time I went back, I tried to open it up to see a little more. I didn't see his face, but I could sense an essence of my father.

Sometimes visual memories are more complete. A survivor who's had them both ways explained the difference:

A flashback is like a slide compared to a film. It's the difference between getting one shot or one look into a room and getting the expanded version. A full memory is more like panning over the whole scene, with all the details, sound, feeling, and visuals rolled into one.

But not everyone is visual. One woman was upset that she couldn't get any pictures. Her father had held her at knifepoint in the car, face down in the dark, and raped her. She had never seen anything. But she had heard him. And when she began to write the scene in Spanish, her native language, it all came back to her—his threats, his brutality, his violation.

Regression

Another way to regain memory is through regression. Under the guidance of a trustworthy therapist, it is possible to go back to earlier times. Or you may find yourself going back on such a journey on your own, with only the prompting of your own unconscious.

Most of the regressions I experienced felt almost like going on a ride. They'd last maybe three or four hours at a time. One of the most vivid physical regressions I went through was late one evening, when Barbara and I were talking about her going to visit a friend. All of a sudden, I felt like I was being sucked down a drain. And then I felt like a real baby. I started crying and clinging and saying, "You can't go! You have to stay with me!" And I began to talk in a five-year-old's voice, using words and concepts that a five-year-old might use.

All of a sudden I thought I was just going to throw up. I ran to the bathroom, and then I really started to sob. I saw lots of scenes from my childhood. Times I felt rejected flashed by me, almost in slides.

Barb held me, and kind of coached me through it. "It's okay. You can get through this." Having her just sit there and listen really helped me. I just kept crying, and described to Barbara all these slides that were going by. After about twenty minutes, I fell into the deepest sleep I'd had for months. The next morning when I woke up, I felt a million pounds lighter.

Sense Memory

Often it is a particular touch, smell, or sound that triggers a memory. You might remember when you return to the town, to the house, to the room, where the abuse took place. Or when you smell a certain aftershave the abuser wore.

Thirty-five-year-old Ella says, "It's all real tactile, sensory things that have brought memories back. Textures. Sounds. The smell of my father's house. The smell of vodka on somebody."

Ella had a magic purple quilt when she was a little girl. Her grandmother made it for her. It was supposed to keep her safe—nothing bad could happen to her as long as she was under it. The quilt had been lost for many years, but when Ella finally got it back at twenty-one, it triggered a whole series of memories.

Touch can also reopen memories. Women have had images come up while they were being massaged. You may freeze up and see pictures when you're making love. Your lover breathes in your ear just as your abuser once did, and it all comes spilling back:

Sometimes when we're making love, I feel like my head just starts to float away somewhere. I feel like I literally split off at my shoulders, and I get very lightheaded and dizzy. It's as if someone was blowing a fan down on top of my head. There's a lot of movement down

past my hair. It's like rising up out of my head. I get really disoriented.

The other thing I experience is a lot of splitting right at the hips. My legs get very heavy and really solid. They just feel like dead weight, like logs. No energy is passing through them. Then I get real sick to my stomach, just violently ill. I find the minute I get nauseous, whatever it is is very close to me. And if I pay attention to it, I can see it, and move on.

The Body Remembers What the Mind Chooses to Forget

It is also possible to remember only feelings. Memories are stored in our bodies, and it is possible to physically reexperience the terror of the abuse. Your body may clutch tight, or you may feel the screams you could not scream as a child. Or you may feel that you are suffocating and cannot breathe.

I would get body memories that would have no pictures to them at all. I would just start screaming and feel that something was coming out of my body that I had no control over. And I would usually get them right after making love or in the middle of making love, or right in the middle of a fight. When my passion was aroused in some way, I would remember in my body, although I wouldn't have a conscious picture, just this screaming coming out of me.

WAYS TO REMEMBER

Memories come up under many different circumstances. You might remember because you're finally in a relationship that feels safe. Or because you've just been through a divorce and everything in your life is unraveling. Women often remember childhood abuse when they are raped or attacked in adult life.

Memories don't always surface in such dramatic ways. While talking with her friend, one woman suddenly heard herself saying something she didn't realize she knew. "It's as though I always knew it," she explained. "It's just that I hadn't thought about it in twenty or thirty years. Up until that moment, I'd forgotten."

You may remember seemingly out of the blue. Or because you're having persistent nightmares that reach up through sleep to tell you:

I'd always had a dream about my brother assaulting me. It was a foggy dream, and I had it over and over again. I'd wake up thinking it was really disgusting because I was enjoying it in the dream. I'd think, "You're sick. Why are you having this dream? Is that what you want?" I'd give myself all those kinds of guilt messages, 'cause it was still a dream. It wasn't history yet.

Then, six months ago, I was sitting in a training meeting for working with sexual assault prevention. I don't even remember what the trainer said, but all of a sudden, I realized that it wasn't a dream, and that it had really happened. I can't tell you anything about the rest of the meeting. I was just in shock.

The fact that this woman remembered in the middle of a training session for sexual assault is significant. As the media focus on sexual abuse has increased, more and more women have had their memories triggered.

Media Coverage of Sexual Abuse
Jennierose, who remembered in her mid-forties, was sitting with her lover one night, watching a TV program about sexual offenders in prison. The therapist running the group encouraged the offenders to get very emotional, at which time they'd remember the traumatic events in their own childhoods.

In the middle of the program, Jennierose turned to her lover and said, "I wish there was a therapist like that I could go to, because I know there's something I'm not remembering." As soon as she said that, Jennierose had a vision of the first time her father sodomized her, when she was four and a half and her mother had gone to the hospital to have another baby. "It was a totally detailed vision, to the point of seeing the rose-colored curtains blowing in the window."

Sobbing, Jennierose said to her lover, "I think I'm making something up." Her lover simply said, "Look at yourself! Look at yourself! Tell me you're making it up." And Jennierose couldn't. She knew she was telling the truth.

This kind of memory is common. Often women become very uncomfortable (nauseated, dizzy, unable to concentrate, emotional) when they hear another survivor's story and realize that what's being described happened to them too.

When You Break an Addiction
Many survivors remember their abuse once they get sober, quit drugs, or stop eating compulsively. These and other addictions can effectively block any recollection of the abuse, but once you stop, the memories often surface. Anna Stevens explains:

At the point I decided to put down drinking, I had to start feeling. The connection to the abuse was almost immediate. And I've watched other people come to AA and do the same thing. They have just enough time to get through the initial shakes, and you watch them start to go through the memories. And you know what's coming, but they don't....

When You Become a Mother

Mothers often remember their own abuse when they see their children's vulnerability, or when their children reach the age they were when their own abuse began. Sometimes they remember because their child is being abused. Dana was court-ordered to go for therapy when her three-year-old daughter, Christy, was molested. Dana first remembered when she unconsciously substituted her own name for her daughter's:

I was in therapy talking about Christy, and instead of saying "Christy," I said "I." And I didn't even catch it. My therapist did. She had always suspected that I was abused too, but she hadn't said anything to me.

She told me what I had said, and I said, "I did? I said 'I?' I hadn't even heard myself. It was really eerie.

What came out was that I was really dealing with Christy's molestation on a level of my own. The things that I was outraged at and that hurt me the most were things that had happened to me, not things that had happened to Christy. Part of the reason I fell apart and so much came back to me when I found out about Christy was because my husband was doing the same things to her that my father had done with me.

After a Significant Death

Many women are too scared to remember while their abusers are still alive. One woman said, "I couldn't afford to remember until both my parents were dead, until there was nobody left to hurt me." A forty-seven-year-old woman first remembered a year and a half after her mother died: "Then I could no longer hurt my mother by telling her."

FEELING THE FEELINGS

Although some remembering is emotionally detached, when you remember with feeling, the helplessness, terror, and physical pain can be as real as any actual experience. You may feel as if you are being crushed, ripped open, or suffocated. Sexual arousal may also accompany your memories, and this may horrify you, but arousal is a natural response to sexual stimulation. There is no reason to be ashamed.

You might remember feeling close and happy, wrapped in a special kind of love. Disgust and horror are not the only way to feel when you have memories. There is no *right* way to feel, but you must feel, even if it sends you reeling:

When I first remembered, I shut down emotionally right away. I climbed all the way up into my mind and forgot about the gut level. That's how I protected myself. For a long time it was just an intellectual exercise. "Oh, that's why I have trouble with men and authority. That's why I might not have remembered much about growing up." It took nine months after I first remembered for the feelings to start bubbling up.

I found myself slipping into the feelings I'd had during the abuse, that hadn't been safe to feel at the time. The first was this tremendous isolation. From there, I moved into absolute terror. I got in touch with how frightening the world is. It was the worst of the fear finally coming up. I felt like it was right at the top of my neck all the time, just ready to come out in a scream.

I was right on the edge. I had an encounter with my boss, who said that my performance had been poor. I finally told him what had happened, which was really heavy—telling some male authority figure that you remembered incest in your family. He is a kind and caring person. The best he could do was back off and leave me alone.

I was then carrying around all this external pressure—my job was in jeopardy, my life was falling apart, and I was having all these feelings I didn't know what to do with. In order to keep myself in control, I started compulsively eating. Finally I decided I didn't want to go through this stuff by myself anymore." I got myself into therapy.

Having to experience the feelings is one of the roughest parts of remembering. "It pisses me off that I have to survive it twice, only this time with feelings," one woman said. "This time it's worse. I'm not so effective at dissociating anymore."

Another woman said, "I started off very butch [tough] about remembering. I kicked into my overachiever thing. I was going to lick this thing. I believed getting the pictures was what was important. I got a ton of memories, all on the intellectual level. It was kind of like I was going to 'do' incest, just like I might take up typing."

It was only after a year of therapy that this woman began to realize that *she* was the one who'd been abused. "I finally realized, I finally *felt*, that this was something that had happened to me, and that it had been damaging. I had to realize that just getting the memories was not going to make it go away. *This was about me!*"

LETTING MEMORIES IN

Few survivors feel they have control over their memories. Most feel the memories have control of them, that they do not choose the time and place a new memory will emerge. You may be able to fight them off for a time, but the price—

headaches, nightmares, exhaustion—is not worth staving off what is inevitable.

Not everyone will know a memory is coming, but many survivors do get warnings, a certain feeling or series of feelings, that clue them in. Your stomach may get tight. You may sleep poorly, have frightening dreams. Or you may be warned in other ways:

I always know when they're coming. I get very tense. I get very scared. I get snappy at things that ordinarily wouldn't make me angry. I get sad. Usually it's anger and anxiety and fear that come first. And I have a choice. It's a real conscious choice. It's either I want it or I don't want it. And I said "I don't want it" a lot. And when I did that, I would just get sicker and sicker. I'd get more depressed. I'd get angry irrationally.

Now I don't say I don't want it. It's not worth it. My body seems to need to release it. The more I heal, the more I see these memories are literally stored in my body, and they've got to get out. Otherwise I'm going to carry them forever.

REMEMBERING OVER TIME

Often when you've resolved one group of memories, another will make its way to the surface.

The more I worked on the abuse, the more I remembered. First I remembered my brother, and then my grandfather. About six months after that I remembered my father. And then about a year later, I remembered my mother. I remembered the "easiest" first and the "hardest" last. Even though it was traumatic for me to realize that everyone in my family abused me, there was something reassuring about it. For a long time I'd felt worse than the initial memories should have made me feel, so remembering the rest of the abuse was actually one of the most grounding things to happen. My life suddenly made sense.

The impact new memories have will shift over time. One woman who has been getting new memories for the past ten years says remembering has become harder over time:

My first flood of memories came when I was twenty-five. The memories I get now are like fine-tuning—more details, more textures. Even though there was more of a feeling of shock and catharsis at first, remembering is harder now. I believe them now. It hurts more. I have the emotions to feel the impact. I can see how it's affected my life.

Laura also says new memories are harder:

Just when I felt that my life was getting back to normal and I could put the incest aside, I had another flashback that was much more violent than the earlier pictures I'd seen. I was furious. I wanted to be finished. I didn't want to be starting in with incest again! And my resistance made the remembering a lot more difficult.

Other survivors say memories have gotten easier to handle:

As I've come to terms with the fact that I was abused, new pictures, new incidents, don't have the same impact. The battle of believing it happened is not one I have to fight each time another piece falls into place. Once I had a framework to fit new memories into, my recovery time got much faster. While my first memories overwhelmed me for weeks, now I might only cry for ten minutes or feel depressed for an hour. It's not that I don't have new memories. It's just that they don't devastate me.

And new memories don't take anything away from the healing you've already done. Paradoxically, *you are already healing from the effects of the things you have yet to remember.*

"BUT I DON'T HAVE ANY MEMORIES"

If you don't remember your abuse, you are not alone. Many women don't have memories, and some never get memories. This doesn't mean they weren't abused.

If you don't have any memory of it, it can be hard to believe the abuse really happened. You may feel insecure about trusting your intuition and want "proof" of your abuse. This is a very natural desire, but it is not always one that can be met. The unconscious has its own way of unfolding that does not always meet your demands or your timetable.

One thirty-eight-year-old survivor described her relationship with her father as "emotionally incestuous." She has never had specific memories of any physical contact between them, and for a long time she was haunted by the fact that she couldn't come up with solid data. Over time, though, she's come to terms with her lack of memories. Her story is a good model if you don't have specific pictures to draw from:

Do I want to know if something physical happened between my father and me? Really, I think you have to be strong enough to know. I think that our minds are wonderful in the way they protect us, and I think that when I'm strong enough to know, I'll know.

I obsessed for about a year on trying to remember, and then I got tired of sitting around talking about what I couldn't remember. I thought, "All right, let's act as if." It's like you come home and your home has been robbed, and everything has been thrown in the middle of the room, and the window is open and the curtain is blowing in the wind, and the cat is gone. You know somebody robbed you, but you're never going to know who. So what are you going to do? Sit there and try to figure it out while your stuff lies around? No, you start to clean it up. You put bars on the windows. You assume somebody was there. Somebody could come along and say, "Now how do you know someone was there?" You don't know.

That's how I acted. I had the symptoms. Every incest group I went to I completely empathized. It rang bells all the time. I felt like there was something I just couldn't get to, that I couldn't remember yet. And my healing was blocked there.

Part of my wanting to get specific memories was guilt that I could be accusing this man of something so heinous, and what if he didn't do it? How horrible for me to accuse him! That's why I wanted the memories. I wanted to be sure. Societally, women have always been accused of crying rape.

But I had to ask myself, "Why would I be feeling all of this? Why would I be feeling all this anxiety if something didn't happen?" If the specifics are not available to you, then go with what you've got.

I'm left with the damage. And that's why I relate to that story of the burglar.

I'm owning the damage. I want to get better. I've been very ill as a result of the damage, and at some point I realized, "I'm thirty-eight years old. What am I going to do—wait twenty more years for a memory?" I'd rather get better.

And then maybe the stronger I am, the more the memories will come back. Maybe I'm putting the cart before the horse. Maybe I've remembered as much as I'm able to remember without breaking down. I don't want to go insane. I want to be out in the world. Maybe I should go with that sense of protection. There is a survivor in here and she's pretty smart. So I'm going with the circumstantial evidence, and I'm working on healing myself. I go to these incest groups, and I tell people, "I don't have any pictures," and then I go on and talk all about my father, and nobody ever says, "You don't belong here."

NOTES

1. For sources on the scope of child sexual abuse, see the "About Sexual Abuse" section of the Resource Guide. A number of these books cite recent studies to which you can refer for more complete statistics.

2. Between 500,000 and 1,000,000 children are involved in prostitution and pornography in this country; a high percentage of them are victims of incest. See *Sex Work: Writings by Women in the Industry*, edited by Frédérique Dellacoste and Priscilla Alexander (Pittsburgh: Cleis Press, 1987).

NO

Lee Coleman

CREATING "MEMORIES" OF SEXUAL ABUSE

ABSTRACT: An analysis of a case of alleged recovered memories of sexual abuse is presented to illustrate how such mental images can be created in therapy. The memories, although believed by the woman to be of actual events, were the result of suggestions from both lay persons and professionals.

While, just a few years ago, students of child sexual abuse accusations thought they had seen every imaginable brand of irresponsibility on the part of certain mental health professionals, something new and equally terrible has emerged. To the growing number of children trained to say and believe things which never happened is now added a growing number of adults, usually women, being trained to say and believe that they have suddenly "unblocked" memories of childhood sexual abuse.

Just like allegations coming from children, concern about biased and unprofessional methods of eliciting statements from adults should in no way cast doubt on the reality of sexual abuse. There are countless numbers of adults who were molested as children, who did not speak of it, but who now may reveal their experiences as part of our society's belated recognition of such abuse. But to acknowledge the reality of sexual abuse, and the reality of the silence kept by some of the victims, does nothing to mitigate the harm being done by those therapists who are convincing patients that even if sexual abuse is not remembered, it probably happened anyway.

In this article, I will illustrate the process by which a young woman, moderately depressed and unsure of her life goals, but in no way out of touch with reality (psychotic), came to make allegations which were so bizarre that they might easily be thought to be the product of [a] major mental disorder. In such cases, I have repeatedly seen the falsely accused and their closest family and friends make this assumption. This case will show, as have the others I have studied, that the source is not a disorder in the patient, but a "disorder" in the therapist. The problem is the irresponsible adoption by some therapists of a new fad which will be clarified below.

From Lee Coleman, "Creating 'Memories' of Sexual Abuse," *Issues in Child Abuse Accusations*, vol. 4, no. 4 (1992), pp. 169–176. Copyright © 1992 by The Institute for Psychological Therapies. Reprinted by permission of *Issues in Child Abuse Accusations*.

Here, then, is a report I submitted to the Court hearing the civil lawsuit filed by this woman against her cousin. All names and identifying information have been changed.

* * *

Judge John Q. Smith
    Superior Court, All American County
    Anywhere, USA

The following report concerns the suit between Susan Q. Smith and John V. Public. The opinions expressed are based on a study of the Amended List of Documents of the Plaintiff, dated April 6, 1992, Additional Documents (such as police records and Children's Services Records), Examination for Discovery transcripts of Mrs. Smith and Mr. Public, and my examination of Mrs. Smith on May 4, 1992, which lasted somewhat over three hours. I have also studied several videotapes pertinent to the case, enumerated below.

Based upon all this information, as well [as] my prior professional experience, it is my opinion that the alleged "memories" of Mrs. Smith, relating a variety of sexual and abusive acts perpetrated upon her by Mr. Public and others, are not memories at all. They are, instead, mental images which, however sincerely felt by her to be memories of past events, are nonetheless the result of a series of suggestions from both lay persons and professionals.

That Mrs. Smith has succumbed to these influences in no way implies that she suffers from any mental disorder. By her own account, she has had problems of low self-esteem, depression, and bulimia in her past. She has, however, never suffered and does not now suffer a mental disorder which would imply a loss of contact with reality. If the reliability of her claims are to be best evaluated by the Court, it should be understood that there is another way that a person may say things that may not be true, yet be entirely sincere.

Suggestibility is something we all share as part of our being human, with some persons obviously being more suggestible than others. In this case, Mrs. Smith has been involved with individuals and groups, over a period of years, the end result of which has been to promote a process of accepting the false idea that whatever mental image is conjured up, especially if part of "therapy," is necessarily a valid retrieval of past experience, i.e. a "memory."

Let me now document the evidence which has led me to the above conclusions.

1. Mrs. Smith's Suspicions About John Public and His Daughter Alice.

From several sources, such as her deposition, my interview, and investigative interviews, it seems clear that Mrs. Smith suspected for several years that her cousin John Public was engaging in sexual behavior with his daughter Alice. When asked for examples which led to these suspicions, she mentioned alleged comments from him that "a child's hands" felt so good. She also mentioned that no other adults seemed to be concerned about such comments.

Seeing Mr. Public and Alice (approximately eight years old at the time) lying in bed together, in their underwear, reinforced her suspicion, as did the alleged comment from Mr. Public to Mr. Smith (not heard by Mrs. Smith), that his (Smith's) daughter would make him horny. Mrs. Smith also noted that, until age 18 months, her own daughter would cry if Mr. Public attempted to pick her up or get close to her, and Mrs. Smith noted to herself, "She's a smart child." (It should be noted that such behavior in infants of this age is perfectly normal.)

Mrs. Smith told me that she had informed family members on several occasions of her suspicions, but no one else apparently shared her opinions, or felt anything needed to be reported.

The 1986 video of a family Halloween party was the event that convinced Mrs. Smith she should report her suspicions. It is quite important that the Court view this video, in order to judge for itself whether the material could reasonably lead a person to believe something untoward was taking place. My own opinion is there was nothing happening that was unusual or abnormal. It was Alice who first struck a somewhat playful and seductive pose, and such displays are hardly abnormal for a teenage girl. Police investigators likewise saw nothing untoward on this tape.

The question raised, then, is whether Mrs. Smith had for her own personal reasons, upon which I will not attempt to speculate, developed an obsession about Mr. Public and his daughter, one which was leading her (Smith) to overinterpret ordinary behaviors.

It is not surprising, then, that when the report was investigated by Children's Services, no evidence of abuse was uncovered. Mrs. Smith tells me, however, that she was not reassured, and only felt that she had fulfilled an obligation to report something.

2. Early Influences Promoting in Mrs. Smith a Belief That Prior Sexual Abuse Might Have Occurred but Not Be Remembered.

From numerous sources (deposition, my interview, journals, therapy records), it is clear that Mrs. Smith was strongly influenced by a statement she says Dr. Gwen Olson made to her regarding bulimia, a problem Mrs. Smith had suffered from to one degree or another since early adolescence.

Mrs. Smith states that Dr. Olson told her, sometime in early 1987 (the records indicate this was in December 1986), that "one hundred percent of my patients with bulimia have later found out that they were sexual abuse victims." Whether these words were actually spoken by Dr. Olson, or instead interpreted this way by Mrs. Smith, I of course do not know. But in either case, the words Mrs. Smith took away with her are extremely important, because the words "found out" would imply that a person could have been sexually abused, not be aware of it, and later recover such an awareness. I will later on be discussing the lack of evidence for, and major evidence against, any such phenomenon being genuine.

Mrs. Smith told me she was seriously affected by this, experiencing crying and feelings of fear. She began to wonder if she might have been sexually abused. When I asked her if she had ever before that time had such a question, she said that she "had no memories" of any such abuse. She had, in fact, told Children's Services shortly before, during the investigation of Alice, that John Public had "never before abused me...I was relying on my memory."

At this time, Mrs. Smith was being seen in psychotherapy, first by Edna Johnson, and then by Dr. Abraham, for what seems to have been feelings of anxiety and depression. Sexual abuse was apparently not an issue in this therapy. Instead, Mrs. Smith states that her self-esteem was low, and that she was "not functioning" well as a housewife, even though she felt good about her marriage. Both she and Dr. Abraham apparently felt she was "a bored housewife." She decided to start her own business, but this never happened because events leading to the current accusations against John Public interceded.

Mrs. Smith explains that she went to an Entrepreneurs Training Camp in the Fall of 1987, was doing extremely well, but then "sabotaged myself" by performing poorly despite knowing correct answers on an examination. She felt, after the camp, that she needed to work on herself.

In addition, she saw an Oprah Winfrey program on the subject of child abuse. Mrs. Smith told me that she cried as she watched this program, "for me and not for them... I wondered at my feelings and where they were coming from."

Mrs. Smith confirms that it was shortly after seeing this program, with all of the above background in place, that she called the Women's Sexual Assault Center (WSAC) on September 3, 1987.

After a telephone intake, she had a face-to-face contact with Joan Oliver, and told her that "I had concerns, feelings, but no memory of being sexually assaulted.... I thought it would be better to wait (for therapy) until I had a memory. They said OK, and put me on a waiting list."

The records of WSAC generally confirm this account which I received from Mrs. Smith on May 4, 1992. During the first telephone contact, Mrs. Smith related

> ... strong feelings of abuse as a child came up ... She can't remember specific things ... her GP told her most bulimics have been sexually abused as children ...

A second telephone contact, September 16, include[d]

> ... occluded memories. Sister was abused by neighborhood man as a child. Susan gets very retriggered by this and by shows about child abuse. Her doctor told her that close to 100% of bulimics have been sexually abused. This really brought up a lot of feelings and some images but not really a memory.

Yet another important event happened around Christmas 1987, before Mrs. Smith had entered the treatments (with Mary Brown and Veronica Erickson) where the mental images alleged to be "memories" started. This was something I had not discovered from any written materials, and learned about for the first time from Mrs. Smith on May 4, 1992.

Mrs. Smith had a friend, Valerie White, who told her about her treatments for back problems. Biofeedback was used at the pain and stress clinic she attended, and Ms. White told Mrs. Smith that she had started to remember being abused. When I asked Mrs. Smith how she reacted to this, she said, "I felt... that if she was in therapy, remembering, maybe I should start as well. I had no memory, but if she was in therapy..."

To summarize, then, the suggestive influences to this point: Mrs. Smith is still not reassured that Alice is not being abused by John Public; Dr. Olson either says or Mrs. Smith believes she says that in her experience all bulimics are sexual abuse victims; finally, after she decides she shouldn't go into therapy "until she has a memory" of sexual abuse, a friend tells her "the remembering" can wait, and Mrs. Smith concludes she should give it a try.

It is my opinion, based on the above material, that Mrs. Smith was at this point being victimized by lay persons and professionals who were representing to her that sexual abuse might not be remembered, when in truth there is no evidence to support such a claim. While Mrs. Smith may have had her own personal problems and/or motivations for claiming abuse at the hands of Mr. Public (something I will not speculate upon) she was being profoundly influenced by unsound information. It is my opinion that this has persisted to this day.

3. Suggestive and Unprofessional Therapy Creates the "Memories."

In March 1988, Mrs. Smith started seeing Mary Brown for individual psychotherapy, and also had interviews with Veronica Erickson, a student who was writing a thesis on "Recovering Memories of Childhood Sexual Abuse." On March 9, 1988, Ms. Erickson commented that Mrs. Smith had done

> ... a lot of great body work. Worked on her anger, hurt about being sexually abused. Has a few memories about it and wants more.

On March 28, the WSAC records show that the

> "memory recovery process" was getting into high gear:... had lots of memories come to her which she feels good about; 2 "rapes," 9 sodomies, and 2 oral sex (she has remembered both rapes and 1 sodomy and oral sex), 8 sodomies and 1 oral sex to go. Can't wait.

Further WSAC records of Ms. Erickson show just as clearly that she has lost all professional objectivity.... The June 14, 1988 note gives an insight as to the position Ms. Erickson was taking with regard to whether Mrs. Smith's

increasingly severe claims should be automatically assumed to be accurate:

> ... trying to remember a memory that was just beginning to flash... really scared that this memory is made up... I told her I believed her.

If there is any doubt about the stance being adopted by Ms. Erickson, i.e. that whatever Mrs. Smith "recovers" from week to week is a reliable statement about past events, a reading of her Ph.D. thesis makes it abundantly clear that it was simply a given for her and the selected sources she relies on, that the patient's claims must be taken at face value. She writes, for example:

> Validation, feeling believed, was seen as essential for incest survivors struggling to reconcile their memories.

Nowhere in the thesis is mention made of any concern that false claims may arise in therapy specifically aimed at such "uncovering." Next, she speaks of

> ... the ability of counselor... to facilitate the survivor's recall of the abuse... which of course assumes that abuse has taken place.

Just how broadly based is the source of these allegedly reliable "memories," is indicated by her quoting the book, *The Courage to Heal*, which has been influential in promoting the very ideas at the center of this case:

> "Occluded" memories are vague flashbacks, triggered by touches, smells, sounds, body memories, bodily sensations as "warning signs." Some women just intuitively knew that they had been sexually abused and were struggling to trust their intuition.

It is also clear that the proper role for the therapist, according to Ms. Erickson, is not only to accept all images as "memories," but to actively encourage this process. She writes of her method which

> ... serves to continually promote an atmosphere in which the researcher is spontaneously both receptive and actively stimulating the recollection of the participant.... The participants and researcher... create the world within which this study is revealed.

Ms. Erickson says of "Victoria" (pseudonym for Mrs. Smith),

> She thought about who might have abused her and when she said his name, she knew who the offender was but she still had no memories as proof (p. 56 of Erickson thesis).

Let me now turn to her other therapist, Mary Brown. Ms. Brown in her intake notes of March 1, 1988 refers to Mrs. Smith having

> ... flashbacks of childhood sexual abuse experiences, she believes by this same cousin.

Ms. Brown's treatment plan was to "assist Susan express and release the emotions associated with the sexual abuse experience." This is important, because it shows that Ms. Brown, from the beginning, assumed the truth of the allegations.

It wasn't too long after this, the night of March 12/13, that Mrs. Smith's calendar indicates she had a "nightmare," and her "first memories." When I asked Mrs. Smith about this, she said it was

> ... the nightmare which triggered the memory.... In the nightmare, the neighbor had shot her husband in the chest. Her cleaning up his blood, I recalled John blotting up my blood after raping me.

There are, of course, no reputable data which would indicate that a patient or therapist can use dream material to reliably "recover memories" of real events. Ms. Brown, however, seems to have utter confidence in the process, for she wrote to the police on August 3, 1988:

> The treatment methods I use enable clients to express and release the very deepest feelings that may have been stifled.... It is precisely because the emotional intensity of sexual abuse in childhood is greater than what most children can integrate that these experiences are quickly lost to memory. The ensuing, forgetting and denial are the mind's way of protecting the individual from total disruption of their cognitive functioning. This was particularly true of survivors of sexual abuse whose experiences occurred more than ten years ago. The reason for this is that there was not the social awareness nor the professional expertise for dealing with these problems at that time. Children instinctively know when the adults around them are going to be able to help them. When they find themselves in situations where they may either be disbelieved... this forgetting and denial comes into play even more strongly....

> Memories tend to return in fragments and to be unclear or non-specific in the beginning... the blocks in the way of memory are gradually removed.... This is precisely what occurred... with Susan Smith. It is my clinical judgment that Susan had reached a point in her healing process when the memories that were returning were completely reliable.... She was unprepared to report until she herself was certain and until she received validation from me that I was in agreement that the memories could be trusted...

That Ms. Brown was not only accepting all statements as real events, but actively encouraging them, is seen by the following passage from the same letter:

> Susan herself questioned any inconsistency.... It took some education on my part for her to... understand the whole process of how it is that the recall process works...

Ms. Brown was even willing to assure the police that the other persons that Mrs. Smith was gradually naming as victims during that Spring and Summer of 1988 would also need "help" in remembering.

> ...It is highly likely that most or all of the children that Susan remembers... will be unable to remember these experiences. This does not mean they did not occur any more than Susan's former amnesia means that these events had not happened to her. One of these (youngsters) may be precipitated to remember and recapture the experiences through a process similar to what occurred for Susan.

There is, of course, absolutely no evidence that this whole process has anything to do with memory, or a recall of past events. The only professionals who advocate these ideas are those making up a small, fringe group who hold themselves out as "specialists in treating sexual abuse," but who (as this case shows) seem to assume that it is permissible to pass off wild theories, like the ones above, to both patients, families, and investigative agencies.

Most important, however, is that outsiders evaluate the possible impact of such ideas on persons like Mrs. Smith. The evidence is clear that she has raised doubts from time to time, but each time, these "specialists" have told her that her mental images must represent real events. In this sense, I believe the professionals (Brown, Erickson, and others to be mentioned) are most responsible for creating the unreliable information in this case.

Not only do the ideas promoted by Brown and Erickson hold great potential to contaminate information coming from such counseling, but the techniques used with Mrs. Smith would likely heighten this possibility. Mrs. Smith described pounding pillows and being encouraged to express her anger in sessions with Ms. Erickson, and in individual and group sessions with Ms. Brown, she described exercises in which she was using hyperventilation or bending from the waist. The many group sessions she has attended, focusing on "recovery from sexual abuse," have a potentially profound influence on the participants.

In addition, Ms. Brown had a technique, which she called the "denial game," that was used when Mrs. Smith expressed caution about whether her mental images were reliable. This process had the intended effect of causing Mrs. Smith to once more *assume that whatever she could think of had actually happened.*

The police investigation was dropped for lack of evidence, for lack of corroboration from any of the many alleged victims named by Mrs. Smith, and because an outside consultant told the police that the impact of the therapy might be contaminating the information....

Mrs. Smith's statements to police include "trying to see" alleged events, having

> a flash... (a) visual memory of a spirit part of me coming out of me via my mouth and sitting on a head board. I now understand this to be dissociation....

The police, quite understandably, wondered whether this might be a sign of major mental disorder, like a psychosis. Instead, such statements reflect not that Mrs. Smith was suffering a major mental disorder, but simply that she was absorbing unsupported ideas from her therapists. I have studied the process by which some mental health professionals are passing these ideas to patients, via articles, speeches, and in therapy sessions. Many, if not most, patients, will accept these ideas as accepted scientific information, coming as they do from a professional therapist.

Just how much Mrs. Smith had come to believe in this process, already by April, 1988, is seen by her telling the police on April 20, 1988 that

> These are not complete memories at this point but there are bits and pieces of which I would like to tell you now and when I have the complete memory back I will talk to you again.... I would like to add that I expect to have further recall of incidents as I have just begun to have recall in the last five weeks or so....

4. The Growth of the Allegations.

The process described above will often lead to a virtual flood of allegations which grow and grow. Particularly if there are emotional rewards for producing more claims, the sky is the limit. In this case, it ultimately led to claims of ritual abuse, animal killings, gang rape, multiple personalities, etc. which Mrs. Smith now seems to disavow but which she at the time was claiming as legitimate memory. A brief review of these developments offers important perspective on the unreliable nature of this entire process.

Dr. Wagner saw Mrs. Smith from May 20, 1988 to January 27, 1989. He used a method Mrs. Smith describes as "regression," and which she now does not trust. She feels that some of the things she said as a result of these methods may not have happened.

For example, Dr. Wagner's notes of November 24, 1988 speak of "... memory of John and 'Joe.' Tying her up—raping her. Two others came in, Evan and [unreadable]." Mrs. Smith says she doesn't recall saying this to Dr. Wagner, doesn't believe she said it to him, believes his records are incorrect, and believes she talked about "Sam."

Dr. Wagner, while nowhere in his records expressing any doubt about the reality of these statements, did mention at the outset (June 3, 1988) that he thought Mrs. Smith was: "I suspect getting a lot of mileage out of sexual abuse. Attention and support from home she never got from mom and dad?"

When I questioned Mrs. Smith about other examples of statements drawn from the notes of the many therapists she saw in the coming months, I noted an interesting pattern. Whenever a statement in therapy records referred to events which she now says may not have happened, like seeing a boy with slits for eyes and no face, she says that she cannot recall saying any of this. She repeatedly said it was only her study of the therapy records which allows her to remember what she might have said in therapy.

However, when I asked her about a note from Morton Hunt's evaluation of January 15, 1991, she was quite clear that she did not say the following "... Then had nightmare. Chose John. Just knew it was him (reviewed possible men)."

Such selective "memory" merely reinforces my opinion that these multiple therapy contacts, of the nature described, make a mockery of the idea that claims growing out of the sessions, or growing out of the mental images of a patient between such sessions, are reliable.

The fact that Mrs. Smith was in much more therapy than I have yet summarized, only deepens the dilemmas. She was in group therapy with Ms. Summers, for 32 sessions, from March 21, 1989 to December 1, 1989, and Ms. Summers, who is another of those who specialize in "working mainly with women recovering from childhood sexual abuse," wrote in her records that "Susan's abuse was the most cruel and degrading I have encountered."

Once again, unquestioning acceptance seems to be the *sine qua non* of many of the therapists in this case. Sadly, such an attitude may be quite destructive to patients. A review of her journals, which I will highlight, shows that (as Dr. Wagner had indicated) Mrs. Smith was getting a lot of positive feedback from more and more "memories." A patient might feel good at the time of such feedback, but the encouragement of this process does not bode well for the long-term welfare of such patients.

> May 24, 1988—"Another memory came back—arms tied,... I know there are things I can't even imagine yet that they did to me. I know I still have a lot of memories to go... I know I'll have the strength to handle them... I'm on my way to a happy successful life... I love my strength.
>
> May 26, 1988—This morning at the Mom's Group... another memory came back.... I called WSAC. The more I discover about what I've been through the more I wonder how I ever survived.... You're so strong Susan, so wonderful. You're capable of whatever you believe in. You're OK, Susan Smith. You're

strong, you're a survivor, and a winner, you're going straight to the top, head of the class. You're OK, you're a winner. I'm really truly beginning to like myself and I really like that—all these years I hated myself.

> May 27—I begin my workshop with my therapist. (Mary Brown)
>
> May 28—... we did rapid breathing... I went to my sexual abuse... my body was twitching and squirming just as if it were tied up by the hands... I started getting these vague recollections of this blond male being Warren and some occurrence happening.... I wasn't ready to look at it until I could intellectually figure out how this could be...
>
> May 31—Describes Dave* meeting with Smith—He explained to him that these memories had been undisturbed for twenty years and had not been distorted... and that I was not making it up... I knew Dave was not ready to look at his abuse... at WSAC I went into denial mode... Veronica played the denial game with me just to show me that I was crazy to believe I was making this up.
>
> June 14, 1988—Saw Veronica, talked about Yellowstone incident with Gretchen involved, how I was blocking everything because I had no proof John was in Yellowstone and the fact that Gretchen must have repressed and that she would probably deny remembering such an incident... so she had me "hang" and it took a much longer time for the feelings to come, but they did, I cried, pound pillows, yelled, and got back more memories... so much doesn't make sense. Where is everyone else?
>
> Nov. 9, 1988—What I learned in therapy today: When I was abused it happened to my body. It happened to a part of me that I dissociated from. I have separated from and disowned the part of

---

*A cousin of Mrs. Smith, and one of the other alleged victims, none of whom had any memories of abuse.

me that it happened to.... I am ashamed of my body... so I abuse it.

April 18, 1989—I love myself and that's something I couldn't have said a year ago. I've come a long way.... Signed Terrific Susan.

May ?, 1989—... I let my little girls talk... etc.

June 8, 1989—attended Conference on Child Sexual Abuse... I learned a lot... talked to Gretchen two weeks ago. More about her "other personalities."... Memories, memories. Where are they. I want to remember all the mean sadistic things John did to me.

July 5, 1989—I know I am going to go on and achieve great things in my life... speak out against abuse of children, especially sexual abuse. I know I'm strong, a survivor, and a successeder. (sic)

Oct. 16, 1989—I got back memories of what happened after John gave my body to the two "tough men" in exchange for drugs.

October 29, 1989—I don't think this can happily, successfully end for me unless I have power over him.

Nov. 29, 1989—Cousin Joe called and told me Warren had memories of being sexually assaulted by John. The memories are just beginning... I told Warren... I was really proud of him.

Nov. 27, 1990—... I don't want any more memories!!! ... I called WSAC this afternoon and bits of memories came up. One was John beside me, and about 5 men, in black robes, or gowns—full length with hoods on their heads.... These men had swordlike daggers in their hands... a memory of John slitting the throat of a cat with a knife... telling us that this is what would happen to us if we ever told about him.

Dec. 16, 1990—I think I might have multiple personalities. It is something I've wondered about before, but believed you only developed multiples if you

were severely abused before age 8.... My first day with Veronica there was this other part of me talking. She named herself Julie... it was really weird cause I knew what was happening... I'm going to get to the other side of this—new and improved. But in the mean time, I'm a nuttsy basketcase.

Dec. 25, 1990—I started back in therapy mid-December, I could no longer contain the memories within me.... I want to write about and keep track of my memories. I've had a feeling for several months now that there might have been ritual abuse. When I started having flashes of white candles, lots of them, burning, I thought well, this is probably just an image I've seen on TV.... My 2nd day in therapy (3rd time I'd seen June) I had this memory—a faceless boy,... he had no nose and only slits for eyes.... They told us if we didn't behave, or if we ever told they would burn our faces with an iron.... They told the girls they use their genitals as eyes, then when they grow older they'd have furry, hairy eyes and everyone would laugh.

Toward the end of our meeting, I asked Mrs. Smith how she distinguished between the many allegations which she insists took place, and the many allegations which she made but now says she cannot remember saying and isn't sure they are real. The gist of her answer (the tape is of course available) was that "memories" which were like a "videotape," where a picture is complete, from start to finish, and which occurred to her sometimes in therapy but often by herself, are reliable. Brief images, or "flashes," which are incomplete, and which were often in response to therapeutic techniques she now is critical of, like those of June Schreiber and others, she distrusts.

I find this distinction, which I must assume to be sincere on Mrs. Smith's part, to be utterly unreliable. First, the therapy from the beginning has been manipulative, even though I have no doubt that all the therapists were sincere in wanting to help. They all, nonetheless, adopted the position that "the more memory the better."

While this might be interpreted to mean that this is standard practice in the therapeutic community, since so many therapists in this case acted in this manner, it is instead an artifact which resulted when Mrs. Smith sought out or was referred to a selected group of therapists who "specialize in recovery from sexual abuse." Amongst this group, whose work and education I have studied intensively, it is common practice to assume abuse occurs if anyone claims it has, common practice to encourage as many "memories" as possible, common practice to encourage anger and "empowerment," and common practice to accept all allegations, however unlikely, as being real.

All this is terribly unscientific, without general agreement from the mental health community, and in my view highly destructive to many patients. Perhaps most important here, in the context of litigation, is the fact that these techniques absolutely fly in the face of reliable fact-finding.

I cannot emphasize strongly enough how important it is for the Court, in studying this case and deciding what is reliable and what is not, to understand that if commonsense leads to one conclusion about where the truth lies, the use of psychiatric labels and esoteric explanations should not cause the Court to abandon what the facts otherwise seem to show.

* * *

As of this writing, the Court has yet to render a verdict. But whatever is decided in this case, it should be clear that our society is about to experience yet another wave of unreliable sexual abuse allegations. Once again, it is the promulgation of faulty ideas by a small segment of the mental health community (see for example Bass & Davis, 1988; Blume, 1990; Briere & Conte, in press; Cozolino, 1989; Maltz, 1990; Herman & Schatzow, 1987; Summit, 1987; Young, Sachs, Braun, & Watkins, 1991), coupled with the apathy of the bulk of the mental health community, which promises to create a new form of abuse of patients, families, and the falsely accused. The moral and economic costs are incalculable, and the promotion of pseudoscientific ideas which confuse memory with mental imagery is already confusing the scientific literature.

Fortunately, clearer heads are also in evidence (see Ganaway, 1991; Lanning, 1989 and 1992; Mulhern, 1991a, 1991b, 1991c; Nathan, 1989, 1990, 1991; Passantino, Passantino, & Trott, 1989; Price, 1992; Putnam, 1991; Wakefield & Underwager, 1992 and undated). Given our society's tendency to become infatuated with all manner of fads, it should be obvious that this latest development in the child sexual abuse circus is not going to go away quickly or easily. It will take insight and perseverance to counteract the tendency of the media and most lay persons to uncritically accept the "blocked memory" claims now emerging with increasing regularity. If our society is serious about responding to the reality of childhood sexual abuse, a critical ingredient is the avoidance of irresponsible empire-building by some mental health professionals who have abandoned both science and reason.

REFERENCES

Bass, E., & Davis, L. (1988). *The courage to heal.* New York, Harper & Row.

Blume, E. (1990). *Secret survivors: Uncovering incest and its aftereffects in women.* New York: J. Wiley & Sons.

Briere, J., & Conte, J. (in press). Self reported amnesia for abuse in adults molested as children. *Journal of Traumatic Stress.*

Cozolino, L. (1989). The ritual abuse of children: Implications for clinical practice and research, *The Journal of Sex Research, 26(1),* 131–138.

Ganaway, G. K. (1991, August 19). *Alternate hypotheses regarding satanic ritual abuse memories.* Presented at the 99th Annual Convention of the American Psychological Association, San Francisco.

Herman, J. L., & Schatzow, E. (1987). Recovery and verification of memories of childhood sexual trauma. *Psychoanalytic Psychology, 4(1),* 1–14.

Lanning, K. V. (1989, October). *Satanic, occult, ritualistic crime: A law enforcement perspective.* National Center for the Analysis of Violent Crime, FBI Academy, Quantico, VA.

Lanning, K. V. (1992). *Investigator's guide to allegations of "ritual" child abuse.* National Center for the Analysis of Violent Crime: Quantico, VA.

Maltz, W. (1990, December). Adult survivors of incest: How to help them overcome the trauma. *Medical Aspects of Human Sexuality,* 42–47.

Mulhern, S. (1991a). *Ritual abuse: Defining a syndrome v. defending a belief.* Unpublished manuscript.

Mulhern, S. (1991b). [Letter to the Editor]. *Child Abuse & Neglect, 15,* 609–610.

Mulhern, S. (1991c). Satanism and psychotherapy: A rumor in search of an inquisition. In J. T. Richardson, J. Best, & D. G. Bromley (Eds.), *The Satanism scare* (pp. 145–172). New York: Aldine de Gruyter.

Nathan, D. (1989, June 21). The Devil and Mr. Mattox, *Texas Observer,* pp. 10–13.

Nathan, D. (1991). Satanism and child molestation: Constructing the ritual abuse scare. In J. T. Richardson, J. Best, & D. G. Bromley (Eds.), *The Satanism scare* (pp. 75–94). New York: Aldine de Gruyter.

Nathan, D. (1990, June 20). The ritual sex abuse hoax, *Village Voice,* pp. 36–44.

Passantino, G., Passantino, B., & Trott, J. (1989). Satan's sideshow. *Cornerstone, 18(90),* 23–28.

Price, L. (1992, April 20). Presentation at the Midwest Regional False Memory Syndrome Foundation Meeting. Benton Harbor, Michigan.

Putnam, F. (1991). The satanic ritual abuse controversy. *Child Abuse & Neglect, 15,* 175–179.

Summit, R. (1987, July). Declaration of Roland Summit, MD, Regarding *People v. Dill.*

Wakefield, H., & Underwager, R. (1992, June 20). *Recovered memories of alleged sexual abuse: Lawsuits against parents.* Presentation at 4th Annual Convention of the American Psychological Society, San Diego, CA. (Also, *Behavioral Sciences and the Law,* in press.)

Wakefield, H., & Underwager, R. (undated). Magic, mischief, and memories: Remembering repressed abuse. Unpublished manuscript. (Also see *Issues in Child Abuse Accusations,* 1991, Vol. 3, No. 3.)

Young, W. C., Sachs, R. G., Braun, B. G., & Watkins, R. (1991). Patients reporting ritual abuse in childhood: A clinical syndrome of 37 cases. *Child Abuse & Neglect, 15,* 181–189.

CHALLENGE QUESTIONS

Are Memories of Sex Abuse Always Real?

1. Can a psychologist or other mental health professional lead a patient to believe something that is not true? If so, how can this happen?

2. Can you think of any explanations for the "instances" described by Bass and Davis other than prior sexual abuse?

3. How would you go about "proving" that someone had been sexually abused? What evidence would you need?

4. What are your beliefs about how memories are stored and retrieved?

CONTRIBUTORS
TO THIS VOLUME

AUTHORS

ELLEN BASS is a nationally recognized counselor, lecturer, and professional trainer who works with survivors of child sexual abuse.

FRANCES M. BERG is a nutritionist and the founder, publisher, and editor of *Healthy Weight Journal*. She is also an adjunct professor in the Department of Community Medicine and Rural Health of the School of Medicine at the University of North Dakota in Grand Forks, North Dakota. She is the author of eight books, and she writes a weekly "Healthy Living" column, which is syndicated in over 50 newspapers.

DENNIS BERNSTEIN is an associate editor for *Pacific News Service* and a co-producer of KPFA's *Flashpoints* radio show.

PATRICK J. CARNES is the primary architect of an inpatient program for sexual dependency at the Golden Valley Health Center in Minneapolis, Minnesota. He is the author of *Out of the Shadows: Understanding Sexual Addiction* (CompCare, 1985) and *Counseling the Sexual Addict* (CompCare, 1986). He received a Ph.D. from the University of Minnesota.

LEE COLEMAN is a psychiatrist in Berkeley, California, and a critic of the role of mental health professionals in legal settings. His current research interests focus on false accusations of child sexual abuse.

LAURA DAVIS is an expert on healing from child sexual abuse and a nationally recognized workshop leader.

PATRICK H. DeLEON, a psychologist and a lawyer, is a staff member for Senator Daniel K. Inouye (D) of Hawaii.

GARLAND Y. DeNELSKY is head of the psychology section and director of the Psychology Training Program at the Cleveland Clinic, where he provides training and supervision for psychology fellows and psychiatry residents. His clinical and research interests include the enhancement of coping skills, facilitation of smoking cessation, and treatment of performance anxiety. He received his Ph.D. from Purdue University in 1966 and was recently awarded the Outstanding Alumni Award from Grinnell College, where he received his bachelor's degree.

MICHAEL FUMENTO, a former AIDS analyst and attorney for the U.S. Commission on Civil Rights, is the science and economics reporter for *Investor's Business Daily*. He has written two books, *The Myth of Heterosexual AIDS* (New Republic Books, 1990) and *Science Under*

Siege (William Morrow, 1993), and he is the author of numerous articles on AIDS, which have appeared in publications worldwide.

WILLIAM A. HENKIN is the coauthor of *Bodywise* (Wingbow Press, 1991) with Joseph Heller.

EVE C. JOHNSTONE is a professor in the Department of Psychiatry at the University of Edinburgh.

ANDREW G. KADAR is an attending physician at Cedars-Sinai Medical Center in Los Angeles, California, and a clinical instructor in the School of Medicine at the University of California, Los Angeles.

THEA KELLEY is a freelance journalist based in San Francisco.

PETER D. KRAMER is a psychiatrist and the author of *Moments of Engagement: Intimate Psychotherapy in a Technological Age* (W. W. Norton, 1989).

LESLIE LAURENCE is a health and medical reporter.

PAUL A. LOGLI is the state's attorney for Winnebago County, Illinois, and a lecturer with the National College of District Attorneys. A member of the Illinois State Bar since 1974, he is a nationally recognized advocate for prosecutorial involvement in the issue of substance-abused infants. He received a J.D. from the University of Illinois.

JAMES MAURO is a former senior editor of *Psychology Today*.

JOAN McCORD is a professor of criminal justice at Temple University in Phila-

delphia, Pennsylvania, where she has been teaching since 1987. She has received the Prix Emile Durkheim Award from the International Society of Criminology and the Edwin H. Sutherland Award from the American Society of Criminology for her research. A former president of the American Society of Criminology, she has authored or coauthored more than 100 articles, books, and essays on theory, treatment effects, crime, alcoholism, protective factors, and socialization.

NATIONAL TASK FORCE ON THE PREVENTION AND TREATMENT OF OBESITY of the National Institutes of Health in Bethesda, Maryland, was composed of nine scientific members from universities throughout the United States. Among their goals was to address concerns about the effects of weight cycling and to provide guidance on the risk-to-benefit ratio of attempts at weight loss, given current scientific knowledge.

MAUREEN A. NORTON-HAWK is a research fellow in the Center for Alcohol and Addiction Studies at Brown University in Providence, Rhode Island. She has written numerous articles on the prosecution of pregnant drug addicts, and she continues to do research on the interrelationship between law and medicine.

D. L. ROSENHAN is a professor of law and psychology at Stanford University and a social psychologist whose focal concern has been clinical and personality matters. He has also been a faculty member at Princeton University, the University of Pennsylvania, and Swarthmore College.

THEODORE R. SARBIN is an emeritus professor of psychology and criminology at the University of California, Santa Cruz.

ROBERT L. SPITZER is affiliated with the New York State Psychiatric Institute in New York City. He is a former chairman of the American Psychiatric Association and its Task Force on Nomenclature and Statistics.

MURRAY A. STRAUS is a professor of sociology and codirector of the Family Research Laboratory at the University of New Hampshire in Durham, New Hampshire. He has held academic appointments at Cornell University, the University of Minnesota, the University of Wisconsin, and Washington State University, as well as at universities in England, India, and Sri Lanka. He is the author or coauthor of over 150 articles and 15 books on the family, research methods, and South Asia, including *Physical Violence in American Families: Risk, Factors, and Adaptations to Violence in 8,145 Families* (Transaction, 1989), coauthored with Richard J. Gelles.

CAROL TAVRIS is a social psychologist and an author based in Los Angeles, California, and a member of the American Psychological Association. Her publications include *The Longest War: Sex Differences in Perspective*, 2d ed. (Harcourt Brace, 1984), coauthored with Carole Wade, and *Anger: The Misunderstood Emotion* (Simon & Schuster, 1989).

NANCY WARTIK is a contributing editor for *American Health*.

BETH WEINHOUSE is a health and medical reporter.

INDEX